# RADICAL MAN

*The Process of Psycho-Social Development*

IN *Radical Man* CHARLES HAMPDEN-TURNER HAS UNDERTAKEN the extraordinarily ambitious task of outlining the human process of psychosocial development. His model not only organizes thousands of individual research findings from nearly two hundred research studies, but it conceptualizes a large number of contemporary social and political events: student rebellion, Vietnam protest, the psychology of violence and militarism, the vogue for "Sensitivity Training," the anomie which plagues advanced industrial society, and the destructive effect of technology upon our lives.

Among his conclusions, all the more devastating for the array of evidence he marshalls, is that perhaps for the first time in American history there has arisen a Left-wing movement which represents, at least in part, the dynamics of human development, and that this fact terrifies and enrages millions of those whose lives have been narrowly constrained by the demands of industrial enterprise.

He traces the failure of many institutions to respond to this evolving dynamic, but his special indictment is reserved for bureaucratic social science, which routinely betrays the compassion of its own young recruits in its ambition to achieve the status of a physical science.

Hampden-Turner most convincingly restores human conscience and moral impulse to the very center of social science, from which they were banished years ago by behaviorism. He argues that only a human concern which is translated into principled action can maintain our mental and social integration, and that technocratic society has debased these truths.

He sees brilliant promise in a small creative minority of mostly young Americans, shadowed by the prospect of destruction, and often crippled by despair, but still representing the sole source of renewal in an emotionally desensitized culture.

# RADICAL MAN

*The Process of Psycho-Social Development*

BY

CHARLES HAMPDEN-TURNER

Schenkman Publishing Company
Cambridge, Massachusetts

# PREFACE AND ACKNOWLEDGMENTS

In the four and a half years it took me to complete this book I occasionally basked in one particular fantasy. I would imagine myself as some kind of existential hero confronting a hostile multitude of academic Know-Nothings. This vision of myself was extraordinarily pleasing and when frustrated in the least degree I would mutter to the great pillars which uphold the Baker Library at the Harvard Business School.

I did but urge the age to quit its clogs
By the known laws of Ancient Liberty
When lo! A barbarous noise environs me
Of owls and cuckoos, asses, apes and dogs.

Unfortunately my pet vision does not survive even a partial enumeration of those who went out of their way to help me. When I read an early paper to Fritz Roethlisberger he actually jumped with excitement, a demonstration which did more for my subsequent morale than hours of sage advice from august persons. At a time when my ideas were jumbled, to put it mildly, Maurice Stein was unbelievably kind and patient in reading my work. The chairman of my thesis committee, "By" Barnes, encouraged me to write the first ever theoretical dissertation at the Harvard Business School, thereby inviting a lot of trouble for himself.

I am especially grateful to Carl Rogers who rescued me from despair at a time when my fellowship aid had been suspended. In two hours he showed so great a comprehension and support for my work that my finances and morale were sustained for months afterward.

Thanks must also go to Warren Bennis who frequently rescued me from self-delusion during T-Groups. Abraham Maslow praised me so effusively to publishers that at least one accepted this manuscript. Maslow was also an intellectual inspiration to me as well as an example of courage. Most valued support and encouragement came from Adam Curle; Denis Goulet and Merrill Jackson with whom I worked at the Center for Education and Development. Dr. Nolan Penn, a visiting professor at Brandeis not only enthused about my work but tried out the models with his class. I was tremendously encouraged by the students' response.

Dick Rosenbloom and Paul Lawrence showed great tolerance for an ambiguous employee in their research group on ghetto corporations and took the risk of letting me alone to germinate. Without an enthusiastic letter of praise from Robert Guest at Dartmouth, I might have been unemployed these last years.

Quite out of the blue, Professor William Davenport offered to edit my manuscript, and David Scondras of *Resist* acted as kind of spontaneous publicity agent among his friends. Both showed me the greatest kindness and encouragement. In the last few months before publication I have been indebted to the keen but friendly criticism of Silvan Tomkins, the unfailing courtesy and consideration of "Jack" Seeley, who found time to help me when he was in the midst of a personal crisis. Alfred Schenkman, my publisher, has dealt patiently and skillfully with the obsessive egotism that grips me on the subject of my own creations. Madelyn Wisnia and Carol Bangs struggled bravely with typing endless drafts of my effulgence.

Finally, I owe much to Gar Alperowitz and Don Devereux of the Cambridge Institute where I may at last have found a home. They not only encourage my work, they pay me, and I much appreciate this evidence of sincerity. Of the several other persons who ignored or disparaged my work for its "naive idealism," and of those whose main preoccupation when evaluating me was the maintenance of their own status, I shall say nothing that might rescue them from obscurity.

The Cambridge Institute<br>Cambridge, Massachusetts<br>September, 1969

## CONTENTS


| CHAPTER | | PAGE |
|---|---|---|
| PREFACE AND ACKNOWLEDGMENTS | | vii |
| HOW TO READ THIS BOOK | | xii |
| I. | THE BORROWED TOOLBOX AND CONSERVATIVE MAN | 1 |
| | Science and power | 2 |
| | Prediction, control and experimentation | 3 |
| | The null hypothesis, detachment and technique | 5 |
| | Science pure and applied | 6 |
| | Precision and invariability | 7 |
| | Empiricism and physicalism | 8 |
| | Mathematics and reductive analysis | 9 |
| | Value free science | 12 |
| II. | THE EXISTENTIAL PERSPECTIVE | 19 |
| | The synthesizing capacity | 20 |
| | The symbolizing capacity | 22 |
| | The exploring capacity | 23 |
| | A field theory | 24 |
| | The concept of freedom within the law | 25 |
| | Relational facts not objective facts | 26 |
| | Alternate involvement with self and others | 27 |
| | Value full investigation – not value free | 27 |
| III. | A MODEL OF PSYCHO-SOCIAL DEVELOPMENT | 31 |
| | (a) PERCEPTION | 37 |
| | (b) IDENTITY | 39 |
| | (c) COMPETENCE | 43 |
| | (d) INVESTMENT | 43 |
| | (e) SUSPENSION and RISK | 45 |
| | (f) BRIDGING THE DISTANCE | 48 |
| | (g) SELF-CONFIRMING, SELF-TRANSCENDING IMPACT | 50 |

(h) Dialectic and SYNERGY . . . . . . . . . . . . . . 53
(i) FEEDBACK, INTEGRATION and COMPLEXITY . 56

IV. ANOMIE – THE FAILURE OF EXISTENCE . . . . . . . . 67

(a) PERCEPTION narrow and impoverished . . . . . . 69
(b) IDENTITY "locked in" and stagnant . . . . . . . . 74
(c) In COMPETENCE and anticipated loss . . . . . . . 75
(d) Failure to INVEST . . . . . . . . . . . . . . . . . 76
(e) Non-SUSPENDING RISK-reducing . . . . . . . . . 79
(f) Avoidance of DISTANCE . . . . . . . . . . . . . . 81
(g) Failure of CONFIRMATION and TRANSCENDENCE . . . . . . . . . . . . . . . . 86
(h) Non-dialectical failure of SYNERGY . . . . . . . . 88
(i) DisINTERGRATION and lack of COMPLEXITY. . 91

V. DISSENT AND REBELLION IN THE LABORATORY . . . 97

VI. DEVELOPMENT AND THE SOCIAL STRUCTURE OF FORMAL SYSTEMS . . . . . . . . . . . . . . . . . . 127

The formal system and the loss of humanity . . . . . . . 131
The formal system as conservative . . . . . . . . . . . . 134
The formal system as a safety net . . . . . . . . . . . . . 135
Anomic men cling to the formal system. . . . . . . . . . 140
Problems of system design – complexity and simplicity. . 141
The dangers of specialization and technique. . . . . . . . 150
The formal system as the servant of man and his development . . . . . . . . . . . . . . . . . . . 151

VII. REBELLION, GROWTH AND REGRESSION IN TRAINING GROUPS . . . . . . . . . . . . . . . . . . . 155

Existential nothingness – an encounter with the absurd. . 157
The small group climate . . . . . . . . . . . . . . . . . 160
The enforced confrontation . . . . . . . . . . . . . . . . 161
The moratorium . . . . . . . . . . . . . . . . . . . . . 163
The rebellion against authority . . . . . . . . . . . . . . 164

VIII. CORPORATE RADICALISM . . . . . . . . . . . . . . . . . . . 183
The bungled experiment – Hawthorne revisited . . . . . . . 184
Existentialism for workers – Scanlon Plan . . . . . . . . 192
The manager as a healer of anomie . . . . . . . . . . . . 207

IX. THE RADICAL-CONSERVATIVE DIMENSION IN AMERICAN POLITICS . . . . . . . . . . . . . . . . . . 217
The inadequacy of conventional explanations . . . . . . . 217
Problems in defining a developmental radicalism . . . . . 219
The dogmatic left, the dogmatic right and the new left . . . . . . . . . . . . . . . . . . . . . 220
Legitimacy and the battle against anomie and repression . 225
Basic polarities in ideology and psycho-social development 229

X. CONSERVATIVE AND RADICAL ISSUES . . . . . . . . . 269
Conservatism as an antidote to the pathologies of the left. 269
The "situational conservative" . . . . . . . . . . . . . . 273
The need for a radical-conservative dialogue . . . . . . . . 273
Problems in the use of violence by Radical Man . . . . . . 277
Radical-conservative issues in Congress . . . . . . . . . . 281
The humanists and the custodians . . . . . . . . . . . . 292
Democracy and psycho-social development . . . . . . . . 295

XI. THE CRYPTO-CONSERVATISM OF TECHNOLOGICAL THINKING . . . . . . . . . . . . . . . . . . . . . . . 303

XII. THE STUDENT RADICALS . . . . . . . . . . . . . . . . 349
A research profile of student radicals . . . . . . . . . . . . 349
The years of unrest – why now? . . . . . . . . . . . . . . 363
The developmental themes in radical tactics . . . . . . . . 377
The rationales for repression . . . . . . . . . . . . . . . . 383
The dominant culture's thesis and the radicals antithesis . . . 390
The choice of fires . . . . . . . . . . . . . . . . . . . . 392

BIBLIOGRAPHY . . . . . . . . . . . . . . . . . . . . . . . . . 397

SUBJECT INDEX . . . . . . . . . . . . . . . . . . . . . . . . 411

NAME INDEX . . . . . . . . . . . . . . . . . . . . . . . . . . 427

## HOW TO READ THIS BOOK

It is especially important to start at the beginning of this book, go on to the end, and then stop. In Chapters III and IV, I present models of psycho-social development and underdevelopment, respectively, and these are systematically applied to various social and political problems in every subsequent chapter. Halfway through Chapter III, a radical student in the social sciences may sense betrayal. "*Another* of those abstract schemes where you go up into the clouds, never to come down." Take heart. We come down in every chapter from V to XII, and upon very relevant and topical issues.

Persons like myself tend to "ransack" books in the social sciences, selecting just those pieces which are of special interest. The reader may hinder his own comprehension if he does this, since my models are supposed to gather credence and pick up more and more of the environment, like expanding snowballs rolling down a hill.

For hardened "ransackers" may I suggest the following? If you already object to the basic premises of traditional social science you may omit Chapter I, which will provide you only with extra ammunition. If you are familiar with the premises of existential and normative psychology, or are bored with philosophy of science, skip Chapter II. But Chapters III and IV should be read by anyone seeking to get the most out of the rest of the book.

If you are first and foremost a *political* radical, rather than a social and cultural one, you may skip Chapters V to VII. If you have not the time to read this book but seek a nodding acquaintance with its conclusions, or if you want evidence as to whether you should take the trouble to get into it, then Chapters I, VIII, and XII are the more entertaining and easier to read than others. You will also be minimally handicapped by not having read Chapters III and IV, which are more complex.

*Chapter 1*

# The Borrowed Toolbox and Conservative Man

In this book I shall attempt to model the human process of psycho-social development and to lay the foundations of a humanistic psychology. When embarking on this task I had hoped to apply in modified forms the many tools and methodologies in current use. It was here that I encountered difficulties – so many that I eventually concluded that the tools themselves functioned in a manner reductive to man and were impeding the emergence of a fully human science.

Man is the maker of tools which shape his environment, guide his vision, claim his energies, and through this process make his destiny.[1] When he uses these tools on himself and his fellow men, then it becomes especially important to ask how these tools affect his vision of humanity. Do the present methodologies, borrowed from physical science, do justice to the full range of human endowments?

In this chapter I shall contend that they do less than justice, that the borrowed tools distort and deemphasize the very properties of life. In later chapters I shall outline an alternative method designed to avoid the injurious aspects of the borrowed tools.

I shall now list some cornerstones of scientific tradition and methods. I shall then take each assumption on the list and discuss its application to human affairs.

1 Science and power
2. Prediction, control and experimentation
3. The null hypothesis, detachment and technique
4. Science pure and applied
5. Precision and invariability
6. Empiricism and physicalism
7. Mathematics and reductive analysis
8. Value free science.

While only a minority of social scientists abide by every one of these assumptions, there are few who can do without at least some of them. We shall see how very central a number of these assumptions are to any investigation regarded as "scientific."

A word should first be said about the "liberal style" of many social scientists. The shortcomings of their methodologies are frequently commented upon. It is a mark of the aware researcher to pay the customary tribute to the imperfection of his instruments and to show knowledge of the recurrent criticisms. But once these official regrets have been made it is business as usual, with perhaps a few skillful circumlocutions which leave chrome plated, updated versions of the borrowed tools intact. If one persists in criticism these same scientists accuse one of "flogging a dead horse," but as Arthur Koestler has remarked, there has never been a dead horse with such a vicious kick.[2] The old assumptions remain. A liberal rhetoric substitutes for radical revision.

### *1. Science and power*

Bacon's adage that "knowledge is power" was the central theme behind "the marriage of Mind and of Universe," which he foretold in *The Great Instauration.* From this marriage was to spring

> a line and race of inventions that may in some degree subdue and overcome the necessities and miseries of humanity. . . . And so these twin objects, *human knowledge* and *human power*, do really meet in one.[3]

Few would deny that Bacon's vision has been realized in the advanced industrial countries. Where once man cringed fearfully before the assaults of Nature, the cry is now raised that Nature has been so polluted and debauched that every effort must be made to prevent a total subjugation and conserve what remains. Yet the relationship of human science to nature is still one of domination. Four hundred years after Bacon the American philosopher Hans Jonas can still say:

> Not only is man's relation to nature one of power, but nature herself is conceived in terms of power. Thus it is a question either of ruling or being ruled; and to be ruled by a nature not noble, kindred or wise means slavery and hence misery. The exercise of man's inherent right is therefore also the response to a basic and continuous emergency: the emergency of a contest decreed by man's condition.[4]

The use to which science and technology can be put usually follows straight from the fact that the researcher has demonstrated his capacity to predict and control key variables. His feat can be replicated and then disseminated in the form of technical power over identified physical elements. The actual uses may be multifarious and include applications regarded as good or evil. However, the human power developed by physical science is widely regarded as at least a potential opportunity and resource for all mankind.

But can the social sciences make this claim? Suppose certain men gain the power to predict and control variables in the behavior of other men, could we then assume without further reflection that such knowledge is a power which all mankind could share? The usefulness of learning to manipulate the physical universe is self-evident, but if I can control aspects of A's behavior have we increased the sum of our joint powers? Great power in the hands of a few experts is generally regarded as *reducing* the overall potency and freedom of the citizenry. And if the techniques of power over men are broadly disseminated in common with the traditions of science, who then would willingly *be* controlled when the knowledge to control others is at hand?

In short, the adage that knowledge is power requires extensive redefinition in social science, for the kind of power that comes from the scientific knowledge of things is *physical* power *over* those things. In order to share freely among ourselves the fruits of psychological research, the fruits themselves must make possible the kind of power which mutually enhances both giver and receiver – that is, power *through* people. It is difficult to see how most current interpretations of "the scientific method" in the social sciences would permit the study of mutuality between scientist and subject.

*2. Prediction, control, and experimentation*

While there are non-predictive theories such as the Theory of Evolution, it is widely felt that the capacity to predict and control the outcome of studies is a measure of how "scientific" an investigation is. Prediction is the basis of the hypothetico-deductive method. We test a theory or proposition by deducing that in those conditions covered by our proposition the predicted events will occur. In a controlled experiment we can create the conditions, vary them systematically, and thereby test the range of our proposition, filling in our theory like a tapestry and adapting the objects of interest to the progressive logic of our own calculations, instead of waiting perhaps for years for the natural combination of events.

To deduce a future event is considered superior to an *ex post facto* induction, since by induction (from the concrete event to abstract theory), we may unconsciously select those pieces of evidence that fit our predetermined notions. Systematic prediction of hypothesized phenomena is at best a form of disciplined open-mindedness. We place our propositions "at risk," and we must account for the verdict which nature renders.

When "the objects of interest" become the human subjects of experimental social science the relationship between the investigator and his universe appears rather one-sided. The requirement that the conditions of the experiment be carefully controlled so that they can be replicated or systematically varied, places the experimental subjects in an environment entirely of the experimenter's choosing and where he unilaterally controls nearly all the variables. While the subject retains the capacity to confirm or to disconfirm the experimental hypothesis this "feedback mechanism" is totally inadequate as judged by our customary social norms.[5] What *constitutes* confirmation or disconfirmation of the hypothesis is not usually arrived at by mutual consent so that the "object" is "reacting" within a theoretical framework of which he has little understanding and which is nine-tenths fixed in advance by the unilateral fiat of the investigator.

I would be rash to claim that no knowledge valuable to humanity will emerge from such experiments. I might even defend the continued right of scientists to carry them out where ethical safeguards were present. What concerns me much more is the knowledge *that could not possibly emerge from such procedures*. You can only get answers to those questions you are asking. Questions about relationships of trust, equality and dialogue between the investigator and his subject are not being asked, since they offend against current conceptions of good methodology. But power over people in a laboratory can *only* lead (if it leads anywhere) to a technology of behavior control. The results which flow from the unilateral inputs of the experimenter are only applicable to those exercising unilateral inputs in our culture. If, on the other hand, men have the capacity freely to exchange knowledge and support in ways that enrich their respective personalities, then the highly controlled experiment is not going to uncover this process – not this year, next year, or ever.

When we search the literature of socio-psychological experiments what do we find? We find an astonishing number of experiments on pain inflicting, prejudice, obedience, conformity, cheating, aggression, inauthenticity, and scapegoating.[6] Only rarely do we find experiments on affection or on independence and when we look more closely at these we discover that the "affectionate monkeys" were those the experimenter left alone and the "independent students" were those who *resisted* the experimental pressures to conform, cheat, and obey.[7] In nearly every case *it is the anti-social subjects who confirm the experimental hypothesis and confirm the experimenter as a scientist*. The dissenters who resisted these pressures are shown to be creative, impulsive, affectionate, intelligent, interpersonally skillful, tolerant, imaginative, philosophical, self-aware, humorous, etc.

Need we be surprised? It is not that the investigators themselves have a savage eye, but rather that their predicting and controlling tools demand the predictable and controllable man in order to consummate the Good Experiment! And what a misery the man turns out to be! The highly respected Dr. Jekyll discovers Mr. Hyde, the beast in man uncovered by inhuman instruments.

I am weary of hearing these experiments described as an *ethical* problem. How we use the atom bomb may not be a problem *in physics* but the capacity of "scientific methodology" to generate and then "discover" unethical behavior is a problem *in psychology.*[8] Experimental psychologists are producing results referred to as "data" but better described as *capta,*[9] aspects of man taken or seized by methods which screen out other more valued aspects. What such experiments do their best to suppress is the ethical nature of man which, as we shall see in later chapters, manifests itself more strongly in relationships of equal power and mutual comprehension.

While only a minority of social scientists use strictly controlled laboratory experiments, the ideal of the experiment is extremely influential. The search for prior independent variables which may have caused the subjects to respond is still the pervasive paradigm in field surveys, change studies, and "natural" experiments. The image of man is of one who obeys natural laws by reacting to prior events or conditions.

*3. The null hypothesis, detachment and technique*

Part of the discipline a scientist must learn is skepticism and caution. Anyone who commits his time and effort to hypothesizing certain relationships may too easily assume that he has discovered a justification for his labor. Physical objects are little influenced by our hope, impatience, or desire, and scientists have learned to guard against the all-too-human tendency of wishful thinking. Objects or events must be regarded as random – that is, unrelated until correlation at a high degree of significance justifies the disproof of the *null hypothesis*.

For similar reasons, detachment and technique are often considered essential. Methods should be detachable from the personality of the scientist and be capable of dissemination in the form of research technique. If science is to be distinguished from magic, the knowledge of the scientist must be fully separable from his personality, to be tested and used by others.

These excellent principles translate themselves rather disagreeably into social life. The assumption that a patient will not improve and that therapy is ineffective will go a long way to create the fact. To assume until the opposite is proved, that a community is a random collection of unrelated individuals whose words are unconnected to their acts is to assume meaninglessness, pessimism, and disintegration until those powerless persons whom we usually choose as experimental subjects have persuaded us otherwise.[10] No wonder social scientists are being ejected unceremoniously from the ghettos!

Scepticism and the detachment of practicing a technique are not communicated to dead objects, but they do influence the relationships of human investigators with their subjects, and while social scientists frequently refer to the "self-fulfilling prophecy," they less often comprehend that so-called "neutrality" and "scientific detachment" are self-fulfilling too. The voluminous literature on alienation, anomie, and conformity is in part the mirror-image of scientific techniques used in gathering the information.

One philosopher of science has recently argued that many good scientists are not detached at all, but often show the greatest enthusiasm for their methods.[11] What is not permissible is to exhibit enthusiasm for concerns external to the method itself. But this streamlined version of neutrality hardly removes the previous objection. Instead of being faced with a dispassionate researcher, we are now offered one who is bubbling with enthusiasm *for his own perspectives* – but is obliged to treat the perspectives of the other with a contrasting coolness.

*4. Science Pure and Applied*

One of our most fundamental traditions is the division between pure and applied science. Practitioners of the former have usually earned the right to do "basic research". By reason of their excellence society gives them a mandate to search for truth and does not impose the condition that the truths be immediately valuable. Brilliant scientists have traditionally journeyed far from public comprehension to make fantastic discoveries. Generally speaking the lesser scientists have then worked on the practical applications of these discoveries. These applied scientists are much closer to public comprehension and human concerns.

This distinction between pure and applied science seems to have had a most unfortunate side effect on the social and life sciences. Edmund Leach expressed it well in a recent Reith Lecture.

> Mathematicians have always been eminently respectable, and so are those who deal with the hard lifeless theories about what constitutes the physical world – astronomers, the physicists, the theoretical chemists. But the more a scientist interests himself in matters which are of direct human relevance, the lower his social status. The real scum of the scientific world are the engineers and sociologists, and the psychologists. Indeed if the psychologist wants to rate as a scientist he must study rats, not human beings. In zoology the same rules apply. It is much more respectable to dissect muscle tissues than to observe the behavior of a living animal in its natural habitat.[12]

This tradition that any pure science must by definition be distant from the layman's comprehension not only militates against a psychology of human experience, it tempts social scientists to obfuscate their work so as to create social distance between themselves and critics. So successful have they been in this that some recent research found that sociology although using simpler words was less comprehensible to laymen than pharmacology![13]

Many social scientists have withdrawn into the mists on the mountain tops and can occasionally be seen mysteriously rotating factors and making multivariate analyses. Many instruments of science are there, and the incantations in jargon, but not the results.[14] It is becoming quite embarrassing.[15]

I believe that the mystique in which social science tries to envelop itself is actually a sign of failure. I regard it as one of those false shirt fronts liable at any moment to roll up under the wearer's chin. We need to question whether a science *about* human beings should be incomprehensible *to* human beings, for it seems unlikely that an incomprehensible social science can help human beings to heal, nurture, and enlighten one another. This being so, a "pure" social science, remote from lay understanding, will continue in its failure to uncover the growth inherent in giving and receiving such understanding, and we will still regard as "merely applied" the work that is done with real human beings.[16] Degrees of abstraction, reification, and deadness have become the status symbols of those who study living humanity – an extraordinary state of affairs.

*5. Precision and invariability*

Another reason for the pecking order among scientists discussed above is that the more physical and less humane the investigation, the more precise, invariable, replicable and hence "scientific" the predicted results will tend to be.

There are two ways in which a social scientist can increase the precision and invariability of his results. The first we have already discussed. He can so completely control the experimental subject that the possibilities of alternative action are reduced. Hence a hungry pigeon in a cage will peck at corn with a high degree of invariability since he cannot get out and the alternative is starvation. The dogs constrained in harness in Pavlov's experiments with meat powder periodically blasted into their mouths had to salivate or choke. Another way to increase precision is to study the *least* conscious or salient activities in the lives of subjects, e.g., the eyeblinks of beagle puppies or the unreflective purchase of detergents by housewives.[17]

Human skills, as Arthur Koestler has observed, are consciously learnt but later become "fixed sub-assemblies."[18] We drive a car automatically while thinking about our next appointment, although at first driving absorbed our total attention. What human beings regard as important and salient in their lives are their *novel and non-repetitive* activities, but what gives social investigators the feeling of being scientists is their precise and invariable patterns of behavior.

This is why social science is so frequently accused of triviality in its findings. The moment anything of import to mankind is introduced we are likely to encounter exploratory and unpredictable behavior. Consider the observation of Archimedes taking his bath. He sits down with a heavy plop as he has done many times before, soaps himself in an identical sequence of actions: all this is precise, predictable, invariable. Then to our great annoyance he shouts Eureka!, jumps to his feet, and runs naked and dripping through the doorway, completely wrecking our experiment and falsifying our hypotheses. Solemnly we determine to institute "better controls" next time and we write a short article on "the ever present danger of the Eureka-effect." The most noble aspects of man are thereby classified as a hazard for researchers.[19]

In the perspectives of psychotherapists a person who behaves repetitively in the most important areas of his life is compulsive, obsessive, and ritualistic and we should fear for his health. But if the social sciences are to build a predictive theory of high precision and invariability then healthy and creative personalities are a major snag, while the sick, the incarcerated, and the conforming will be in great demand.

*6. Empiricism and physicalism*

A respectable science is expected to have an "empirical base" consisting of unambiguous and individualized observations of "the data." While no science has been able to prosper without less visible constructs and inferences, the expectation remains that an infant science must gather, classify and account for fully observable entities. Hence the widely used term *behavioral* science owes its popularity to the visibility of outward behavior while "mental science" or "studies of consciousness" are rarely referred to.

When science spreads its mantle of prestige over all those aspects of social life which lend themselves most easily to observation, then outward behavior and appearance are elevated above inner conviction. It is no use for Martin Luther King to declare movingly, "I have a dream – that one day men will be judged not by the color of their skins but by the content of their characters" – as any proponent of the scientific method will explain, content of character and dreams are extremely inferential and represent at best "soft data." In contrast, skin color, ethnic group, income position and role in the organization, property and concrete behavior are all visible, measurable and therefore the potential ingredients of a science. There are twenty social research programs which deal with physical externalities for every one that attempts to explore the depths of human feelings and experience.

We know from the everyday social judgments which we make of people that their external appearances are not only misleading but often trivial compared with deeper knowledge of their character. It was Herman Melville who urged us to look at a single man alone,

> and he seems a wonder, a grandeur and woe. But from the same point take mankind in the mass, and for the most part, they seem a mob of unnecessary duplicates.[20]

That which is most precious and fundamental to every man is not lightly exposed to the general gaze. To do so is to risk being hurt. Nothing about the scientific methodology which I have discussed so far could lead us to suppose that men would willingly bare their innermost selves to its probings.

The use of external data located in "public space" permits hundreds of social scientists to work with identical raw materials, and this is supposed to hasten the process by which a science can be built. But if a few of these building blocks are central to men's deepest needs then the psycho-social theory which emerges may be of very limited use.

The selection of visible externalities also contains a strong bias in favor of the status quo. The existing scheme of things can be observed and measured but the aspiration in men's minds, the dream of Martin Luther King, is rarely given attention – notwithstanding the 500,000 who flocked to his funeral inspired by that dream. The current problem in the ghettos – the desperate poverty, unemployment, and anomie – are visible, quantifiable and hence scientific, but the social philosophies which galvanize the poor into a struggle against their fate have not since Marxism been accorded the accolade of science. This means that only the darkness of the present hour can receive the stamp of scientific authority. About the validity of visualized alternatives the strict empiricist can have little of authority to say until they come to pass.

*7. Mathematics and reductive analysis*

Mathematics is an excellent example of a tool so potentially valuable and prestigious that it is put to work without reflecting on the basic premises which underlie its applicability. As a symbolic language it permits such compression of thought and parsimony that it has come close to being regarded as the hallmark of scientific endeavor.

There is an old story of the drunk who searched for his lost wallet beneath the lamppost because the light was better. In deference to the "light" of mathematics we traditionally analyze the physical world into discrete observations and smaller and smaller pieces. Atomistic reduction can often reveal how the pieces combine, and the combinations are expressed mathematically. Thus two parts of hydrogen combine with one part of oxygen to form water.

The expectation that we shall explain social phenomena by analysis is prominent in behaviorism, where an apparently fluent and purposive action is broken up into a number of antecedent reinforcements under stimulus conditions. Even in psychoanalysis the personality is split into the components consisting of superego, ego and id, which comprise a limited energy mechanism.

In order to use mathematics to express the combination of separate parts, we must assume that figures are additive, commutative, and associative. Commutative means that a series of numbers taken in any order will come to the same result, while associative means that the numbers though grouped in various ways will make the same total, so that 2 and 6 and 3 are identical to 6 and 3 and 2.

There are two major problems in the analysis of social reality into its supposed parts. In the first place, the parts may not retain all the qualities of the whole. In the second place, the parts, though measurable in quantitative terms, may be neither additive, commutative, nor associative.[21]

Michael Polanyi has patiently explained that even a machine capable of reduction into parts, is not explicable by its parts.[22] All the knowledge of physics and chemistry in the world could not explain a clock to us, unless *we identify with the purpose of the creator in making the clock*. Its "clockness" is a human and holistic phenomenon which is lost sight of when taken apart. Only if we know the purpose of the creator can we use our knowledge of physics to improve its function. The same is true of an animal or a human being. Our recognition of humanity depends upon a *norm of rightness*. "This is how a human being should look and function." A human is indivisible – which is what the word "individual" originally meant.

The habit of scientific analysis has led social investigators into the "Humpty Dumpty dilemma." Humpty Dumpty not only labeled social reality unilaterally and arbitrarily, "the question is . . . which is to be master – that's all," he finished up in thousands of fragments which no one could put together again. Social science breaks the human mold into parts – and of course the parts can have nothing to say about this because only a whole can talk back – but then the attempted resynthesis fails, and we are left with the same problem as all the king's horses and all the king's men.

What social science has done is banish human *purpose* from its universe of discourse. Purpose and process are destroyed in analysis, and a mathematical combination of the parts cannot bring them back. Today a social scientist who uses human purpose as an organizing entity will likely be accused of "vitalism," "anthropomorphic subjectivism" and "normative thinking," only a few of the epithets in the arsenal. Hence while life processes face forwards towards greater complexity, variety, and higher synthesis, the vast majority of social scientists face backwards, searching for the causes of present behavior in a myriad of separate incidents, group affiliations, economic conditions, and occupational roles.

The practice of analysis assumes that the primitive can explain the complex – what Ludwig von Bertalanffy has called the "ratomorphic fallacy."[23] This tends to degrade man in many ways. Not only are the behaviors of rats, pigeons, flat-worms, and apes accepted as paradigms of human functioning, but the analytic framework will focus on fragmentation to the exclusion of integration. This is why we have such detailed knowledge of mental illness, alienation, anomie, isolation, delinquency, sensory deprivation and every kind of human and social disintegration. But we know next to nothing of integration, wholeness, personality development, and complex mental syntheses and functionings. This situation recalls the tale told by Herbert Butterfield of the professor who diced a piece of cheese with a kitchen gadget, pondered long and hard over the pieces, and then wrote a learned treatise on the cubic structure of cheese.[24]

What social scientists are ever loath to concede is that two and two can make five or even more. One of the most obvious experiences of social life is that human beings can mingle their competences to create a surplus of knowledge, love, confidence, and self-esteem. We find this in religious teachings again and again, from the parable of the talents to the feeding of five thousand. When human beings meet and interact, both may part wiser and emotionally richer. The addition of a single word to a sentence may immeasurably enrich the meanings in that sentence, just as a single additional connection between neural circuits in the brain may permit a hundred additional syntheses of knowledge. Only recently have social scientists come up with a word for this process and grudgingly enough they refer to it as "negative entropy" which is like referring to life as "undeath."

Alvin Gouldner has remarked on the extraordinary pessimism of social science, which he calls "metaphysical pathos."[25]While Romeo can say to Juliet "The more I give you the more I have," here is Peter Blau a very prominent sociologist in a rare "Excursus on Love:"

> The individual who is less deeply involved in a love relationship, therefore, is in an advantageous position, since the other's greater concern with continuing makes him or her dependent and gives the less involved individual power. . . .The lover who does not express unconditional affection early, gains advantages in the established interpersonal relationship.[26]

This is no quotation out of context but the recurring theme of much of the book.[27] It is not about love at all, of course, but about exploitation, and yet this is one of the very few attempts to treat the subject of love scientifically. Why this taboo and the absurdity of the few attempts?[28]It is because love flowing from one person to another destroys the logical distinction between A and not-A, strikes at the computer's binary code, creates more resources than were present initially, thereby upsetting laws on the conservation of energy, changes both "independent" and "dependent" variables simultaneously and has multiple meanings for the persons involved. Those whom God hath joined together, methodologists must somehow keep asunder if their tools are to work.

*8. Value-free science*

What wraps up this sad state of affairs with a pink ribbon is the assurance of scientific methodologists that they are making no value judgments. "You cannot get an ought from an is, a prescription and description. . ." so runs the catechism. What if the tools of description are injuring the social system as they take its measure? For even in the micro-physics, Heisenberg tells us, we affect the data by our tools. It is even more so in social science where the system experiences the scientist while the scientist experiences the system.[29]

What is meant by value free science is that tools can make no final judgments as to ends. But tools can, as we have seen, bring certain ends nearer by their application, make other ends nearly impossible to attain, and leave vast areas of human endeavor undiscovered. If we value integrity and wholeness then the process of analysis without synthesis will create disvalues. If we value love, then a detached technique can hinder both its study and its consummation. The controlled experiment will not enable us to examine freedom or spontaneity.

Those who work on war games and the simulations of megadeath try to persuade us that their tools are neutral and can be plugged in to many policies and national goals,[30] but I doubt this. Two nations or persons locked into a mutual antagonism and competing for scarce resources both constrain each other's moves and monopolize each other's attention. Like the marital games which people play,[31] the game of war is a large scale neurosis, wherein the two sides, neatly separable, mutually frustrating and rigidified by fear will respond predictably and defensively to each other's inputs. The formidable pile of statistics on zero sum games and the Prisoner's Dilemma game[32] could not possibly simulate creative and trusting relationships, for it is precisely the glory of man that mutually enhancing behavior obviates the need for repetition and brings on emancipation from games through endless elaborations and explorations. War games and like simulations represent a massive investment of brainpower and money in the psychological (not technical) status quo. The game *as currently conducted* is enshrined in scientism with a vested interest in its continuance. But if, as I shall argue in this book, the most valuable outcomes to man are inherently the most uncertain, then the insistence upon containing foreign policy within a "scientific" framework is a vote for everlasting enmity and mutual constriction on behavior. Where tools of science demand certain conditions for their "best application" we must first assure ourselves that these conditions are also best for us. In the meantime we should not delude ourselves that the borrowed toolbox is neutral. Those tools regarded as most "scientific" uncover selectively those aspects of man that most resemble the dead mechanical universe for which the tools were originally designed.

Tools of science are an extension of our senses and soon become part of us. We know from research that the pupils of our eyes will contract when we see distasteful things and expand to take in what we value.[33] It behooves us therefore to be aware not only of what our liking or disliking enables us to see but to consider that tools act like an expanding pupil to let in some phenomenon *as if we liked it*. And since science is itself a prestigious authority what its tools screen out will be less valued by the culture as a whole.

But is there any consistent political bias within the borrowed toolbox? I am not talking about social scientists as a group but rather about the political direction in which an insistence on strict methodology would oblige them to lean. I have argued that power over things turns into unreflective power over people, that the need to predict and control produces detachment, an unequal relationship and a self-fulfilling prophecy which makes the unequal appear undeserving of equality. I have argued that the demand for precision and invariability attracts the investigator to the more trivial and repetitive activities of man, that empiricism focuses on stereotyped externalities, ignores depth of experience and emphasizes the status quo above visions of the future. We have seen that analysis fragments without being able to reintegrate, looks to the past instead of facing forward, regards man in the light of animals and fails to respect his complexity. The "games" which simulate life view it as a competitive struggle for scarce resources, rather than the synergistic creation of abundance.

Now there is a simple political term which sums up this orientation. It is *conservative*. And those who doubt me can examine McClosky's painstaking research on the conservative personality, which is detailed in Chapter IX of this book. An American conservative is elitist, hierarchical, and anxious to control others. He tends to see mankind as animalistic and as an unorganized rabble. He is often vigorous but is obsessive and repetitive in his habits. He values consensus and discipline. He is suspicious of unpredictable people and has little tolerance for human ambiguity, sees life as an economic struggle, looks to the past, and tends to stereotype people. He is uneasy with emotion and affect, prefers to put social distance between himself and others and to withdraw into a class of like minded people.

It will be immediately objected that social scientists give little support to conservatism and are actively disliked on the American Right. Quite so. Like any academics they need the liberal ideology of free inquiry and the search for truth. We have seen that investigators tend to regard *themselves* as "independent variables" as purposive, creative, and free. Their social conservatism is *for others*, the objects of investigation. Moreover their conservatism is unaware, non-ideological, unowned, and is latent in the tools they employ. It comes about less by valuing conservatively than by the "value-free" selection of the less than human.[34] As Maurice Stein has observed, the attempt to be value-free in social contexts can end up by making one value*less*. He who is silent assents, and to describe the *status quo* with detailed and passionless precision is usually to dignify it.

Social scientists with a social conscience, and there are many, have reacted to the dilemma of the borrowed toolbox in several ways: Some eschew methodology all together and take the role of essayists and social critics. Others make a whole career out of protesting against current orthodoxies. Still others accept parts of the methodology but can be heard consecrating parts of it towards the betterment of the poor. However, as with the Moynihan Report, the *style* remains conservative and the poor do not relish a description of the problem as being *inside them* – when in fact the problem is one of *relational elitism*, of which the report is itself an example, and which is endemic in the "scientific methodology" employed.[35] If dedication to the poor on the part of these tool bearers is sometimes suspect, no one can doubt the humanism of that small minority of social scientists who study such phenomena as creativity and self-fulfillment. Yet for the most part they work in a methodological vacuum and are widely ignored in their professions. Watching all these strategies I get the impression of a virgin science attempting to free itself from the mechanism of a chastity belt.

What is required is a new philosophy for the social sciences – a complete reassessment of what a science of humanity should be. This is not accomplished by cultivating an awareness of criticism or by acknowledging humanity in the shape of "intervening variables" between stimulus and response – but by a total reversal of the mechanistic, reactive, and physicalist treatment of man. What the borrowed toolbox uncovers and helps to create is Conservative Man. Current methodology is like a weighted coin which can only come up "tails." When we look at Conservative Man we cannot see the other side of the coin – but when we turn it over we discover Radical Man and then the Conservative image is obscured.

While Conservative Man is caused to behave, Radical Man imagines and reasons autonomously. Where the former responds predictably and obediently, the latter rebels creatively. Where the former is a product of natural forces, the latter defines himself and his environment in dialogue with others and is a radiating center of meaning. Where the former seeks to *conserve* his energy, reduce dissonance and achieve equilibrium, the latter seeks to create more energy, and values the tension and excitement of disequilibrium. While the former obeys the law of entropy by running down like an old clock, the latter diverges, converges, and emerges as a life force. What we have, then, is a principle of complementarity in which two opposing conceptualisations of man are required to organize the findings of social science. This could be analogous to the principle proposed by Niels Bohr. He argued that the ultimate nature of matter could be regarded as waves *and* as particles but that these must be viewed in alternation since it was impossible to see both "sides" simultaneously.

It is hardly surprising that social science students, who more than those in any other field, value altruism[36] are in open revolt from campus to campus, as their schools attempt to drill the humanity out of them and force them into the conservative cast. Not since the Children of Israel were required to make bricks without straw has a generation been faced with such a ludicrous disproportion between the social tasks and the tools provided. The revolt began at the Berkeley campus at the University of California, where nearly 40% of the students study the social sciences and where over 50% of the Free Speech Movement were majoring in this area. The French student revolt of May 1968 began in the department of Sociology. Early in the Columbia University revolt social science students spontaneously seized their own Fairweather Hall. At Harvard, students of Social Relations were disproportionately represented among those arrested in University Hall in the Spring of 1969. During this term the most popular course in the entire University was Social Relations 149, a student-run break-away course with over 800 members, that deliberately eschewed formal disciplines in order to attain human relevance.

What testifies to the present bankruptcy of the social sciences is that formal disciplines and human relevance are so difficult to reconcile, that our best students are obliged to sacrifice the first in choosing the second. This book will attempt a reconciliation between the two.

## NOTES FOR CHAPTER I

1. Emmanuel G. Mesthene, "Man and His Tools," Address to Grinnell College. Harvard University, Program on Technology and Society, Mimeo., 1967.

2. In *The Ghost in the Machine,* Macmillan, 1967, see especially Chapter I and Appendix II.

3. From "The Prooemiom of Francis Bacon," *The Great Instauration* quoted by Hans Jonas in "The Practical Uses of Theory," *Social Research,* Vol. 26, No. 2, 1959, p. 127.

4. "The Practical Uses of Theory," *op. cit.,* p. 131.

5. That experimental procedures violate our social norms is evident in the fact that experimental subjects are so frequently deceived and made to believe that they are in a cooperative relationship with the experimenter when in fact they are being unilaterally manipulated.

6. See for example Leonard Berkowitz (1964) on violence, Richard Crutchfield (1955) on conformity, Stanley Milgram (1963) on obedience, Grinder (1964) on cheating, and Allport (1954) for a summary of experiments on prejudice and scapegoating.

7. The experiments with monkeys are by Harlow (1964), for the characteristics of rebels in experiments see Chapter V of this volume.

8. This and many other telling critiques are made by John R. Seeley in "Social Science? Some Probabitive Problems," in *Sociology on Trial,* Maurice Stein and Arthur Vidich (eds.), Englewood Cliffs: Prentice-Hall, 1963.

9. For a discussion of this distinction see R. D. Laing, *The Politics of Experience,* New York: Pantheon, 1967.

10. For a good account of a revolt by investigated persons see *The Moynihan Report and The Politics of Controversy* by Lee Rainwater and William L. Yancey (1967).

11. See Abraham Kaplan, *The Conduct of Inquiry,* (1964).

12. *Runaway World?*, British Broadcasting Company, London, 1968, p. 10.

13. "Are Sociologists Incomprehensible?" by F. E. Cheek and Maureen Rosenhaupt, in *Amer. J. Sociology,* Vol. 73, No. 5, 1968, pp. 617-627.

14. Admissions of failure come not just from critics but from The Establishment. George Homans recently complained that social scientists between them had been unable to agree on any single general proposition which could form a basis for research. The field was in "intellectual chaos." He thereupon offered his proposition of social exchange, whereupon many colleagues disagreed and the chaos continued. See *Social Behavior: Its Elementary Forms,* New York: Harcourt, Brace & World, 1961.

15. Robert K. Merton writes beautiful apologies for sociology, explaining, in a delightful prose style, why the style of others is necessarily so dull and how much work is still to be done before the science can be relevant. However he makes some crucial admissions. Sociology has yet to find its Kepler, much less its Newton. See *Social Theory and Social Structure,* Glencoe: Free Press, 1949. No sign of a Kepler has since appeared. Twelve years later Fritz Machlup was still complaining that "Many Sociology departments have been notorious for their role as a refuge for mentally underprivileged undergraduates." See "Are the Social Sciences Really Inferior" in *Philosophy of The Social Sciences,* M. Natanson (ed.), New York: Random House, 1965, p. 176.

16. Alfred Schutz is particularly enlightening on this issue, see "Concepts, Constructs and Theory Formation" in *The Journal of Philosophy,* April, 1959, pp. 257-273.

17. Anyone wishing to sample the "best" research in the social sciences can scan the prize-winning dissertations of The Creative Talents Awards Program, sponsored by The American Institutes for Research, and described in their annual publication. The 1967 award winners included, "The Development of Visually Evoked Responses in Kittens," "The Effect of Errors on the Reaction Time in a Serial Reaction Task," and "The Effects of Independent Manipulations of Central Stimulation and Nasal Air Flow on Induced Activity Recorded from Olfactory Structures." When I offered an early version of this manuscript to the awards committee they declined even to read it.

18. *The Act of Creation,* New York: Macmillan, 1964, p. 38f.

19. See my discussion at the beginning of Chapter VIII on The Hawthorne effect.

20. *Moby Dick,* New York: Rinehart and Co., 1948, p. 461.

21. See Abraham Kaplan, *The Conduct of Inquiry, op. cit.*, p. 67.

22. For an excellent discussion of this issue see *Personal Knowledge,* New York: Harper Torchbook, 1964, pp. 328-331.

23. *Robots, Men and Minds,* New York: George Braziller, 1967, pp. 14-18.

24. *History and Human Relations,* London: Collins, 1951.

25. See "Metaphysical Pathos and The Theory of Bureaucracy" in *Amer. Pol. Sci. Rev.,* 49 (1955), pp. 496-507.

26. *Exchange and Power,* New York: Wiley, 1964, p. 78.

27. We are told that "A woman who readily gives proof of her affection to a man, therefore, provides presumptive evidence of her lack of popularity and thus tends to depreciate the value of her affection for him. Her resistance to his attempts to conquer her, in contrast, implies that she is in great demand and has many alternatives to choose from, which is likely to enhance her desirability in his eyes." Blau frequently cites research done among high school adolescents and delinquent gangs, giving ample evidence of the entrapment and misery of those who think in terms of this model which likens human interaction to the exchange and mutual marketing of attractive goods.

28. Blau draws his principle idea of exchange from George C. Homans, *Social Behavior: Its Elementary Forms,* New York: Harcourt, Brace & World, 1961. Homans sees "liking" as a function of geographical proximity, conformity, positive reinforcement, and status congruence.

29. John Seeley asks, "How could a love relationship survive, for instance, an extended equitable enumeration of the characteristics of the beloved? How does other-directed behavior survive its categorization (stigmatization) as such? What becomes of an organization man, once he is identified by self and others as such? See "Social Science? Some Probative Problems," *op. cit.,* p. 58.

30. One of the best discussions is in *Deadly Logic: The Theory of Nuclear Deterrence* by Philip Green, New York: Schocken Books, 1968. See also Anatol Rapoport, *Strategy and Conscience,* New York: Harper & Row, 1964.

31. E. Berne, *Games People Play,* New York: Grove Press, 1964.

32. *Strategy and Conscience,* op. cit., pp. 41-58.

33. Eckhard H. Hess and James Polk, "Pupil Size as Related to Interest Value of Visual Stimuli," *Science,* 132, 1960, pp. 349-50.

34. See "Anti-Minotaur: The Myth of Value-Free Sociology" by Alvin W. Gouldner in *Sociology on Trial, op. cit.,* pp. 35-52.

35. This issue is thoroughly discussed in *The Moynihan Report and The Politics of Controversy* by Lee Rainwater and William L. Yancey, Cambridge: M.I.T. Press, 1967.

36. See Figure 2 in Chapter XI.

*Chapter II*

## The Existential Perspective

I have argued that we need a fresh perspective in the social sciences in order to appreciate the radical, creative and integrative side of human personality. In this Chapter I shall explore the full ramifications of the words "man exists freely," which will form the basis of my model of psycho-social development introduced in the next chapter.

Existence comes from the Latin ex-istere meaning to *stand out*. I shall later be referring to the process of *investment* or man investing personal meanings, since what I wish to convey is the transitive nature of the process. The human personality is invested beyond the mind into the social environment, so that man is conceived as a radiating center of meaning.

In the diagram below, the box in the center represents the human mind with inputs on the left and outputs on the right. The top half of the diagram is expressed in existential terms. The lower half with dotted lines is expressed in the terms of behavioral learning theory.

| INPUTS | MIND | OUTPUTS |
|---|---|---|
| Confirmations of experience and novel perceptions | Synthesing Symbolizing and Exploring Capacities | Investments of personal meanings and experience |
| Various reinforcements under certain stimulus conditions | Basic Drives and Intervening Variables | Responses in the form of physical and verbal behavior |

Under the following heads I shall explore the evidence for man's existence and the ramifications thereof.

1. The synthesizing capacity
2. The symbolizing capacity
3. The exploring capacity
   (which require:)–
4. A field theory – not a monadic one
5. The concept of freedom within the law – not strict determinism
6. Relational facts not objective facts
7. Alternate involvement with self and others – not detachment
8. Value full investigation – not value free.

In the bottom half of the diagram above we see that behaviorists work with the concepts of "stimuli," "reinforcements," the "basic drives" of the person such as hunger and sex, and the characteristics of his "responses," such as strength, frequency and direction. Lately neo-behaviorists have been more and more concerned with "intervening variables" – e.g., age, intelligence, personality type, I.Q., and diagnostic categories. They believe that "reinforcement" under certain "stimulus conditions" will "shape the drives" of specified types of people so that their "responses" can be predicted. The more sophisticated of these experiments have multiple intervening variables.[1]

The advantage of this technique is that it permits the application of most of the traditional scientific principles outlined in Chapter I, including the hypothetico-deductive method, fairly strict empiricism (depending on the nature of the "intervening variables"), replication, precision, mathematics and analysis. Its disadvantages, as we saw in Chapter I, are that it ignores, minimizes, or distorts the radical human capacities for synthesizing, symbolizing, and exploring. I hope to show that these capacities are so salient that they justify a reversal of the behavioral perspective itself.

*1. The synthesizing capacity*

There has been a series of experiments by José Delgado thought by many to usher in a new millenium for behaviorism. By implanting electrodes in certain parts of the brain, angry bulls have been halted in mid-charge to become as docile as Ferdinand, monkeys have eaten ravenously at the press of a button and then rejected the food when other parts of their brains were stimulated. But after detailed study of neural pathways and the synapses which permit new connections between circuits Delgado wrote:–

> . . .it should be emphasized that the source of mental information is totally *extracerebral*. The brain can accept, reject or react against received information, or establish associations between past and present sensory inputs. Originality and invention are merely a novel combination of old data, and original thought could not be produced by the naive brain of a newborn baby. Shakespeare did not invent English, nor Einstein, mathematics. . . . The elements which form our personality are borrowed from the environment and from the past. Only their combination and the feelings they create within us are unique.[2]

Here, then, from the pinnacle of S-R achievement we have an admission (hedged around with "merely's" and "only's") of man's capacity to select information, synthesize and resynthesize it. We know that even apes can do this. Wolfgang Kohler describes how an ape which he had observed from birth and which had never used a stick as a tool and never seen one used (although he had played with one), suddenly broke a branch from a bush growing within his cage and, stripping it of leaves and twigs, pushed it through the bars of the cage to retrieve a banana. He accomplished this not by trial and error, but by one fluent series of actions following a period of seeming reflection.[3] Cats have been faced with the problem of obtaining a piece of meat which is suspended in the middle of a closed cage by a piece of string which passes through the top of the cage and is attached to the ceiling. They survey the situation, pause a moment, then leap upon the top of the cage and draw up the string with the meat at the end.[4]

Arthur Koestler has described these elementary acts of creation as "bi-sociation" of two or more "thought matrices".[5] The wanting-to-reach-and-eat-the-banana matrix is suddenly visualized as capable of combination with the playing-with-sticks matrix and in the absence of a stick "the bush-consisting-of-sticks" is seen as relevant too. The animals can *select* only a stick from out of the "bush matrix" and only the raking in motion from the "playing matrix." Coded information from one neural circuit travels across the synapse into another circuit, and two images are combined.[6]

From apes let us move to Gutenberg and his invention of the printing press. He recollected seeing the carved wooden blocks which were used to stamp playing cards. Later he watched molten coins poured into moulds, and he recalled that seals could be used to stamp paper. But none of these could solve his problem of how to mass produce bibles for a pilgrimage – until months later when he watched a wine press in action. In a flash he saw the solution. "A simple substitution which is a ray of light. . . God hath revealed to me the secret. . ." he wrote. He visualized moulds for every letter of the alphabet in which type could be cast like coins, the type face like a giant seal could be attached to a press, and the press could stamp vellum "like your foot when it multiplies its print. There is the Bible!"[7]

Let us return to the diagram for a moment. Behaviorists would argue that every part of Gutenberg's "response", the printing press, can be traced to prior "reinforcements" and "contiguous stimuli," or to quote Delgado, we have "merely a novel combination of old data." But this combination is no less than revolutionary *so that the input has been totally transformed by this human brain into a novel output*.

What do I mean by "totally transformed"? In the first place there is a transformation in human significance. Print technology was perhaps our greatest leap into modernity and rang up the curtain on the Renaissance. We cannot say this of playing cards or winepresses – a fact that illustrates how incredibly more significant can be the combination of parts than the parts themselves. Combination can produce totally new entities – neither a bush, a plaything, nor the need for a banana is a tool – but the selective syntheses of these matrices can produce the idea of a tool, with its endless ramifications leading up to space technology.

A synthesis can increase energy output a thousandfold or more. How long would it have taken to carve every word of the Bible on wooden blocks? This synthesis transformed the capacity to communicate, helped to fashion the notion of information storage and retrieval, disseminated the Bible so widely that a moral Reformation soon swept Europe. Finally it led to vast increases in the human capacity to symbolize and transmit symbols.

*2. The symbolizing capacity*

If man stands out from his past "reinforcements" by weaving remembered experiences into a personal synthesis, then he stands out also when he chooses symbols to *stand for* those experiences.

Suppose that one were thrown by Nazis into a death camp, as was Viktor Frankl[8] or that like Albert Camus and Jean Paul Sartre one were forced to live under the Occupation. It would be hard to conceive of more "negative reinforcements" designed to obtain predictable "responses" from victims. And to some extent the predictions were correct, for thousands collaborated, perished, and gave up hope: but a sizable minority found the courage to rebel and this they did by finding fresh meanings, by relabelling the same reality that was overwhelming their compatriots.[9]

For existentialists like Sartre and Camus the absurdity and horror of their environment instead of forcing them to be products of absurdity convinced them of their freedom and that human beings themselves were the sole source of value. "We were never more free than under the Nazis." wrote Sartre. Here he is using "free" in the special existential sense as *the discrepancy between the tyrannical pressures upon him and his capacity to generate meanings which contradicted this environment.*

Similarly Frankl had to experience the degradation of a concentration camp to discover how powerful was his human capacity to emit meaning in the face of chaos. His light shone all the more brightly because the darkness was so total. When aid and comfort were finally extinguished in his surroundings he discovered a personal power which not only sustained him and his companions but laid the ground work for his Third Psychiatric Revolution.[10]

Existential philosophies have a way of strengthening themselves in the face of adversity, for the more evil and inchoate is the environment, the more is the existentialist convinced that only his own affirmation of value and his rebellion in the face of death itself (the final absurdity) can project meaning into the world. He only needs a few memory traces whose combination is meaningful to combat a contemporary assault of "negative reinforcements." Man is free to choose between symbols, and to label pressures upon him as legitimate or illegitimate, free to resymbolize, and free to synthesize and resynthesize those symbols into structured fields of meaning by which he exists.

*3. The exploring capacity*

Man stands out in yet another way. Instead of passively waiting to be bombarded with "stimuli" he actively explores his environment, using his incomplete knowledge in search for the missing elements in his mental "map."

Behaviorists have never been comfortable with the "exploratory drive." While "hunger drives" in animals can be "shaped" almost completely in controlled conditions, the drive for exploration which *seeks the unknown* cannot be be "shaped" by events *known* to be "reinforcing." Even were I to admit that "novelty is reinforcing," this would not enable me to predict that a certain "reinforcement" would produce a certain "response" since that "response" might still be seeking the unknown – that is something different from what was previously "reinforced." Whichever way you stretch the elastic concept of "reinforcement," the exploratory capacity introduces an unpredictable element, and where exploration is combined with man's synthesizing and symbolizing capacities this produces an intentional and a focused capacity to search.

Even in caged animal experiments – and these conditions minimize the freedom to explore – it has long been known that rats will learn a maze merely by being placed in it without reward.[11] They will run the gauntlet of an electrified grill for the sake of exploring strange objects[12] and leave food unfinished when their curiosity is aroused.[13] Rhesus monkeys solve manual puzzles more easily when *no* food or "reinforcers" are inside.[14] Indeed appetite makes them clumsy and impatient. Similarly hungry babies and unmothered monkeys are notoriously unexplorative. The need to know emerges when physiological and emotional needs reach some level of satisfaction.

When man searches he may be looking for a piece to link two or more information matrices and so create a systemic body of thought. He may have a symbol and be seeking the experience for which it stands. Successful exploration can expand his symbolizing, synthesizing, and experiential capacities, and this expanded consciousness can in turn guide his further exploration. In view of the total transformation of incoming messages wrought by the human mind, its capacity to seek out certain messages in preference to others, and its astonishing freedom to synthesize and code its store of memories, I submit that "man exists freely."

In light of this existence let me pause to restate the opening question in this book. If with Bacon we seek a knowledge which is power, then what would most contribute to the knowledge and power of man – a psychology that traced *backwards* from a radio telescope to dim memories of jungle drums and smoked glass, or a psychology that reveals the synthesizing, developing, and expanding process of the human mind in dialogue with other minds? Even were I convinced (and I am not) that man was nine-tenths "caused to behave" and one-tenth seeking, synthesizing and symbolizing, I would still explore the latter realm and thereby make my existential choice of being as responsible as the human condition allows. As Arthur Miller once put it.

> What is needed are people who, quite simply, know how to think, who know how to synthesize knowledge and find connections between distantly related phenomena, who seek constantly to relate rather than isolate experience.[15]

Given this existential perspective a number of ramifications follow that profoundly affect the usual assumptions of psychosocial investigation.

*4. A field theory – not a monadic one*

Once we accept that man is a synthesizer of fragmentary experience and a synthesizer of his own earlier syntheses, then analysis, the breaking down of the life field into fragments, must be recognized as a potentially regressive process[16] and one that can blind an investigator to the struggle of living organisms to achieve higher levels of developmental organization.

For the basic property that differentiates living matter from dead matter is not found in a physical or chemical description of the constituents. A heap of dead ingredients can have the same chemical properties as a live organism. Life is a peculiar *state of organization* – a vital synthesis of parts.[17]

Most attempts at theory building in the social sciences assume a *monadic* theory – one in which the relationships *between* unit entities are explained by some property of the *units themselves.*[18] In other words first you analyze social reality into separate units – making sure they are "mutually exclusive and collectively exhaustive" – and *then* you discover how these units interact and relate. What is overlooked in this almost standard procedure is the possibility that the overall organization of the pieces is what imparts to them the very property of life and that their meanings are not intrinsic but depend on how they are synthesized.

Suppose we meet a man who proclaims loudly and often that his home is his castle. Depending on how he organized this attitude into an overall *gestalt* he might for all we know:

be a radical protesting illegal seizure of his pamphlets by the police,
be a racist objecting to open housing ordinances,
be a psychotic convinced that he is William the Conqueror,
or be an English peer of the realm attempting to attract tourists to his ancestral seat. To treat such statements as "basic data" and "building blocks" for a science could be extremely hazardous.

What a psychology of existence needs is a *field* theory rather than a monadic one. Our symbolic language is comprehended through its overall structure which carries the meaning, so that we retain the meaning while often forgetting the verbal units in which it was expressed, and we substitute our own units when we relay the meaning to others. Hence an existential perspective is holistic in the sense that *the whole must be grasped in order to comprehend the function of the parts.*[19]

Much of social science is getting laboriously nowhere by trying to correlate artificially separated units of attitude and behavior whose intrinsic meaning is at best ambiguous and inconstant. And the attempt to invent a private language where words have only one precise meaning leads to some very simple ideas being expressed in turgid prose at extraordinary length.[20] In fact the multi-faceted symbol with several contiguous meanings plays a vital part in creating a synthesis between matrices. When social science purges itself of ambiguity it may reduce the capacity of its researchers to think creatively, which might explain why so many of its writings hardly keep the mind alive.

*5. The concept of freedom within the law – not strict determinism*

"The freedom of living things is a freedom not *without* the law but *within* the law," writes Floyd Matson.[21] In contrast to this view the polarity of freedom *versus* determinism is commonly expressed along with conviction that science rests squarely upon determinism.

The existential perspective regards this and many other polarities as reconcilable. The capacity to synthesize, symbolize and explore, though leading to unique results, is still a lawful process containing measurable uniformities. In existential philosophy man is free yet bound by his human condition, recognition of the certainties of this condition is regarded as the springboard of freedom, and all free men may still be required to regard certain truths as inalterable.[22]

In biology the concept of equipotentiality recognizes that while an organism will unfold and seems directed by a genetic code to seek an end state of maturation – there are still many degrees of freedom in the paths taken to this end.[23] If parts of an organism are removed other parts will take over their function. Minced and scrambled tissues reorganize themselves while certain organs regenerate. Where normal paths are blocked ingenious and circuitous paths will be substituted. In some organisms, for instance the mushroom, the tangle of fibres is quite unpredictable but not the final smooth curvature to which these fibres aim. In man codes of thought and morals seem to have supplemented the genetic code and while we can seldom predict on the basis of his ideological or his genetic code the exact behaviors a man will emit, we can predict *the direction* and understand to what ends the partial processes are being subordinated.

This subordination of man's motor skills, verbal units, and fixed sub-assemblies to the overall style and purpose of his existence is completely missed by those who regard freedom as some unreliable link in an otherwise flawless chain of cause and effect.[24] Existentially man lives in a "world of freedom." Everything in that world is directed and triggered into action by the structures of his existence. Even if Delgado were to intrude upon my brain and stimulate it so that I poured out an endless succession of cups of tea, I might still combine this with my own value matrix and pour it over him and his contraptions. My body and my world though hedged on many sides by compulsion are freed by my capacities for existence to serve overall ends.[25]

*6. Relational facts not objective facts*

The old habits of mind also contrast objectivity with subjectivity – usually to the detriment of the latter. This originates in the habit of detachment and analysis, but specifically in the Cartesian dichotomy between the mind and external reality. So thoroughly has this view permeated our discourse that we are seldom aware of how narrowly it channels our thought. The eye is regarded as a retinal mirror, reflecting what is out there in the "real world" of physical objects located in public space.

After summarizing many research studies that demonstrate the impact of human thought and knowledge upon perception, Arthur Koestler bids us trace with soap the outline of our faces reflected in the mirror.[26] The image is actually much smaller than our heads. That we do not exclaim, "My God, my head has shrunk!," testifies to the fact that we *know* our heads remain of constant size and this knowledge adjusts our vision. In many other ways our knowledge and expectancy, our symbols and syntheses, control the way we see.

Instead of facts being "out there" separate from me and passively reflected in my brain, the existential perspective regards all perceived facts as organized by my style of existence – an integrated structure of *relational facts,* which thus transcend another false dichotomy – that between subjective and objective. As Rollo May has put it:

> Existentialism, in short, is the endeavor to understand man by cutting below the cleavage between subject and object which has bedeviled Western thought and science since shortly after the Renaissance. This cleavage Binswanger calls "the cancer of all psychology up to now . . .[27]

So while all behaviorists regard "reinforcements," "stimuli," and "responses," etc. as separate objective facts, the existentialists see the creation, investment and confirmation of meanings as a total process radiating from the individual. Labelling the parts of this process is purely for convenience, as we might draw attention to different aspects of a total organism without ever assuming its separateness.

It is often assumed that existentialism is wholly subjective – an error which springs from a Cartesian cast of mind unable to suspend its structures. From here the conclusion is drawn that only objectivity can be validated. But most existentialists regard objectivity as nothing more than a consensus among investigators as to how a phenomenon is to be regarded and measured. Hence calls for objectivity are like calls for consensus politics – they affirm the most obvious and the least controversial. In fact, creative styles of existence tend to be self-validating. A creative man will have distinctive kinds of thought processes that we can measure, will report his experience in certain ways, communicate that experience to others, and leave impacts on his environment. Every stage of this process is validated by earlier or later stages so that they are *congruent.* Lack of congruence alerts the investigator to pseudo existence, misreports, or unreliable instruments. The particular fault can often be identified by which of the measures are out of line.

*7. Alternate involvement with self and others – not detachment*

The existential knower cannot by definition practice the traditional scientific detachment. He is studying relational facts, and the attempt to detach himself could destroy these. Even where he is observing the mutuality of others, the source of his insight will run dry with the source of his concern, since his own feelings and powers of identification are important clues to the shared human condition. If man exists he inevitably influences what he studies, and his only choice is to become aware of what he contributes to the relationship and to ensure that it facilitates the developmental process in which he himself is involved.

Yet there is one kind of "detachment" which *is* necessary. In order to understand others one must achieve at least a momentary suspension of self-concern in order to comprehend *their* perspectives – to switch from self-involvement to other-involvement. A man with the disciplined capacity to understand why his most cherished idea is a dead duck from the perspectives of his listeners is still attached to human concerns.

*8. Value full investigation – not value free*

Were men caused to behave only by previous "reinforcements" and "stimuli" and were these enough or almost enough to predict the human "responses," then the professed values of such men would be only verbalized noises for what had actually "reinforced" them. The investigators would then be wise to discard such values as explanations for behavior since description carries no prescription and you cannot get an "Ought" from an "Is." If, on the other hand, men are synthesizers of symbols and these totally transform "reinforcements" into novel existence then *personal values are the partial blueprints for these transformations.* Where men choose between aspects of their past experience to create their preferred combinations then moral choice is at the very heart of existence and cannot be exorcised from the investigator or his subjects. To detach oneself and treat others like so many objects is not to be value-free but to choose to devalue others.

The moment we conceive of creativity and communication as mediated by codes of values, then we must ask which values facilitate successful and creative communication and which impede this process. The thousands of values which we urge one another to adopt can only be fashioned and exchanged if those *core* values supportive of creativity and communication themselves are constantly affirmed. In this existential view, radical man daily invests prescriptions in his environment which can become descriptive realities. In every "Ought" lies an embryonic "Is."

It is because I dispute the norms of value-free science, detachment, and objectivity that I am not writing this book with the usual academic inhibitions. My core values are better conveyed if they less resemble an apology on stilts. Since affirmation and involvement are appropriate to existential inquiry, it seems appropriate to reveal them in these pages.

## NOTES FOR CHAPTER II

1. The most convincing summary and exposition of current neo-behaviorism is contained in *Social Learning and Personality Development* by Albert Bandura and Richard H. Walters, New York: Holt, Rinehart and Winston, 1965.

2. "Manipulation of Behavior by Direct Stimulation of The Brain." Paper presented at the Columbia University Seminars on Technology and Social Change, Nov. 1966, Mimeo., p. 19.

3. See *The Mentality of Apes,* Harmondsworth: Pelican Books, 1957.

4. See E. R. Hilgard, *Theories of Learning,* London: Methuen, 1958, p. 65.

5. *The Act of Creation, op. cit.,* p. 35f.

6. "Manipulation of Behavior by Direct Stimulation of The Brain," *op. cit.,* p. 10.

7. Quoted by Arthur Koestler in *The Act of Creation, op. cit.,* p. 123.

8. A description of his conversion to existentialism is in *Man's Search for Meaning* (formerly entitled *From Death Camp to Existentialism*) New York: Washington Square Press, 1963.

9. This process is well described by Camus in *Resistance, Rebellion, and Death,* New York: Modern Library, 1960, see especially pp. 1-25, "Letters to a German Friend."

10. *Man's Search for Meaning, op. cit.*

11. Harlow, H. F., *Psychol. Review,* 60, 1953, pp. 23-32.

12. See H. W. Nissen's contribution in *Current Theory and Research in Motivation,* Jones, M. R. (ed.), University of Nebraska Press, 1954.

13. See D. E. Berlyne, *Conflict, Arousal and Curiosity,* New York: McGraw-Hill, 1960, p. 119.

14. Harlow, H. F., *op. cit.*

15. Quoted by Penelope Gilliat in the London *Observer,* 1965. Exact reference mislaid.

16. For a persuasive and scholarly account of man fragmented by scientific premises, see *The Broken Image* by Floyd W. Matson, New York: Braziller, 1964.

17. Ludwig von Bertalanffy was making this and related points as early as 1927. His views are at last gaining a respectful hearing and are well summarized in *Problems of Life,* New York: Harper Torchbooks, 1960.

18. The distinction between monodic and field theories is well made in *The Conduct of Inquiry, op. cit.*

19. This idea is developed by Arthur Koestler in his distinction between The Chain of Words and The Tree of Language, see *The Ghost in The Machine, op. cit.,* pp. 19-45.

20. C. Wright Mills has teased grand theorists, especially Talcott Parsons. He cites whole pages from Parsons and then summarizes them in one short paragraph each. See *The Sociological Imagination,* New York: Grove Press, 1961, pp. 25-49.

21. *The Broken Image, op. cit.,* p. 76.

22. This and similar points are made in John Wild's excellent exposition on *Existence and The World of Freedom,* Englewood Cliffs: Prentice Hall, 1963.

23. See *Problems of Life, op. cit.*

24. *The Ghost in The Machine, op. cit.,* p. 19 *et. seq.*

25. *Ibid.,* pp. 45-58.

26. *The Act of Creation, op. cit.,* p. 120.

27. See "Origins of the Existential Movement" by Rollo May, in *Existence: A New Dimension in Psychiatry and Psychology,* Rollo May (ed.), New York: Clarion Books, 1967, p. 11. For an excellent summary of the arguments for and against behaviorism and phenomenology, see *Behaviorism and Phenomenology,* T. W. Wann (ed.), University of Chicago Press, 1964.

## *Chapter III*

## A Model of Psycho-Social Development

Not only does man exist, but he does so in relation to others who receive his communications and witness the investment of his personality in the human environment. Hence the development of existential capacities in one man is interdependent with the development of such capacities in other men and the total relationship may be regarded as a continuous process. My model of this process reads as follows:

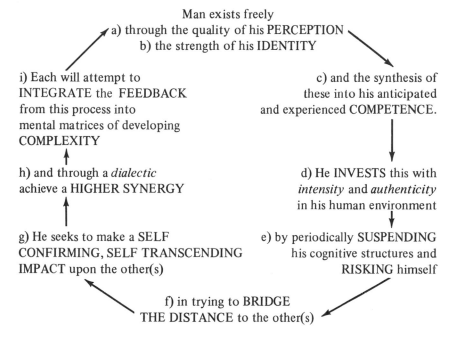

Man exists freely
a) through the quality of his PERCEPTION
b) the strength of his IDENTITY

c) and the synthesis of these into his anticipated and experienced COMPETENCE.

d) He INVESTS this with *intensity* and *authenticity* in his human environment

e) by periodically SUSPENDING his cognitive structures and RISKING himself

f) in trying to BRIDGE THE DISTANCE to the other(s)

g) He seeks to make a SELF CONFIRMING, SELF TRANSCENDING IMPACT upon the other(s)

h) and through a *dialectic* achieve a HIGHER SYNERGY

i) Each will attempt to INTEGRATE the FEEDBACK from this process into mental matrices of developing COMPLEXITY

Let us recall from the discussion in Chapter II some of the characteristics of this model.

1. Every segment of the model is permeated by man's existence and the values thereof. He *chooses* how to perceive and whom to perceive. He defines himself and his competence, and invests this competence with a chosen degree of risk and purpose. From the synergy of his existence with that of others he chooses what to recall and how to symbolize and synthesize it. He is free *within* the process of his development which is the necessary condition

of his freedom.
2. The model foreshadows a field theory and not a monadic one. Each segment derives its meaning from its place in the total field. If I wish to define precisely what I mean by "the quality of PERCEPTION" in segment (a) of the model, then I must point *to each of the other segments which qualify it.* By perception I mean the cognitive capacity that enables a man to invest and risk his competence by investing in distant others . . . etc. The same rule applies to all the other segments. They are defined by their function in thc totality, strcngthened in that function by the strength of that totality, and weakened in definition and in strength by a malfunction in any segment of the totality.

3. It follows that the "different" segments are but parts of a continuum of relational facts which comprise a whole of living and hence inseparable parts, which are separately identified purely as a matter of convenience.

This much followed from Chapter II. Here are some additional points.

The model is cyclical and because "the other" who receives the investment also exists we may think of a *double cycle* which intersects at segments (g) and (h) of the processes. This is illustrated below.

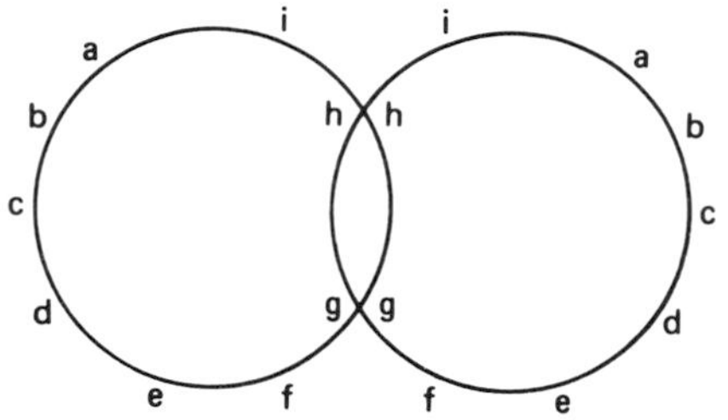


With continual revolutions of the intersecting cycles it is possible for perceptions to be improved, identities strengthened and invested competences to be confirmed. It is possible for each party to the interaction to receive support and information from the other, so that *every segment of the two cycles is enhanced and developed.* This being so, one may think of each cycle as a helix spiraling upwards and of the model as a *double helix.* (See Figure 1.) I do not wish to push the analogy of the double helix with the D.N.A. molecule too far. Here I would only say that the psycho-social helixes are the basis of psycho-social development as the D.N.A. molecule is the basis of organic development, that in both cases a helix is capable of detaching itself temporarily for the purpose of reattaching itself to another helix, and that messages transmitting the coded instructions for growth can flow between both kinds of double helix.

Figure 1

The Double Helix

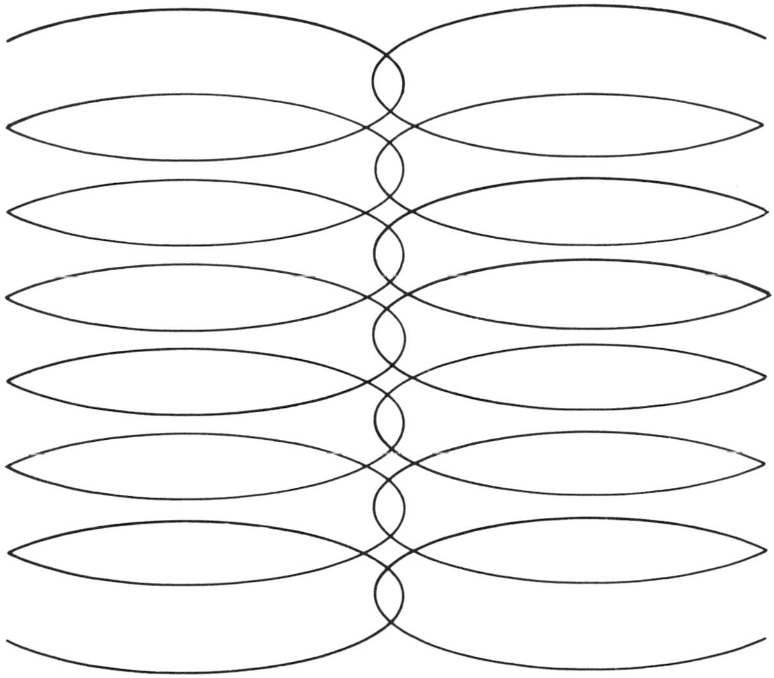

The individual can only grow in relationship to "significant others" with whom he forms synergistic relationships.

The upper reaches of the helix represent more mature relationships. The lower reaches represent frustrating, debilitating, neurotic, and alienated levels of development.

Each individual helix can divide from the other and enter fresh relationships, taking with it what it has learnt.

The image of cycles and spirals appears in the writings of psycho-biologists. Just recently Ludwig von Bertalanffy wrote:

> So evolution appears to be more than the mere product of chance governed by profit. It seems a cornucopia of *evolution creatrice,* a drama full of suspense, of dynamics and tragic complications. Life spirals laboriously upwards to higher and ever higher levels paying for every step . . . It passes into levels of higher differentiation and centralization, and pays for this by the loss regulability after disturbances. It invents a highly developed nervous system and therewith pain. It adds to the primeval parts of this nervous system a brain which allows consciousness that by means of a world of symbols grants foresight and control of the future . . .[1]

Every segment of my cycle model has been cited by five or more theorists of psychological development as a criterion for "positive mental health" and mature human functioning. Table 1 summarizes these clinical insights. Instead of joining in the usual dispute about which of these theorists are right or wrong and instead of complaining that each criterion is inadequate by itself, I submit that all these insights can be reconciled by the cycle and qualify each other in a total description of psycho-social development.

I will now proceed "around the cycle" and discuss in more detail each segment of the helical process. I will also show that knowledge of the state of development in any one part of the process provides clues to the development of all the other parts, so that research studies wherein subjects score high on one particular segment will show them scoring high in other segments as well. This is *not* because the segments are independently correlated as was assumed by most of those researchers I will cite – but because the segments were never actually separate in the first place. It is the sure mark of integrated-personalities-in-relation that every part of their mutual processes overlaps and synergises . . . It is the mark of alienated and disintegrating persons that the parts of their personality and their behaviors seem largely independent.

*"Man exists freely"*

I argued this proposition in Chapter II. There we saw that man frees himself from being "stimulus bound" by his capacity for synthesizing, symbolizing, and exploring. This permits him to rebel against the absurdity of atrophying cultures, empty forms, and the repressive banality of physical coercion, and permits him to create new meaning and renew himself and his environment. The supreme test of radical man "lies in his decision to be stronger than his condition and if his condition is unjust, he has only one way

**Table 1**

**CONCEPTS OF POSITIVE MENTAL HEALTH AND MATURE INTERPERSONAL RELATIONSHIP**

| *Segment of Cycle* | *Criteria of Positive Mental Health* | *Theorists* |
|---|---|---|
| Man exists freely | Productive | Erich Fromm |
| | Productive | G.T. Barrett Lennard |
| | Creative | G.T. Barrett Lennard |
| | Creative | Frank Barron |
| | Conscious Moral Decision | Carl Jung |
| | Conscious Moral Decision | Paul Tillich |
| | Independence from immediate impact of present stimuli | Heinz Hartmann |
| | A chosen personal direction | Viktor Frankl |
| a) through the quality of his PERCEPTION | Telic Sensitivity | T. L. Moreno |
| | Awareness of interpersonal relations | H.S. Sullivan |
| | Empathy | Foote and Cottrel |
| | Respect | Erich Fromm |
| | Sociocentricity | Bernard Overstreet |
| | Ability to see stark reality | Karen Horney |
| | Cognitive control | G. A. Kelly |
| b) the strength of his IDENTITY | Stabilization of ego identity | Erik Erikson |
| | Self-acceptance | Erich Fromm |
| | Self-knowledge | C. Binger |
| | Self-insight | Gordon Allport |
| | Self-insight | Lawrence Kubie |
| | Clear concept of self | G. Engel |
| c) and the synthesis of these into his anticipated and experienced COMPETENCE | Competence | R. W. White |
| | Interpersonal competence | Chris Argyris |
| | Self-esteem | Karen Horney |
| | Sense of adequacy | Combs and Snygg |
| | Self love | Erich Fromm |
| d) he INVESTS this with . . . . . . . . . . . . . . . | Investment in living | M. Mayman |
| | Inputs of psychic energy | Chris Argyris |
| | Self-expression | J. Rof-Carballo |
| *intensity* | Live intensely | Erich Fromm |
| and | Participation with ego involvement | Gordon Allport |
| *authenticity* in his human environment | Authenticity | J.F.T. Bugental |
| | Congruence | Carl Rogers |

**Table 1 (Continued)**

| | | |
|---|---|---|
| e) by periodically SUSPENDING his cognitive structures and RISKING himself | Suspension of self concern | Herbert Fingarette |
| | Self-surrender | Andras Angyal |
| | Surrender | Kurt H. Wolff |
| | Allo-plastic ego | Isidor Chein |
| | Toleration of insecurity | Erich Fromm |
| | Existential anxiety | Paul Tillich |
| f) in trying to BRIDGE THE DISTANCE to the other | Overcoming aloneness | Erich Fromm |
| | Relationship with one set at a distance | Martin Buber |
| | Resolution of subject – object split | Ludvig Binswanger |
| | Being-in-the-world | Ludvig Binswanger |
| g) He seeks to make a SELF CONFIRMING | Consensual Validation | H. S. Sullivan |
| | Self-Confirmation | Martin Buber |
| | Self-consistancy | Prescott Lecky |
| | Self-actualization | Abraham Maslow |
| SELF TRANSCENDING IMPACT upon the other | Self-extension | Gordon Allport |
| | Self-transcendence | Medard Boss |
| h) and through a *dialectic* acheive a . . . . . | Problem-solving | Robert Blake |
| | Coping mechanism | Theodore Kroeber |
| | Problem centering | Gordon Allport |
| HIGHER SYNERGY | Synergy | Abraham Maslow |
| | Mutuality | H. Guntrip |
| | Mutuality | W. R. Fairbairn |
| | Transcendence of dichotomies | Thomas Hora |
| | Transcendence of dichotomies | Abraham Maslow |
| i) Each will attempt to INTEGRATE the . . . . . . . . . . . . FEEDBACK from this process into mental matrices of developing COMPLEXITY | Integrity | Erik Erikson |
| | Unifying Philosophy | Gordon Allport |
| | Well integrated and balanced | B. Boelen |
| | Responsibility | J.F.T. Bugental |
| | Expansion of consciousness | Frank Barron |
| | Inner organization of beliefs and accomplishments | M. Mayman |
| | The richer, most organizable universe, the more inclusive whole | William James |

**Selected Sources**


1. Vispo, R. H. — "On Human Maturity" *Perspectives in Biology and Medicine,* vol. ix, 4. 1966

2. Jahoda, Marie — *Current Concepts of Positive Mental Health.* New York Basic Books. 1958

3. White, R. W. — "Motivation Reconsidered: The Concept of Competence" *Psychological Review.* v. 66. 1959.

to overcome it, which is to be just himself."[2]

Characteristics which accompany this state of free existence were enumerated at conferences on research into creativity, held at the University of Utah. The conclusions of three conferences were summarized by Calvin Taylor. In Table 2 we can see that creative persons tend to score higher than the less creative on every segment of the helix for which data were gathered. Creative existence is a vital dimension of "all round" psycho-social development.

*a) Through the quality of his PERCEPTION*

To gaze upon absurdity while recognizing its full horror and not permitting this nightmare to dull one's sensitivity is part of the radical vision. Our culture is always "discovering" things which have been there for centuries without stirring our anger and compassion. The starving children in Mississippi and Appalachia have been there for hundreds of years but only recently have we chosen to see them. Earlier generations tolerated with equanimity the flogging of mental patients and the lynching of black Americans. Charles Grenville, the English diarist observed some small boys being hanged at Tyburn and "was astonished by the incomprehensible attitude of some of the boys sentenced to be hanged. Never did I see boys cry so!"[3]As the Second World War broke over Europe Arthur Koestler wrote of the fascist horror he had seen, suffered and warned against for years.

> Perhaps it is we, the screamers, who react in a sound and healthy way to the reality which surrounds us, whereas you are the neurotics who totter around in a screened fantasy world because you lack the capacity to face the facts. Were it not so, this war would have been avoided, and those murdered within sight of your day-dreaming eyes would still be alive.[4]

Our cities must explode before we acknowledge their discontent, and the Kennedy brothers must die in front of television cameras to still for a few moments the fatuous babble of commerce in our mass media which "distracts us from distraction by distraction."

Amidst this tin and kite paper a few men have the courage to perceive the discrepancy between absurdity and what they know ought to be done. They look, knowing full well how the discrepancy between their creative perception (segment a) and current impacts (segment g) will hurt and enrage them. Most of us have as much compassion and recognition of problems as we can easily solve and discharge. But radical man gazes into the face even of nuclear annihilation, knowing as he does so, that once the full enormity has permeated his conscience, he may never rest again but must live in ceaseless agitation for a saner world. Scott Fitzgerald wrote:

**Table 2**

**A PROFILE OF THE CREATIVE PERSON**

| *Segments of the cycle* | *Findings on Creative Processes and Personalities* |
|---|---|
| a) PERCEPTION | "More observant . . . more emotionally sensitive . . . broadly diffused attention." |
| b) IDENTITY | "More self-accepting . . . more introverted yet bold" |
| c) COMPETENCE | "A strong need for mastery . . ." |
| d) INVESTS . . . *authentically* and *intensely* | "More devoted to autonomy . . . divergent thinking: moral committment . . . self-assertive . . . more involved and impulsive |
| e) SUSPENDING and RISKING | "More adaptive, more spontaneously flexible . . . long range risks for greater gain" |
| f) BRIDGING THE DISTANCE | (no data collected) |
| g) SELF CONFIRMING SELF TRANSCENDING impact | "Excites, disturbs, and threatens people . . . behavior controlled by self-concept . . ." |
| h) Dialectic towards HIGHER SYNERGY | "More often making supervisors angry" "Capacity to make richer syntheses" |
| i) INTEGRATION of FEEDBACK COMPLEXITY | "More complex solutions . . . insatiability for intellectual ordering . . . resistance to idea reduction . . . more complex as a person" |

*Source:* Calvin W. Taylor "A Tentative Description of the Creative Individual" in *A Source Book for Creative Thinking:* Sidney J. Parnes and Harold F. Harding (eds). New York: Charles Scribner's Sons, 1962

Although no data were available on segment (f), one useful way of measuring creativity is by the "remote associations test". It is arguable that a person capable of making remote associations could more easily discover the relevance of the perspectives of others who were distant or remote from himself and could better "bridge the distance" to them.

> The test of a first rate intelligence is the ability to hold two opposed ideas in the mind at the same time, and still retain the ability to function. One should, for example, be able to see that things are hopeless yet be determined to make them otherwise.[5]

The highest stage of Kohlberg's Moral Judgment Scale comes the closest of any instrument to measuring my concept of radical perception. We shall explore the full wealth of this scale later. Here we may note that "Stage 6 perceivers" choose to respect the human and moral principles of their consciences while fully realizing that in the situation confronting them these conflict with shared values and role expectations, with laws, with personal convenience and with avoiding punishment. Table A shows the characteristics of Bay Area students with "Stage 6 perception." Their style is radical and they are developed in every segment of the cycle model. (The letters A, B, etc., of each Table correspond with segment a, b, etc., of the cycle model.)

*b) "The strength of his IDENTITY"*

The man who exists carves out a radical identity for himself, deliberately fashioning it in dialogue with others. It represents:—

> The accrued confidence that the inner sameness and continuity are matched by the sameness and continuity of one's meaning for others . . .[6]

When existentialists stress the absurdity of man's "thrown" condition the effect is to urge upon him and acceptance of this unalterable condition. He can never struggle to transcend the finiteness of his condition if he waits upon Godot[7] or God to lend him extra grace or strength. He can spend his whole life like the man in Kafka's parables,[8] waiting outside the gate to receive the law or waiting for the messenger from the dying king. Yet the knowledge that he is alone, that *he* is all he can be certain about, convinces him that the projection of his unvarnished *limited* self is his only path to the *limitless* extension of dialogue and consciousness. He can transcend the absurd limitations of humanity until like the blind pianist at the concert he evokes an admiration from others which is heightened by their knowledge of his handicap and his lack of pretense.

Abraham Maslow has described patients who spent their whole lives lamenting this or that part of their human condition, their personalities crippled by the need to pretend that they did not sweat, or age or defecate. In contrast to these neurotics are those who obey the Delphic command "Know Thyself!" and define and redefine themselves in a process of becoming which is radical, self-knowing, and emerging. In Table B we see that where previously delinquent youngsters achieved self- insight into their condition this existential capacity was accompanied by renewal of strength in

**Table A**

**CHARACTERISTICS OF YOUNG ADULTS IN THE BAY AREA WITH THE HIGHEST CAPACITIES FOR MORAL JUDGMENT**

| *Segments of the Cycle* | *Measured Characteristics of Young Adults as Compared with Other Groups* |
|---|---|
| *Existence* | More radical politically, more likely to support the Free Speech Movement at Berkeley, high level of protest activity, rejection by females of traditional feminine role, more agnostic. |
| | Most likely to reject experimental conditions which require them to torture another human being. (See discussion of Milgram's Experiment in Chapter V.) |
| | Idealizes: – Creativity, Rebellion, Artistry, Individualism, and Freedom. |
| a) PERCEPTION | (Achieves the highest stage in Kohlberg's Moral Judgment Scale, which measures the cognitive resolution of moral dilemmas.) |
| | Idealizes: – Perceptiveness, Sensitivity, Responsiveness, Idealism, and Empathy. |
| b) IDENTITY | Honest with self. |
| c) COMPETENCE | Higher occupational focus than most comparison groups. |
| d) INVESTMENT | Highest levels of socio-political activity, especially Demonstrating, Peace Marching. Sit-ins, picketing, leafletting and tutoring. |
| *authentic and intense* | Idealizes: – Impulsiveness. Sympathy and authentic Self-Expression. |
| e) SUSPENSION and RISK | More likely to have interrupted college career, to devalue orderliness, practicality, and self-control. More likely, to risk others' disapproval, to doubt on occasions their own rectitude, to idealize such doubt. Idealizes altruism and the suspension of self-concern. |

| | |
|---|---|
| | Encouraged as children to experiment, to take chances and to try new things. |
| f) BRIDGING THE DISTANCE | Relationship with parents more loving *and* more conflictful than most other groups (see segment h). |
| g) SELF CONFIRMING SELF TRANSCENDING IMPACT | Small Self-Ideal discrepancy. Greater preference for teaching, petitioning and tutoring. Impresses teachers and peers as fair-minded and morally mature. |
| h) *Dialectic* leading to SYNERGY | High level of conflict over the years with parents, *but* . . . . High level of achieved agreement with mother and moderate level with father. |
| | Their parents insisted on their own rights while respecting the needs of their children. |
| | Idealizes Love, rejects Competitiveness (parents also de-emphasized competitive games). |
| | More likely to be influenced by equal status associates than by authorities. |
| | Greater attendance at meetings. |
| i) INTEGRATION of FEEDBACK and COMPLEXITY | Tendency toward feeling responsible and self-condemnation for mistakes. |
| | Much more complex understanding of moral dilemmas and arguments. |

Sources: Norma Haan, M. Brewster Smith and Jeanne Block, "Moral Reasoning in Young Adults." In *Journal of Personality and Social Psychology* Vol. 10, No. 3, 1968.

Lawrence Kohlberg, "Stage and Sequence: The Cognitive – Developmental Approach to Socialization." In *Handbook of Socialization Theory and Research* David A. Goslin (Ed.) Chicago: Rand McNally, 1969

**Table B**

**THE DYNAMICS OF SELF-INSIGHT**

Two prediction studies on the future development of juvenile delinquents found that items on two scales measuring "self-insight" and "social experience" together predicted the juvenile's subsequent social development and emancipation from crime. Intercorrelated items from the two scales were as follows:

| | |
|---|---|
| *Existence* | Has social initiative, is choosing own future |
| a) PERCEPTION | Now understands persons in his environment |
| b) IDENTITY | Has achieved self insight and understanding of his dilemma |
| c) COMPETENCE | Shows planfulness and willingness to act for himself |
| d) INVESTMENT *authentic and intense* | Tells facts frankly |
| e) SUSPENSION and RISK | Objectively self-critical and undefensive |
| f) BRIDGE THE DISTANCE | Capacity to relate to adults |
| g) SELF CONFIRMING SELF TRANSCENDING IMPACT | Socially skillful, leadership capacity |
| h) *Dialectic* leading to SYNERGY | no data<br>Friendships with own and opposite sex. Acts cooperatively. |
| i) INTEGRATION of FEEDBACK and COMPLEXITY | Takes responsibility for events and has intellectual and emotional understanding. |

Source: Carl R. Rogers, Bill L. Kell and Helen McNeil. " The role of self understanding in the prediction of behavior" in *The Self in Growth, Teaching and Learning.* Don E. Hamachek (Ed.) Englewood Cliffs: Prentice Hall, 1965.

several segments of the cycle and predicted their subsequent emancipation, far better than did all the causational variables studied.[9]

*c) and the synthesis of these into his anticipated and experienced COMPETENCE*

Radical man takes his perceptions along with his own inner awareness and combines these into a personal sense of anticipated, goal-directed competence. "Each becomes great in proportion to his expectation," wrote Kierkegaard. In his *Autobiography,* John Stuart Mill reflected on the pleasure he had discovered in anticipating the radical accomplishments of his lifetime.

> . . . In this frame of mind it occurred to me to put the question directly to myself: 'Suppose that all your objects in life were realized; that all the changes in institutions and opinions which you were looking forward to, could be completely effected at this very instant: would this be a great joy and happiness to you?' And an irrepressible self-consciousness distinctly answered, 'No!-' . . . All my happiness was to have been found in the continual pursuit of this end.[10]

In research literature the notion of competence is partly covered by such concepts as "ego strength" and "self-esteem." Unfortunately these tend to be rather gross instruments which pick up forceful behavior *per se* and do not separate out the persuasiveness which arises from an intuitive grasp of other people's needs and mere manipulative skills. Thus high "ego strength" in a group of bomber pilots was found to include a number of aggressive and manipulative extroverts,[11] but when the same scale was used to measure creative writers, the profile was much closer to the segments of my helix. Perhaps the most comprehensive data on self-esteem were collected by Morris Rosenberg among 5,000 adolescents and some normal hospital volunteers. Those with the highest sense of self-esteem also tended to score highest on the segments of the helix – see Table C.

*d) He INVESTS with intensity and authenticity in his human environment.*

The *act* of investing into the environment, creative and moral choice is a crucial dimension of existence. While we begin to exist merely by perceiving and construing, we deepen our commitment and add significance to our being-in-the-world by the projection into social reality of our personal syntheses. The "outside view" sees "freedom" as residing in *acts* of investment, but the inner, the existential view regards freedom as pervading the entire helix with action as its most obvious and intense manifestation. Experientially an investment is the vehicle of inner conviction so that men feel *compelled* to act on the basis of the moral synthesis they perceive. "No

**Table C**

**RESEARCH ON ADOLESCENT SELF-ESTEEM**

Adolescents scoring in the top seventh of a "self-esteem scale", as compared to those scoring lower, were likely to report.........

| | |
|---|---|
| *Existence* | Leading in voluntary rather than formal activities, personally valuing the activities in which they excelled (little self-esteem accrued from unvalued, unvoluntary activities – even when well performed). Joining clubs which permitted maximum autonomy and minimum supervision. |
| a) PERCEPTION | Wider knowledge of national and international affairs and wider knowledge of peers |
| b) IDENTITY | Ability to examine and criticize selves |
| c) COMPETENCE | Ease in talking and making friends, more ambition, less fear of competition, greater social success, more anticipation of success |
| d) INVESTMENT *authentic* *intense* | More self-disclosure, more assertive, more straightforward and direct, less pretentious, greater intensity of political discussion |
| e) SUSPENSION and RISK | Greater faith in people<br>Bigger risk-takers, less self-concern and self-consciousness |
| f) BRIDGING the DISTANCE | Good relationships with many different kinds of people |
| g) SELF CONFIRMING SELF TRANSCENDING IMPACT | Parents much more interested in adolescent's expressed opinions, more parental reaction, positive and negative, to school work. Student personally values self-realization and is more influential among his peers. |
| h) *Dialectic* leading to SYNERGY | Enjoys competition, little fear of criticism, rated "firm but just" "can be strict where necessary"<br>Close and supportive relationships with significant others.<br>Childhood friends known and liked by parents |
| i) INTEGRATION of FEEDBACK and COMPLEXITY | Much higher memory of significant experiences. Stable, rather than unstable self-system. (No data on complexity) |

Source: Morris Rosenberg, *Society and the Adolescent Self-Image* Princeton University Press, 1965 man should do ought against conscience," declared Martin Luther. "Here stand I . . . I cannot do otherwise." Yet the decision to invest oneself is crucial to the cycles as a whole and to communicating the coded instructions for growth. Where such acts are suppressed the whole helix atrophies. In the words of a group of black clergymen pleading the cause of Black Power

> The conscience of black men is corrupted because having no power to implement the demands of conscience, the concern for justice in the absence of justice becomes a chaotic self-surrender. Powerlessness breeds a race of beggars. We are faced with a situation where powerless conscience meets conscienceless power, threatening the very foundations of our Nation . . .
> . . . Without the capacity to have some organized and economic strength to really influence people with whom one interacts, integration is not meaningful.[12]

But there are obvious problems in defining investment as a visible act. An act, though energetic may be overconforming, compulsive, and "mechanical" – like the energy of Eichmann filling cattle trucks with Jews marked for extermination. An act may carry no conscious moral choice and represent nothing of the actor's true feelings. Hence in order to ensure that the term investment is replete with existential commitment, we must ensure that the act is *authentic* and has *intensity*. The act may take many forms – a gift, a job, a gesture, a poem, a magnum opus, a passionate affair or the sheer effort of imaginatively and selectively confirming another. Whatever the unique contents, "all existing persons have the need and possibility of going out from their centeredness to participate in other beings."[13]

One measure of authentic and intense investment could be the degree of self-disclosure. Much work has been done on this dimension by Sidney Jourard. Once again, however, his measure is a rather gross one from the point of view of estimating psycho-social development. Included among the highly developed relationships picked up by this instrument are certain persons with a strong urge to confess who seem to have crawled into his calculations on their hands and knees, willingly exposing their very humble selves. Despite this, however, there are significant if modest relationships between high self-disclosure and strength in other segments of the cycle. (See Table D.)

*e) By periodically SUSPENDING his cognitive structures and RISKING himself*

When a man invests his personal synthesis, or competence, in others he must be prepared to modify his competence in the light of their reactions. But because it consists of an ordered and purposeful structure of meanings

**Table D**

**PERSONALITY AND BEHAVIOR CORRELATES OF SELF-DISCLOSURE**

| | |
|---|---|
| *Existence* | (no data) |
| a) PERCEPTION | More sensitive |
| b) IDENTITY | More aware of the self that is disclosed |
| c) COMPETENT | More interpersonally competent |
| d) INVEST *authentic* *intense* | Higher self-disclosure to significant others |
| e) SUSPENSION and RISK | More tension felt while genuine self disclosure takes place |
| f) BRIDGE THE DISTANCE | Better able to establish communicative relationships |
| g) SELF CONFIRMING SELF TRANSCENDING IMPACT | Disclosers raise other's self concept Make greater impact on instructors and staff. |
| h) *Dialectic* leading to SYNERGY | (no data) More nurturant, better as healers and nurses of patients. Have "dyadic effect" on others leading them to disclose and engage in mutual help. |
| i) INTEGRATION of FEEDBACK and COMPLEXITY | More knowledge obtained through mutual disclosure (no data on complexity) |

Source: Sidney M. Jourard. *The Transparent Self.* Princeton: Van Nostrand 1964 this modification cannot take place without a temporary suspension of his syntheses so that new meanings can enter the "open" mind and the totality can be reintegrated.

Suppose that I am trying to convey to a friend the value I see in a new social policy. In order to comprehend how it is impinging upon his needs and interests I must temporarily suspend the structure of meanings that it has for me and imagine myself in his place. I must do this in spite of the frightening consequences for myself. The risk I undertake is permitting my structure to crumble, with the knowledge that a new element supplied by him may prevent the logical restructuring of my beloved ideas. I risk being ridiculed by him at a moment when my competence is not firmly in my grasp. By investing my undefended worth I am risking the verdict that I am worthless. I tell him something which shows that I value his judgment but leave him free to disconfirm and devalue my judgment and so alter the definition of our relationship. I do this because I am seeking confirmation from him and the expansion of my ideas – *yet I cannot gain these without temporarily "surrendering" and risking permanent loss.*

Existentialists have insisted that it is painful and frightening to face this risk of self-suspension. Herein they see the source of existential anxiety. Tillich referred to "ontological insecurity," Kierkegaard to the dizziness of freedom and of "dread . . . the womanish debility in which freedom swoons."[14] Nietzche insisted there are no half-willing, all-comfortable virtues "one must still have chaos in one, to give birth to a dancing star."[15] Christ warned, "He that shall save his life shall lose it – but he that shall lose his life, for my sake, shall find it."

But we must distinguish suspension for the sake of higher synthesis from suspension for its own sake which *seeks* (rather than acknowledges and rebels against) chaos and nihilism. The lover who suffers *la petite mort* does so for the sake of greater life and love, or as Kurt Wolff has put it

> The lover must lose himself in order to find himself – not to lose himself.[16]

The existential preoccupation with death – the final suspension – is not a morbid hankering after the inevitable but a call to man to invest and risk himself *for something of value to humanity* while there is still life in him.

We have already seen that the perception of radical man must stare unflinchingly into the face of absurdity and death. Here we see that he must also take some of this absurdity into himself. By suspending and risking his personal synthesis he *evokes in himself continual imitations and intimations of death,* but he does this in the name of life in defiance of death like a man on a tight-rope, and when old age overtakes him, he will "burn and rave at close of day; rage, rage against the dying of the light."[17]

We see in Christ's radical existence and rebellion against entrenched authority the outline of the helix. There was "the word of God," a new moral synthesis, the investment of its meaning in men through word and act; the suspension of meaning in a "descent into Hell" where all forsook Him as He made a leap into despair; the dialectical conflict between Him and the world, and within Him, symbolized by the cross, and the eventual "resurrection" or reintegration of the Word. One does not have to be a Christian to admit that Christ's death made him supremely competent and self-transcendent. Few men have had so profound an impact on our social reality.[18]

The weakness of most concepts of positive mental health is that they treat the individual in the medical tradition of being bounded by his skin and they do not permit any degree of anguish or "unadjustment." But if we regard man's existence as *relational,* then many creative geniuses have been "sane" even in their death or despair, since the meanings flowing from them enriched the lives of thousands and their own bodies were destined to wither anyway.

Only if radical man has periodically "immolated" himself in the purging fires of his own anxiety, conflict, and self-suspension can he also transcend his "final" death, and rise like a Phoenix from the ashes, so that those who know him may "have life and . . . have it more abundantly."

An important product of this "unselfish" suspension of personal syntheses and the acceptance of risk is the building of *trust.* I am not referring here to childlike or dependent trust, but of mature trust, learned by putting one's suspended and undefended self temporarily into the power of the other and discovering whom one can trust and how to build trust. This effort may even involve a peaceful demonstration in the face of brutality and violence. Hence trust is not a naive belief that a specific person will not beat you with his billy club, it is a determination to create a trustful relationship through "holy insecurity" and an attempt to persuade the authoritarian conscience that his fear of you is groundless. It involves not only a determination to create or maintain trust with others but is a trust in one's own powers of resynthesis, which neither negative feedback nor physical beatings will prevent.

One could measure this capacity for self-suspension and risk in several ways. Faith-in-people scales are quite useful but tend to pick up some naive dependency. Flexibility scales may include the chronically suggestive and indecisive. One researcher who seems to have captured the crucial combination of deliberate *daring* self-suspension is Frank Barron in an investigation of creative writers. In Table E we once more see the pattern of strength throughout the helix.

*f) In trying to BRIDGE THE DISTANCE to others.*

By distance I mean the experienced remoteness of the other's needs and characteristics of one's own. Several psychological theorists have pointed to the fact that man develops through a process of "individuation," and opens

## Table E

## THE "PHOENIX EFFECT" IN CREATIVE WRITERS

This usually talented group of established writers and student writers were found to score very high on the following scales and to posess the following characteristics:

| | |
|---|---|
| *Existence* | *Independence of Judgment Scale*<br>"Originality"<br>"Strong moral attitudes" |
| a) PERCEPTION | *Intuition Scale*<br>*Psychological Mindedness Scale*<br>"Creative vision" |
| b) IDENTITY | *Self-Acceptance Scale* |
| c) COMPETENCE | *Ego Strength Scale*<br>*Achievement through Independence Scale* |
| d) INVESTMENT<br>*intense*<br>*authentic* | "A profound commitment to larger meanings of an esthetic and philosophic sort..." |
| e) SUSPENSION and RISK | *Flexibility Scale*<br>"Deliberate, periodic regression into schizoid, depressive, and hysterical conditions. Act of rejection preceding act of construction. . . More troubled psychologically, but they also have far greater resources with which to deal with their troubles. . . both sicker and healthier psychologically than people in general. . . vision suffused with intense feeling: horror, awe, ecstasy, desolation". |
| f) BRIDGING THE DISTANCE (and make) | (no direct evidence but. . .)<br>*Social Presence Scale*<br>*Capacity for Social Status Scale* |
| g) SELF CONFIRMING SELF TRANSCENDING IMPACT | ". .personally effective. . .handle themselves with pride and distinctiveness". |
| h) *Dialectic* leading to SYNERGY | "personal dominance and intellectual effeciency"<br>no data collected |
| i) INTEGRATION of FEEDBACK and COMPLEXITY | *Terman's Concept Mastery Scale*<br>*Verbal Intelligence Scale*<br>"Constant creation of private universes of meaning:: |

Source: Frank Barron. *Creativity and Psychological Health* Princeton: Van Nostrand, 1963 up the distance between himself and others through his creativity, divergence, and the division of labor in society. Henri Bergson observed that man gains freedom at the price of isolation. Erich Fromm pictures man as struggling to overcome this consequent aloneness.

It is across this "abyss" between man and man that each must make his "existential leap" to reach others. We may think of the helix as a spiral staircase, with one segment missing in every revolution. But this missing step gets wider and the abyss deeper as the subject climbs – taking greater risks and longer leaps. The dread that grips him is of finding nothing, of leaping into non-being, with no confirmation but only emptiness, hollowness and void. The images of outer darkness, the bottomless pit and the hell fire of burning frustration have haunted men from the earliest time, along with the dreadful finality of The Fall, from which comes all knowledge, but knowledge which brings an awareness of pain, nakedness, and severance from primal bonds.

Man's one hope is to leap the abyss which his own quest for the knowledge has created, for then "the birth of individuality and the pain of aloneness – is dissolved on a higher plane by man's spontaneous action." To make this leap each man must search for what William James called "new truth" that "marries old opinion to new fact."[19] The "leap of faith" said Kierkegaard is one from the aesthetic to the ethical. Before he leaps, man beholds the aesthetic. When he has leapt, the aesthetic can be consummated to become the ethical. In this way he can overcome the dichotomy between the subjective and objective to resolve all those polarities that originate in Cartesian dualism.

The wider the abyss, the more hesitant are men to enter into relationships. The distance between white and black Americans has strained this nation's moral and social capacities to the very limit, as did the shorter distance between managers and workers a half-century earlier. But radical man as defined in this chapter, strains every nerve to bridge the distance to those who are deviant or despised, an effort that so anguishes the populace at large, that America seems unable to prevent her advocates of dialogue from being murdered by those terrified out of their wits by the prospect of dialogue.

One way of estimating this capacity to bridge wide distances is by scales which measure "internationalism." Those who wish to enter cooperative relationships with feared groups like the Russians or Chinese are generally more developed throughout the helix,[20] but perhaps the best instrument was the Tolerance Scale devised by James A. Martin, who conceived of tolerance as the reverse of ethnocentricity[21] (the refusal to confront those distant from oneself). In Table F we see that more "tolerant" persons so defined are generally stronger throughout the helix.

*g) He seeks to make a SELF-CONFIRMING, SELF-TRANSCENDING*

**Table F**

**THE TOLERANT PERSONALITY**

Subjects scoring highest on "tolerance scale" have .....

| | |
|---|---|
| *Existence* | A more idealistic outlook, idiosyncratic, unconservative ways. They support their country only when they judge her to be acting morally. Can criticize their parents. |
| a) PERCEPTION | Humanitarian perception, highly empathic, tolerant of ambiguity, sympathetic |
| b) IDENTITY | Greater self-insight |
| c) COMPETENCE | Stronger self-confidence and belief in ability to influence events. |
| d) INVESTMENT *authentic* | Greater concern with self-expression Readier admission of weaknesses |
| e) SUSPENSION and RISK | Undogmatic, trustful and altruistic personalities. Give others benefit of doubt. Tolerate uncertainty, modify their judgments easily. Can detach themselves more. |
| f) BRIDGE THE DISTANCE | Sympathy for underdog, supports immigration of aliens, international assistance, support for Negroes. |
| g) SELF CONFIRMING SELF TRANSCENDING IMPACT | More popular in the community but otherwise no clear findings. |
| h) *Dialectic* leading to SYNERGY | no data collected Greater stress on mutual assistance and cooperativeness |
| i) INTEGRATION of FEEDBACK and COMPLEXITY | More education, and greater valuation of intelligence, greater capacity to abstract from concrete experience, prefers complex and abstract art |

Source: James G. Martin. *The Tolerant Personality,* Detroit: Wayne State University

*IMPACT upon the other(s)*

Many theorists have defined development as the capacity to make upon others the impression one anticipates and desires. Man consummates the act of creation when others confirm the value of his investment and make it their own, so that it *transcends* the personality of its creator. Paul Tillich regarded this existential process as the measure of vitality. "Man's vitality is as great as his intentionality. Vitality is the power of creating beyond oneself without losing oneself."[22] We find this capacity in the earthy character of Zorba the Greek, who could "make external laws conform to the internal laws of the soul, to deny all that is and create a new world according to the laws of one's own heart . . . "[23]

But a self-confirming impact could be achieved with high certainty and little skill by kicking someone hard on the shin. Even self-transcendence can be accomplished, rather laboriously, by brainwashing. Yet the more spectacular impact and the readier transcendence come from communicating to the other thoughts and feelings which propel him in the direction of his own growth – then is his growth force harnessed to that of the investor and the joint impact is great indeed. Martin Buber describes this as an *I-Thou* relationship. It is direct, mutual, present, sharing rather than possessing; valuing the relationship for itself, not imposing upon the other but helping him unfold.

Since the other is unique only my uniquely wrought synthesis could fashion an investment tailored to his needs. There can be no successful impact, then, without creative existence and without rebellion.

> In order to exist, man must rebel, but rebellion must respect the limit it discovers in itself – a limit where minds meet and, in meeting begin to exist.[24]

An illustration of this is found in Camus' story of the dying artist who leaves on his canvas the scrawled word "solitary"– or is it "solidary"?[25] Camus intends us to see that it is both. In the solitary act of rebellion, investment, suspension, risking and leaping the distance between men, man creates and recreates his solidarity with other men. He may also fail and leap forever into obscurity. Radical existence is not guaranteed to succeed.

The impact made by the investor on social reality is regarded as central by American pragmatists such as Dewey and William James. "By their fruits shall ye know them" was a favorite quotation of Dewey's. "We take it as our point of departure that ideas have consequences . . . that which truly guides us is true."[26] But pragmatism tends to emphasize this single segment of the helix to the detriment of other segments. If we are only to think thoughts which have a high probability of immediate implementation and acceptance by others, or if the immediate reactions of others to a new investment are sufficient to discredit us, then our radical existence and creativity will be greatly impoverished.

It is part of the competence and solitariness of man that he invests and leaps again and again into the face of absurd discouragement, hoping that he will eventually communicate while risking that it is all for nothing – that his light shines in a darkness that will never comprehend him – or worse still – that he *has* no light – that his own convictions are nothing but the absurd twitchings of an isolated organism.

In the eventual meeting of minds there is a healing of this despair and there is self-fulfillment, and self-consistency[27] from which the participants gather strength to invest their syntheses afresh in the face of more incomprehension. Abraham Maslow has combined the two notions of self-confirmation and self-transcendance into the concept of *self-actualization.* The individual fulfills his potentiality and becomes extended and actualized through entering into the perceived reality of others and thus joining the two strands of the double helix. Maslow undertook extensive research into some highly creative and self-actualizing subjects. His findings in Table G bear the unmistakable outline of the helix. (Indeed his findings greatly influenced me to devise this model.)

*h) and through a dialectic achieve a HIGHER SYNERGY.*

If a man's existence is highly creative, his vision, identity and competence radical, his risk-taking considerable, and the distance he seeks to bridge wide, then he is unlikely to achieve *immediate* confirmation from others – rather, he must struggle for this understanding through *a dialectical process that seeks to reconcile apparent opposites.*

Why the dialectic? Firstly because the thought objects, which are organized into matrices by individuals and groups striving for competence, differ markedly both in content and structure. The world view of A, in which *he* is the center, will seldom fit snugly into a world-view centered on B, in which A is a periphery construct. Sartre has contrasted being-for-itself, the experienced identity of the investor, and being-in-itself, this same identity perceived by the other as an object and "fixed" so as to impede development. The two matrices will therefore clash in dialectic and can be successfully meshed only if "shaken loose" and partially suspended, so that new larger totalities can be reassembled (segment i). Sartre, in adapting the Hegelian dialectic, refers to "totalizations" (competences) which by "praxis" (investment) clash together before each is "depassed" and absorbed into a larger synthesis.[28]

There can be no *larger* synthesis than before without an initial dialectic, for no man can judge another from afar or know precisely how he will react. One cannot know persons *in general,* not with all the psychological knowledge yet compiled, but only particular persons here and now. The variable patterns of strength and weakness in the other's helix call for the "right" balance of

## Table G

## CORRELATES OF SELF-ACTUALIZATION

Self-actualizing persons have: . . . . . . . . . . . . . . . . . .

| | |
|---|---|
| *Existence* | Highly creative, inventive, original capacities. Strongly ethical and lives off own latent resources. Ruled by laws of their own characters, essentially and internally unconventional with acute richness of subjective experience. Radical potential. |
| a) PERCEPTION | More efficient perception of reality with unusual capacity to detect the spurious and fake. Greatly pained by, but still conscious of, the discrepancy between "is" and "ought". Can see confused and concealed realities. |
| b) IDENTITY | Accepting of "animal self" as part of total self. Self-insight, self-knowledge and self-acceptance. |
| c) COMPETENCE | Unconventional ambitions – a mission to improve some aspect of the world – very strong personality. |
| d) INVESTMENT *authentic* and *intense* | Great powers of work and concentration, strong need for self-expression, absence of pose, cant and guile, with great depth of feeling, spontaneity, impulsiveness, and naturalness. |
| e) SUSPENSION and RISK | Fresh and "innocent" perspectives, can face the unknown with less fear than most, can be tentative. Likes ambiguity and unstructured situations. Capable of mystic, ecstatic and oceanic feelings. |
| f) BRIDGING THE DISTANCE | Deep feeling of sympathy and identification with all humanity – *gemeinshaftsgefuhl* – feels a basic underlying kinship with most distant persons. |
| g) SELF CONFIRMING IMPACT and SELF TRANSCENDENCE | Achieve considerable self-actualization along with a high capacity for frustration and deprivation. |
| h) *Dialectic* leading to SYNERGY | Capacity to take blows and knocks, with a "situational hostility" towards the pretentious, hypocrytical and self-inflated, and willingness to fight others for their own good and for what is right. Combined with *synergistic* powers, the capacity to reconcile opposites and achieve deeper, more profound interpersonal relationships. |
| i) INTEGRATION of FEEDBACK and COMPLEXITY | Concern with eternal and basic issues – widest frame of reference – intellectual – superior capacity to reason and to form an autonomous code of ethics. Deep sense of responsibility for events. |

Source: A.H. Maslow. *Motivation and Personality,* New York: Harper, 1954 strengths in one's own. Hence the intensity and risk of one's own investment will be governed by Buber's doctrine of *quantum satis* – the sufficient amount and quality of one's resources to meet the unique situation. The unique situation is discoverable only *after* we have leapt the distance to the other, clashed in dialectic, and then engaged with him.

In the teeth of this confrontation between personal syntheses is discovered "a morality which, far from obeying abstract principles discovers them only in the heat of the battle and in the incessant movement of contradiction."[29] As the confrontation continues, contradiction gives way to what Buber has called "a unity of contraries" and I shall be calling *synergy.*

Synergy is a state of mutual enhancement between two or more helixes, so that their respective segments are developed and strengthened. It consists of an affective and intellectual synthesis which is *more* than the sum of its parts, so that each party to the interaction can win a "return on investment" that is greater than the competence risked. Abraham Maslow has argued that synergy applies not only to the relationships between people and groups but that synergy *within* the person promotes a synergy *between* persons and vice versa. Translated into the terms of the helix this means that *all* segments of both helixes can ideally achieve an *optimal organization of strengths that will lead the double helix to "spiral upwards."*

The segments of the helix are full of *potential* conflict and imbalance. I may have a perception of the world's wrongs which is so much greater than my capacity to invest help and make an impact that I am near suicide. I may have such an exaggerated sense of my own competence that confirmation could never be achieved. I may suspend my assumptions and risk myself more completely than my powers of reintegration can sustain. My radical existence may so increase the distance between myself and others that the gulf is unbridgeable. All these unreconciled opposites within me will impede my reconciliation with others. But in the heat of the dialectic with the other each can exchange impressions and can come to experience which of his segments are out of line and are impeding communication. The *I-Thou* relationship, as Buber conceives it, brings conflicting and "unbalanced" parts of oneself into active unity.

The degree of synergy can range from very high to very low. The lowest form of synergy is close to compromise, wherein each partly frustrates the other and partly gains agreement. There may be no synergy at all but a totally frustrating, negantropic form of deadlock, wherein each party loses the competence he invested and thus weakens the segments of his helix. The attainment of synergy and its quality will depend upon the strengths of the helixes and the resources of the parties. Weakly developed persons can withstand only small disagreements to win equally small synergy.

But the possibility of synergy has been widely acclaimed in literature, psychology, religion, and philosophy from the earliest time. Herbert Marcuse refers to "the ancient idea of a state where Being attains fulfillment, where the tension between "is" and "ought" is resolved in the cycle of an eternal return . . . The reconciliation of Logos and Eros."[30] Camus calls for "the free exchange following rebellion . . . I rebel, therefore we exist." The human capacity to create a surplus of affection and wisdom is found in the biblical parables of the talents and the feeding of the five thousand. The multitude of ways in which synergistic processes have been understood are summarized in Table H.

*i) Each will attempt to INTEGRATE the FEEDBACK from this process into mental matrices of developing COMPLEXITY'*

The concept of the integration of feedback follows closely on the heels of synergy. If individuals can reconcile dichotomies and bring the various segments of their helixes into synergistic combination, they are half way towards discovering how these and other experiences can be integrated into a greater complexity.

This desire for larger unity was seen by William James as the very core of choice and values.

> He knows that he must vote always for the richer universe, for the good which seems most organizable, most fit to enter into complex combinations, most apt to be a member of a more inclusive whole. . .[31]

Through a process of dialectic, one-dimensional men confront one another to become two-dimensional men or better, and discover additional configurations of thought with transitive meanings.

We may think of the structure of thought and language as represented by "inverted trees" – see Figure 2. These structures are differentiated and integrated by a series of *holons.* (This term was originated by Arthur Koestler and refers to junctions in the trees which are wholes to the branches beneath them and parts to the junctions above them.)

Two persons (or cultures) which I will call "East" and "West" have an idea at the top of their integrated pyramids. East, let us suppose, expresses the idea of human brotherhood and cooperation, by translating the idea into sentence structures, which are broken up into phrases, words and phonemes. West expresses the idea of human individualism and translates it down the pyramid also. In each case the sentences and words chosen clarify but also narrow the respective ideas by submitting them to the orderly discipline of language construction. Benjamin Whorf argued that we actually think in words and phrases, preparatory to uttering them, and that where words needed to convey ideas are missing, the ideas will not be there either – or are being deliberately suppressed. For some ideas only malodorous words may be available.

**Table H**

**SYNERGY BETWEEN PERSONS AND THE RECONCILIATION OF OPPOSITES WITHIN THEM**

| Description of Synergy | Author and his work | Explanation in terms of the double helix |
|---|---|---|
| As balance and justice | Albert Camus *The Rebel, An Essay on Man in Revolt* | Justice equals the balance in segments of the cycle which permits growth. |
| Solitary and solidary is one | "The Artist at Work" in *Exile and the Kingdom* | Existence and rebellious investment (d) can create synergy (h). |
| A unity of contraries in meeting and dialogue Relationship is only possible with one set at a distance | Martin Buber *Between Man and Man. Distance and Relationship.* | Dialectic and bridging the distance (g) leads to synergy (h). Synergy (h) is only possible through the distance (f) created by existence. |
| Balance between the Yogi and the Commissar, the Saint and the Revolutionary | Arthur Koestler *The Yogi and the Commissar* | The capacity to invest (d) and to obtain the desired impact (g), must be balanced by self-insight (b) and nurturant relationships (h) |
| The way up is the way down. Truth is realized through paradox. Time future and time past united in the moment of time present | T. S. Eliot *4 Quartets* | Temporary suspension (e) is required for greater synthesis (i) Those segments of the cycle which anticipate the future (a),(b) and (c), and those which recall and reintegrate the past (segment h) are unified in present investment (e) and synergy (h). |
| Unity between the "inner" and the "outer" | Carl Jung *Memories, Dreams and Reflections* | The inner sense of identity (b) and existence can create an outer impact and transcendence (g). |
| Fusion between means and ends and between prizing and appraising | John Dewey *Reconstruction in Philosophy* | Cognition (a) and investment (d) are fused in the pragmatic impact (g) and its consequences for human growth |
| Overcoming the dichotomy between "I" and "Me". This fusion is the source of sympathy for others. | George Herbert Mead *Mind, Self and Society* | Identity (b) makes a self confirming impact (g). Synergy between helixes accompanies synergy within them. |

**Table H (Continued)**

| | | |
|---|---|---|
| The fusion between "is" and "ought" | Erich Fromm *Man for Himself* | Moral existence and cognition (a) translated into impact and transcendence (g) |
| Individuality and separation dissolved in action | *The Sane Society* | The loneliness of rebellion and existence is overcome by the capacity to invest (d) and bridge the distance (f) |
| The experience of oneness overcoming paradox | *The Art of Loving* | Synergy (h) and integration (i). |
| Discovery of inner being and other simultaneously | Jean Paul Sartre *Existentialism* | Self- confirming impact on the other (g). |
| Thesis and antithesis fused in synthesis | G. F. Hegel *Philosophy of Right* | The competences (c) of self and other are integrated through dielectic (h) |
| Divergence and convergence meet in a novel emergence | Teilard de Chardin *The Phenomenon of Man* | Creative existence and investment (d) bridge the distance (f) and lead to greater synergy (h) and novel integrations (i) |
| Unification of the "within" and "without" | Teilard de Chardin *The Phenomenon of Man* | The inner sense of identity (b) can become the outer impact and transcendence (g) |
| Shared knowledge forms a "noosphere" | | The shared integration of feedback between men will become increasingly complex |
| Unification of subjective and objective | Rollo May *Existence; A New Dimension . . .* | This is inherent in bridging distance to other (f) |
| Lose yourself in order to find yourself | Kurt Wolff "On Surrender" | Suspension and risk (e) for the sake of better reintegration (i) |
| Maintenance of due balance among the faculties | John Stuart Mill *On Liberty* | Balance within segments of the helix |
| Orchestration and harmonizing of value experiences | Ralph Barton Perry *Realms of Value* | Synergy |
| Fusion between the Modern Promethean and the Modern Job | Maurice Friedman *To Deny Our Nothingness* | Prometheus rebelled and shouted defiance, segments (a) to (d) – but Job entered a dialogue of protest, segments (e) and (i) |
| In myth, religion and fable, contradictions and opposites are reconciled | Alan Watts *The Two Hands of God . . .* | The exercise of imagination and holistic perception (a) are necessary to achieve Synergy. |

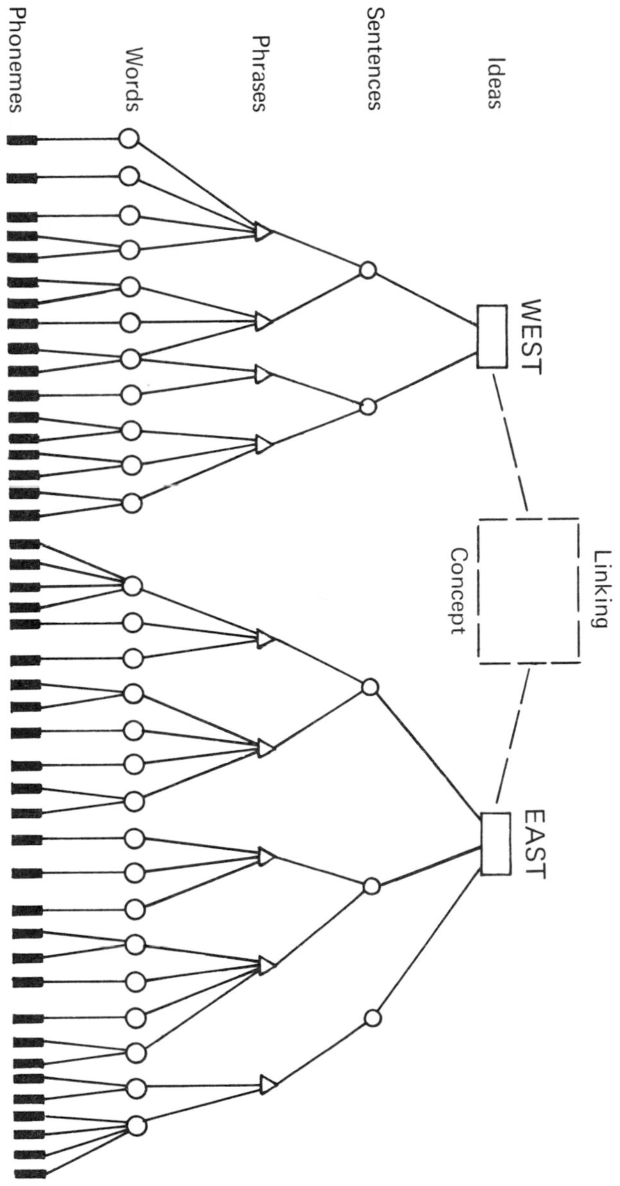
Ideas
Sentences
Phrases
Words
Phonemes
WEST
EAST
Linking
Concept

Figure 2

Now in the confrontation and verbal dialectic between East and West, the former extols his idea of comradely cooperation, contrasting it with the exploitive individualism of West. West extols individualism while denouncing as the road to serfdom the "socialist" pleas on behalf of the disadvantaged. But, as we have seen, both individualism (which is implicit in existence and in segments (a) to (e) of the helix) *and* cooperation (which is implicit in segments (f), (g) and (h)) are vital to the overall development of the helix. Through a dialectic between sufficiently developed individuals can emerge a linking concept that integrates individualism and cooperation at higher levels of thought: the linking concept could be "man should use his liberty for new relatedness – his right to *de*tach himself for more effective *at*tachments." With this synthesis *East and West could integrate into an expanding consciousness much of the other's thought.* It is no coincidence that the radical intellectuals of the Western Bloc plead for compassion and cooperation for the disadvantaged, while radical intellectuals in the Eastern Bloc push for personal liberties. Each is trying to supply the "missing element" in his own culture, while conservatives decry these elements as the work of the enemy.

What, then, are the obstacles to this larger synthesis? We find clues in every segment of the cycle.

1) Can West (or East) bear to *perceive* the other who seems so contrary to himself?

2) Are his *identity, competence* and *investing* skills such that they can withstand the *risk* and shock of *dialectic.*

3) Can he *suspend* the automatic translation of his ideas into rigidified and polemical structures, and reconsider the meanings of "individualism." Can he then relinquish permanently those aspects of individualism incompatible with cooperation?

4) Can he tolerate the delay in *self-confirmation* until *dialectic* gives way to *synergy?*

If the answer to these questions is "yes" then a more complex integration of ideas can be accomplished which in turn will provide the perspectives for more developed interpersonal relations. Individualism and cooperation are of course only two of the false dichotomies over which men deadlock and thereby proclaim their psycho-social infancy. Other reconcilable opposites are freedom versus determinism, objective versus subjective, concrete versus abstract and the numerous polarities synergized within Table H.

This reconciliation of a polarized world through dialectical reason is a unique accomplishment of the radical personality, seeking a balance or *justice* that will unify the segments of the cycle. Camus put it well: –

> The metaphysical rebel . . . attacks a shattered world in order to demand unity from it. He opposes the principle of justice which

> he finds in himself to the principle of injustice which he sees being applied in the world . . . Metaphysical rebellion is a claim, motivated by the concepts of complete unity, against the suffering of life and death, and a protest against the human condition . . . for its incompleteness . . .[32]

Arthur Koestler has argued that the "inverted trees" of thought and language (see Figure 2) are always open "at the top." Hence a new idea can be added which links, reorganizes and subordinates ("depasses," Sartre would say) the branches and holons beneath it. Herein lies not only man's freedom but the integrative power of personality.

Some important research into this integrative capacity has been undertaken on young college women with personally wrought, unified, and complex philosophies of life. As can be seen in Table I, they show great strength throughout the helix.

This completes our journey around the cycle. An additional word needs to be said about variations of strength in different parts of the helix. It follows from my argument thus far that if the segments are not *relatively* even in potential strength, the relationship will suffer, and the development of the interacting individuals will be blocked. For instance, any serious deficiency in the capacity to suspend existing structures, or in the capacity to integrate feedback *must* adversely affect the entire process.

Nevertheless, human beings get their distinctive personalities not only from the infinite variations in the content of investing, but also from special emphasis on one or more segments. Following around the cycle we can recognize:

a) The reporter or observer
b) The "character"
c) The power seeker
d) The man-of-action
e) The mystic
f) The emissary or mediator
g) The pragmatist
h) The "do gooder," therapist, co-operator
i) The intellectual

Radical man is, of course, all these and more. To summarize: –

His radical existence projects its own moral and creative synthesis into the world.

a) He is radical in his vision, which can stare into the face of injustice and absurdity without yielding in determination to "balance" and make it just.

b) He fashions periodically new and daring facets to his identity which he

**Table I**

**RESEARCH ON COLLEGE WOMEN WITH COMPLEX , ENLIGHTENED PERSONALLY WROUGHT RELIGIOUS PHILOSOPHIES**

| **Segments of the Cycle** | **Variables** | **r** |
|---|---|---|
| Existence | Autonomy | .38 |
| | Internalized morality | .35 |
| | Originality | .34 |
| | Independence of judgment | .42 |
| a) PERCEPTION | Social perceptivity | .37 |
| | Awareness of others | .39 |
| | Tender-mindedness | .32 |
| | Aesthetic appreciation | .48 |
| b) IDENTITY | Self-insight | .43 |
| | Self-awareness | .35 |
| | Intraception | .39 |
| c) COMPETENCE | Strong motivation (C.P.I.) | .36 |
| d) INVESTMENT | General intellectual capacity | .36 |
| *authentic* | Movement towards autonomy | .29 |
| *intense* | Naturalness | .29 |
| | Affection towards parents | .46 |
| e) SUSPENSION and RISK | Flexibility (C.P.I.) | .31 |
| | Ability to accept anxiety | .34 |
| f) BRIDGING THE DISTANCE | Staff role nomination for: – | |
| | leadership in refugee camp | .40 |
| | women's prison | .31 |
| | labor/management mediator | .30 |
| g) SELF CONFIRMING SELF TRANSCENDING IMPACT | Meets college's expectations | |
| | intellectually | .39 |
| | aesthetically | .45 |
| | ideologically | .44 |
| | morally | .41 |
| | achieves need gratification | .37 |
| | Life diversified | .30 |
| h) Dialectic leading to SYNERGY | Staff role nomination for: – | |
| | representative state legislature | .38 |
| | citizen's committee leader | .35 |
| | marriage counsellor | .45 |
| | marriage companion | .36 |
| | likeableness | .43 |
| i) INTEGRATION of FEEDBACK and COMPLEXITY | Organizes experience | |
| | intellectually | .34 |
| | aesthetically | .30 |
| | large life space | .40 |
| | capacity for further growth | .36 |

Source: Frank Barron *Creativity and Psychological Health.* Princeton: Van Nostrand, 1963 examines and understands.

c) He forever seeks fresh and greater competence for himself.

d) He invests and commits himself to others authentically and intensely.

e) He risks himself by deliberately suspending his assumptions and exposing his undefended self to friends and to the forces of reaction.

f) He bridges the great distances to the deviant, the despised, the minority groups, and the "enemies" of his country, to make contact, to bring compassion, and to discover novel life.

g) He finds self confirmation; and the new meanings he invests transcend his own personality and enter into the consciousness of the community.

h) He forms cooperative relationships of higher synergy, but only after a desperate dialectical confrontation and struggle to understand.

i) He integrates these experiences by using the radical and unifying concepts which emerged from the dialectic to expand his consciousness.

## NOTES FOR CHAPTER III

1. *Problems of Life, op. cit.*, p. 103, also *Robots, Men and Minds, op. cit.*, p. 87.
2. *The Rebel: An Essay on Man in Revolt* by Albert Camus, Trans. by Anthony Bower, New York: Vintage, 1956, p. 30.
3. Quoted by Bryan Magee in *The New Radicalism,* New York: St. Martin's Press, 1962, p. 60.
4. *The Yogi and the Commissar,* New York: Macmillan, 1945, p. 89.
5. *The Crack-up,* New York: New Directions, 1945.
6. *Childhood and Society* by Erik H. Erikson, New York: Norton and Co., 1950, p. 228.
7. See *Waiting for Godot* by Samuel Beckett, New York: Grove Press, 1954.
8. See "Before the Law" and "An Imperial Message" in *The Penal Colony* by Franz Kafka, New York: Schocken Books, 1945, pp. 148f and 158f.
9. The "causational variables" included Family Environment, Physical Health, I.Q., and Heredity. The correlations between these four factors and subsequent emancipation were .36, .25, .39, and .37 respectively. But the correlation between Self-Insight and emancipation was .84, and the correlation with Social Skill and Experience was .55.
10. *Autobiography,* New York: Oxford University Press, 1924, p. 112.
11. *Creativity and Psychological Health* by Frank Barron, New York: Van Nostrand, p. 137-143.

12. *New York Times,* July 31, 1966, also quoted by Stokely Carmichael and Charles Hamilton in *Black Power, The Politics of Liberation in America,* New York: Vintage Books, 1968, p. 48.

13. "Existential Bases of Psychotherapy" by Rollo May in *Existential Psychology,* New York: Random House, 1961.

14. *The Concept of Dread,* Trans. with Introduction by Walter Lowrie, Princeton University Press, 1944, p. 55.

15. *Thus Spoke Zarathrustra,* Trans. by Thomas Common, New York: The Modern Library, p. 11.

16. "On 'Surrender' " in *Interpersonal Dynamics,* Warren G. Bennis, *et. al.* (eds.), Homewood, Ill.: The Dorsey Press, p. 48.

17. "Do not go gentle into that good night." *The Collected Poems of Dylan Thomas,* New York: New Directions.

18. This is not, of course, exclusive to Christ. Arthur Koestler notes in *The Act of Creation, op. cit.,* p. 466, "I have mentioned the perennial myth of the prophet's and hero's temporary isolation and retreat from human society – followed by his triumphant return endowed with new powers. Buddha and Mohammed go into the desert; Joseph is thrown into a well. . . Jung's "death and rebirth" motif, Toynbee's "withdrawal and return" reflect the same archetypal motif."

19. Quoted by Maurice Friedman in *To Deny Our Nothingness,* New York: Delacorte Press, 1967, p. 212.

20. "Some psychological correlates of world mindedness and authoritarianism," Smith, H. P. and Rosen, Ellen W., *J. Pers.,* 26, 1958, pp. 170-183. Internationally, "world-minded" students were higher in self-expressiveness, independence and capacity to criticize parents. They were less stereotyped in thinking and perception, less submissive and obedient, and more egalitarian.

21. However, ethnocentricity is not an entirely satisfactory measure either, since persons may or may not regard ethnicity as a symbol and a good predictor of distance between perspectives. Milton Rokeach (1960) presents evidence to show that perceived difference in beliefs is the fundamental source of distance and that different political groups on the Right and Left react to different warning symbols of such distance.

22. *The Courage to Be,* New Haven: Yale University Press, 1959, p. 81.

23. Quoted by Maurice Friedman in *To Deny Our Nothingness, op. cit.,* p. 75, here and elsewhere I am greatly indebted to Friedman's work.

24. *The Rebel. An Essay on Man in Revolt, op. cit.,* p. 22.

25. "The Artist at Work" in *Exile and the Kingdom,* New York: Vintage, 1958, p. 158.

26. That which truly guides us is true.

27. There are numerous theories of cognitive consistency which assert that men are motivated to create impacts on their environment roughly consistent with their prior expectations. Such theorists include George A. Kelly, David C. McClelland, Donald W. Fiske and Salvatore R. Maddi, Leon Festinger, C. Osgood and H. Tannenbaum, and Fritz Heider. Their thinking is well summarized in *Personality Theories* by Salvatore R. Maddi, Homewood, Ill.: The Dorsey Press, chapter IV, and in *Attraction and Hostility* by Albert Pepitone, New York: Atherton, chapter II.

28. Sartre is not easy to follow. A good exposition of *Saint Genet, Question de Methode,* and *Critique de la Raison Dialectique,* may be found in *Reason and Violence, A Decade of Sartre's Philosophy* by R. D. Laing and D. G. Cooper, London: Tavistock Publications, 1964.

29. *The Rebel, op. cit.*, p. 283.

30. See *One Dimensional Man,* Boston: Beacon Press, 1964, p. 167.

31. *Essays in Pragmatism,* New York: Haffner Publishing Co., 1949, p. 83.

32. *The Rebel, op. cit.*, p. 23.

*Chapter IV*

## Anomie – The Failure of Existence

If, as we have seen, Radical Man chooses, if he synthesizes and resynthesizes his resources into unique combinations and directs these towards the development of unique others, how then do we describe the failure of such existence? The opposite to free existence is the incapacity to choose and create the "right" behavior in the "right" circumstances. Ultimately this leads to a disgust and despair since the "right rules" if not used selectively and appropriately are experienced as useless. The unchoosing person must then reject *either* the rules themselves *or* the "wicked human beings" who constitute an offense against "sacred laws." In this way anomie will typically lead to a polarization of the Left wing rule-rejectors and the Right wing rule-worshipers. Among those who reject will be some radical men who came not just to destroy laws but to fulfill some, renew others, and create additional ones.

The failure of this process of updating and renewal is neatly summed up in the concept of *anomie,* as defined in some recent studies by Herbert McClosky and John Schaar.[1] Those suffering from anomie complain that "everything is so uncertain," that "the old kind of friendship" is lacking, that a person cannot know "where he stands from one day to the next," "which are the right rules to follow" and "just how he is expected to act." "The trouble with the world is that people really don't believe in anything . . . (but) other people find it easier to decide what is right than I do."

Note that the anomic person shares with radical man the view of an environment which is often absurd – but with an important difference. With anomie there is no capacity to rebel and create meaning. As the "little priest" discovered in the novel by Georges Bernanos, it was not the night *outside* him that terrified him most.

> God! I breathe, I inhale the night, the night is entering into me by some inconceivable, unimaginable gap in my soul. I, myself, am the night.[2]

The anomic fail to conceive of themselves as lights shining in darkness or to experience themselves as norm choosers, norm makers, and norm testers.

If anomie is the opposite of free existence, then an anomic cycle may be conceived as the opposite of the developed cycle described in Chapter III. Hence anomie may be defined as *a severe state of underdevelopment with relative weakness instead of strength in the segments of the helix.* It reads as follows.

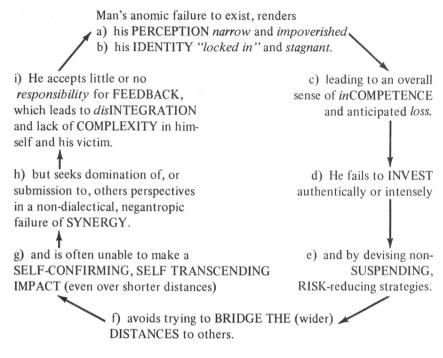

Man's anomic failure to exist, renders
a) his PERCEPTION *narrow* and *impoverished*
b) his IDENTITY *"locked in"* and *stagnant.*

c) leading to an overall sense of *in*COMPETENCE and anticipated *loss.*

d) He fails to INVEST authentically or intensely

e) and by devising non-SUSPENDING, RISK-reducing strategies.

f) avoids trying to BRIDGE THE (wider) DISTANCES to others.

g) and is often unable to make a SELF-CONFIRMING, SELF TRANSCENDING IMPACT (even over shorter distances)

h) but seeks domination of, or submission to, others perspectives in a non-dialectical, negantropic failure of SYNERGY.

i) He accepts little or no *responsibility* for FEEDBACK, which leads to *dis*INTEGRATION and lack of COMPLEXITY in himself and his victim.

The above cycle represents a very low level of development on the single helix which is capable of "doubling up" only with persons of very similar perceptions who are short "distances" away (see segment f). It fails to communicate at all with living helixes differentiated from itself, and when confronted with distant yet unavoidable persons is actively destructive.

In his various studies over the past ten years, Herbert McClosky and his co-workers have found over fifty variables significantly and substantially related to anomie (or anomy, as he calls it). We can see in Table 3 that high scores on the anomy scale tend to accompany weakness and failure on every segment of the cycle. I shall now proceed "around the cycle," describing each segment of the underdeveloped helix.

*Man's anomic failure to exist*

Anomie is the cultural wasteland lamented by T. S. Eliot with its inner deadness and sterility and its artificial crust through which no living thing can burst and bud. Where men fail to "stand out" and renew themselves; the culture is left only with dead things fashioned for earlier generations and now either discarded or manipulated for purposes never envisaged in their creation. Christ had a brilliant metaphor for the authorities of his time:

> Whited sepulchres, which indeed appear beautiful outward, but are within full of dead men's bones.

With no creative decisions to renew personality, life seeps away. "If there were a devil," wrote Martin Buber, "it would not be one who decided against God, but one who, in eternity came to no decision . . ."[4] Anomie is generally defined as meaninglessness and normlessness, for only individuals who choose between norms, combine them, and invest them into the human environment can discover in them a human meaning and thereby convert dead cliches into living truths. As McClosky's study shows in Table 3, anomic persons are preponderantly conventional, clinging to borrowed axioms. They score high on Religiosity, expressing fear at "losing my religion," and higher still on Conservatism, which I shall discuss in detail in later chapters. Finally they score poorly on Independence.

*a) PERCEPTION, narrow and impoverished*

Without personal choice and its active implementation, a man's perception of the human environment shrinks into parochial pleasantries and crude stereotypes. Consider George F. Babbitt and his family.

> He liked three kinds of films: pretty bathing girls with bare legs; policemen or cowboys and an industrious shooting of revolvers; and funny fat men who ate spaghetti. He chuckled with immense, moist-eyed sentimentality at interludes portraying puppies, kittens and chubby babies; and he wept at deathbeds and old mothers being patient in mortgaged cottages. Mrs. Babbitt preferred the pictures in which handsome young women in elaborate frocks moved through sets ticketed as the drawing-rooms of New York millionaires. As for Tinka, she preferred, or was believed to prefer, whatever her parents told her to.[5]

For many people politics begins and ends with the P.T.A. and Cub Scouts. The struggles of ghetto residents and the pock-marked face of Vietnam are of little concern – until one of "our boys" is killed and turns out to be the son of a neighbor. As Charles Silberman has observed, the most ominous thing about the American Dilemma, or the crisis in black and white,[6] is that so many whites, a majority in the early sixties, *experienced no dilemma at all!* Why let the federal government push you around when there isn't any problem?

When those with poor perception do become aroused, their perception often takes on an obsessive character of "false concretness." What is visible to the eye is too multifaceted, ambiguous and threatening and so it is rejected in favor of One-Great-Conspiracy-That-Explains-It-All.[7] Beneath the appearance of things lies the Jesuit Conspiracy, the Freemason Conspiracy, the Capitalist Conspiracy, the Communist Conspiracy, and the Protocols of the Elders of

Table 3

**RESEARCH STUDIES ON "ANOMY"**

| *Segments of the Cycle* | *Scales & Correlations* | *r* |
|---|---|---|
| | "Anomy" scale correlated with . . . . . . | |
| Anomic failure to exist . . . . . . . . . . . . . . . . . . . . . . . . | Conventionality | .40 |
| | Conservatism | .59 |
| | Independence (negative) | .22 |
| | Religiosity | .36 |
| a) PERCEPTION, narrow and impoverished . . . . . . . . | Intolerance for Ambiguity | .51 |
| | Political Indifference | .38 |
| | Political & Moral Indulgence | .45 |
| | Awareness (negative) | * |
| b) IDENTITY, "locked in" and stagnant . . . . . . . . . . | Need Inviolacy | .56 |
| c) INCOMPETENCE and anticipated loss . . . . . . . . . | Political Impotence | .54 |
| | Guilt | .59 |
| | Pessimism | .44 |
| | Self Confidence (negative) | * |
| d) Fails to INVEST authentically or intensely . . . . . . | Aquiescence | .58 |
| | Political Cynicism | .59 |
| | Obsessive (compulsive) | .27 |
| e) Non-SUSPENDING RISK-reducing strategies . . . . . | Elitism | .35 |
| | Political Suspicion | .55 |
| | Chauvinism | .59 |
| | Rigidity | .41 |
| | Inflexibility | * |
| | Faith in People (negative) | * |
| f) Avoidance of BRIDGING THE (wider) DISTANCES | Isolationism | .57 |
| | Contempt for Frailty | .42 |
| | Calvinism | .34 |
| | Ethnocentrism | .58 |
| | Anti-Semitism | .39 |
| | Segregation | .27 |
| | Grew up in Small Community | .21 |
| | Toleration (negative) | – .33 |

**Table 3 (Continued)**

| | | |
|---|---|---|
| g) Inability to make SELF CONFIRMING SELF TRANSCENDING IMPACT .......... | Sense of Futility | * |
| | Alienation | .60 |
| | Status Frustration | .42 |
| | Life Satisfaction (negative) | .41 |
| h) Domination of, or submission to, others perspectives, in a non-dialectic, negantropic, failure of SYNERGY ............. | Contempt of Human Weakness | .45 |
| | Paranoid Tendencies | .66 |
| | Authoritarianism | .67 |
| | Hostility | .53 |
| | Dependency | .22 |
| | Mysticism | * |
| | Populism | .68 |
| i) No responsibility for FEEDBACK, hence DisINTEGRATION and lack of COMPLEXITY | Social Responsibility (negative) | –.47 |
| | Disorganization | * |
| | Bewilderment | * |
| | Intellectuality (negative) | –.47 |
| | Education (negative) | –.42 |

N.B. Scales marked thus* were not included in the National Sample of 1484 persons, but in a Minnesota Sample of 1082. Results from this latter sample were divided into those "high", "middle" and "low" on the Anomy Scale, and the corresponding scales were similarly divided. The findings were as follows:

**(In Percentages)**

| | Minnesota Sample Anomy | | | |
|---|---|---|---|---|
| | **High** | **Middle** | **Low** | **(N)** |
| Manifest Anxiety | | | | |
| High | 52.4 | 35.1 | 12.5 | (248) |
| Middle | 26.4 | 35.5 | 38.1 | (533) |
| Low | 10.3 | 29.2 | 60.5 | (301) |
| Stability-Disorganization | | | | |
| High | 51.8 | 32.6 | 15.6 | (365) |
| Middle | 21.6 | 36.7 | 41.7 | (393) |
| Low | 8.6 | 31.2 | 60.2 | (324) |
| Bewilderment | | | | |
| High | 61.0 | 26.9 | 12.1 | (331) |
| Middle | 22.9 | 43.0 | 34.1 | (393) |
| Low | 2.8 | 29.6 | 67.6 | (358) |

**Table 3 (Continued)**

| | | | | |
|---|---|---|---|---|
| Awareness | | | | |
| High | 8.1 | 30.9 | 61.0 | (295) |
| Middle | 23.6 | 33.6 | 42.8 | (381) |
| Low | 46.3 | 35.7 | 18.0 | (406) |
| Mysticism | | | | |
| High | 47.2 | 33.7 | 19.1 | (413) |
| Middle | 21.9 | 39.9 | 38.2 | (406) |
| Low | 6.8 | 24.0 | 69.2 | (263) |
| Inflexibility | | | | |
| High | 48 | 41 | 11 | (157) |
| Mid-High | 34 | 35 | 31 | (325) |
| Mid-Low | 23 | 35 | 42 | (346) |
| Low | 12 | 27 | 61 | (242) |
| Self-Confidence | | | | |
| High | 13.4 | 33.9 | 52.7 | (336) |
| Middle | 28.1 | 34.7 | 37.2 | (449) |
| Low | 44.1 | 31.7 | 24.2 | (297) |
| Faith in People | | | | |
| High | 6.3 | 29.7 | 64.0 | (300) |
| Middle | 26.0 | 39.4 | 34.6 | (439) |
| Low | 49.3 | 29.7 | 21.0 | (343) |

Source: Herbert McClosky & John H. Shaar "Psychological Dimensions of Anomy", *American Sociological Review* v30.1 1965. Also personal communications.

**Table 4**

**RESEARCH STUDIES ON "NEED INVIOLACY"**

| *Segments of the Cycle* | *Scales and Correlations* | *r* |
|---|---|---|
| | "Need Inviolacy" scale correlated with . . . | |
| Anomic failure to exist . . . . . . . . . . . | Conventionality | .39 |
| | Conservatism | .42 |
| | Anomie | .56 |
| | Religiosity | .23 |
| a) PERCEPTION, narrow and impoverished . . . . . . . . . . . . . . | Intolerance for Ambiguity | .42 |
| | Political Indifference | .21 |
| | Political & Moral Indulgence | .36 |

**Table 4 (Continued)**

| | | |
|---|---|---|
| b) IDENTITY, "locked in" and stagnant . . . . . . . . . . . . . . . . . | (Need Inviolacy) | |
| c) INCOMPETENCE and anticipated loss . . . . . . . . . . . . . . . . . . . . . | Political Impotence | .41 |
| | Guilt | .42 |
| | Pessimism | .33 |
| | Self Confidence (negative) | * |
| d) Fails to INVEST authentically or intensely . . . . . . . . . . . . . . . | Acquiescence | .53 |
| | Political Cynicism | .47 |
| | Obsessive–compulsive | .27 |
| e) Non-SUSPENDING RISK-reducing strategies . . . . . . . . . . . . . . . . . | Elitism | .29 |
| | Political Suspicion | .39 |
| | Chauvinism | .48 |
| | Ridigity | .29 |
| f) Avoidance of BRIDGING THE (wider) DISTANCES . . . . . . . . | Isolationism | .46 |
| | Contempt for Frailty | .40 |
| | Calvinism | .31 |
| | Ethnocentrism | .48 |
| | Anti-Semitism | .32 |
| | Segregation | .22 |
| | Toleration (negative) | –.30 |
| g) Inability to make SELF CONFIRMING SELF TRANSCENDING IMPACT . . . . . . . . . . . . . . . . . | Alienation | .42 |
| | Status Frustration | .36 |
| | Life Satisfaction (negative | –.24 |
| h) Domination of, or submission to, others perspectives, in a non-dialectic, negantropic, failure of SYNERGY . . . . . . . . . . | Contempt of Human Weakness | .40 |
| | Paranoid Tendencies | .51 |
| | Authoritarianism | .51 |
| | Hostility | .45 |
| | Populism | .51 |
| i) No responsibility for FEEDBACK, hence DisINTEGRATION and lack of COMPLEXITY | Social Responsibility (negative) | –.34 |
| | Intellectuality (negative) | –.36 |
| | Education (negative) | –.38 |

Source: Intercorrelation Matrix, research by Herbert McClosky. Survey Research Center, University of California at Berkeley.

Zion. If Reuther says he is not a Communist, this proves that he is because they are all "masters of deceit," and if he admits it, well there you are! This type of thinking is a protection for impoverished perception, enabling the anomic person to maintain his beliefs despite any evidence to the contrary.

Kenneth Keniston studied some highly intelligent but extremely anomic Harvard students[8] and found that they were attracted to notions attributed to Freud, namely that values and ideologies were mere rationalizations for libidinal gratification. They also embraced the arguments of Logical Positivists that value judgments were mere exclamations of preference without testable content. For such persons, modern social science must be a veritable "Feast of Anomia."

No wonder, then, that the Politically Indifferent on McClosky's scales were overwhelmingly anomic, as were those Intolerant of Ambiguity. We saw that radical man looked unflinchingly into the face of injustice without weakening in his resolve to transform its absurdity. In contrast anomic man shows Political and Moral Indulgence of corruption and wrongdoing, explaining that it's "more important to get things done than worry about methods," that "bribes are necessary," "you have to cut corners sometime" and certain people must "have a rake off." Not surprisingly this scale corresponds with weakness in every segment of the cycle: segment (a) Political and Moral Indulgence not only correlates +.45 with anomie but +.36 with segment (b) – Need Inviolacy, +.45 with segment (c) – (unsatisfied) Need for Status, +.46 with segment (d) – Acquiescence, +.35 with segment (e) – Elitism, +.37 with segment (f) – Isolationism, +.39 with segment (g) – Alienation, +.41 with segment (h) – Authoritarianism, and –.36 (negative) with segment (i) – Social Responsibility.[9]

The anomic person does not see and does not want to know. It is all too big and too complicated and besides what can he do?

*b) IDENTITY "locked in" and stagnant*

While the radical identity was "opened up," risked, and offered to others, anomic man is afraid to let his true self be revealed either to others or to himself. Camus describes the Roman emperor Caligula in this condition, within him "an abyss of silence, a pool of stagnant water and rotting weeds."[10] Kierkegaard spoke of "demonic shut-inness." But perhaps the most telling description is one by the English theologian, Harry Williams.

> The root of sin . . . is the identification of my total self with the self of which I am aware. Two consequences follow from this identification. First of all, the known self is too narrow to be satisfying to me and is felt in its constriction to be intolerable. Secondly, the unknown self which, for mistaken reasons of

> security, I keep imprisoned and in exile, becomes a savage as a result, like a man locked for life in a dark dungeon seeing nobody.[11]

One of the most common experiences in anomie is of becoming "a thing." The self when unexposed and unexpanded loses the very experience of humanity with its accompanying initiative and tension. People in this state will speak of their "terrible temper" or "inferiority complex" as if it were an alien intrusion stuck upon them by fate.[12] Others will manufacture a false self, a thing deliberately fashioned to gain approval like a marketed product.[13] But the false self can only gain a confirmation and acceptance which is attributable to its falsity. The frightened thing behind the *persona* remains unacceptable and unloved until one day perhaps the facade itself cracks open, as when the Wizard of Oz, breathing fire, smoke, and majesty, turned out to be a small, fat man pulling on levers. It is a similar realization that came to Pietro in the aptly named novel by Ignazio Silone, *The Seed Beneath the Snow.*

> Every mask and every pretense can be reduced to one great evasion: the desire to overcome the sorrows of life with palliatives and tricks of imagination rather than with sincerity and manly impulsion . . . But there is a sorrow inherent in our human fate which we must learn how to face and make into our friend. We must not fear even despair . . . as long as it is serious and sincere and has some fundamental reason. We must not fear to ask ourselves: Who am I?[14]

Research studies have found that those who are "anti-intraceptive," that is, fearful of looking into themselves and examining their motives, show weaknesses corresponding with every segment of the cycle.[15] McClosky measured Need Inviolacy, the disinclination to have one's inner feelings known by others or oneself. In Table 4, we see substantial correlations between this scale and the other scales which correspond to the segments of the anomic cycle.

*c) INCOMPETENCE and anticipated loss*

Sometimes beneath a surface optimism and sometimes clearly visible is the crippling sense of helplessness, guilt, and incompetence experienced by anomic man. By lack of competence is *not* meant the inability to coerce other people and terrify them into compliance – as Stalin did very effectively. Nor do I mean the ability to do technical work and strenuous feats of athletics – all this the Nazis excelled at. By incompetence is meant the failure to communicate one's personal thought and meanings in ways that enhance the development of others – an incapacity which Stalinists and Nazis exemplified.

A number of existential writers have portrayed anomic man as burdened by existential guilt. For Sartre guilt comes from a self-deceived identity (segment b) and from "bad faith" or inauthentic investment (segment d).[16] According to Heidegger it comes directly from a failure of existence and inability to invest (segment d) according to one's conscience. Erich Fromm sees it as stemming from a failure to achieve fulfillment and transcendence (segment g), while Martin Buber traces it to a failure to answer the call from the other and enter into a unique synergy with him (segment h).[17] The anomic cycle enables us to reconcile all these viewpoints.

We can see from the data in Table 3 that the anomic are Politically Impotent and strongly doubt their capacity to influence events. They are characterized by Guilt, are Pessimistic about the outcome of attempts to communicate and lack Self Confidence.

*d) Failure to INVEST authentically or intensely*

Although the anomic person may be as "cheery" and active with his friends as Babbitt and his Zenith Boosters, nothing of meaning or great significance passes between them. Conversation is amiable, palliative, and shallow. Much of our commercial culture is intended to soothe customers into moods for maximum consumption. TV networks will forego a coverage of the Senate Foreign Relations Committee investigating Vietnam policy, to give us the sixth rerun of the Lucy show. There is no absence of noise or activity, but it signifies next to nothing.

> And the key to all is the SMILE, wide, youthful and brilliant, and everything is GOOD and GLAD, day after endless day, hour after hour, program after program . . . and the fat and the fatuous are interchangeable and are labeled the *full* life! Grown men are shown behaving like children at play – all giggly with cuteness and delight, until we sicken and die of it, SMILING no doubt![18]

Another source of repetitive and meaningless activity is the work that many people must do.

In Arnold Wesker's play *The Kitchen,* the cooks and workers slave compulsively in the steam to produce inferior food, driven by the lure of high wages to empty their lives of meaning. But what kind of men do all these "kitchens" produce? One of the characters explains

> . . . When the world is filled with kitchens you get pigs – I'll tell you. Next door to me. . . is a bus driver. . . he's my age, married and got two kids. He says good morning to me, I ask him how he

is. . . That's our relationship. Somehow he seems frightened to say too much, you know? God forbid I might ask him for something. . . Then one day the busmen go on strike. He's out five weeks. Every morning I say to him "Keep going mate, you'll win! Every morning I give him words of encouragement. . . I got to get up earlier to get to work but I don't mind. We're neighbors. We're workers together. . . Then, one Sunday, there's a peace march. I don't believe they do much good but I go, because in this world a man's got to show he can have his say. The next morning he comes up to me. . . "Did you go to that peace march yesterday?" So I says, Yes. . . So he turns round to me and he says "You know what? A bomb should have been dropped on the lot!". . . And you know what's upsetting him? The march was holding up the traffic, the buses couldn't move so fast! Now I don't want him to say I'm right. . . but what terrifies me is that he didn't stop to think that this man helped me in my cause so maybe, only *maybe*, there's something in his cause. I'll talk about it. No!. . . and you should have seen the hate in his eyes, as if I'd murdered his child. Like an animal he looked. And the horror is this – that there's a wall, a big wall between me and millions of people like him. . . and I look around me, at the kitchen, at the factories, at the enormous bloody buildings going up with all those offices and all those people in them and I think, Christ!. . ."[19]

Other forms of pseudo-investment are those in which we act in bad faith. Camus tells of *The Misunderstanding* wherein a son returning to his mother after a twenty year absence does not reveal to her his true identity. Seeing him as a stranger she murders him for gain – thereby illustrating the theme of our anomic cycle that weakness in segments (b) and (d) is followed by inability to bridge distances (segment f) and destructiveness (segment h). Camus notes in the preface

Everything would have been different if the son had said, "It is I, here is my name." It amounts to saying that in an unjust or indifferent world man can save himself, and save others by practicing the most basic sincerity and pronouncing the most appropriate word.[20]

In Table 3 we see that anomic man is often obsessive and compulsive in his hyper-activity. Alternatively, or in addition, he is Acquiescent, a scale which measures a general orientation towards "avoiding unpleasantness" through the inauthentic straddling of issues and avoidance of making a definite choice.

Table 5

RESEARCH STUDIES ON "ACQUIESCENCE"

| *Segments of the Cycle* | *Scales and Correlations* | *r* |
|---|---|---|
| | "Acquiescence" scale correlated with . . . | |
| Anomic failure to exist . . . . . . . . . . . | Conventionality | .44 |
| | Conservatism | .61 |
| | Religiosity | .26 |
| a) PERCEPTION, narrow and impoverished . . . . . . . . . . . . . . . . | Intolerance for Ambiguity | .52 |
| | Political Indifference | .27 |
| | Political & Moral Indulgence | .46 |
| b) IDENTITY, "locked in" and stagnant . . . . . . . . . . . . . . . . . | Need Inviolacy | .53 |
| c) InCOMPETENCE and anticipated loss . . . . . . . . . . . . . . . . . . . . . | Political Impotence | .42 |
| | Guilt | .41 |
| | Pessimism | .32 |
| d) Fails to INVEST authentically or intensely . . . . . . . . . . . . . . . | (Acquiescence) | – |
| | Political Cynicism | .56 |
| | Obsessive–compulsive | .38 |
| e) Non-SUSPENDING RISK-reducing strategies . . . . . . . . . . . . . . . . . | Elitism | .37 |
| | Political Suspicion | .47 |
| | Chauvinism | .55 |
| | Rigidity | .43 |
| f) Avoidance of BRIDGING THE (wider) DISTANCES . . . . . . . . | Isolationism | .54 |
| | Contempt for Frailty | .45 |
| | Calvinism | .36 |
| | Ethnocentrism | .53 |
| | Anti-Semitism | .31 |
| | Segregation | .19 |
| | Toleration (negative) | –.26 |
| g) Inability to make SELF CONFIRMING SELF TRANSCENDING IMPACT . . . . . . . . . . . . . . . . . . | Alienation | .46 |
| | Status Frustration | .36 |
| | Life Satisfaction (negative) | –.24 |
| h) Domination of, or submission to, others perspectives, in a non-dialectic, negantropic, failure of SYNERGY . . . . . . . . . . | Contempt of Human Weakness | .45 |
| | Paranoid Tendencies | .58 |
| | Authoritarianism | .69 |
| | Hostility | .48 |
| | Populism | .59 |
| i) No responsibility for FEEDBACK, hence DisINTEGRATION and lack of COMPLEXITY . . . . . . . . . | Social Responsibility (negative) | –.45 |
| | Intellectuality (negative) | –.39 |
| | Education (negative) | –.34 |

Source: Intercorrelation Matrix, research by Herbert McClosky. Survey Research Center, University of California at Berkeley.

In Table 5 we find Acquiescence strongly correlated with scales representing every segment of the anomic cycle.

*e) Non-SUSPENDING RISK-reducing strategies*

Ways of reducing risks and not suspending one's assumptions are numerous. Some we have already touched upon. If you do not let out of your perceived identity those true individual feelings that differentiate you from others, risk is largely avoided. Men who wrap themselves tightly in the American Flag, who use borrowed quotations from the Bible as a kind of "holy hatchet" of incontrovertible truth, who label their own personalities and utterances as patriotic and disagreement with them as traitorous and Un-American – all these techniques are running from self-suspension and risk.

There persists a superstition that words *in themselves,* carry some kind of supra-human authority, so that quotations from the Constitution or the scriptures are true *ab initio.* The anomic man, unable to choose the right combination of norms to suit the uniquely human problem before him, clutches at some prestigious, all-purpose truism which is usually delivered at such a level of generality that its application to the current situation cannot be disproved. In *The Devils of Loudon* Aldous Huxley warns us that words are but working hypotheses and must always be compared with the consequences of their use. Without this constant comparison between intensional and extensional meanings, *e.g.,* between one's experienced competence and its impact upon others, words and the men who utter them become abstracted idols.

The reduction of personal risk so cheaply bought by reliance on pre-fabricated "wisdom," turns out in the end only to "stock pile" the anxiety for later reckoning, for soon the unsuspended, prefabricated "wisdom" must be defended against its visible misapplication by anomic men. But in any dispute, these men will not admit to personally choosing and desiring the specific application of the prefabrications. They regard them, rather, as unquestionable truths – not *capable* of being corrupted by their supporters. To argue with the House Un-American Activities Committee is not, then, to question the motives of anomic men, but is conceived as an attack on "Americanism," "Congress," "Patriotism," and "The Flag." There is no possibility of a dialogue with these unsuspended, non-human abstractions, only submission to what they supposedly represent and of course submission to the anomic little men hiding behind these abstracted idols. These manipulators of idols not only crush the human development of others, but deprive themselves of the capacity or the excuse for ever changing their minds, and abandoning their policies. "Every idol," wrote Aldous Huxley, "however exalted, turns out in the long run, to be a Moloch, hungry for human sacrifice."[21]

Another form of anxiety reduction is elitism, which defines the actor as superior to the other person. The white master talking to the Negro "boy" is trying to guarantee himself against being disconfirmed. By acting in a superior manner he hopes not only to dissuade the other from disconfirming him, but is preparing himself to devalue the disconfirmation if and when it *does* come. Elitists typically value aspects of themselves which *cannot* be forfeited by their atrophying capacities to invest and communicate. They seldom pronounce themselves Superior Communicators or Superior Sympathizers because the person they are addressing has the last say on *that* subject! Rather they trace their superiority to Breeding, Race, Nationality, Color, Religion, Title, Property, Money, and alleged access to God. All these will shore up a precarious sense of identity and competence because they are difficult to disconfirm and do not depend for their maintenance upon reaching new understandings with others.

There are, of course, myriads of different techniques for evading risk and suspension. They stretch from sadism and masochism through numerous neurotic and psychotic devices, such as hysterical paralysis, drug addiction, and the tangential yet evasive responses by schizophrenics. Sometimes they are subtle like the "double bind" which forces the other to incriminate himself by offering him a choice between outcomes equally destructive to himself.[22] Thus the strategy of H.U.A.C. in demanding that those they investigate must demonstrate their loyalty to America by denouncing and informing against their friends or go on record as contemptuous of Congress and America, is a perfect double bind. The victim must either be faithless to those Americans he loves, or appear faithless to "America" the abstraction. In either event the "double binder" risks nothing and avoids suspending and reconsidering his militant sense of patriotism or righteousness.

Richard Wright, the black writer, recalls being offered employment as a teen-ager in an optical company in Jackson, Mississippi. Two senior employees, Pease and Reynolds, ran him out, by the following technique which illustrates the "double bind." First Reynolds accused Richard of saying "Pease" instead of "*Mr.* Pease."

> "Now be careful, nigger," snorted Reynolds, baring his teeth. "I heard you call 'im *Pease.* And if you say you didn't, you're calling me a liar, see?" He waved the bar threateningly. . .
>
> "I don't remember calling you *Pease,* Mr. Pease," I said cautiously. "And if I did, I sure didn't mean. . ."
>
> "You black sonofabitch! You called me *Pease*, then!" He spat, rising and slapping me till I bent sideways over a bench.
>
> Reynolds was on top of me demanding:
>
> "Didn't you call him *Pease*? If you say you didn't, I'll rip your gut string loose with this f------g bar, you black granny dodger! You can't call a white man a liar and get away with it.'

> I wilted, I begged them not to hit me. I knew what they wanted. .
>
> "I'll leave," I promised. "I'll leave right now!"[23]

All kinds of risk reduction, whatever their variety, include the themes of moving away from the other and/or moving against the other. By "away" is meant away from comprehension, and not necessarily physical evasion. Nearly all risk reduction devices also evade the need to suspend one's perspectives and competence, and they thereby partake of *prejudice* (literally judging before the confrontation) and stereotypy. The failure to risk and suspend is always accompanied by at least some of the weaknesses in the anomic cycle. For instance in Tables 3 to 5, we find that the Anomic, the Need Inviolate and the Acquiescent are (despite their surface acquiescence) high in Rigidity and Inflexibility, which also makes them inauthentic. They lack Faith-in-People, which I argued in Chapter III was a product of risk taking, but are high in Political Suspiciousness. They are also high in Elitism and Chauvinism, clinging to non-human reified idols of superiority.

A brilliant evocation of the humble, risk-reducing Common Man, is contained in the drama *The Man for All Seasons.* Here we witness the destruction of Sir Thomas More – "a man of angel's wit and singular learning. . . As time requireth a man of marvellous mirth and pastimes, and sometimes of as sad gravity: a man for all seasons."[24]His destruction, by an anomic culture whose conduct he will not confirm, is undertaken with the collusion of the Common Man –– too humble to risk the disapproval of his fellows. More is first jailed with the Common Man as his jailor, tried on perjured evidence with the Common Man as his juror, and then executed with Common Man as his headsman. As the curtain rings down on More's execution and the complicity of all anomic men – their prototype takes off the headman's mask that hid his identity and confides ingratiatingly to the audience:

> I'm breathing. . . Are you breathing too? It's nice, isn't it? It isn't difficult to keep alive, friends – just don't *make* trouble – or if you must make trouble, make the sort of trouble that's expected. Well, I don't need to tell you that . . . If we should bump into one another, recognize me.[25]

Perhaps this final plea for recognition is the most pathetic of all – for anomic man *is* what he risks – nothing. "They give birth astride a grave, the light gleams an instant, then its night once more."[26]

*f) Avoidance of BRIDGING THE (wider) DISTANCES TO OTHERS.*

The concept of "distance" between the perspectives of one man and another is crucial to understanding the dynamics of the anomic cycle. An individual may seem relatively effective in "short distance" situations and show the severity of his anomie only when confronted with new situations which require creative investments. A strange and distant other – be he poor, black, brilliantly clever, Jewish, or in any way deviant or creative – severely threatens the precarious competence of the anomic man.

The crisis of growing up with its lengthening distances is romantically portrayed in Doris Lessing's play *Each His Own Wilderness.* Myra, a 50 year old radical, is desperately trying to wean her twenty-two year old son Tony from a clutching dependence upon her. He despises her interest in nuclear disarmament and is jealous of her political friends and would-be suitors, demanding her exclusive attention and refusing to leave home. The final catharsis comes when she sells the house and gives him the money to go sow his wild oats. Feeling his whole world is falling to pieces, he screams at her in fury:

> My God, my mother's done that to me! She's done that to me. She's my mother and she might just as well have taken a knife and stabbed me with it. She's my mother and she knows so little about me that she doesn't suspect that there's one thing I love in this world, and it's this house... God, but you're destructive, destructive, destructive. There isn't anything you touch which doesn't go to pieces. You just go on from mess to mess... you live in a mess of love affairs and committees and... you live in a mess like a *pig,* Mother... you're all over everything like a great crawling spider...[27]

This passage is particularly telling because it illustrates the reaction of the anomic man to radical man. The demands that the radical makes on the anomic *are* experienced as destructive and terrifying. Tony is without the capacity to engage a world of strangers and is haunted by nuclear catastrophe which his mother faces daily and brings to his attention, but which is "too big" for him to imagine. His mother, Myra, bitterly hurt by his tirade, announces that she is leaving home to sail a boat into the nuclear testing area. Tony yelps his fear that she will be killed.

> Myra: Dear me, I might get killed! And what of it? I don't propose to keep my life clutched in my hand like small change...
> Tony: Mother, you can't just walk off into – *nothing.*
> Myra: Nothing? I don't have to shelter under a heap of old bricks – like a frightened mouse. I'm going. I'll come back and collect what I need when I've decided what I'm going to do.
> Tony: Mother, you're crying.
> Myra: Why not? I'm nearly 50 – and it's true there's nothing

> much to show for it. Except that I've never been afraid to take chances and make mistakes. I've never wanted security and safety and the walls of respectability – you damned little petty-bourgeois. My God, the irony of it – that *we* should have given birth to a generation of little office boys and clerks and . . . little people who count their pensions before they're out of school . . . little petty-bourgeois. Yes, I am crying. I've been alive for fifty years. Isn't that good enough cause for tears?[28]

But many an anomic man can stave off the day of reckoning by retreating into groups of like-minded persons. George Babbitt and his fellow Boosters were united in their horror of working men attempting to organize.

> When Babbitt drove west from his office at ten that morning, he saw a drove of shabby men. . . He hated them because they were poor, because they made him feel insecure "Damn loafers! Wouldn't be common workmen if they had any pep," he complained. He wondered if there was going to be a riot.[29]

But Babbitt sees a professor whom he admires marching with the workers and later offers a half-hearted backing for their cause. His fellow Boosters are aghast, and Babbitt soon feels the ostracism that comes from his small venture in autonomy. Later the Boosters haze George F. Babbitt by teasing him about his middle name Follansbee – another deviation for which he must be ridiculed in order to keep "distances" short. The President of the Boosters asks the assembled company what they had thought F stood for.

> Flivver, they suggested, and Frog-face and Flathead and Farinaceous and Freezone and Flapdoodle and Foghorn. By the joviality of their insults Babbitt knew he had been taken back to their hearts. . . He knew by the cheer that he was secure again and popular: he knew he would no more endanger his security and popularity by straying from the Clan of Good Fellows.[30]

The more an individual shelters within fraternities, monasteries, patriotic groups, and organizations which demand conformity, exclude diversity, and move away from confrontation with strangers, the more strange and terrifying the external world becomes. What was once an imagined peril becomes real because the individual's resources for dealing with ambiguity have atrophied. This situation is illustrated in *Bread and Wine,* a novel by Ignazio Silone. Pietro Spino, the hero, has become a radical. He has forsaken the Church because it has detached spirituality from materialism and has failed to bridge the distance to the poor, leaving them destitute. But he finds the same lack of diversity and compassion within the Party. He realizes what is needed – a true dialogue between differentiated persons. Through dialogue with the peasants he emancipates himself from party ties and sends his dialogues to his beloved Christina, who is preparing to become a nun. Greatly moved by his writings, she runs to him across the mountain side, at last convinced that there was no real virtue in her detached and closeted spirituality. But on leaving her shelter she is greeted by the howls of a wolf pack which descends the mountain to devour her. Anomic man, unpracticed in the ways of humanity, may lose the capacity to leap the abyss between man and man, and in trying, perish.

This "distance" is becoming wider and wider as society increases its pluralism and diversity. We have become a "temporary society" highly mobile and highly complex, with a continued breaking of old relationships and the reforming of new ones. Peter Laslett reminds us of "The World we Have Lost":

> Time was, and it was all the time up to 200 years ago, when the whole of life went forward in the family, in a circle of loved familiar faces, known and fondled objects, all to human size. That time has gone forever. It makes us very different from our ancestors.[31]

Anomic man tries desperately to conserve the past, romanticizing the small town, preaching States Rights, fighting for continued segregation, and celebrating the imagined superiority of his small group of companions with its short "distances."

We saw in the last chapter that radical man will leap the widest distances to confront even the Russians and Chinese in open dialogue. No wonder, then, that anomic man rates high in Isolationism, as he tries to move *away* from others (where he cannot move away he will move *against* them, as in authoritarianism). In Table 6 we see that Isolationists are weak on every segment of the anomic cycle, as they desperately try to keep their muddled ideas free of "foreign powers" and shrink from the U.N., free trade, and "foreign goods."

In view of Pietro's experience with "the Party" it is hardly surprising to find Party Loyalty correlated with anomie. Babbitt's Contempt for Human Frailty helped him to avoid the poor as unworthy of his attention and his Calvinism urged the poor to help themselves, thereby saving him from discovering his own impotence to help them. Table 3 shows that both these measures are related to anomie in the population at large. In addition Ethnocentrism, Chauvinism, and lack of Tolerance are obvious attractions to those who must keep distances short in order to survive. Finally anomic men have moderate tendencies to Anti-Semitism and support for Segregationist

**Table 6**

**RESEARCH STUDIES ON ISOLATIONISM**

| *Segments of the Cycle* | *Scales & Correlations* | *r* |
|---|---|---|
| | Isolationist scale correlates with . . . | |
| Anomic failure to exist . . . . . . . . . . . | Anomy | .57 |
| | Conventionality | .37 |
| | Conservatism | .35 |
| | Religiosity | .27 |
| a) PERCEPTION, narrow and impoverished . . . . . . . . . . . . . | Intolerance for Ambiguity | .47 |
| | Political Indifference | .26 |
| | Political & Moral Indulgence | .37 |
| b) IDENTITY, "locked in" and stagnant . . . . . . . . . . . . . . . . . . | Need Inviolacy | .46 |
| c) InCOMPETENCE and anticipated loss . . . . . . . . . . . . . . . . . . . | Political Impotence | .44 |
| | Guilt | .35 |
| | Pessimism | .32 |
| d) Fails to INVEST authentically or intensely . . . . . . . . . . . . . . . . | Acquiescence | .54 |
| | Political Cynicism | .54 |
| | Obsessive–compulsive | .35 |
| e) Non-SUSPENDING RISK-reducing strategies . . . . . . . . . . . . . . . . . | Elitism | .37 |
| | Political Suspicion | .50 |
| | Chauvinism | .52 |
| | Rigidity | .38 |
| f) Avoidance of BRIDGING THE (wider) DISTANCES . . . . . . . . | (Isolationism) | |
| | Contempt for Fraility | .39 |
| | Calvinism | .33 |
| | Ethnocentrism | .57 |
| | Anti-Semitism | .36 |
| | Segregation | .33 |
| | Toleration (negative) | .32 |
| g) Inability to make SELF CONFIRMING SELF TRANSCENDING IMPACT . . . . . . . . . . . . . . . . . | Alienation | .33 |
| | Status Frustration | .26 |
| | Life Satisfaction (negative) | .22 |
| h) Domination of, or submission to, others perspectives, in a non-dialectic, negantropic, failure of SYNERGY . . . . . . . . . . | Contempt of Human Weakness | .39 |
| | Paranoid Tendencies | .52 |
| | Authoritarianism | .62 |
| | Hostility | .45 |
| | Populism | .64 |
| i) No responsibility for FEEDBACK, hence DisINTEGRATION and lack of COMPLEXITY . . . . . . | Social Responsibility (negative) | .43 |
| | Intellectuality (negative) | .45 |
| | Education (negative) | .38 |

Source: Intercorrelation Matrix, research by Herbert McClosky, Survey Research Center, University of California at Berkeley.

policies. They also tend to have had less *practice* in "long distance" investing, having grown up in Smaller Communities.

*g) Frequent inability to make SELF CONFIRMING, SELF TRANSCENDING IMPACT*

What happens to the man who launches himself across the widening chasm between man and man but fails to reach the other's side? He reaches for confirmation but grasps at thin air – or what existential writers have variously referred to as nothingness, the great emptiness, the hollow space, non-being, the abyss; in addition to nothingness there is sometimes traumatic rejection, disconfirmation, and the painful frustration of desire.

Just as clumsy, inappropriate action can lead to nothingness, so too will the failure to invest when action is called for. In his appropriately named novel, *The Fall,* Camus tells of Clamence, who is crossing a bridge at night when a young girl throws herself over the parapet but then screams to be saved. Clamence walks on and from that moment he loses all meaning and purpose in life. Maurice Friedman comments on this situation.

> It is his rejection of the call to his real self that is the basis of his retreat from the common world to his private hell. The girl's attempt to commit suicide was probably motivated by her own encounter with the absurd, and so was her cry to be saved, once she hit the water. Yet if Clamence had tried to save her, he would have wrested meaning from the absurd – for her and for him.[32]

Clamence looks back upon his lost opportunity with misery but also with the knowledge that he has now so debilitated himself that he would probably let her die again.

> O young woman, throw yourself in the water again so that I may a second time have the chance of saving both of us!. . . eh what a risky suggestion! Suppose. . . that we should be taken literally? Brr. . .! The water's so cold! But let's not worry! It's too late now.[33]

One thinks of the whole apartment house in New York whose residents let a young girl scream to them in vain for help, as her killer returned twice to finish her off in the courtyard below, and of the crowds that shout "Jump! Jump!" to those on the edge of self-destruction.

Despite all the attempts of men to huddle in groups and keep on good terms with "the authorities," they will sooner or later find themselves confronted by persons they do not know and distances that are too wide. Kafka portrayed the nightmare of the humble office worker who awakes one morning to find himself widely and hideously differentiated from the rest of humanity. He has been metamorphosed into a giant dung-beetle![34] He is lying on his scaly back, his many legs struggling in the air. From this moment on, all his obsequious approaches to his employer and family, begging for their understanding of his condition, are rebuffed with repugnance. His family first try to hush up the disgrace and then neglect him until he subsides into death.

If the avoidance of others' needs, clumsy investment, and overwide distances between perspectives all lead to the failure to make a self-confirming impact, so too do the various techniques for reducing risk and avoiding self-suspension. Where nothing is ventured, nothing can be won. He who does not pause to consider that he might be mistaken can never experience genuine confirmation either. If, as an Elitist playboy, I communicate safely downwards to my "bunny" girl friend, who has been personally selected for me by Hugh Heffner, and guaranteed to be non-threatening, sweet-tasting product of vacuous and pneumatic bliss, then I can only receive the confirmation of this prepackaged imbecile – and what is *that* worth to me?[35]

Or again, if I coerce the other, obligate him with indebtedness, moralize to him, and invite him to weekly denunciations of the income tax, I do, by the very act of social control, limit the range of his investment in me. I may never know what he *really* thinks of me, or what he would have honestly replied had I permitted him the freedom to reinvest as he wished. Those dark doubts inside me remain because I never gave the other a real chance to affirm or reject those doubts. My Klansman's hood covers my identity and limits my sense of responsibility for what I do, but it also limits the public impact of any *favorable* impact I might make. It shields me from life itself, anxiety as well as satisfaction. Within, I am dying by degrees, and I am *still* nothing.

Men have many tricks to try to guarantee their own confirmation. One is to "close ranks" and mobilize for war, calling on all citizens to repel the "enemy" at the gates. Not only does this trick evade the leaping of wider distances to the "enemy" and hence those in any way resembling him, it creates a common overriding purpose, hierarchical structures decreed by the emergency, the elevation of the group survival above individual rights, and the celebration of conformity. War psychology is a short-lived paradise for anomic "patriots," who march off to mutual annihilation, temporarily invigorated.

At the opening of World War I, a number of giant war machines rumbled toward each other on collision course, each a great "iron lung" for anomic men. How they cheered! "All over by Christmas! Oh what a lovely war! We don't want to fight but by *jingo* if we must!" General Haig felt God was at his shoulder. The patriotic women of England, tearful but resolute, commanded their husbands to "Go!" while the home fires were kept burning. And how the world paid for this cheap, easy affection between ethnocentric comrades at arms!

War psychology is that "quick fix" jabbed into cultural arteries – later nine million dead, millions maimed and unemployed, the quickening fever of fascism, and then another "fix." And after the second massacre a strange stillness, for confidence in the future seemed to have died too. Camus looked out on the graveyards and the living dead and commented:

> The most striking feature of the world we live in is that most of its inhabitants – with the exception of pietists of various kinds – are cut off from the future...
> Today no one speaks any more (except those who repeat themselves) because history seems to be in the grip of blind and deaf forces which will heed neither cries of warning, nor advice nor entreaties. The years we have just gone through have killed something in us. And that something is simply the old confidence man had in himself, which led him to believe that he could always elicit human reactions from another man if he spoke to him in the language of a common humanity. We have seen men lie, degrade, kill, deport, torture – and each time it was not possible to persuade them not to do these things because they were sure of themselves and because one cannot appeal to an abstraction, *i.e.*, the representative of an ideology.[36]

Do our research findings in Table 3 confirm this portrait of anomic man? They do. He is markedly alienated and overwhelmed by a Sense of Political Futility. When he is not segregating himself from distant others or denouncing the weak, his need for confirmation encounters Status Frustration, and his Life Satisfaction is low. As we shall see in a moment, this also leads him into aggression against others.

*h) Domination of, or submission to, others' perspectives in a non-dialectical, negantropic failure of SYNERGY*

I argued in the last chapter that synergy involves the reconciliation of our own needs for growth with those of other autonomous persons distant from ourselves and this balancing or "justice" was a dialectical process wherein matrices of thought and feeling were first suspended (segment e) then meshed (segment h) and then reintegrated and held fast (segment i). The capacity of two or more competences-in-relation to extend themselves in mutual optimization is what constitutes synergy.

What, then, can we say of anomic men? In the first place, they fail to reconcile and keep in just balance the segments of their own cycles. (This is inevitable, for any failure within the double helix involves all segments in the contiguous cycles.) Hence where injustice reigns *between* men it will reign also *within* them. The failure to communicate is accompanied by *an obsessive concern with one or more segments of the cycle at the expense of other segments.* Arthur Koestler has drawn attention to the organic analogues of this disturbance

> Hyper-excited organ-systems tend to get out of control. During the repair of physical injuries, the injured part tends to monopolize the attention of the whole organism; in periods of starvation, the digestive system asserts itself to the detriment of other parts; in rage and panic, the sympathico-adrenal apparatus tyrannizes the whole... The over-excited part... (is) released from its restraints; it asserts its autonomy and sometimes tends to usurp the functions of the whole.
> Analogous situations occur at the cognitive level, where the 'hyper-excited part' appears in the guise of an idée fixe, or a 'closed system' of beliefs...[37]

Not only does obsession with protecting and enhancing any single segment cause the others to atrophy, but the atrophying segments also *pull down the very segment with which the actor is obsessively concerned.* Consider the "Acamemic Observer" who with a moderate emphasis on segment (a) Perception, can probably develop as a person, but as his obsession with detached observation increases, it kills commitment, risk-taking, and synergistic relationships with the wider culture. The "fly on the wall" becomes precisely that, and soon he must face the rage of students contemptuous of his pusillanimity.

Or consider the obsessive concern with identity and status (segments b and c). He who would never lose face can never gain either, for he dare not practice risk and self-suspension. We have already seen that the hyper-active investor (segment d) rapidly loses meaning, but so too does the passive mystic who is forever suspending himself (segment e) in trances and contemplation until he has no real convictions left to suspend. Those men obsessed with the need to bridge the distance (segment f) will institute purges of deviant persons and proclaim their own patriotism, but what a sorry image of patriotism emerged from Joe McCarthy's efforts! Perhaps the greatest source of corruption in American life is the obsession with vulgar pragmatism, the insistence on what "works" and will make an immediate impact (segment g) on the American public. From this perversion of the cycle come Richard Nixon's "Checkers speech," the assurances of imminent victory in Vietnam, the repeated false hopes held out to Black Americans, and the sorry list of broken election promises. For obsessive concern with immediate impact can end up by sacrificing every other segment of the cycle including existence itself.

Even synergy (segment h) can be worshipped to the detriment of the whole. It is not difficult to agree if nothing very novel is conceived and little passion or personal stake is invested. A sacrifice of competence and intellectuality can facilitate the meaningless meeting of little minds. Many Black Americans must have been deterred from making tough demands by the beaming faces and pumping hand-shakes of white "liberals." Finally, the same objections can be made to detached intellectuality (segment i) as were made to detached perception (segment a).

Every segment of the cycle has the capacity to become an unsuspended idol and obsession, cut off from the living whole. Civilizations and cultures abuse and kill each other as the Communist idolators of cooperation (segment h) war with thc Capitalist idolators of individualism (segment d). Within America the Hippie idolators of self-suspension and inward looking identity are persecuted by the representatives of an "up-tight" business culture which worships at the shrine of unreflective hyper-activity and pragmatism. Intellectuals who have solved the world's ills on paper regard with contempt the "mere" men of action, while the latter buy cheap votes by jeering at intelligence. And the appalling irony for all these combatants is *that they need each other to become whole men.* Each has the missing piece which the other requires if he is to be more than a psychological cripple. Each strives either to kill or avoid the quality in the other which he himself lacks and whose presence in the other reproaches him. Thus Hippies exaggerate spontaneity into "Happenings" so devoid of reason that they goad the over rationalized business culture into repressive measures. The bourgoisie, scrambling to work five days a week, forty-five weeks a year, like so many mechanical toys are enraged by the suggestion that they have lost something. Hippies are perhaps equally resentful that those who are planfully active, rather than passive, get the upper hand in this world. In this situation dialogue gives way to shrieking monologue, equality to elitism, democratic synergy to authoritarian relationships of domination/submission and just balance to cruel imbalances and injustices. Camus observed

> If injustice is bad for the rebel, it is not because it contradicts an eternal idea of justice, but because it perpetuates the silent hostility that separates the oppressor from the oppressed. It kills the small part of existence that can be realized on this earth through the mutual understanding of men... The mutual understanding and communication discovered by rebellion can survive only in the free exchange of conversation.[38]

The real struggle for life against death is not between aborted part-men and their part truths – these are all on the side of death, it is between Socratic dialogue on the one hand, and napalm, night sticks and the hee-haw of Presidential monologues on the other. Camus saw it clearly back in 1948.

> Between the forces of terror and the forces of dialogue a great unequal battle has begun. I have nothing but reasonable illusions as to the outcome of the battle. But I believe it must be fought, and I know that certain men at least have resolved to do so. . . I fear. . . that they are in fact alone, and that after an interval of two thousand years we may see the sacrifice of Socrates repeated several times. The program for the future is either a permanent dialogue or the solemn and significant putting to death of any of us who have experienced dialogue.[39]

McClosky's research results appear to support the arguments above. I have described anomic combatants as Obsessive concerning certain segments of the cycle. Their obsession with competence is revealed in a Need for Status, their obsession with investment in Calvinism (and hyper-active items on the Obsessive scale); their surfeit of self-suspension is revealed in Mysticism, their concern with distance by Ethnocentricity, and their determination to make *some* sort of impact on others by a punitive Hostility. Finally many strive for a low level "folksy" synergy between "simple, down-to-earth people," which is reflected on the Populism scale.

In view of the Elitism, Dependency, Authoritarianism and Hostility scales, all of which strongly correlate with anomie, the conclusion that anomic people drive each other into submission and stamp on each other's perspectives is also supported by the data.

*i) No responsibility for FEEDBACK, hence DisINTEGRATION and lack of COMPLEXITY*

Anomic men, whose actions and relationships are rarely effective or fulfilling, are faced either with painful memories, or with experience so shallow and peripheral that in either case they fail to integrate the feedback and to learn from their activities. The acceptance of responsibility is often painful because so many choices are made in circumstances where undesirable outcomes are influenced by fate and by the unpredictable reaction of the other.

It goes without saying that the authoritarian, the hostile, the chauvinistic, and those contemptuous of human weakness, will often blame fate and even more often will blame the other for any unpleasantness. It is usually *his* fault. His "filthy provocation" is entirely responsible for my "defensive precautions" in breaking his skull. I am not responsible for clubbing him – the Maintenance of Law and Order, not me, decreed it. By subduing him forcibly I can close his mouth so that no words of his disturb my few simplistic ideas. As a detective and an inspector explained about the New York policemen who beat up Columbia students:

> Most cops I know will walk into the mouth of a cannon. But they're terrified of words. Don't forget, most cops don't have any education. They're inarticulate... The police feel much more challenged by the words of Columbia students than by any threat they may have actually been...
>
> I think the student contempt of patriotism and materialism is, in some ways, much more difficult for the police to understand than the problems confronting a poor Negro... They really became outraged and confused when they hear some kid question the guts of those fighting in Vietnam or hear some Barnard girl shouting dirty words. Their idea of a woman is a nice, quiet young Catholic girl from Queens.[40]

Here we see that the integration of the authoritarian anomic is very rudimentary, with black and white dichotomies – pure girls and bad girls – long haired "perverts" and regular guys – Free World and Communist Conspiracy, etc. The rigid hierarchies *within* his mind are one with domination/submission relationships which he seeks on the outside with others. Within his cycle certain segments will be subordinated to other segments. Thus he may put Patriotism (short distances) *above* the freedom of investment, the status of the police force *above* perceiving the needs of others, Police morale (synergy) *above* social accountability (integration of feedback), etc. In this way he prevents balance within himself and justice in his relationships, thus perpetuating his own anomie.

If some anomic men refuse to allow "subversive ideas" to enter their minds, others have heads which are rag-bags of unintegrated cliches. John Osborne drew a vivid picture of personal disintegration in his drama *Inadmissible Evidence.* The lawyer, Maitland, being tried in the courtroom of his own imagination, refuses to swear by the Bible and is then asked to affirm by whatever he believes in:

> *Maitland:*
>
> I hereby swear and affirm... By my belief. My belief in... in the technological revolution, the pressing, growing, pressing, urgent need for more and more scientists... schools and universities... the theme of change, realistic decisions based upon the highly developed and professional study of society by people who really know... the overdue need to adapt ourselves to different conditions, the theme and challenge of such rapid change, change... rapid change...[41]

His voice falters and we understand the hollowness not only of his own spirit – but of the social and technical sciences whose authority he has tried to borrow, but which remain inhospitable to his quest for meaning. Keniston in his research with anomic Harvard students described them as suffering from *inundation.*[42] Like Maitland, they let in experience but then found themselves drowning in it.

McClosky's research substantiates several facets of the incapacity to integrate feedback. Anomics are very low on Social Responsibility, as we would expect. They are less well Educated, reject Intellectuality, and suffer from Disorganization and Bewilderment. Finally many of them are Totalitarian – for when segments of the cycle become detached, the whole disintegrates, and men long for a superior authority to repair them by force.

## NOTES FOR CHAPTER IV

1. See "Psychological Dimensions of Anomie," *American Sociological Review,* 30:1, 1965.

2. *Diary of a Country Priest,* New York: Macmillan, 1937, p. 105. Also quoted by Maurice Friedman, *To Deny Our Nothingness, op. cit.* I have been unable to find better illustrations of my theme than in the hundreds of quotations he has culled from existential writers. See also *The Worlds of Existentialism,* Maurice Friedman (ed.), New York: Random House, 1964.

3. St. Mathew's Gospel, Chapter XXII, verse 27.

4. *I and Thou,* Trans. by R. C. Smith, New York: Charles Scribner's Sons, 1958, p. 52.

5. *Babbitt* by Sinclair Lewis, New York: Signet Classic, 1961, p. 130.

6. *Crisis in Black and White* by Charles E. Silberman, New York: Vintage, 1964, p. 10.

7. "Anxiety and Politics" by Franz Neumann in *Identity and Anxiety,* Maurice Stein, Arthur J. Vidich and David M. White (eds.), Glencoe: The Free Press, 1960, pp. 277-284. See also *The Democratic and The Authoritarian State,* by Franz Neumann, Glencoe: The Free Press, 1957, p. 280f.

8. *The Uncommitted: Alienated Youth in American Society,* New York: Harcourt, Brace and World, 1965.

9. I obtained these numbers from an intercorrelation matrix at The Survey Research Center at The University of California at Berkeley.

10. See *Caligula and Three Other Plays,* New York: Vintage, 1958. Also quoted by Maurice Friedman in *To Deny Our Nothingness, op. cit.,* p. 322.

11. "Theology and Self-Awareness" in *Soundings: Essays Concerning Christian Understanding,* A. R. Vidler (ed.), Cambridge University Press, 1963, p. 95.

12. "On Alienated Concepts of Identity," by Ernest G. Schachtel in *Man Alone, Alienation in Modern Society,* Eric and Mary Josephson (eds.), New York: Dell Publishing, 1962, pp. 73-83, or *The American Journal of Psychoanalysis,* Nov. 1961.

13. "Alienation under Capitalism" by Erich Fromm in *Man Alone, op. cit.*, pp. 56-73 or *The Sane Society,* New York: Holt, Rinehart and Winston, Inc., 1955.

14. *The Seed Beneath The Snow*, Trans. by Frances Frenaye, New York: Harper, 1942, p. 209, also quoted in *To Deny Our Nothingness, op. cit.*, p. 55.

15. See *The Authoritarian Personality* by Adorno, et. al., New York: Harper and Row, 1950. Anti-intraception is an ingredient of the California F-scale measuring (right-wing) authoritarianism.

16. See "Portrait of an Anti-Semite" in *Existentialism from Dostoyevsky to Sartre*, Walter Kaufmann (ed.), New York: Meridian Books, 1956.

17. These contrasts are discussed by Friedman in *To Deny Our Nothingness.*

18. *The Vulgarians* by Robert Osborn, Greenwich, Conn.: New York Graphic Society.

19. *The Kitchen,* London: Jonathan Cape, 1961, pp. 57-58.

20. See "The Misunderstanding" in *Caligula and Three Other Plays, op. cit.*, p. VII (introduction).

21. *The Devils of Loudon,* New York: Harper Torchbook, 1959, last page.

22. See "Toward a Theory of Schizophrenia" by Gregory Bateson, *et. al., Behavioral Science,* V. 1, no. 4, Oct. 1956, pp. 251-64, also in *Interpersonal Dynamics,* Warren G. Bennis, *et. al.*, (eds.), *op. cit.*, pp. 141-161. The double bind theory features prominently in the work of R. D. Laing, *The Self and Others,* London: Tavistock, 1961, and in the work of David Cooper, *Psychiatry and Anti-Psychiatry*, London: Tavistock, 1967. It is seen as a major source of psychological violence, miscommunication and schizophrenia.

23. See *Black Boy,* New York: Harper and Row, 1945, also excerpted under "The Price of Keeping One's Place" in *Sociology Through Literature,* Lewis A. Coser (ed.), Englewood Cliffs: Prentice Hall, 1963, p. 307.

24. Quotation by Robert Whittinton, preceding the preface of *A Man for All Seasons* by Robert Bolt, New York: Vintage Books, 1966.

25. *Ibid*, p. 95.

26. *Waiting for Godot* by Samuel Beckett, New York: Grove Press, 1954, p. 57.

27. "Each His Own Wilderness" by Doris Lessing in *New English Dramatists,* Harmondsworth, Middlesex: Penguin Books, 1959, p. 92.

28. *Ibid.*, p. 94.

29. *Babbitt* by Sinclair Lewis, *op. cit.*, p. 252.

30. *Ibid.*, p. 315.

31. See *Man Alone: Alienation in Modern Society, op. cit.*, p. 93, originally in *The Listener*, April 7, 1960.

32. *To Deny Our Nothingness, op. cit.*, p. 342.

33. *Ibid.*, see also *The Fall*, New York: Alfred A. Knopf, 1957, p. 147.

34. *Metamorphosis and Other Stories*, Harmondsworth, Middlesex: Penguin Classics, 1961, pp. 7-64.

35. See an excellent discussion of "The Girl" in *The Secular City* by Harvey Cox, New York: Macmillan, 1965.

36. See "Neither Victims nor Executioners" trans. by Dwight MacDonald in *Seeds of Liberation*, Paul Goodman (ed.), New York: George Braziller, 1964, p. 26f. See also *The Human Dialogue*, Floyd W. Matson and Ashley Montague (eds.), New York: The Free Press, p. 300f.

37. *The Act of Creation, op. cit.*, p. 460.

38. *The Rebel, op. cit.*, p. 283f.

39. *Resistance, Rebellion, and Death*, p. 55.

40. "Police Violence: A Changing Pattern," *New York Times*, July 7, 1968.

41. *Inadmissable Evidence*, London: Faber and Faber, 1965, p. 10.

42. *The Uncommitted: Alienated Youth in America, op. cit.*, p. 99f.

*Chapter V*

## Dissent and Rebellion in the Laboratory

I argued in Chapter I that the conditions of a carefully controlled laboratory experiment were hardly conducive to human development. In Chapter III we saw that development involves a sharing and then enlarging of perspectives – yet the typical experiment keeps the subject naive and the experimenter in complete control. Development requires mutual disclosure and authenticity and a generally egalitarian relationship in which both parties are prepared to suspend their assumptions to permit a synergistic mutuality of influence. But in many experiments the fact of unilateral unsuspended manipulation is disguised beneath an inauthentic facade of mutual cooperation. If the naive subject *thinks* that he is being treated as a colleague and has some control over the situation he will be less anxious and more "natural" in his behavior. Hence in such experiments the authoritarian element with its "double bind" conflict is sprung upon the unsuspecting subject, who is first lulled and gulled into the role of a "collaborator."

We saw in Chapter IV that anomic man was frequently deluded, helpless, obedient, hostile, conforming, and cruel. Upon such personality traits there has been a plethora of experiments yielding a rich harvest of data. The reasons are not far to seek. Since experimental procedures delude, render helpless, and set out to predict and control the obedient reactions of subjects, the "discovery" of behavior they have "scientifically" engendered is hardly an earth shaking surprise.

But if these experiments engender and focus upon the anomic and conservative characteristics of man, they also provoke rebellion from those who reject these experimental assaults upon human development. Radical man, as I argued in Chapter III, struggles against absurd and oppressive conditions and rebels against being stimulus bound. Hence a number of these experiments *have* discovered radical man, *indirectly,* by classifying and describing those who have resisted pressures to conform, obey, torture, and cheat. In some cases, it has proved possible to measure rebellion and dissent against the experimental procedures themselves.

Let us take three experimental situations. In the first, known as the "Asch technique,"[1] half a dozen or more subjects are invited to render verdicts on the relative length of two lines, the relative size of two circles, or some similar diagram. The task of discriminating the larger one is varied in difficulty, but usually verdicts are near unanimous when control subjects are permitted to answer freely. In the experimental session all subjects save one are the hired confederates of the experimenter and agree to a false consensus. The single member is left with the dilemma of rendering a true account of what he sees, thereby registering a lone dissent, or conforming quietly to a unanimous verdict.

A significant elaboration of the Asch technique was undertaken by Richard Crutchfield. He put the experimental subjects in separate booths facing imposing looking signal boards, which ostensibly flashed the verdicts of all other subjects. In fact, (oh the subtlety of science!) everyone was being deceived by the investigator and was receiving a unanimous and false consensus. Crutchfield included political and social topics in addition to geometric figures. Only 19% of a sample of college students expressed private agreement with the statement, "Free Speech being a privilege rather than a right, it is proper for society to suspend free speech whenever it feels itself threatened." But when faced with "unanimous approval" of this statement, 58% overtly supported it. The percentages were generally increased when an authority figure in the shape of the experimenter announced the "right" answer after every trial – in each case supporting the contrived consensus. Similarly when the group was shown a list of political problems facing the country only 12% expressed private agreement that "subversive activity" was the most serious of the problems, but under pressure to conform, 48% revealed themselves as at least potential allies of a Joe McCarthy.

If these results cast doubt on the private, attitudinal "liberalism" of many Americans, whose convictions seem to wither before the prestigious technology of signal boards and the declaration of scientists, then the experiments of Stanley Milgram at Yale University provide data which are positively nightmarish.

Milgram set up an experimental procedure which ostensibly studied the effect of punishment on memory and learning. In reality degrees of obedience to the command to torture a third party were being measured. Pairs of "volunteers" – which in fact included one genuine volunteer and one confederate of the experimenter – were divided into "trainers" and "learners." In each case the genuine volunteer was the "trainer" and the confederate was the "learner." Both received $4.50 in payment before the experiment began. The "trainer" was then shown an electrical switching apparatus replete with blue and red lights and thirty levers marked 15 volts, 30 volts, 45 volts, etc. up to and including 450 volts. He was invited to test the apparatus by giving himself a small 45 volt shock (which in fact came from a low voltage battery).

The "purpose" of the experiment was explained to him as follows. The "learner" will be given a series of paired words; later when only one word of an original pair is repeated he must remember the other word. If he remembers correctly no shock is given. If he makes a mistake, a series of *escalating* shocks is administered following each mistake. This will enable the experimentor to discover how much pain is associated with the greatest learning. Then comes the following general procedure.

The "trainer" watches the "learner" being strapped into an electric chair. While doing this the experimenter observes that the shocks can be "extremely painful but leave no permanent tissue damage." Electrode paste is smeared on the subjects hand "to avoid blisters and burns." The "trainer" takes up his position behind the switching apparatus where he can hear but not see the "learner," and the experiment begins. According to a prearranged schedule the "learner" makes repeated mistakes which require the trainer to shout "30 volts!" "45 volts!" etc. and then pull down the lever with that marking upon it. The "learner" pretends to feel the shock in the following gradations.

At 75 volts he gives a light grunt. At 120 volts he shouts out that the shocks are becoming painful. At 135 volts he groans painfully. At 150 he demands to be released "Get me out of here. I refuse to go on!" At 180 he shouts that he cannot stand the pain and repeatedly asks to be released until at 270 volts he screams in agony. At 300 he screams that he will not continue the test. The "trainer" is then told that failure to answer is equivalent to a mistake and that higher shocks must be administered. At 315 volts the "learner" repeats his refusal and in fact ceases to perform in the test. He then shrieks and struggles with increasing intensity with every shock up to 450 volts. The experiment is designed to measure at what stage the "trainer" will rebel.

The levers are elaborately marked not only with the voltage but with legends like, "strong shock," "very strong," "intense shock," "extremely intense," "Danger! severe shock," and "XXX." Later it was found that virtually all "trainers" believed the situation. Although a panel of psychiatrists predicted that only 4% would go beyond 300 volts, in fact 78% did so, and although the psychiatrists predicted that only 1/10th of 1% would go to 450 volts, 65% did so. Originally the experiment was set up with no voice audible but only desperate knocking sounds on the wooden cubicle in which the "learner" sat. In this condition so many shocked their victim to the bitter end that cries of increasing agony had to be added, as well as increasing degrees of proximity between "learner" and "trainer," in order to produce a large enough sample of dissenters. Nearly 30% would continue to torture their victim to the end while grappling with him and *holding his squirming hand down upon the shock plate,* while he screamed about a weak heart!

However, very few subjects enjoyed inflicting the pain. Nearly all were highly agitated and pleaded with the experimenter to let them stop. He repeated monotonously "the experiment requires that you continue," and where this and harsher commands were not enough to achieve compliance, his final words were: "You have no choice, you *must* go on."[2]

The degree of obedience seemed incredible to Milgram and his associates, and incredible to the psychiatrists and the scientific fraternity. All this was before Vietnam. Now we know what this country will do when Asian "learners" cannot be taught that "aggression does not pay." There is something both pathetic and familiar to a student of these experiments in the pleading of President Johnson for "a sign from Hanoi." Just a sign, any sign, the *smallest* sign, *that we were justified in torturing you in order to teach you a lesson.* Perhaps just one more volt and one more scream, and the earlier screams and the volts will be justified! How elusive is the search for forgiveness as we twist and gouge the environment to make it confirm our initial judgments concerning it.

The misery of those who shocked their victims while bewailing the necessity and obeying orders is captured in this young soldier's letter from Vietnam to his parents:

> Dear Mom and Dad:
>
> Today we went on a mission and I am not very proud of myself, my friends or my country. We burned every hut in sight!
>
> It was a small rural network of villages and the people were incredibly poor. My unit burned and plundered their meager possessions. Let me try to explain the situation to you.
>
> The huts here are thatched palm leaves. Each one has a dried mud bunker inside. These bunkers are to protect the families. Kind of like air raid shelters.
>
> My unit commanders, however, chose to think that these bunkers are offensive. So every hut we find that has a bunker, we are ordered to burn to the ground. . .
>
> So, everyone is crying, begging and praying that we don't separate them and take their husbands and fathers, sons and grandfathers. The women wail and moan.
>
> Then they watch in terror as we burn their homes, personal possessions and food. Yes, we burn all rice and shoot all livestock.
>
> Some of the guys are so careless! Today a buddy of mine called "La Dai" ("Come here") into a hut and an old man came out of the bomb shelter. My buddy told the old man to get away from the hut and since we have to move quickly on a sweep, just threw a hand grenade into the shelter.
>
> As he pulled the pin the old man got excited and started jabbering and running toward my buddy and the hut. A GI, not understanding stopped the old man with a football tackle just as my buddy threw the grenade into the shelter. (There is a four-second delay on a hand grenade.)
>
> After he threw it, and was running for cover (during the four-second delay) we all heard a *baby* crying from inside the shelter!
>
> There was nothing we could do. . .
>
> After the explosion we found the mother, two children (ages about 6 and 12, boy and girl) and an almost newborn baby. That is what the old man was trying to tell us!
>
> IT WAS HORRIBLE!!

> The children's fragile bodies were torn apart, literally mutilated. We looked at each other and burned the hut.
>
> The old man was just whimpering in disbelief outside the burning hut. We walked away and left him there.
>
> My last look was an old, old man in ragged, torn, dirty clothes on his knees outside the burning hut, praying to Buddha. His white hair was blowing in the wind and tears were rolling down. . .

Finally, as the soldier was urged on and on to burn and destroy, he managed one small rebellion against his fate, and thereby began to exist as a human being and found, perhaps, the courage to write this letter.

> We kept on walking, then the three of us separated. There was a hut at a distance and my squad leader told me to go over and destroy it. An oldish man came out of the hut.
>
> I checked and made sure no one was in it, then got out my matches. The man came up to me then, and bowed with his hands in a praying motion over and over.
>
> He looked so sad! He didn't say anything, just kept bowing, begging me not to burn his home.
>
> We were both there, alone, and he was about your age Dad. With a heavy heart, I hesitatingly put the match to the straw and started to walk away.
>
> Dad, it was so hard for me to turn and look at him in the eyes, but I did.
>
> I wish I could have cried, but I just can't anymore.
>
> I threw down my rifle and ran into the now blazing hut and took out everything I could save food, clothes, etc.
>
> Afterward he took my hand, still saying nothing and bowed down touching the back of my hand to his forehead. . .
>
> Excuse the poor writing but I was pretty emotional, I guess, even a little shook.
>
> YOUR SON. . .[3]

What is even more grim in its implications for our world is that fully 90% of the "trainers" in Milgram's experiment would repeatedly pull a master switch that then permitted a second person to pull the various shock levers. This is much closer to the kind of situation encountered in warfare. With our advanced technology we have burnt thousands of people alive, without going through the distasteful process of arranging faggots around each victim. Thanks to the patriotism of Dow Chemical we possess new, improved, incenderjel (not to be confused with old napalm). Now it's all done automatically by a man 1,000 feet above the ground, who drops the "miracle substance" with its self-spreading, self-sticking, long burning ingredients, and we don't even have to look. Needless to say, the victim is just as agonized and just as dead whether we use the old fashioned technology of Torquemada or whether the pilot is back at base drinking a chocolate soda before the pyre subsides.

But this chapter is chiefly about radical men – those few who recognized that Public Opinion, Scientific Authority, Up-to-date Technology, and Yale University were being at best ridiculous and at worst obscenely cruel. In the Asch and Crutchfield experiments these men recorded lone dissents. In the obedience experiment they argued, often angrily with the experimenter before thrusting their payment back in his face and demanding the "learner's" release.

I shall contend in this chapter that the three experiments tested to the fullest *every segment of the cycle of radical man.* Hence, those, who survived these tests by their public dissent or rebellion were more developed, psycho-socially, than those who obeyed and conformed. I shall now go around the developed cycle, showing how each segment was challenged by and survived the experimental conditions. Let me first restate the developed cycle from Chapter III.

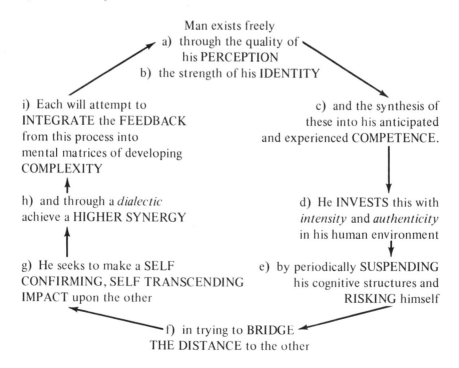

Man exists freely
a) through the quality of his PERCEPTION
b) the strength of his IDENTITY

c) and the synthesis of these into his anticipated and experienced COMPETENCE.

d) He INVESTS this with *intensity* and *authenticity* in his human environment

e) by periodically SUSPENDING his cognitive structures and RISKING himself

f) in trying to BRIDGE THE DISTANCE to the other

g) He seeks to make a SELF CONFIRMING, SELF TRANSCENDING IMPACT upon the other

h) and through a *dialectic* achieve a HIGHER SYNERGY

i) Each will attempt to INTEGRATE the FEEDBACK from this process into mental matrices of developing COMPLEXITY

*A test of man's free existence*

I argued in Chapter II that man is not obliged to internalize the directions, the ideologies, "fixed sub-assemblies" and the pressures to conform which bombard him daily. Rather, he is free to screen out, to accept but label as illegitimate, and to "dismantle" incoming messages, so as to select only that which contributes to his shared existence with others. In so doing he plucks meaning out of Absurdity and thrusts his own valued synthesis out into the chaotic environment to make it meaningful and just.

It would be difficult to think of three experiments which more aptly exemplify encounters with the Absurd. Imagine being faced with a roomful of people, all solemnly proclaiming that large objects are small and broad is narrow. Imagine facing the unanimous opinion, reinforced by authority, that the very processes of free speech, and tolerance of diverse viewpoints, which have been the mainstay of one's intellectual and social development up to this moment, should now be suspended! Finally imagine answering an advertisment to assist scientific research in a prestigious university, and receiving payment for it. Now you are there assisting a Top Scientist in the search for truth. You are proud, perhaps, and a little excited. He seems to be paying you considerable respect and attention. Then suddenly the vision changes to the grim and senseless torture of a bound man, desperate to withdraw from the experiment, and too agonized to learn anything.

In each case the rebellious subjects rejected the absurdity but in no case did they reject *all* the elements in the environment – that would be nihilistic. In the Asch and Crutchfield experiments they chose to affirm that small part of the environment that was consistent with the inner laws of their own development, rejecting the idiotic choruses of agreement. In the obedience experiment they chose to uphold and succour a screaming victim being overwhelmed by trickery and force. Each dissenter in each situation found something of value to rescue from its insane context and to uphold.

*a) A test of the quality of perception*

I argued that radical man looked into the face of absurdity without flinching. He succeeded in holding two sets of contradictory ideas in his mind at the same time, the love of justice and the sight of injustice, meaningfulness and meaninglessness, the tragedy of the current predicament and his determination to make it otherwise. Radical man *sees the contradiction.* In the Asch and Crutchfield experiments it was the contradiction between his conviction and what everyone else appeared to be saying. In the obedience experiment it was the contradiction between the orders he had agreed to and been paid to obey on the one hand, and the desperate appeals to his humanity on the other.

The anomic and conforming man with his exclusive and narrow obsessions and his intolerance for ambiguity (see Table 3, Chapter IV) seems unable to confront the contradiction and tries to push out of sight and out of mind that discrepant element which is easier and safer to ignore. In a version of the obedience experiment where the "trainer" was made to face his writhing victim, the obedient "trainers" would twist their heads to the right and to the left, upwards or downwards, anywhere to avoid the pleading face and eyes of their victims. It was just *after* the young soldier in Vietnam had found the courage to look into the face of his victim, that he first rebelled against his pitiless assignment. "Dad, it was so hard for me to turn and look at him in the eyes, but I did." To look allowed him to save some small dignity and humanity from the situation. The same point was made by Bernard Shaw in *Saint Joan,* in the conversation between two priests, De Stogumber and Cauchon.

> DE STOGUMBER: I tell my folks they must be very careful. I say to them, "If you only saw what you think about you would think quite differently about it. It would give you a great shock. . . I am not cruel by nature, you know. . . I did a very cruel thing once because I did not know what cruelty was like. I had not seen it, you know. . . you must see it. And then you are redeemed and saved.
> CAUCHON: Were not the sufferings of our Lord Christ enough for you?
> DE STOGUMBER: No. Oh no! Not at all. I have seen them in pictures, and read of them in books, and been greatly moved by them, as I thought. But it was no use: it was not our Lord that redeemed me but a young woman whom I saw actually burned to death. It was dreadful: oh, most dreadful. But it saved me. I have been a different man ever since. . .
> CAUCHON: Must then a Christ perish in torment in every age to save those that have no imagination? [4]

*b) A test of the strength of identity*

I defined a strong sense of identity as an awareness of and an accrued confidence in, one's own presence before others. This included an acceptance of one's own bodily apparatus and the limitations of one's human condition. Those who dissented in the Asch and Crutchfield experiments seemed willing to look inside themselves, exposing and being prepared to consider possible limitations in their eyesight, hearing, developmental experience, and logical capacities, and to have these examined by others. Alternatively, or in addition, they may have been more accepting of whatever human limitations they possessed and somewhat more confident about their thoughts, faculties, and feelings. Given a choice between *inside* feelings and *outside* pressures, they chose to prolong rather than shorten the conflict by affirming their own sense of rightness and inner continuity.

*c) A test of competence*

Clearly these experiments pitted the subject's accrued confidence in his own resources against the competence he attributed to those who disagreed with him. Hence those who had previously learned from open disagreements and had prevailed to some extent over opposed viewpoints would be the most likely to support their own judgments in these experimental situations.

Obversely, those with a hunger for status and continually deprived of the standing to which they aspired would "snuggle up" to the experimenter and in the harrowing circumstances of the obedience experiment cling more closely than ever to his mantle of prestige and all-knowing wisdom. The mounting sense of guilt and inner panic can yet be assuaged by sharing the experimenter's power *over* people, that will force them to acknowledge the harsh necessity of one's own cruelty. Interpersonal competence is thereby discarded for the lure of a unilateral power that can expunge the evidence of one's own failure and command unwilling confirmation from others.

*d) A test of authentic and intense investment*

I have argued that the active investment of one's personal synthesis involves the translation of the human personality into the reality experienced by others, and that the strength of such investments can be estimated by their intensity and by their authenticity. In the Asch and Crutchfield experiments we know that few if any of the conformers privately believed in their public affirmations, while the dissenters were clearly authentic and were staking their own views against all odds.

In the Milgram experiment, the obedient subjects displayed an extraordinary disassociation between words and acts. Some would laugh unaccountably and uncontrollably while administering torture, but nearly all kept up a running commentary on their own compassion and good intentions. "He's getting hurt. I'm stopping this. No sir – I'm not going to kill that man! What about his bad heart? I'm not going to give him 450 volts!" But they did, again and again.

Fantastic? It would have seemed so a few years ago, but recently we have watched such disassociations almost nightly on television. If any student cares to compare President Johnson's repeated affirmations of peaceful intention, healing and building, and brotherly love between nations, with the number of bombs dropped, civilians killed, and similar indices of agony, he would probably find a positive correlation. If there is anything in the techniques of conditioning human behavior by appropriate stimuli, then the words, "peace," "honor," "heal," and "build" must make the Vietnamese duck whenever we utter them.

In such situations only determined dissent can bring our investments back into authentic congruence with the values we proclaim and our social impulses. Rebellious subjects in the laboratory were sometimes furious, sometimes calm, but there was no mistaking the voice of conscience. "I'm sorry – but I have to call it as I see it." "There is no money in the world that will make me hurt another individual. Here take your check! . . . This is one hell of an experiment!" Ultimately it is upon these rebellious and "disorderly" people that our civilization and so-called law and order depend. Harold Laski put it well:–

> Civilization means, above all, the unwillingness to inflict unnecessary pain... Those of us who needlessly accept the commands of authority cannot yet claim to be civilized men.
>
> Our business, if we desire to live a life, not utterly devoid of meaning and significance, is to accept nothing which contradicts our basic experience merely because it comes to us from tradition or convention or authority. It may well be that we are wrong; but our self expression is thwarted at the root unless the certainties we are asked to accept coincide with the certainties we experience. That is why the condition of freedom in any state is always a widespread and consistent skepticism of the canons on which power insists.[5]

*e) A test of self-suspension and risk taking.*

Were these experiments also tests of the readiness with which the dissenting subjects could suspend their personal syntheses, so that new and seemingly contradictory messages could enter their "open" minds? I submit that they were. I have argued that suspension can only be achieved by those who risk and thereby tolerate the sharp anxiety of loosening their own thought-matrices, to let in new material.

To risk a lone dissent in the Asch and Crutchfield experiments was also a decision by the dissenter to open up the floodgates and let a wave of criticism burst upon him. Once he explored honestly the differences between himself and a united opposition, he might never be the same again. Most of the conformers may privately have questioned and suspended their judgments, *but they did not risk them by investment in others,* and where nothing is ventured nothing can be won. The conformer cannot achieve confirmation because he has run from disconfirmation.

Physiological tests of anxiety arousal which were run during a Crutchfield experiment revealed one of the few perfect correlations found in social science. *All* experimental subjects suffered strong anxiety in the face of this concentrated assault on their own capacities.[6] But the conformers quickly lowered their anxiety by the inauthentic act of agreement. The dissenters endured and endured high levels of existential anxiety in their attempt to explore and learn from the disagreement. Not until the purpose of the experiment was explained to them did their tension fall – and then they learned of their own strength while conformers discovered their own weakness.

In the obedience experiment the dissenters showed a similar kind of flexible self-suspension. They entered the room believing in Yale University, believing that they were promoting science, and had assumed the role of research assistants on an important project. Minutes later all these assumptions were open to serious question as the authority figure was seen to demand both cruelty and stupidity. How *quickly*, then, could subjects resynthesize and "juggle" their perspectives on this situation to comprehend the enormity of the commands and the complicity of their roles?

There is a second facet to this suspension, the capacity to cut losses, to suspend and reject one's previous behavior as mistaken. The flexible person follows Christ's axiom, "If thine eye offend thee cut it out." The unflexible person uses torture to try to recoup his losses, clinging desperately, against mounting evidence, to the image of himself as justified, and thereby has "two eyes to be cast into hell fire."

There is even a third facet to this self-suspension. The situation calls for the "unselfish" sacrifice of one's own perspectives and self-esteem, in order to enter the perspective of the victim and heed his appeal. A little of oneself must be lost and condemned forever, in order to reconcile oneself with the man wronged. It is not impossible to do this in a small room with few spectators. But to do it on television before millions when the wrong involves thousands of lives and with all the political penalties of publicly acknowledging a mistake – there it would take unusual courage. And besides, the apologists for war have a totally different concept of courage.

The rebellious subjects seem to have found the capacity to suspend all these assumptions, to endure the momentary, anxious inner chaos of rearranging their perspectives, and to reintegrate their assumptions into an emphatic rejection of the torturing role.

*f) A test of bridging wide distances to others*

I have defined "distance" as the experienced remoteness of the other's perspectives and characteristics from one's own. Nearly every subject in the Asch and Crutchfield experiments felt individuation thrust upon him. "I longed to agree." "I felt strange and absurd... inferior in some way... puzzled, separated, as if I'd been cast out!" These and more were typical comments on the experience. By their dissent the subjects acknowledged and thereby opened up the distance between them and a unanimous opposition, and at the same time took the first steps in exploring the chasm. They leapt into nothingness, knowing in advance that they would meet with absurd disconfirmation, yet hoping against hope to snatch some meaning from the absurd dilemma in which they now found themselves.

In the obedience experiments those who volunteered had come to partake of the perspectives of the experimenter. It was upon his needs and requirements that they were concentrating, and they relied upon him to guide them through the strange territory of a psychological laboratory. They had agreed with him to inflict punishment on a "distant" stranger, whom in contrast to the experimenter they had not come to the laboratory to help and had not been paid to help.

The experiment escalates in cruelty, and the "distant" stranger pleads for mercy, while the "close" experimenter insists on proceeding. What is being tested, therefore, is the subject's capacity to *imaginatively identify and communicate with a distant other.* Clearly the stranger is in need, but he is "further away," an underdog, less prestigious, and he is interfering with joint enterprise of the experimenter and the "trainer."

Although "psychological" distance is not identical with spatial distance, there is an obvious tendency for those out of sight to be out of mind, and for persons visibly confronting one another to achieve some measure of mutual influence. Milgram systematically varied the spatial distance between the "trainer" and his victim and between the experimenter and the "trainer." The more the "trainer" was moved toward his victim, the more likely he was to refuse to torture him and to defy the experimenter. But the closer the experimenter stood to the "trainer" the more the trainer was likely to obey. Maximum obedience occurred with a close experimenter and a distant victim. Minimum dissent occurred with a close victim and a distant experimenter. In our society, social victims are nearly always distant and are dimly perceived by the popular culture as being horribly dressed, foul smelling, riotous and dangerously perverse. To answer their call for help is usually to enrage authority, and one forfeits much more than $4.50 for doing so. Yet in this experiment, as in life, radical man goes to the help of the distant victims of authority.

*g) A test of the capacity to make a self-confirming, self-transcending impact.*

Considering that the dissenters in the Asch and Crutchfield experiments know *before* they answer, that they are unanimously disconfirmed, can I really argue that they are persons who habitually seek and find confirmation? I think I can. In the first place, self-confirmation is not remotely meaningful unless it is one's authentic existence and capacities which achieve confirmation. The conformers win no jot of justification from their timidity. The dissenters know that they have little chance for immediate confirmation or transcendence, but they have learnt that when they are true to their experience, they will generally achieve fulfillment in the end. And in variations of the Crutchfield experiment they do achieve it. Where a single man dissents, others will often follow him. In the obedience experiments a variation was introduced in which groups administered the torture. When the first group member rebelled he was usually followed by about ninety percent of the group – thereby illustrating the axiom of Albert Camus that "I rebel, therefore we exist," and that solitariness is the path to a truer solidarity.

*h) A test of the capacity to achieve a higher synergy through dialectic.*

If the dialectical process involves a reconciliation of opposites, then the conformers and the obedient are eliminated in the first round, through their failure to affirm the opposite. Only the rebellious have any personal thesis capable of confronting its antithesis. Actually the Crutchfield and Asch experiments are terminated before a reconciliation can be attempted, and the antithesis is revealed as a contrived one. In the obedience experiments there is nothing *in* the experimenter's antithesis that is worth reconciling. He is the authoritarian villain, an embodiment of the mad scientist. What dissenters do in this situation is to reject anomic authoritarianism and form synergistic relationships with the victim.

I have argued that synergy between people demands "justice" – which I defined as a just balance between all segments of the double helix, so as to optimize their life-giving and creative combination. In rescuing the helpless victim, the rebels in the obedience experiment make just the unequal, deceitful relationship between the "learner" and his environment. They even returned their payments to the experimenter to balance *that* relationship, thereby following the dictim of Camus that if one's condition is unjust one can nonetheless resolve to be just oneself.

A variation of the Crutchfield technique illustrates the capacity of dissenters to reconcile and synergize opposites within the cycle. In this variation the most liked and admired persons in a work group were confronted by the unanimous "consensus" of their group upon a decision which would actually have impeded the group's goals and values. The most admired persons tended to dissent, and tried to sway the group towards its own best interests. Here we see that the most individualistic persons, segment (d), were also the most confirmed and transcending, segment (g). Those willing to bridge the distance, segment (f), were also the best synergists, segment (h). They combined distance with relationship, rebellion with existence, affection with independence, heart with head, and perception with action. In short, *they reconciled potential opposites both within themselves and the group.*

*i) A test of the integration of feedback, and developing complexity.*

I have argued that radical man takes social responsibility for his action and its impacts as well as for his failures to act. In the obedience experiments there is a straightforward case for asserting that the escalating appeals for mercy are heeded by the dissenters who assume responsibility for their acts and are ignored by the obedient, who refuse to allow the piteous feedback to modify their behavior.

There is also ample reason to suppose that dissenters are more complex persons with more expanded consciousness. This is likely to be true not only because the acceptance of feedback is a precondition for its integration, but because self-confirming impacts which are consistent with the perceptions, identity and investments of the actor, possess a continuity and an *integrity* which make personality *integration* possible. Consider, in contrast, the dilemma of the conformist. What he thinks privately contradicts what he says publicly, but having said it publicly he is now stuck with it and is treated by others as holding opinions which he does not have. The discontinuity and disintegration inherent in this dilemma are obvious. Moreover Crutchfield found that some conformers refused to revert to their private opinions. Having publicly assented to such ludicrous propositions as "60% to 70% of U. S. citizens are over 65 years of age," they clung to this belief with tenacity. There was tendency for conformers to go from one rigidly asserted position to the opposite opinion, again rigidly asserted.[7]

Earlier I characterized radical man as voting "for the richer universe, for the good which seems most organizable. . . " The dissenters in the Asch and Crutchfield experiments knew that richer universes are found by exploring rather than denying disagreements. In the obedience experiments, they recognized intuitively that this procedure was not an enlargement of experience but a brutal constraint of it. They faced a dilemma similar in some respects to that of the Maid in Shaw's *Saint Joan.* Joan was a simple peasant girl, overawed during her trial by the mock kindliness of priestcraft, an authority equivalent to modern science. She was in severe conflict because her "voices" had promised her she would not be burnt at the stake, but outside the courthouse the stake awaited her. Surely, she thought, her voices could not wish a young girl to perish so cruelly? So she acceded to the priests who seemed so genuinely desirous of saving her, and signed a recantation. But then the court solemnly condemned her to a lifetime of perpetual imprisonment and she saw in a flash that her recantation was to save *their* paternalism and to provide for *their* confirmation. Behind their masks of piety they feared and hated her youthful existence.

> JOAN Give me that writing (she rushes to the table; snatches up the paper; and tears it into fragments) Light your fire!. . . My voices were right. . . Yes they told me you were fools, and that I was not to listen to your fine words nor trust to your charity. You promised me my life; but you lied. You think that life is nothing but not being stone dead. It is not the bread and water I fear. . . But to shut me from the light of the sky and the sight of fields and flowers; to chain my feet so that I can never again ride with the soldiers nor climb the hill; to make me breathe foul damp darkness, and keep me from everything that brings me back

Table 7

**THE PERSONALITY CORRELATES OF INDEPENDENCE OF JUDGMENT (USING ASCH EXPERIMENT)**

| *Segments of the Cycle* | *Characteristics of Dissenters* | *Characteristics of Conformers* |
|---|---|---|
| Man exists freely.... | High on Originality Scale<br>sees Rebellion as adult<br>Hates taking orders<br>Describes self as:–<br>original<br>artistic<br>idealistic<br>reckless | Low on Originality Scale<br>Rebellion as childish<br>Likes taking orders<br>Describes self as:–<br>efficient<br>obliging<br>patient<br>kind |
| a) PERCEPTION | Values cognitive originality<br>Highly empathic | Values surface characteristics<br>Low in empathy |
| b) IDENTITY | Highly intraceptive<br>High Personal Soundness Scale | Anti-intraceptive<br>Low Personal Soundness Scale |
| c) COMPETENCE | High Ego Strength | Low Ego Strength |
| d) INVESTMENT *authentic and intense* | High in personal involvement<br>Not affected in manner<br>Understands demonstrative men<br>Often feels like crying | Likes poised "outgoing" personalities. Is affected in manner<br>Embarrassed by demonstrative men<br>Does not feel like crying |
| e) SUSPENSION and RISK | Feels lack of social ease<br>Enjoys uncertainty<br>Values open-mindedness | Values courtesy and self-control<br>Likes certainty<br>Values determination |
| f) BRIDGING THE DISTANCE | Could cut moorings and quit home<br>Prefers individual contests | Could not cut moorings<br>Prefers team contests |
| g) SELF-CONFIRMING SELF-TRANSCENDING IMPACT | Prefers few intimate relationships to many casual ones | Prefers many contacts, and values practical applications |
| h) *Dialectic* Leading to SYNERGY | Predicts resolution of world conflicts<br>Rejects solutions imposed by authority<br>Responds to the other's inner integrity | Sees perpetual unresolved conflict<br>Calls for authoritive leaders to impose solutions<br>Rejects those with superficial imperfections |
| i) INTEGRATION of FEEDBACK and | Receptive to new ideas<br>Preference for Complexity | Unreceptive to new ideas<br>Preference for Simplicity |

Source: *Creativity and Psychological Health,* Frank Barron. Princeton: Van Nostrand. 1963. Chapter 14

## Table 8

## THE PERSONALITY CORRELATES OF INDEPENDENCE OF JUDGMENT (USING CRUTCHFIELD EXPERIMENT)

| *Segments of the Cycle* | *Dissenters* | *Conformers* |
|---|---|---|
| *Existence* | Choice of creative careers<br>artist, writer, architect<br>Richness of novel ideas<br>Associates ideas imaginatively<br>Females reject traditional role<br>Likes to break rules. | Choice of conventional careers<br>banker, salesman, clerk<br>Poverty of ideas<br>Conventional attitudes<br>Accept feminine role |
| a) PERCEPTION | Good social perception<br>Tolerance for ambiguity<br>Aesthetic and sensuous<br>High Concept Mastery | Poor social perception<br>Intolerance for ambiguity<br>Narrow interests<br>Low Concept Mastery |
| b) IDENTITY | Insight and self-awareness | Low self-awareness<br>Fear of being found out |
| c) COMPETENCE | High Ego Strength<br>Self-Confidence | Low Ego Strength<br>Inadequacy and guilt |
| d) INVESTMENT<br>*authentic*<br>*and*<br>*intense* | Expressive, ebullient<br>Natural, and forthright<br>Impulsive<br>Spontaneous | Sometimes passive, sometimes<br>"business like" but *emotionally*<br>constricted and<br>overcontrolled |
| e) SUSPENSION and RISK | Undogmatic and<br>relatively open<br>Trustful | Rigid and dogmatic<br>Moralistic, legalistic<br>Distrustful and anxious |
| f) BRIDGING THE DISTANCE | Social but less socialized | More socialized.<br>Desire to return to childhood |
| g) SELF-CONFIRMING SELF-TRANSCENDING IMPACT | Makes impression on staff consistent with self-evaluation. Persuasive leader. | Self-evaluation and impact upon staff are highly discrepant. |
| h) *Dialectic* leading to SYNERGY | Challenges those who take advantage of him<br>Expresses hostility directly<br>Is turned to for advice and reassurance.<br>Anti-authoritarian | Over-responsive to others evaluations<br>Withdraws in adversity<br>Is often exploited by others<br>Somewhat authoritarian |
| i) INTEGRATION of FEEDBACK and COMPLEXITY | Concern with philosophical problems.<br>Unusual association of ideas.<br>More Intellectual | Is easily confused and disorganized.<br>Simple and dichotomous mental constructs. |

Sources: *Individual in Society* by David Krech, Richard S. Crutchfield and Edgerton L. Ballachey. New York. McGraw-Hill 1962. pp. 525-529

"Conformity and Character" by Richard S. Crutchfield. *American Psychologist,* 10, pp. 191-198. 1955

> to the love of God when your wickedness and foolishness tempt me to hate Him. . . I could do without my war-horse. . . if only I could still hear the wind in the trees, the larks in the sunshine, the young lambs crying through the healthy frost. . . But without these things I cannot live; and by wanting to take them away from me. . . I know that your counsel is of the devil, and that mine is of God.[8]

Like the "trainers" in the obedience experiment, Joan heard contradictory voices urging her to comply, and ultimately it was *her* human judgment which had to choose between the voices of life and expansion of meaning on one hand and the beguiling voices of false charity and underlying repression on the other. Her rebellion was one of intuitive humanism. She chose to die because the alternative extinguished not only her freedom but also the meaning of her life and "voices" up to that moment.

This concludes my argument that the three experimental conditions test each and every segment in the cycle of radical man. This being so, we would expect consistent differences in the level of psycho-social development between those dissenters who survived these tests and those conformers who failed them.

Fortunately all three experiments have been adequately researched. Frank Barron made a detailed study of the personalities of dissenters and conformers in an Asch type experiment. His findings are set out in Table 7. Here we see that on every segment of the cycle the dissenters were on average more developed than conformers. An interesting side light is that there were *no* differences in "mental health" as measured on the Minnesota Multiphasic Personality Inventory. The occasional tendencies towards neurotic and psychotic symptoms were equally prevalent in both groups. This finding reinforces my earlier observation that the developmental helix has a "growth factor" and a "stability factor." Two men can be equally stable and adjusted to the expectations of their environments, while having very different *levels* of adjustment. The dissenter balances highly developed segments of the cycle, the conformer balances poorly developed segments. The dissenter "unbalances" himself more through his capacity to suspend and risk himself, but he has a superior capacity to "rebalance" and reintegrate himself. Were the conformers obliged to take the same order of risks they might well become neurotic or worse. This helps us to understand with what panic and unbridled rage the forces of conformity and reaction beat and abuse radical men. It is the very sanity of conforming men which radicals threaten when they urge upon others their own life style.

In Table 8, we see the comparative styles of dissenters and conformers in the Crutchfield experiments. The findings on dissenters not only replicate Barron's work, they also confirm the profile of radical man which emerged from the nine research studies in Chapter III. In contrast, the conformers in both Tables 7 and 8 clearly resemble the profile of anomic man in Chapter IV.

There are some interesting elaborations of the two images. Dissenters tend to locate themselves in the more creative professions – art, writing, architecture – while conformers sit stolidly in the middle-class business culture, preferring the roles of banker, real estate salesman, clerk, office worker, etc. Dissenting females tend to resent the conventional female roles of housewife, sex symbol, and the automatic "confirmer" of males. Just as conforming women are eager to play this expected role, so conforming men are insistent that "generosity and kindness" must be the supreme values of their wives and girl friends. This would function to provide a guaranteed confirmation for the "outgoing" and "virile" investments of insecure men. The American culture virtually trains the adolescent female in the role of automatically rewarding male advances so that she

> . . . pules a kind of "made-up" sex which mocks *true* sex, and *surely* love, and sounds more like the pretend deep- breathing exercises for a class of chirping, nubile girls. . . that the *sellers* may interrupt.[9]

A revolt against cuteness and the breathy "sincerity" of soap-opera teenagers was found both in the laboratory and more recently in the wider culture:

> "No more Miss America."
> That's the rallying cry for a group of feminine activists who plan to picket the Miss America pageant. . . They say the contest presents a phony, degrading, ludicrous image of American womanhood.
>
> The feminists see the beauty queen as. . . mindless girlie symbol. . . forced daily to compete for male approval, enslaved by ludicrous beauty standards we ourselves are conditioned to take seriously. . . (it) represents the pop culture obsolescent theme of spindle, mutilate and discard tomorrow. . .
>
> Highlight of the demonstration will be a "huge freedom trash can," into which girls will throw such items as bras, girdles, curlers and false eyelashes. All these. . . are symbols of a false beauty standard and "they're bloody uncomfortable."[10]

These results are also consistent with Crutchfield's finding that conformers were more *socialized* while less socially effective. They lived in pre-structured systems, performing as was expected of them. Where life consists of well defined games and rituals, the personal risks of rebellion, creativity and self-suspension can be minimized, so as to simplify the task of perception and investment. For example, Babbitt and the Boosters (with their Zip, Zoom, Zowie, and Zenith!) would meet regularly in a highly ritualized atmosphere of bonhomie

> The second March lunch of the Zenith Boosters was the most important of the year, as it was to be followed by the annual election of officers. . . As each of the four hundred Boosters entered he took from the wallboard a huge celluloid button announcing his name, nickname, and his business. There was a fine of ten cents for calling a Fellow Booster by anything but his nickname at a lunch, and as Babbitt. . . checked his hat the air was radiant with shouts of "Hello, Chet!" and "How're you, Shorty!" and "Top o' the mornin' Mac!"[11]

Crutchfield also found that repeated conformity led to a progressive deterioration of perception. Having failed to translate their convictions into action and into social reality, the conformers ended up by blurring their own perception and confusing themselves as disintegration spread through their cycles.

Imagine the nightmarish dilemma of a man too weak and anxious to confront severe differences with another, but who nonetheless diminishes himself by denying these differences. Then comes a Messiah in the shape of Senator Goldwater, who says in effect: "Follow me and you can be honest men once more. Put an end to your conformity and "me-toism" and act authentically *in a simpler society without such wide discrepancies in opinion.* It is a vision of personal salvation for which idealists will struggle arduously. But it is also a doomed vision, because you cannot simplify the task of communicating to distant others without shortening the distance, stamping on free existence, and dragging down more developed persons to the level at which you feel comfortable.

Conformers, Crutchfield found, were often authoritarian, as measured by the California F-scale. The progressive inner deterioration of the conformist leads him to desperate, periodic rebellions and "backlashes" against those who by their innovative behavior force him into a hollow, meaningless compliance.

Finally, in Table 9, we see that obedience to cruel and senseless commands, and contrasting rebellion against these commands, have once again discriminated the psycho-socially immature from the psycho-socially developed. The obedient are clearly anomic. The rebellious in this situation closely resemble radical man.

It is ironic that those forced to hurt others finish up disliking their *victim* – and approving of the experimenter who made them do it! Not so the dissenters who felt warmly for the victim and less so for the experimenter. But this is what we would expect, for only the rebellion which is man's existence can dismantle incoming commands and respond to them selectively. The obedient torturers seldom liked their work. Typical was one elderly man who wailed, "God, let's stop it!" while going to the limit. But once they had done it, the hollow, guilty feelings inside were *not* blamed on the authority figure who had rigged up the whole thing. In what was perhaps an *ex post facto* attempt to make social reality fit their behavior, the victim was described as weak, slow, passive, and stupid – and presumably deserving of his punishment.

Another point of note is the more trustful personalities of the rebellious subjects. As I argued in Chapter III, the capacity to trust others, which comes from openness, self-suspension and vulnerability, is *not* a blind trust of authority, but an extremely discriminating capacity to perceive trustworthiness in others and to create a climate of trust. One can afford to trust if one has spare competence to risk and a high survival capacity. And it is just such capacities which would discriminate and reject the infantile and unilateral trust demanded by the experimenter.

A somewhat chilling piece of data is that those who reported having killed men while on active military service were much more likely to torture their victim to the end. We saw in Crutchfield's research that compliance led to progressive deterioration in judgment along with destructive impulses. Here we see that those who had killed men in wars – however "just" those wars might have been – were also much more prepared to obey again, this time in grotesquely unjust circumstances. In view of these findings one must seriously entertain the possibility that warfare severely and permanently cripples the human capacity for psycho-social learning.

Throughout the discussion of these three experiments, I have suggested that conformity and obedience in the laboratory give us important clues to the same conditions in the culture at large. Many social scientists regard it as both brash and unscientific to leap from laboratory results to the wider culture. Yet there is a coherence in personality by which we recognize a subject's thoughts and actions across many contexts. It is possible for strictly controlled experiments to create simulations of at least the more oppressive aspects of daily life that challenge our developmental capacities. Broad leaps from different contexts are also a measure of our capacity to think and make creative syntheses. For these reasons I believe it is possible to leap from American laboratory simulations of conformity and obedience clear across the Atlantic to the British Campaign for Nuclear Disarmament. In Table 10 we see an analysis of the social backgrounds, life styles, and attitudes of the members of this movement. Although the data are sociological rather than

**Table 9**

**THE PERSONALITY CORRELATES OF OBEDIENT AND REBELLIOUS "TRAINERS"**

| *Segments of the Cycle* | *Rebellious Subjects* | *Obedient Subjects* |
|---|---|---|
| *Existence* | Favors rebellion in young.<br>Unhostile to creative artists and thinkers<br>Unconventional<br>Dislikes taking orders | Hostile to rebellion in the young.<br>Hostile to artists and thinkers<br>Conventional<br>Positive about accepting orders |
| a) PERCEPTION | Greater concern for social and moral issues.<br>Viewed orders as harsh<br>Does not stereotype | Less concern for social issues<br>Viewed orders as not so harsh<br>Stereotypes people |
| b) IDENTITY | Sees own conscience as strong.<br>Relatively intraceptive | Sees own conscience as less strong.<br>Anti-intraceptive |
| c) COMPETENCE | Conversationally confident and persuasive | Less confident |
| d) INVESTMENT authentic and intense | Favors verbal expression with subjective and imaginative content | Hostile to "talk", prefers action, dislikes subjectivity and imagination |
| e) SUSPENSION and RISK | Relatively flexible<br>Only moderately concerned with law. More trustful | Rigid adherence to middle class morality. Cynical. Favors strong laws. Less trustful. |
| f) BRIDGING THE DISTANCE | Low in ethnocentrism<br>Does not condemn deviation | Ethnocentric, condemns immoral, crooked, feeble minded persons, homosexuals, etc. |
| g) SELF-CONFIRMING SELF-TRANSCENDING IMPACT | No tabu on disconfirming close friends and relatives<br>Closer and more intimate with father.<br>Believes in intimacy | Tabu on disconfirming close friends and relatives.<br>More hostile and more distant to father<br>"Familiarity breeds contempt" |
| h) *Dialectic* leading to SYNERGY | Prepared to talk things over.<br>Low Authoritarianism<br>Feels warmer towards victim in experiment<br>Seldom reports killing others in military service | Hostility to words and ideas generally.<br>High Authoritarian<br>Feels cooler towards victim in experiment<br>More often reports killing others in military service |

**Table 9 (Continued)**

| | | |
|---|---|---|
| i) INTEGRATION of FEEDBACK and COMPLEXITY | Higher in Social Responsibility More Educated. Rejects simple and dichotomous structures. | Lower Social Responsibility Less Educated Has Simple and dichotomous thought structures. |

Source: Elms, Alan C. and Milgram, S. "Personality Characteristics Associated with Obedience and Defiance Toward Authorative Commands." *Journal of Experimental Research in Personality*, Vol. 1, No. 4, 1966.

**Table 10**

**BACKGROUNDS, OCCUPATIONS, ROLES, AND ATTITUDES OF MEMBERS OF THE BRITISH CAMPAIGN FOR NUCLEAR DISARMAMENT**

| *Segments of the Cycle* | *Description of Activists* |
|---|---|
| Existence | 58% of activists reject organized religion. Unusual number of highly creative persons, unattached to an institutional supports. Especially dramatists, writers, artists, intellectuals, architects, poets, etc.<br>86% support protest against evils even if no visible result emerges. |
| a) PERCEPTION | Strong focus on suffering humanity, with evils treated *sui generis,* and *not* ideologically reduced or simplified. Moral concerns much stronger than economic or family concerns. |
| b) IDENTITY | High valuation upon the expression of personal thoughts and feelings. |
| c) COMPETENCE | 90% have strong confidence and optimism that they can influence political events. They come from those sectors of society with *highest* control of environment and life opportunities. |
| d) INVESTMENT *authentic* and *intense* | High occupational preference for "people oriented" work. Strong beliefs in the implementation of decisions of conscience. 83% drawn from the more active and successful sections of middle class, professional managerial, etc. Unusually high committment to an ideal normative order. |

**Table 10 (Continued)**

| | |
|---|---|
| e) SUSPENSION and RISK | Dissents made in face of severe social criticism and ostracism by middle class friends. 79% do not work in profit oriented or commercial activities. Strong dedication towards objectives outside self and immediate family. |
| f) BRIDGING THE DISTANCE | Wide preference for international issues (56%) over national issues (29%) and over local and parocial issues (1%) Over 85% advocating compassion for homosexuals, and greater material aid for poorer countries. Over 60% advocate increased (colored) immigration. |
| g) SELF-CONFIRMING SELF-TRANSCENDING IMPACT | 46% elected to leadership positions of some kind. Over 70% believe that talent is rewarded in current environment. 62% of youthful demonstrators have the agreement and support of at least one parent. |
| | Over 70% employed in welfare or creative occupations. |
| h) *Dialectic* leading to SYNERGY | 87% believe that warring opposites can be peacefully reconciled. Over 65% advocate mutuality between managment and workers. Youthful demonstrators have had less authoritarian and *more* "moderate" and "liberal" relationships with their parents. |
| i) INTEGRATION of FEEDBACK and COMPLEXITY | Strong emphasis on personal accountability. Relatively large participation by Intellectuals. Membership unusually well educated and largest proportion of youthful members receiving full time education. |

Source: Frank Parkin. *Middle Class Radicalism.* New York. Frederick A. Praeger. 1968.

psychological, although the subjects live in a different political culture, are acting in natural rather than experimental conditions, and are protesting world wide events and not some immediate stimulus, the profile of radical man is immediately recognizable, and is remarkably similar to the experimental results in Tables 7 to 9.

Once again it is the more creative professions, unoriented to the conventional, profit motivated culture, that emerge with strength throughout the cycle. Another point to note is the *success* rather than the failure of these rebels in the pursuit of self-expression, influence, education, and leadership. Of young persons in the campaign, the vast majority had won the support of at least one parent, and had won admission to higher education. These were very seldom rebels against personal misfortune, parental repression, or blocked opportunity. These were protestors for life and sanity, those living much fuller lives than most of their contemporaries in a world suddenly darkened and absurdly menaced by the Bomb. And menaced too my anomic men willing to obey, even in the destruction of all life. For the root trouble is man's psycho-social infancy. One nuclear disarmer wrote:

> A few men seem possessed by a devil. . .
> And some have a stomach for sacrifice
> Corrupted by a secret appetite for death.
> But many more – and alas we women blind ourselves to this
> obscenity –
> Many more have remained as boys, just boys
> Heedlessly playing. But the spring of the toys
> They are winding
> Is Death.
> We must take power from these madmen,
> These prisoners, these perilous children. [12]

In Chapter III I briefly referred to Kohlberg's Moral Judgment Scale. This instrument is of particular interest here since it clearly discriminates rebellious persons from obedient ones. Subjects are given a number of stories illustrating moral dilemmas and they are forced to choose between differing moral claims which these dilemmas force upon them. Depending on this choice subjects fall into the following classifications.[13]

Stages of development

Stage 1: Obedience and punishment orientation. Egocentric deference to superior power or prestige, or a trouble-avoiding set. Objective responsibility.

Stage 2: Instrumental Relativists (IR) Naively egoistic orientation. Right Action is that instrumentally satisfying the self's needs and occasionally others'. Awareness of relativism of value to each actor's needs and perspective. Naive egalitarianism and orientation to exchange and reciprocity.

Stage 3: Personal Concordance (PC) Good-boy orientation. Orientation to approval and to pleasing and helping others. Conformity to stereotypical images of majority or natural role behavior, and judgment by intentions.

Stage 4: Law and Order (LO) Authority and social-order maintaining orientation. Orientation to "doing duty" and to showing respect for authority and maintaining the given social order for its own sake. Regard for earned expectations of others.

Stage 5: Social Contract (SC) Contractual legalistic orientation. Recognition of an arbitrary element or starting point in rules or expectations for the sake of agreement. Duty defined in terms of contract, general avoidance of violations of the will or rights of others, and majority will and welfare.

Stage 6: Individual Principles (IP) Conscience or principle orientation. Orientation not only to actually ordained social rules but to principles of choice involving appeal to logical universality and consistency. Orientation to conscience as a directing agent and to mutual respect and trust.

I would submit that Kohlberg's scale and my double-helix model are measuring approximately the same process of development. Consider, for example, the psycho-social qualities required of an individual making a Stage 6 moral judgment based upon conscience and principle. He is likely to be a person. . . .

Whose radical *existence* enabled him to make the appropriate moral synthesis to fit the unique situation.

a) Whose PERCEPTION was courageous enough to focus upon the full range of the dilemmas, and was accurate enough in gauging the needs of the other to regard this specific judgment as superior to existing laws and contracts which conflicted with it.

b) Whose IDENTITY was strong enough to override the role expectations thrust upon him by the culture (Stage 3)

c) and d) Whose COMPETENCE at authentic INVESTING was great enough to communicate and to act upon the principle he saw despite the likelihood of conflict and opposition.

e) Who would RISK SUSPENDING social contracts (Stage 5), laws (Stage 4), role-expectations (Stage 3), and RISK personal inconvenience (Stage 2) and punishment (Stage 1) in order to express a better principle than custom enshrined.

f) Who would BRIDGE THE DISTANCE created between himself and others, consequent upon his breaking of laws and conventions at stages 3 to 5.

g) Whose selected principle is so well chosen and communicated that it calls forth a CONFIRMING response in others, and TRANSCENDS not only the communicator himself but previous contracts, laws and role expectations (stages 3 to 5).

h) Whose selected principle is capable of becoming *a new social contract* (Stage 5) and later a new law (Stage 4), and a role-model (Stage 3). He would thereby eventually *reconcile the opposites between law and conscience* and through a dialectic between the two achieve a HIGHER SYNERGY of justice and universalized principles.

i) Whose experience of moral choice and action would increase his COMPLEX INTEGRATION of the principles of conscience.

Assuming that I am correct in arguing that Kohlberg's model and my own focus upon different facets of the same developmental phenomenon, we would then expect that persons highly developed on the segments of the cycle model would also have achieved higher stages in Moral Judgment. This appears to be so.

One research study measured Ego Development (defined in a manner approximating to segments b, c, and d of the cycle) and Conceptual Development (roughly equivalent to segment i). Both Ego and Conceptual Development indices correlated with Moral Judgment ($r = .66$ and $.62$ respectively).[14]

In a second study it was found that fully 75% of those persons with a stage 6 capacity for Moral Judgment *declined to torture the bound victim in Milgram's Obedience Experiment*, while only 13% of those at lower stages of Moral Judgment refused to electrocute "the learner."[15]

We have already seen in Table A, Chapter III, that Bay Area students at Stage 6 were also characterized by development in every segment of the cycle. The same study revealed that 80% of these students had sat in at Sproul Hall during the Berkeley Student Revolt of 1964. 50% of the Stage 5 students were also in Sproul Hall, but only 10% of those at Stages 4 and 3. Finally 60% of Stage 2 students also sat in, which suggests that there is a "dark side of rebellion" so that protests attract both the highly moral and the pre-moral.

I have taken the characteristics of dissenters and conformers organized by my cycle model in Tables 7 to 9, and reorganized these same characteristics into Kohlberg's stages of development. Thus in Table 11 we see that many of the non-conformists and rebels in the three experiments show distinctive "Stage 6" characteristics, while the conformers and the torturers are the law-abiding, "good boy," All-American types at Stages 3 and 4. The pre-moral rebels do not seem to have registered. Perhaps there were too few of them.

What clearly emerges from research with Kohlberg's scale is that the vast majority of American adults and school-age children have only reached Stages 3 to 4. They are rarely capable of making principled moral judgments and do not even comprehend these judgments when others make them. As a rule people can comprehend only *one* stage above their own customary level of judgment.[16] No wonder, then, that the "Law and Order Brigade" (Stage 4) regards the Constituency of Conscience (Stage 6) as a clique of disreputable traitors, anarchists and "Nervous Nellies," deserving to be gassed from helicopters, thrashed by policemen and indicted by Attorney Generals. Indeed Stage 4 persons would be likely to interpret acts of conscience in terms of what they *do* understand, e.g., selfish acts of rebellion at Stage 2. The mentality of those who tapped the telephone of Martin Luther King becomes easier to understand as do the utterances of police chiefs and conservative governors who broadcast their fear and disgust across this land of technological giants and moral pygmies.

**Table 11**

**THE CHARACTERISTICS OF REBELS AND CONFORMERS IN THE THREE EXPERIMENTS CLASSIFIED BY KOHLBERG'S STAGES OF MORAL DEVELOPMENT**

| *Kohlberg's Stages* | *Characteristics of Conformers* | *Characteristics of Rebels* |
|---|---|---|
| *Stage 6* Conscience or principle orientation to shared or shareable standards. Orientation to conscience as a directing agent and to mutual respect and trust. | | Sees own conscience as strong, concern for philosophical ideas and social/moral issues. Richness of novel ideas. More trustful, empathic and responsive to the other's inner integrity. Personally involved. |
| *Stage 4* Law, order and authority maintaining orientation to "doing duty" and maintaining the given social order for its own sake. | Rebellion regarded as dangerous or childish. Calls for authoritative leaders to impose solutions. Somewhat authoritarian, moralistic, legalistic. Enjoys taking orders. | |
| *Stage 3* Personal concordance and "good boy" orientation to pleasing and helping others. Conformity to stereotypical images of majority or natural role behavior. | Chooses conventional male careers or accepts traditional feminine role. Describes self as "obliging, patient, and kind." Stereotypes other people and adheres closely to conventional middle class morality. Overresponsive to the evaluations of others. | |
| *Stage 2* Instrumental relativism. Naively egotistical orientation towards action which is instrumentally satisfying to self's needs and occasionally others. | A few neurotics, some punitive, hostile persons who see long term irreconcilable conflict between themselves and others. | A few neurotics, some reckless, moody, artistic persons, who express their hostility directly and hate taking any orders. |

N.B. Two of the stages have been omitted. Stage 1 is omitted because few of the subjects, if any, were at this stage. Stage 5 is omitted because Milgram's experiment would tend to place "Fives" among the conformers, since they had *contracted* to go through with the experiment, while the Asch and Crutchfield experiments would put "Fives" among the dissenters because they had contracted to render true verdicts. Apart from this, stage 5 is intermediate in the development from 4 to 6, so that omitting it sharpens the contrast.

Source: Tables 7, 8 and 9.

## NOTES FOR CHAPTER V

1. "Opinions and Social Pressure" by Solomon E. Asch, *Scientific American,* 193, 1955, pp. 31-35.

2. The procedure is more fully described in *The Journal of Abnormal and Social Psychology,* Vol. 67, No. 4, 1963, pp. 371-78.

3. *In The Name of America* published by Clergy and Laymen Concerned about VietNam, distributed by Dutton and Co., New York, 1968, pp. 151-152. Originally appeared in *Akron Beacon Journal,* March 27, 1967.

4. *Saint Joan* Leipzig: Tauchnitz Edition, 1924, pp. 245-6.

5. Quoted by Stanley Milgram in "Some Conditions of Obedience and Disobedience to Authority," *Human Relations, 18, 1965, p. 76.*

6. M. D. Bogdonoff, *et. al.,* "The modifying effect of conforming behavior upon lipid responses. . .," *Clinical Research,* 9, 1961, p. 135.

7. *Individual in Society* by David Krech, Richard S. Crutchfield and Egerton L. Ballachey, New York: McGraw-Hill, 1962, p. 519f.

8. *Saint Joan, op. cit.,* pp. 221-222.

9. *The Vulgarians, op. cit.*

10. Is "Miss America" Phony? by Louise Cook, *Boston Globe,* Sept. 6, 1968.

11. *Babbitt, op. cit.,* p. 120.

12. "Now at Last" by Jaquetta Hawkes, *The New Statesmen,* July 5, 1958, also in *Voices from the Crowd,* David Boulton (ed.), London: Peter Owen, 1964, pp. 83-84.

13. See "Stage and Sequence: The Cognitive – Developmental Approach to Socialization" by Lawrence Kohlberg, in *Handbook of Socialization Theory and Research,* David A. Goslin (ed.), New York: Rand McNally, 1969, p. 376.

14. A Developmantal Study of the Relationship between Conceptual, Ego, and Moral Development by E. V. Sullivan, G. McCullough and M. Stager, Ontario Institute for Studies in Education: University of Toronto, Mimeo, 1969.

15. "Education for Justice. . .," Ernest Burton Lecture on Moral Education delivered at Harvard University, April 23, 1968, Lawrence Kohlberg (Harvard School of Education, Mimeo).

16. "Developmental Hierarchies of Comprehension and Preference in Moral Thinking," by James R. Rest, paper read at the meeting of The Society for Research in Child Development, Santa Monica, Calif., March 1969.

*Chapter VI*

# Development and the Social Structure of Formal Systems

It will have occurred to many who have followed my argument thus far that the helix model can apply to groups in relationship to groups, or organizations in relationship to organizations, just as easily as it applies to an individual in relationship to another individual. It is only necessary to change the subject of the sentence from "Man exists freely. . ." to "Group A exists freely. . ." Any ongoing group of individuals usually has:—

a) A shared outlook or PERCEPTION on the world.
b) An IDENTITY, e.g., a research group or a "good fellowship" group.
c) An overall purpose and COMPETENCE.
d) A series of INVESTMENTS in the external environment.
e) A degree to which it is willing to RISK and SUSPEND its reputation, its cohesion and the agreement of its members in order to develop.
f) A degree of differentiation or DISTANCE between itself and other groups which it is prepared to BRIDGE.
g) A desired impression or SELF CONFIRMING IMPACT which it seeks to make on other groups or individuals.
h) A series of *dialectical* encounters with neighboring groups from which a degree of SYNERGY will emerge.
i) A group consciousness, belief-system, body of knowledge, and shared INTEGRATION of FEEDBACK of varying degrees of internal coherence and COMPLEXITY.

This group culture is built up by the several contributions of past and present members interacting over a period of time. Suggestions as to group identity, purpose, and style are offered explicitly or implicitly by different group members, and those suggestions which are confirmed by the group transcend the mind of the particular individual to enter the group consciousness. The diagram below shows five "individual cycles" interacting to form one "group cycle" comprised of the inputs and personal syntheses of each member.

Alternatively we could regard the diagram above as five *group* cycles, for instance the research, production, marketing, finance and personnel departments, all interacting to form a *corporate cycle.* An "open system" is one in which a novel synthesis wrought by one individual moves swiftly through the "nest of cycles" to enlighten first his friends, then his group, then the organization and then the larger culture into which the organization itself invests.

But the intersecting cycles of groups and organizations do not come together by a kind of spontaneous impulse occurring simultaneously in a thousand minds. Seldom do they forge their identities and purposes from a state of initial vacuum. Men do not usually face each other in an empty room and say "Let's become a research group." We are born into a society filled with *social structures* and formal systems of political institutions, bureaucracies, laws, and myriad networks of official, reciprocal expectations.

Take, for example, an office worker in a large corporate bureaucracy. For most segments of his cycle there are formal system structures to guide and channel his existence.

| *Segments of the Cycle* | *Formal System Structures* |
|---|---|
| Man exists freely | (no structural equivalent) |
| Segment (a) PERCEPTION | Structure (A) Official policies, information and plans. |
| Segment (b) IDENTITY | Structure (B) Roles, formal positions, and job descriptions. |
| Segment (c) COMPETENCE | Structure (C) Status, marks of privilege, hierarchical levels. |
| Segment (d) INVESTMENT | Structure (D) Required job activities and interactions. |

| | |
|---|---|
| Segment (e)<br>SUSPENSION & RISK | (no structural equivalent since this involves *the suspension of structure* itself.) |
| Segment (f)<br>BRIDGING THE (wide) DISTANCE | Structure (F) Degree of differentiation required by division of labor between units which must be coordinated. |
| Segment (g)<br>SELF CONFIRMING<br>SELF TRANSCENDING<br>IMPACT | Structure (G) Formal techniques for evaluation, recognition and integration. |
| Segment (h)<br>*Dialectic* leading to SYNERGY | Structure (H) Coordination procedures, collective bargaining, committee meetings, official liaison activities. |
| Segment (i)<br>INTEGRATION of FEEDBACK & COMPLEXITY | Structure (I) Periodic accounting, control, analyses of variance, all integrated into the *formal system.* |

The fact that most segments of the cycle have their structural equivalents is no occasion for surprise. Man models organizations upon an image of himself. They are intended as giant replications of his own functioning into which he and others fit.

It is because these structures are designed to fit men and their needs that the structures themselves must develop, or more accurately, must *be* developed in order to support higher and higher levels of psycho-social development.

In underdeveloped cultures the amount of differentiation permitted between persons and the divisions of labor (Structure F) are typically narrow so that coordination and integration (Structure G) can be achieved with little difficulty. In more developed cultures differentiation is extremely wide and diffuse so that integration may require considerable bargaining and the institutionalization of conflict (Structure H). An underdeveloped culture may not have any institutions in which synergistic solutions can be forged, rather conflicts are solved by the enforced will of the chief.

Hence in order for a group to develop psycho-socially, structures must be periodically reformed to reflect the increasing growth in social relationships. Much has been said in earlier chapters of the rebellious existence of radical man, who dismantles incoming information and transforms the data into concepts which facilitate his further development. Now we can see *against what* radical man rebels. He periodically rejects those social structures which constrain his activity and legitimize lower levels of development than those which he feels able to attain. Thus he will attack the practice of *de jure* or *de facto* segregation because he believes that he and others should and can BRIDGE THE DISTANCE to Black Americans and that social structures impeding this also impede the psycho-social development of society.

When men enter into corporate and structured relationships every cycle in the intersecting "nest of cycles" carries its own load of formal system structures. An official like Pooh-Bah in *The Mikado* may have roles and job definitions within his group, another series of structures when representing his group to other groups, and yet other roles in relation to the total enterprise. Hence when Ko-Ko asks Pooh-Bah whether he can spend freely at his approaching marriage feast, the latter replies:

> *Pooh-Bah:* Speaking as your Private Secretary... don't stint yourself, do it well.
> *Ko-Ko:* Exactly – as the city will have to pay for it.
> *Pooh-Bah:* As Private Secretary... as Chancellor of the Exchequer, I am bound to see that due economy is observed...
> *Ko-Ko:* I see. Come over here, where the Chancellor can't hear us. (They cross the stage.) Now as my Solicitor, how do you advise me to deal with this difficulty?
> *Pooh-Bah:* Oh, as your solicitor, I would have no hesitation in saying "Chance it –"... if it were not that, as Lord Chief Justice, I am bound to see that the law isn't violated.[1]

While the example above has obviously been stretched to the point of absurdity, the proliferation of social structures in modern society makes conflicts extremely likely, and the human capacity continually to suspend old or conflicting structures and to create new ones becomes extremely important to social development.

Every pair of intersecting cycles, then, whether individual, group, or corporate, has "outer cycles" of formal system structures A, B, C, etc., corresponding to segments (a), (b), (c) etc. on the "inner cycle." This is illustrated below.

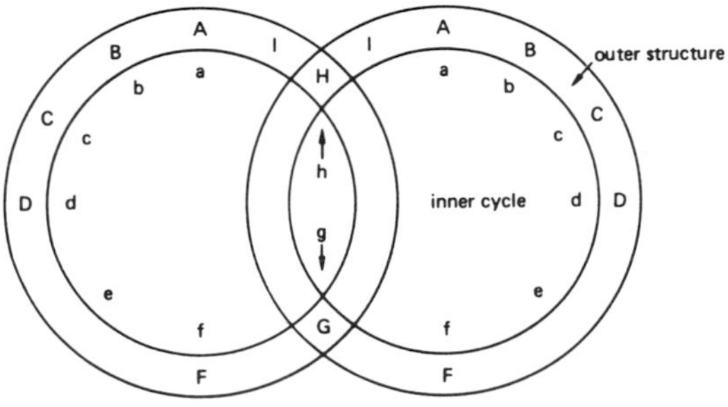

How does the existence of these structures help or hinder man's long struggle to achieve higher states of synergy? I shall argue that much of the drag upon our capacities for development derives not so much from formal systems themselves as from a widely misconceived relationship between human needs and formal systems in general. The problems arising from this misconception will be discussed under the following heads:

1. The formal system and the loss of humanity.
2. The formal system as conservative.
3. The formal system as a "safety net."
4. Anomic men cling to the formal system.
5. Problems of system design – complexity and simplicity.
6. The dangers of specialization and technique.
7. The formal system as the servant of man and his development.

1. *The formal system and the loss of humanity.*

A most elementary mistake in the process of translating the "inner cycle" into formal system structures is to forget that the duplication is not in itself *alive.* Structure is but a social tool, similar to man and shaped in his image, but a *thing* nonetheless.

As with all non-human things made by man it lacks at least two of the vital qualities of the "inner cycle." There is no way to duplicate free existence, a quality which pervades the entire cycle and differentiates human life from the dead universe. And there is no way to duplicate the capacity for self-suspension and risk (segment e) and reitntegration in an altered form. Only man creates himself, suspends himself, and recreates himself, *none of the things he makes can do that for themselves.*

This simple truth is often denied. It is currently fashionable to assert that a servo-mechanism has "purpose" and "autonomy" because it can receive signals and change direction by means of a feedback loop. But no cybernetic system can suspend the assumptions upon which it was created. A guided missile, however sophisticated, cannot suspend the misguided assumptions of strategic deterrence which brought it into existence.

Similarly many corporations have analyses of variance from expected operations which automatically draw managerial attention to indices which are out of line with projections. But these "steering mechanisms" are but the palest imitations of man's capacity to resynthesize his ideas. They are little more than mechanical idols of human functioning.

> They have mouths but speak not
> Eyes they have but they see not. . .
> . . . They that make them shall be like unto them
> Yea, everyone that trusteth in them. [2]

For many social scientists the various formal systems and social structures are the starting points and basic data of social science. Believing that science must separate the "objective" from the "subjective" they see status, role, and structural forms as universal facts untainted by subjective distortion and similar to physical objects located in "public space." Believing that a science starts by generalizing and classifying, they abstract from human experience those elements on which there is common agreement and which lend themselves most readily to analysis, separation, and manipulation. Believing, above all, that science must be "value-free," they regard the "inner cycle" as a dark pool of passionate subjectivities and unbridled affects, while the "outer cycle" is a clean statement of logical form, a separation of means from ends.

Unfortunately the "scientific" appeal of formal system structures is due almost entirely to their lack of life and humanity, which produces a resemblance to physical science.

Even this situation might not be so serious if the formal systems were true shadows and semblances of psycho-social development. But this is seldom the case since social structure is usually *for* some purpose. If it is for the mining of bituminous coal then the social structure will be formed by the requirements of technology and the shape of the coal face. In many such situations it is not even possible to talk owing to spatial distance and noise.

Whatever the burdens created by technology, the formal structure may still be predominantly an *economic* system. In a culture where technical knowledge and economic theory are far advanced, but where the need for psycho-social development is scarcely comprehended save intuitively, the design of formal systems will reflect formalized knowledge to the near-exclusion of infant sciences. Corporations and institutions, whether for profit or not for profit, run on financial indices, thereby elevating the countable far above the intangible signs of human betterment. Money is used to provide information (Structure A), to differentiate roles (Structure B), to confer status (Structure C), to reward desired behavior (Structure G) and to take account of the entire system (Structure I). These procedures make certain assumptions about the nature of man which may thrust the formal system into *non*-developmental shapes. John Ruskin had few doubts on this score.

> . . . Political economy has a plausible idea at the root of it. "The social affections," says the economist, "are accidental and disturbing elements in human nature; but avarice and the desire of progress are constant elements. Let us eliminate the inconstants, and, considering the human being merely as a covetous machine, examine by what laws of labor, purchase and sale, the greatest accumulative result in wealth is obtainable. Those laws once determined, it will be for each individual afterwards to introduce as much of the disturbing affectionate element as he chooses. . . [3]

But as Ruskin goes on to point out, a science of human functioning which deprives men of their souls is like "a science of gymnastics which assumed that men had no skeletons."

> It might be shown, on that supposition, that it would be advantageous to roll students up into pellets, flatten them into cakes, or stretch them into cables; and that when these results were effected, the reinsertion of the skeleton would be attended by various inconveniences to their constitution. The reasoning might be admirable, the conclusions true, and the science deficient only in applicability.[4]

When men build formal systems these will inevitably be "stretched" by technology and "flattened" by the assumptions of economic motivation. And there is some research data which suggest that Ruskin was right to warn us! Students high in "materialism" and "careerism" have been found to be significantly lacking in spontaneity, aestheticism, emotional sensitivity, concern with ideas, authenticity, self-realization, and humanitarianism.[5] McClosky, in his research on anomie which was detailed in Chapter IV, found that pro-Business attitudes correlated .18 with Anomie, suggesting that these attitudes are slightly but not severely productive of under-development. A scale measuring economic Ambition and Aspiration was unrelated either with anomie or to its negation, the capacity for creative choice and independence. A major study of those highest in Achievement Motivation[6] found them to be "moderately authoritarian," which is one variation on a mild anomic condition. Studies of workers have found that the least self-fulfilled by their jobs have the highest concern for economic rewards,[7-8] while students of Business Administration have been found lower in their concern for personal independence and the civil liberties of others than any other student group.[9]

At best, the motivation for economic betterment appears to be a distraction from psycho-social development, although it is sometimes argued that personal economic security has provided underpinning for student radicalism. In any event, the belief that a formal system designed with a mixture of economic and technical ends in view, will yet retain the necessary conditions for psycho-social development is at best a perilous assumption. For a social scientist to accept these bruised structures as pure and logical expressions of the human need to develop could be a most egregious error.

2. *The formal system as conservative.*

There are a number of reasons for supposing that a focus on the "outer cycle" of formal system structures will produce a much more conservative view of humanity than a focus on the "inner cycle." While the segments of the "inner cycle" face forward into the future and represent a continuity of past and present experience and future aspiration, the outer structures represent mostly the past and the *status quo.* For example a man's IDENTITY (segment b) includes novel aspects of himself yet to be revealed and realized, but his *role* (Structure B) represents the expectation that others have of him, based on *past* performance and previous arrangements. The same may be said in comparing his COMPETENCE (segment c) with his status (Structure C), or his conscience (segment i) with that which the formal system is designed to record (Structure I). If man, and no one but man, builds, tears down, and repairs the formal systems of society, then the spirit of reform will manifest itself *first* in the inner cycle and only later in the outer structures.

I am *not* saying that manipulation of structures cannot induce development and reform. I *am* saying that those who study social structure to the exclusion or near exclusion of the human needs for development, will be the last to understand or appreciate dissent and rebellion against those structures. Indeed they are likely to rush to the defense of their "data base," believing that since formal systems are the stuff of sociology, their suspension by radical man is an Affront to Science.

Another reason why a concern with formal systems often reflects a conservative viewpoint is that many systems are "left standing" like ghost towns dotting the social landscape, but bereft of human allegiance or habitation. It does not follow that a company's Senior Vice President, though high in formal status, has the actual respect of anyone. Medieval laws remain on statute books long after anyone would dare to apply them. A Trades Union can create chaos by "working to rule," so numerous are the unrepealed encumbrances.

A keen student of formal systems is likely, therefore, to be lumbered with the dead husks of civilization. Many social scientists are marching in perfect step, behind foremost, into the future, ardently examining the spores, minutiae, and nameless objects left in the wake of social progress.

Even where formal systems are widely respected and operational they are designed and used by the dominant forces in the corporation and in society, and may reflect the needs of their makers more than the needs of people at the lower levels. Hence the "economic design" of many factory systems makes workers clock in and clock out and gives them piecework incentives, but top managements never, to my knowledge, use such methods on themselves. Not only, then, are formal systems instruments of control from which the designers exempt themselves, but those most controlled by structures have seldom, if ever, participated in their design.

The social scientist who concerns himself exclusively with social structure has a ready-made and cosy relationship with the dominant powers in society. He does not have to pick sides in any overt manner, for like a distributor of rattan switches he is already on the side of the disciplinarian.

Since the structures and formal systems are but means to certain ends, and since ends, needs, and morals are widely regarded as a bottomless quicksand, into which no self-respecting scientist would venture, those studying social structures will give added *power* to the power elite, without any commensurate increase in self-insight or moral reflection.

Occasionally the elitism of social scientists is baldly stated. Ithiel de Sola Pool, for example, recently informed us.

> Thc social sciences can be described as the new humanities of the Twentieth Century. They have the same relationship to the training of mandarins of the Twentieth Century that the humanities have always had to the training of mandarins in the past.[10]

I shall now turn to another conserving feature of the formal system.

3. *The formal system as a "safety harness."*

Another way in which the formal system structure is used by its inhabitants is as something to fall *back* on – and the word "back" is significant. Men have always experimented more in the intimacy of personal relationships and have dared to change themselves and hatch new ideas among a small circle of friends.

But these novel, passionate, and tentative relationships involve higher risk (segment e) and are more likely to break down. When this happens, frightened men fall back on *previously established communications in the form of social structures.* Thus when married partners fall out there is a resort to the law. Expensive, crude and unsatisfactory – it is at least better than the mutual vindictiveness of their disappointed love. Similarly the failure of a boss and a subordinate to agree in committee will usually lead to the senior "pulling rank" and enforcing his decision. When the meeting cannot stand the anxiety of disagreement any longer, the hierarchical structure comes to its rescue. Those with higher status automatically prevail.

There is a classic story on the theme that law with its formal structure is a compromise between higher moral development and the total disintegration of the social system brought about by attempts to develop. This theme is explored in *Billy Budd* by Herman Melville.

Billy Budd, a handsome and personable young sailor, is removed by impressment from the merchant ship "The Rights of Man" and is taken into service aboard the British naval warship "H.M.S. Indominitable," commanded by Captain Vere. The time is 1798, during the Napoleonic Wars, and shortly after the naval mutinies at Spithead and the Nore.

No sooner does Billy join the crew than the informal relationships and the "inner cycles" of crew members start to develop rapidly. He is so socially effective, so authentic, insightful, charming and affectionate that he influences nearly everyone aboard, officers as well as men, and is soon promoted to captain of the foretop.

But of course the *formal* system cannot keep pace with this development. The system was designed by the Admiralty, which, having impressed its sailors, assumes them to be a cut-throat crew which must be terrorized into a sullen obedience. This authoritarian formal system permits Claggart, the Master at Arms, to beat and bully the men into compliance, while being legally justified in enforcing the system.

Budd is a threat to Claggart, first, because he so improves the morale of the crew that Claggart's methods appear unnecessary and even provoking; second, because he does not fear Claggart's surface appearance, seeing through it into the strange and lonely man inside, "so Claggart, lest his world be proven false, planned Billy's death"; and third, because conservative *status* (Structure C) is the natural enemy of radical COMPETENCE (segment c), as soon as the two start to diverge. As one sailor put it directly to Claggart:

> He usurps the crew: They turn from hating you to loving him and leave you impotent.[11]

Claggart knows that Billy cannot be destroyed by the machinery of the formal system unless he breaks some rule that will trigger that machinery into compulsory action. He therefore plays on the single visible flaw in Budd's character. In moments of intense anxiety Billy stammers so that he cannot communicate. What Melville has so beautifully captured is that *virtue among men depends upon the capacity to communicate.* Billy's flaw is only a variation of what enough anxiety will do to *any* of us. Some will use intellectual defenses, some will become authoritarian, some will conform and submit, yet others become murderous, psychotic, or neurotic. All fail to communicate.

Knowing this, Claggart falsely accuses Billy of hatching mutiny, and the boy, unable to find words, strikes Claggart a fatal blow. Billy has been delivered into the hands of the formal system. The officers are faced with a terrible crisis. A greatly loved and COMPETENT *low* status man, has killed the *least* COMPETENT, most hated, *high* status man.

The split between the inner cycle and the outer structure is total, and from this moment on the conflict tortures the officers assembled at Billy's court-martial. There is the conflict between their IDENTITIES (segment b) as compassionate men, and their *roles* (Structure B) as officers on the ship. Captain Vere tells them to sacrifice the former to the latter.

> The kind of judgment I ask is only this. . . that you recognize your function in this ship. I believe you know it. . . yet you rebel. Can't you see that you must first strip off the uniform you wear, and after that your flesh, before you can escape this issue here?. . . We are the law; law orders us to act, shows us how. . . Acquit Budd if you can. God knows I wish I could. . . Show us how to save him without putting aside our function.[12]

The conflict is also between their own INTEGRATED FEEDBACK or consciences (segment i) and the system of law (Structure I). One officer pleads with the captain.

> How can we condemn this man and live at peace again within ourselves. We have our standards; ethics if you like.
> *Vere*: Challenge your scruples!. . . The gold we wear shows that we serve the King, the Law. What does it matter that our acts are fatal to our manhood, if we serve as we are forced to serve? What bitter salt leagues move between our code and God's own judgments![13]

Note that even Vere regards his own conscience and intuitive judgment as closer to God's than to the law. He actually admits that Budd is morally innocent, "an Angel of God. . . and I must judge the angel."[14]

It remains to be asked *why* Vere and his officers cling to the outer cycle and negate their own consciences. Why prefer the "outer" to the "inner" law? Vere makes it quite clear that the inner law *cannot be communicated to the sailors without misunderstanding.*

> No. Your clemency would be accounted fear, and they would say we flinch from practicing lawful rigor lest new outbreaks be provoked. What shame to us! And what a deadly blow to discipline![15]

Thus the tragedy which began with one failure of communication is perpetuated by a second. But the formal system *can* be communicated because it is rigid, simple and brutal, and represents a previous understanding. Pardoning Billy would weaken the law by providing an exception, ". . . they know the penalty to follow, and yet it does not follow."

Captain Vere knows that reverting to the formal system is a fearful regression and injustice, but he is convinced that once communication has broken down only a reversion to simple codes can save his control over the social system.

> Laws of one kind or another shape our course from birth to death. . . without this lawful tyranny, what should we have but worse tyranny of anarchy and chaos. . . Oh, if I were a man alone, manhood would declare for Billy.[16]

There is one final reason why Billy must die and maintain the consistency of the Mutiny Act. This whole drama has taken place in the context of a failure of communication between Britain and France. This initial breakdown has created such an emergency that there is no time for the communication of subtle ambiguities or the settlement of differences. Moreover, men nurtured by sensitive dialogue might decline to blast and hack other human beings to death. The very capacity to choose militates against militance. As Vere points out,

> This was a wartime cruise and in this ship are Englishmen who fight against their wills, perhaps against their conscience, pressed by war into the service of the King. Though we as fellow creatures understand their lot, what does it matter to the officers or to the enemy? . . . War has no business with anything but surfaces. . .
>
> I repeat, then, that while we ponder and you hesitate. . . the enemy comes nearer. We must act and quickly. The French close in on us: the crew will find out shortly what has happened. Our consciences are private matters. . . but we are public men, controlling life and death within this world at sea.[17]

So the captain and the officers murder Billy and their consciences for the continuance of social control. Faced with death Billy asks the Captain for some words by which to understand why he must die. But it is precisely words and ideas that have failed.

> *Vere:* I give you the judgment of the world. . . deadly constraint, a length of hemp and a yard arm . . . There are no words. We are

> all prisoners of deadly forms that are made to break us to their measure.[18]

Let us take a moment to see whether Kohlberg's classification of the stages of development in Moral Judgment can help to illuminate the dilemma faced by Captain Vere. Reading from the bottom upwards these stages were as follows:

> Stage 6. Individual Principles, conscience orientation towards shareable values and the logical universality of principles.
>
> Stage 5. Social Contract, duty defined in terms of general avoidance of violating agreements which are seen as the bases of shared values.
>
> Stage 4. Law and Order, authority and social-order maintaining orientation.
>
> Stage 3. Personal Concordance, "good boy" orientation and conformity to roles and stereotypes.
>
> Stage 2. Instrumental relativism, right action seen as that instrumentally satisfying to self.
>
> Stage 1. Obedience and punishment orientation. Egocentric deference to superior power.

The first thing to note is that the formal system is represented most strongly at stages 4 and 3, and that insofar as most social scientists concentrate their attention here, to the neglect of stage 5 and especially stage 6, their influence must be regarded not as amoral but as relatively immoral.

Kohlberg's model also illustrates, rather better than my own, the way in which the formal system (stages 3 and 4) acts as a safety harness. These middle stages function so as to "save" the social system when the experimental morality of those at stages 5 and 6 miscarries. Hence when Budd revealed his flaw and failed to communicate, the social system on board H.M.S. Indominatable *retreated from sharing Budd's values and conscience* (stages 5 and 6) and fell back upon stage 4. Captain Vere knowing the mutinous temper of the crew, and fearing a pre-moral abyss (stages 1 and 2) urged the court-martial to uphold stage 4. "Without this lawful tyranny what should we have but worse tyranny and chaos."

Research with Kohlberg's model shows that men can seldom comprehend a moral judgment more than one stage above the stage they themselves habitually use.[19] This would tend to strengthen Captain Vere's argument that the near mutinous crew, teetering between stages 1 and 2, would have misunderstood an act of conscience by the court martial They would have seen Billy's authentic act of uncontrolled indignation as the opening signal for a blood bath, and they would have interpreted his pardon as an act of weakness.

Vere saw the fearful ambiguity currently faced by many college administrations, namely that rebellion involves two major forces, the highly moral (stage 6) and the pre-moral (stages 1 and 2),[20] and that without Law (stage 4) which treats each alike (and hence moral persons unjustly) the two "extremes" have an inherent tendency first to excite and then to destroy each other. They do this because the lower persons cannot comprehend the higher and see acts of conscience as essentially lawless behavior. Mistaking stage 6 behavior for stage 2, the Law and Order advocate cannot see why he, too, should not "take the law into his own hands" and regress from 4 to 2. The persons at stage 1 see the threat of punishment lifted and join stage 2 persons in the opportunity to indulge their every egotistic whim. From one end of campus comes a moving declaration of conviction, from the other comes smoke from the fires of an arsonist. What can the administrator say to the man of conscience who in the crunch has failed to communicate and is widely misunderstood by both his violent enemies and his violent allies?

> There's not much right, Billy. Only necessity. You and Claggart broke man's compromise with good and evil, and both of you must pay the penalty. . . . Yes, it's all wrong, all wrong. . . .[21]

4. *Anomic men cling to the formal system.*

It follows from this argument that among the American population in general, those stage 3s and 4s who are less morally and psycho-socially developed than the stage 5s and 6s would invoke the authority of the formal system most often, and fall back upon it to settle their disputes.

In Chapters IV and V data were reviewed which would support this conclusion. Anomic man clung to fundamentalist religion and the "certainty" of received truths. He was conventional, acquiescent, moralistic, and chauvinistic, in each case rejecting ambiguity of ideas, and supporting the national, social, religious, or party structures instead. He was obsessed with loss of status (Structure C), and often tried to claim an *a priori* elitism based on his position in the structure, rather than on his own interpersonal skill.

The conformers and the obedient torturers in Chapter V obeyed the *outer structure* of the experimental situation while ignoring the communicated pleas and the rebellion of their own senses. Further studies of these conformers revealed a preference for team games (where structure is usually high), a preference for conventional business careers, and an acceptance of the traditional feminine roles. They were legalistic and moralistic in their thought, led lives which were more *socialized* (while displaying less social skill), were hostile to youthful rebellion against the system, and had killed more men in warfare while defending that system.

I also argued in Chapters IV and V that regression into anomic behavior was nearly always accompanied by the abstraction of, and over-emphasis upon, certain segments at the expense of others, which were frozen into unsuspended and obsessive structures and ideologies. Thinking in the terms of the "outer cycle" is a constant temptation to an idolatrous abstraction. How many millions have died to save the status of generals and presidents, and to save the fabric of political institutions? When synergy is abstracted to become the General Will, or when creative existence becomes The Free World, or when the natural tendency to love more deeply those close and familiar to you becomes Patriotism, then certain segments of the cycle have been wrenched from their context and idolized so that thousands grovel before the work of their own hands.

Additional evidence for these contentions comes from a study of six welfare agencies which varied along dimensions of "orientation to rules," "emphasis on hierarchy," and "job codification." Not only were strong rules, coded jobs and hierarchical structures highly and positively intercorrelated, but they also accompanied feelings of inadequate professional competence (segments b and c), low self-expression (segments b and d), failure to influence others (segment g), and low participation in agency affairs (segment h). In contrast, those agencies with less emphasis on structure were much less anomic.[22]

Where rules and structures are particularly oppressive as for instance in prisons or aboard *H.M.S. Indominitable,* then order is maintained only by the systematic destruction of developmental rebellion. One prison study revealed that the most cynical, destructive, dominating, conforming, intolerant and prejudiced prisoners could live with the system and participate in it. Only the more developed suffered excruciatingly and fought actively or passively against the system.[23] Of such places Captain Vere spoke truly – "we are all prisoners of deadly forms that are made to break us to their measure."

5. *Problems of system design – complexity and simplicity.*

I have argued that formal systems were a very long way from being pure expressions of human needs to develop since they are shaped by technological and economic requirements. These requirements take their most oppressive form when they are basically *simple.* So long as the jobs to be performed are complex, human beings can find some measure of fulfillment and freedom in the multitudinous variations by which the total task can be performed. Moreover, where the environment is in rapid flux and high uncertainty it becomes increasingly difficult for authority figures to prescribe rules which could apply in unforeseeable circumstances. The more complex our society becomes and the faster is the tempo of change, the more impossible becomes the conception of external structures as prescriptions for human behavior.

In conditions of uncertainty the development of the "inner cycle" with its intuitive capacity to "home in" upon the needs of the other, however much these needs have changed, becomes the only "law" by which men can reasonably live. But we must differentiate *technological complexity* from the *behavioral complexity* required of employees in various roles. It is common to have "a ship designed by geniuses to be run by idiots", *i.e.*, a complex technology requiring psycho-socially infant behavior. Thus do the few with creative opportunities doom the many to oppressive simplicity.

If we ask, then, whether the success of corporations requires the psycho-social development of employees, part of the answer is set out in Table 12. Of ten corporations, six required complex behavior (chemicals and plastics), two fairly complex (food), and two simple (containers). It was found that of the eight companies in the more complex categories, the four most successful showed developed behavior in every segment of the cycle, and the four least successful, relatively undeveloped behavior.

Moreover, the formal structures in the more successful companies were much looser, with a relatively egalitarian spread of influence and flatter hierarchies. Only in the least successful companies did structure remain high and hierarchy steep. In their attempts to reconcile disagreements the executives from successful companies would struggle in dialectical confrontation until mutually satisfactory solutions were found, but in the less successful companies, people would pull rank and *use the structure* to enforce their wishes.

But the same study revealed a dissolution of these correlations in the cases where simple systems dealt with simple environments. Here the more rigid of the two structures was more productive of sales and profits and the company in which executives were more informal and felt more adequate was *less* economically successful.

These findings suggest that a simple system imposes a severe limit upon the attainable degree of psycho-social development, and that a constraining structure is required to keep the behavior of employees sufficiently simple so that they do not "wastefully" elaborate on the routine behaviors required for maximum economic efficiency.

What is true for overall systems is also true for the lower and more simple levels of complex systems. Studies have shown that the further down the hierarchy one goes the greater are both the simplicity of the system and the unfulfilled needs of workers, who suffer from alienation, anomie, and fatalism.[24] A most comprehensive study of automobile workers at the lower

Table 12

**CHARACTERISTICS OF HIGH PERFORMING AND LOW PERFORMING ORGANIZATIONS IN COMPLEX-DEMAND ENVIRONMENTS**

| *Segments of the Cycle* | *Where the developmental environments ...* | *Then, High Performing Organizations ...* | *But Low Performing Organizations ..* |
|---|---|---|---|
| Existence | are full of innovative contributions and are in rapid flux. | are the most creative in the production of new products. | are the least creative in the production of new products. |
| a) PERCEPTION | Contain much ambiguous information | Contront those who disagree about policy | Evade those who disagree |
| b) IDENTITY | Require innovative persons | Gives prominence to research activities | Give less prominence to research activities |
| c) COMPETENCE | Require considerable expertise | Contain managers who experience themselves as influential and successful | Contain managers who feel less influential and successful. |
| d) INVESTMENT *authentic and intense* | Are constantly changed by novel inputs | Have the most expert also exercise the most influence Have departments which reveal the full extent of their disagreements departments | Have the less expert excercising more influence than the more expert Have departments which hide and suppress the full extent of their disagreements |
| e) SUSPENSION & RISK | Are high in uncertainty | Are less hierarchical, formal or structured | Are more hierarchical, formal and structured. |

Table 12 (Continued)

| *Segments of the Cycle* | *Where the developmental environments ...* | *Then, High Performing Organizations ...* | *But Low Performing Organizations..* |
|---|---|---|---|
| f) BRIDGING THE (wide) DISTANCE | Require "wide" division of labor and highly differentiated | Achieve wide differentiation | Achieve either *less* differentiation or |
| g) SELF-CONFIRMING, SELF-TRANSCENDING IMPACT | Require effective integrations of these sub-systems | Achieve effective integration of these sub-systems Managers (especially coordinators) feel more rewarded. | Achieve less integration (or both) Managers (especially coordinators) feel less rewarded. |
| h) *Dialectic* leading to SYNERGY | Require considerable skill to reconcile complex opposites | Use prolonged confrontation, mutual reasoning, and "digging for the truth" in order to reconcile conflict. Less smoothing over of differences. | Have conflict settled by stronger suppressing weaker or top management imposing forced solutions. More smoothing over of differences. |
| i) INTEGRATION of FEEDBACK & COMPLEXITY | Are exceedingly complex and require equally complex comprehension | Achieve *optimal balance* and reconciliation of: - Differentiation with Integration, Researchers influence with Coordinator's influence, Knowledge commensurate to influence. | Severe *imbalance* with either poorly integrated, over-differentiated sub-systems, or under-differentiated highly integrated sub-systems. Knowledge and influence are typically separated. |

Source: - *Organization and Environment* by Paul R. Lawrence and Jay W. Lorsch. Boston: Harvard Business School, Division of Research, 1967.

levels of corporate hierarchies in Detroit was recently undertaken by Kornhauser. He used degree of skill (or complexity) as a variable and his findings are set out in Table 13.

The overall picture is one of extreme anomie, moderated only in the case of higher skilled workers and overpowering in the case of the lesser skilled, of whom 86% are trapped in a job they want to change but cannot and 80% boil with frustration inside. The destruction of personality by simple repetitive work is nowhere better conveyed than by the scores for young workers (20-29) on the composite mental health index below.

| *Occupational Category* | *% with High Mental Health* |
| --- | --- |
| Skilled and high semi-skilled | 58 |
| Ordinary semi-skilled | 35 |
| Repetitive unskilled | 10 |
| Machine-paced unskilled | 7 |

Kornhauser notes that even where education is held constant little difference occurs in this sharp decrease of mental health with declining skill levels. Even relatively skilled automobile workers are reported in large proportion to be segregationist, authoritarian, cynical, lonely and anomic.

In contrast to these workers imprisoned by the simplicity of technological requirements, we see in Table 14 a comparison of two engineering research departments in two small companies, both pioneering in extremely complex work. Such work requires high levels of psycho-social development, and the company with more mature relationships is clearly ahead.

In summary, only the higher levels of the more complex business enterprises are able to educe from individual employees anything approaching their full developmental capacities. Many other employees, probably a majority, are trapped. They are caught in a vicious circle, producing for consumers who, like them, are so confined by their work that they seek to escape into more and more consumption, which in turn drives them back to work. No one *has* to suffer from excessive simplicity. It is imposed by mechanistic thinkers who seek to maximise the efficiency and parsimony of their technical designs and are too ignorant of the human psyche to comprehend its need for complexity. If corporations began to design their work with a view to their employees' needs for self-expression and meaningfulness, they might *create* a more complex market of consumers, consisting of just such liberated employees.

**Table 13**

**DEGREES OF ANOMIE AMONG HIGHER AND LOWER SKILLED AUTOMOBILE WORKERS**

| *Segments of the Anomic Cycle* | *Indices of Development and Questionnaires* | *%Higher Skilled* | *%Lower Skilled* | *%Increase associated with lower skill* |
|---|---|---|---|---|
| Anomic failure to exist ... | *Would* choose different work but cannot | 52 | 86 | 34 |
| | Restless but don't know what I want | 44 | 67 | 23 |
| | Absolute obedience from children demanded | (58% no breakdown given) | | |
| | High anomie | 27 | 60 | 33 |
| a) PERCEPTION, narrow | Job not complex enough | 15 | 66 | 51 |
| | Don't know who to count on | 34 | 60 | 26 |
| b) IDENTITY, "locked in" and stagnant.... | I boil inside but don't show it | 53 | 80 | 27 |
| c) InCOMPETENCE and anticipated loss. | My full abilities are not used. | 35 | 69 | 34 |
| | Feel unsatisfied at work | 33 | 77 | 44 |
| d) Fails to INVEST authentically or intensely | Against free speech on dangerous ideas* | 40 | 50 | 10 |
| | Withdraws from social relations | 18 | 37 | 19 |
| | Has inactive life style | 24 | 57 | 33 |
| e) Non-SUSPENDING RISK-reducing strategies | Have to live for today | 22 | 53 | 31 |
| | Cynicism & Distrust | 27 | 60 | 33 |
| | Everyone's out only for themselves | 42 | 63 | 21 |
| f) Avoids BRIDGING (wider) DISTANCES | Isolationist** | 43 | 61 | 18 |
| | Pro-segregation | (54% no separate breakdown) | | |
| | Unfavorable feelings towards co-workers | 45 | 80 | 35 |
| g) Inability to make SELF-CONFIRMING SELF TRANSCENDING IMPACT | Nothing is worthwhile | 22 | 46 | 24 |
| | Don't have more than 2 good friends | 34 | 57 | 23 |

**Table 13 (Continued)**

| | | | | |
|---|---|---|---|---|
| h) Domination of, or submission to, others perspectives, in a non-dialectic, failure of SYNERGY | For strict authoritarian leadership* | 35 | 45 | 10 |
| | Interpersonal relationships not good | 43 | 63 | 20 |
| | Officials don't care for average man | 28 | 41 | 13 |
| | More force* less talk | 31 | 41 | 10 |
| i) No responsibility for FEEDBACK, hence DISINTEGRATION and lack of COMPLEXITY | Not scoring high on Mental Health Composite (no data on feedback or complexity) | 42 | 90 | 48 |

Source: *Mental Health of the Industrial Worker* by Arthur Kornhauser New York: John Wiley, 1965.

N.B. All indices except those marked * are for *young* workers 20-29. Results for the older age group were similar.

* signifies both age groups combined.

** signifies older group only (data was not available for younger group).

**Table 14**

**CREATIVE AND UNCREATIVE RESEARCH ENGINEERING DEPARTMENTS**

| *Segments of the Cycle* | *Creative Department* | *Uncreative Department* |
|---|---|---|
| Existence | Outstanding record of creative innovations.<br>Researchers insist upon the integrity of search for truth | Routine, and very conventional work.<br>Researchers relinquish scientific values in favor of business orientation |
| a) PERCEPTION | Humanistic conern and orientation towards development. | Overriding concern with day to day mechanical operations |
| b) IDENTITY | Technicians able to change their identity to become engineers<br>Good utilization of individual backgrounds and skills | Hard and fast insuperable barriers between technicians and engineers.<br>Poor utilization of backgrounds and skills |
| c) COMPETENCE | High levels of aspiration<br>Only 13% of research staff know of better jobs they would like to have on the outside. | Low levels of aspiration<br>57% of research staff know of better outside jobs. |
| d) INVESTMENT *authentic* & *intense* | Many more interactions counted with wide spectrum of persons<br>Head of research department represents his own authentic view to all departments | Relatively few interactions with narrow range of proximate persons<br>Head of research department "faces both ways" and calls for more business values from research and more research values from managers |
| e) SUSPENSION and RISK | Performance diverges from seniority and rank.<br>Low structure<br>No organization chart<br>President is egalitarian and dresses like a machinist<br>Long range view<br>Uncertainty is legitimate | Performance remains congruent with seniority and rank.<br>High structure<br>Much "pulling rank" and identification by seniority.<br>Each man keeps his place<br>Short range concerns<br>High certainty |

**Table 14 (Continued)**

| | | |
|---|---|---|
| f) BRIDGING THE (wide) DISTANCE | High range of upward initiation.<br>High rate of interaction between departments<br>"Misfits" welcomed and their talents stressed. Lower status persons included. | Research department described as "isolated". Complaints of "language gap" between depts.<br>Brilliant and eccentric persons squeezed out.<br>Lower status persons isolated. |
| g) SELF CONFIRMING SELF TRANSCENDING IMPACT | Many engineers with reputations for scientific integrity<br>66% Highly Satisfied<br>Many deep friendship involvements<br>Supervisors act as "sounding boards" | Very few engineers with reputations for scientific integrity<br>37% Highly Satisfied<br>Few deep friendship involvements<br>Supervisors exert pressures for conformity |
| h) Dialectic leading to SYNERGY | Research department reconciles its differences with the rest of the company<br>High number of inter-departmental and intra-departmental mutual friendship choices<br>Pleasure taken in nurturant relationships | Research department complains of domination by business values<br>Low number of inter-departmental and intra-departmental mutual friendship choices<br>No evidence for this |
| i) INTEGRATION of FEEDBACK and COMPLEXITY | Reconciliation of scientific integrity with business values, with needs for friendship, with creativity and deviance, a *balanced* cycle with complex integration | Conflict and subordination of science to business, of creativity to "fitting in", of friendship to status, of satisfaction to coordination.<br>An *unbalanced* cycle with dichotomous structures. |

Source: *Organizational Systems and Engineering Groups,* by Louis B. Barnes. Boston: Division of Research, Harvard Business School.

6. *The dangers of specialization and technique.*

It has been a recurrent theme in chapters III to V that individuals require *balance* within the segments of their cycles in order to develop. Yet most formal systems structures which correspond to segments of the cycle (see p 127) have specialists concentrating on that segment alone.

Take for instance the specialist in the Information Department, Structure (A), corresponding to segment (a). His job is to perceive and gather facts, but not necessarily to act on them, persuade others of their value, or reconcile them with other perspectives. Or take the public relations man whose job is to take the company's self-image (segment b) and make an impact with it on the environment (segment g). As a final example take the corporation's resident "thinker" whose job is to integrate corporate facts, whatever they may be, into complex combinations (segment i), and create new formal systems (Structure I).

The danger for all these men is an abstraction and idolization of their pet segment and the belief that one segment alone can be perfected in the absence of a concern for the other segments. Why are people in advertising and public relations held by many in moral contempt? Because they sacrifice all other segments of the cycle to the overall importance of making a "good" and profitable IMPACT (segment g). They maximize impact by sacrificing any kind of novel or meaningful existence, by declining to perceive (segment a) anything frightening or upsetting, by creating an image (segment b) that is merely bland, and acting in ways bereft of *authenticity* or *intensity* (segment d). Avoiding any genuine RISK or SELF-SUSPENSION (segment e), they indulge in manipulative monologues, instead of *dialectic* and meaningful SYNERGY (segment h).

This capacity for turning one aspect of a living whole into a *dictinct technique* unqualified by the humanity of the whole cycle, is a peculiarly American corruption. Here for instance is an English reporter evidently repelled by the following scene.

> Can this, you find yourself asking, really be a political campaign?... It lacks warmth, emotion even simple humanity. Instead there is an overwhelming aroma of public relations... and the unmistakable mechanistic atmosphere of a big corporation.
>
> There can be no argument about the technical perfection of the instrument that has been forged. Wherever the candidate appears there are 100 to 200 "Nixonettes" – or teeny-screamers as the Press Bus irreverently calls them – carefully filling the space between the platform and the television camera stands...
>
> Everywhere the Nixon caravan makes a stop, the Press is shepherded solicitously to a low visibility area of trestle tables... Invariably, Mr. Nixon begins by announcing that this is "the

> best," "the most thrilling," "the greatest" meeting of the campaign.[25]

Or take as another example our professorial "thinker" nuzzling up to a cold-war corporation like R.A.N.D. or the Institute of Defense Analysis. He is held in gathering contempt by students and peers, because he has abstracted the process of complex thought out of its developmental context and is using it in a context of deliberate oppression. The corporations for which he works do not have a concerned PERCEPTION for the suffering of the world (segment a), their IDENTITIES (segment b) are secret rather than open or shared, their INVESTMENTS are *in*authentic and treacherous (segment d), and they extol national self-interest instead of RISKING and SUSPENDING it on behalf of others (segment e). Their style of relating is the enforced submission of others by death and deceit – an obviously *anti*-SYNERGISTIC process (segment h). What radical students have seen with an untaught perspicacity is that many academics are psycho-socially corrupt, and that so long as a wider war continues between nations, developing students will share, albeit in milder forms, the fate of Billy Budd.

The basic premise of technique is that every human action or faculty is improvable by the process of isolation, calculation, repetition and the reduction of uncertain outcomes until it "works perfectly." In fact psycho-social development consists of being surprised, excited and confounded a large proportion of the time while maintaining a balanced integrity between perception, communication, action and thought. Just as the prostitute is rightly condemned for moving the sexual act from a personal to an economic context, the organizational expert may heedlessly perfect his narrow task until every other value inherent in the cycle is sacrificed to the Moloch of Mechanism – that vision of society as the harmonious arrangement of individually perfected techniques.

7. *The formal system as a servant of man and his development.*

Up to now it might have seemed that the formal system structure is a kind of nursemaid for the immature, who follow the advice of Hilaire Belloc.

> So always keep a hold on nurse
> For fear of finding something worse[26]

But this is not necessarily so. The anti-developmental aspects of social structure come about through the abdication by men in favor of their own social and technical machinery. Because we lack an existential theory in social science or even a widely accepted social philosophy, we tend to cohere around institutions "that work," while neglecting the ongoing human experience which created all of them and which may by this time be considering their reformation.

It is often said that appeals to conscience are purely anarchical and the only way to discipline man is to oblige him to use proper channels and to work within the system. This argument assumes that democracy is chiefly a structural and institutional network – rather than the state of mind capable of creating ever better relationships and new structures. Once conscience is seen to have its own laws, then the terror that grips Americans whenever business institutions are threatened by unions, or students paralyse a university, may subside. We may begin to see social structures for what they are – instruments for our development – to be modified or discarded when their useful life is at an end.

The capacity to create structures may indeed be of crucial importance in the development of societies. Perhaps the most distinguishing feature of economically impoverished cultures is the extreme difficulty they have in forming secondary groups with reciprocal role expectations which can be relied upon. But we shall constantly regress to the "deadly forms" created by our conservative ancestors unless human experience and dialogue are placed in the forefront of our values and we comprehend that all other values flow from these. Only then will we begin to understand – after 2,000 years – that for which Socrates was willing to die.

> I do nothing but go about persuading you, young and old alike not to take thought for your persons or properties but first and chiefly to care about the greatest improvement of the soul. I tell you that virtue is not given by money but that from virtue come money and every other good of man, public as well as private. This is my teaching and if this is the doctrine that corrupts the youth, my influence is ruinous indeed.

## NOTES FOR CHAPTER VI

1. *The Mikado* by W. S. Gilbert, New York: Random House.

2. *The Psalms,* CXV, 6.

3. *Unto This Last,* Drummond C. Monfries and G. E. Hollingworth (eds.), London: University Tutorial Press, p. 7.

4. *Ibid,* p. 8.

5. "The Liberated Generation" by Richard W. Flacks, *Journal of Social Issues,* Vol. 23, No. 3, 1967.

6. *The Achieving Society* by David C. McClelland, Princeton: Van Nostrand, 1961, pp. 154-155.

7. See *The Motivation to Work* by F. Herzberg, B. Mausner and B. Snyderman, New York: Wiley, 1959.

8. Y. Rim found that "opportunity to learn new skills" was inversely related to neuroticism and a desire for high salaries. See *Acta Psychology,* Vol. 18, No. 5, 1961, pp. 332-36.

9. Only 24% of Business Administration students at Berkeley were found "highly libertarian" (in the top 34% of a libertarian index based on The Bill of Rights). This compared with 63% studying social sciences, 62% in the humanities, 39% in physical sciences, and 30% in Engineering. See "Determinants of Support for Civil Liberties" by Hanan C. Selvin and Warren O. Hagstrom in *The Berkeley Student Revolt,* S. M. Lipset and S. S. Wolin (eds.), New York: Doubleday, 1965, pp. 499-512.

10. Pool can be relied upon as a source of many similar statements. This and others are quoted in *The Dissenting Academy,* T. Roszak (ed.), New York: Pantheon, 1968, p. .

11. *Billy Budd* (Drama) written for the stage by Louis Coxe and Robert Chapman, New York: Hill and Wang, 1962, p. 56.

12. *Ibid.* p. 77.

13. *Ibid.,* p. 74.

14. *Ibid.,* p. 63.

15. *Ibid.,* p. 73.

16. *Ibid.,* p. 65.

17. *Ibid.,* pp. 76-77.

18. *Ibid.,* p. 81.

19. "Development Hierarchies of Comprehension and Preference" by James R. Rest, *op. cit.*

20. See "Moral Reasoning of Young Adults" by Norma Haan, M. Brewster Smith and Jeanne Block, *J. of Pers. and Soc. Psychol.,* Vol. 10, No. 3, 1968, pp. 183-201.

21. *Billy Budd, op. cit.,* p. 81.

22. "Organizational Alienation: A Comparative Analysis" by M. Aiken and J. Hage, *Amer. Soc. Rev.,* Vol. 31, No. 4, 1966, pp. 497-507.

23. "Authoritarianism and Effective Indoctrination" by O. Grusky, *Admin. Sci. Quarterly,* Vol. 7, No. 9, 1962, pp. 79-95.

24. At least a dozen studies supporting this conclusion are discussed by Chris Argyris in *Integrating the Individual and The Organization,* New York: Wiley, 1964, pp. 59-92.

25. Anthony Howard, "The Presidential Elections," *The London Observer,* October 18, 1968, p. 6.

26. *Cautionary Verses* by Hillaire Belloc, New York: Alfred Knopf.

*Chapter VII*

# Rebellion, Growth and Regression in Training Groups

In chapters III to VI I have demonstrated that the double helix model of psycho-social development can discriminate between different levels of maturity. But little has been said about how such development might be hastened or induced. Can certain environments or interventions in the cycles encourage the helixes to "spiral upwards"?

Now potentially *any* intervention which increased the strength of *any* segment of the helix model could "feed around" the intersecting cycles to strengthen all segments. Let me restate the cycle, and then illustrate this point.

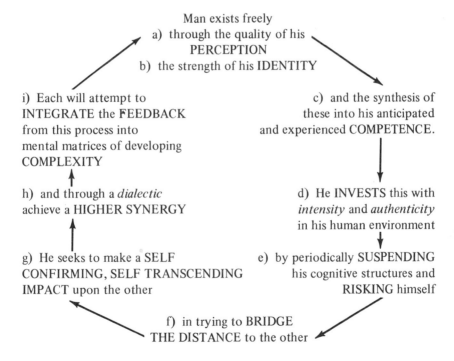

Man exists freely
a) through the quality of his PERCEPTION
b) the strength of his IDENTITY

c) and the synthesis of these into his anticipated and experienced COMPETENCE.

d) He INVESTS this with *intensity* and *authenticity* in his human environment

e) by periodically SUSPENDING his cognitive structures and RISKING himself

f) in trying to BRIDGE THE DISTANCE to the other

g) He seeks to make a SELF CONFIRMING, SELF TRANSCENDING IMPACT upon the other

h) and through a *dialectic* achieve a HIGHER SYNERGY

i) Each will attempt to INTEGRATE the FEEDBACK from this process into mental matrices of developing COMPLEXITY

Now suppose I lend a novel to my friend X which brilliantly portrays the human condition so that X immediately improves, (a) his perception and (b) develops insight into certain aspects of his identity. Following this, he might combine these into a greater sense of competence (segment c), which he then courageously invests (segment d) in distant others (segment f) to confirm and transcend himself (segment g) . . . etc. Why do I say "might"? Because an individual's development is usually held back *by the weakest and least developed segments in his own and other's cycles.*

In the first place X may only comprehend those sections of the book which seem to commend his present life style. Or second, he may realize that the book calls upon him to alter his behavior but he may not communicate this to others. Or, he may communicate verbatim passages, but in no way alter his own style of delivery, so that while the books speak of "The Courage to Be" no greater risk taking or courage is exhibited in X's interpersonal relationships. He talks *about* the book, instead of *living* the book. It takes not one jot of creativity for him to deliver a monologue on the virtues of creativity.

All kinds of moral advice which people give to each other or assemble in church to hear suffers the same fate. "Look people straight in the eyes!" "Know thyself!" "Be more confident!" It is easy to think up a cliché for every segment of the developed helix. They are all true in a general sense but only occasionally are they useful to individual persons, and they *may* be disastrous. If I deliver a sermon to my flock on Humility, Flexibility, and Unselfishness (see segment e) and one listener thereupon suspends his last remaining conviction and shoots himself, then I have scarcely been helpful. Regretting my own recent lack of charity toward an unshaven drunk lurching toward me on the street, I deliver a sermon on the Good Samaritan and the need to succour the outsiders in this world (segment f). Actually I am talking about *myself,* as do most of those indulging in monologues. But suppose a young female parishioner feels that she must now try to save the bums on Skid Row, and through inexperience is assaulted and almost killed? She recovers in body but spends the rest of her life denouncing "do-gooders," "bleeding hearts," and "communists in the clergy." Once again I have scarcely helped. General appeals to strengthen certain segments of the cycle, *may only lead to an unbalancing of the cycle, an obsession with certain segments at the expense of others, severe anomie and regression.* In any event, the conforming and obedient acting out of moral imperatives *could never* succeed in developing the cycle since personal selection of appropriate behavior in never-recurring situations is necessary, as well as a rebellion against predigested thought.

Is it, then, possible to devise an experience for a number of persons which has a chance of developing most of them, despite their differences, and without serious casualties? I believe it is, and that Training Groups or T-Groups, as they are often called, have achieved this. Both T-Groups and the developmental climates I shall discuss in the next chapter have at least one theme in common. They unite theory and activity, intelligence and affect, and strengthen simultaneously various segments of the cycle, according to the special imbalance in each individual.

T-Group training originated in the National Training Laboratories, at Bethel, Maine in 1947, and since then the activity has grown prodigiously, spreading even to Western Europe and parts of Asia. It has many forms, mutations, and imitators. It is variously known as T-Groups, Laboratory Training, Sensitivity Training, Basic Encounter Groups, Group Development, Executive Development, Managerial Grid Seminars, and Workshops.[1] In its more traditional form it usually consists of a two-week or three-week residential course wherein trainees who are strangers to one another come face to face in an unstructured, small group of around twelve persons, plus a resident Trainer.

The purposes of these groups, assembled in confrontation, are deliberately vague, and highly general and existential. Each member is there to discover how he relates to others in a group setting, how he can create purpose, how others will then react to him, and how he can use this knowledge for further learning and development.

Readers who react to the ambiguity of these last two sentences by thinking, "That sounds like a Big Nothing" may be closer to the truth than they imagined. I contend that the following characteristics of T-Groups promote the psycho-social development of participants.

1) Existential nothingness – an encounter with the Absurd
2) The small group climate
3) The enforced confrontation
4) The moratorium
5) The rebellion against authority

Having discussed how T-Groups induce development, I shall next examine some research evaluations to establish their effectiveness in certain circumstances and with certain kinds of people. I shall also discuss circumstances in which such groups can cause regression. Finally, and most importantly, I shall argue that these same techniques for inducing development are being used by radicals of the New Left. In fact, I regard T-Groups themselves as useful but limited aids to development. I am more concerned with the developmental dynamics which their operation has uncovered. These I believe to be of crucial importance.

1) *Existential nothingness – an encounter with the Absurd.*

> The absurd is only too necessary on earth. The world stands on absurdities, and perhaps nothing we know would come to pass in it without them.[2]

The absurd was also necessary in the obedience and conformity experiments for it drove the developed subjects into a rebellious affirmation of their individual humanity. I argued in Chapter V that the mindless cruelty of shocking a victim was absurd, and that a roomful of people acclaiming the palpably untrue as true, was absurd.

Now imagine, if you will, the absurdity of twelve persons, with no purpose or knowledge of one another, save for some vague injunctions to experience one another. It is enough to make the mind rebel from sheer anxiety and embarrassment. Could anything be *less* "scientific"? The whole busy world of business stopped and a long agonizing silence over everything. No cocktail glasses to fiddle with, no flag to salute which will automatically commend you to every "true American," no comfortable task to complete with mechanical pieces behaving predictably. Only *living,* inscrutable people, in a horribly ambiguous situation, for which even Amy Vanderbilt and Dear Abby have no etiquette.

This is the way a T-Group begins – in a social vacuum – literally nothingness. Members are stripped of the complete "outer cycle" I discussed in the last chapter. Official information is removed from each person's perceptions, his identity is stripped of a role, his competence is deprived of formal status, and his investing powers lack job descriptions, etc. Even if participants hastily introduce themselves, there is no overall context to make each man's expertise relevant. What meaning has *anyone* when there *is* no shared meaning?

This social vacuum has a strong stimulant effect upon man's free existence and upon segments (a), (b), (d), (e), (f) and (g) of the cycle.

If radical man develops by snatching meaning out of the Absurd and by tolerating a cultural wasteland prior to existing and transforming it, then the process of radicalization must first begin by a recognition of the Absurd. In order to force this recognition the T-Group creates such overwhelming absurdity that none can deny it.

I have argued that all developing men must rebel against some features of their environment and transform incoming messages into personal, meaningful syntheses. We have seen that conformity and obedience have crippling effects on development. What better device, then, for inducing development than removing from the environment anything to which the participants *could possibly conform*? No one can obey a void. As with Sartre beneath the heels of the Nazis, Viktor Frankl in the concentration camp, Dr. Rieux facing mass fatality in *The Plague*,[3] or Meursault in *The Stranger*[4] facing execution, it comes to participants in the T-Group that since everything around them is a total negation of meaning, *they* must rebel against this or be swept away into oblivion. They must do this even if it means being angrily disconfirmed, since that is, at least, some evidence for their existence. Thus Meursault being led away to execution reflects

> . . . all that remained to hope was that on the day of my execution there should be a huge crowd of spectators and that they should greet me with howls of execration.[5]

As the horror of nothingness is forced rudely upon T-Group participants, its corollary becomes evident also. If nothing external to the group gives it meaning, then the members can choose to become anything they desire and will mutually confirm. Their sweating palms and thumping hearts testify to the "dizziness of freedom." With no existing definitions or meanings in the environment, *every meaningful statement is perforce creative and a denial of nothingness.*

I defined radical vision (segment a) as the capacity to perceive chaos and death while seeking harmony and life, and as tolerating the wrenching discrepancy between "is" and "ought" while still being able to function. The T-Group vacuum produces a longing for meaning and confirmation amidst an undeniable nothingness and in this way "stretches" vision to encompass both ends of the polarity.

In Chapter III we also saw that radical man accepts his identity (segment b) and lets others see and share that which is *inside* him. Could anything better facilitate this process than the abolition of everything *external* to him and stripping him of his role? Into the vacuum of a T-Group are sucked the inner needs and personal identities of the participants. They all desire some external definitions, yet they have only their inner resources from which to produce these definitions.

The translation of inner needs to fill the outer vacuum is, of course, the act of investment (segment d), and this the vacuum also stimulates. Many techniques of risk reduction and non-suspension (segment e) are also rendered difficult. Who can practice elitism without recognized status or social structure? It is difficult to talk down to people or look humbly up to them with no accepted definition of "up" or "down." Those abstracted idols and pre-fabricated wisdoms which so debilitated anomic man in Chapter IV cannot survive in a vacuum, as they require an ongoing tradition to make them powerful. The social vacuum *forces* each participant to suspend his assumptions. Assumptions are always about some context, and with no initial context, followed by a context growing and changing with every passing minute, participants are induced to learn the utmost flexibility in order to keep abreast of the situation.

Since all participants are usually strangers to each other, everyone is faced with the dilemma of *wide* distances to bridge (segment f). Each, though severely anxious, is prodded to leap the abyss. He is like a man on a narrow ledge with the abyss beneath him. What better way to make him jump than *a crumbling of the ledge on which he is standing?* The dissolution of meaning in a social vacuum is the equivalent of that crumbling ledge. Participants leap the abyss because the "Death Fear" as Otto Rank called it, has been made greater than the "Life Fear."[6] We are all afraid of sinking into meaninglessness (death fear), yet we also fear leaping the hazardous distance to others (life fear) and thereby risking disconfirmation. The T-Group works by "crumbling the ledge" and heightening the death fear until many leap with a kind of desperation.

T. S. Eliot expressed the same idea, using the analogy of two fires, that of hate and loneliness and that of love. Our only choice is to go through the torment of anxiety to consumate human love.

Who then devised this torment? Love.
Love is the unfamiliar name
Behind the hands that wove
The intolerable shirt of flame
Which human power cannot remove.
We only live, only suspire
Consumed by either fire or fire.[7]

Another way of seeing this "dreadful choice" is via Kohlberg's stages of Moral Development. These were:— 6. Conscience orientation, 5. Social Contract, 4. Law and Order, 3. Personal Concordance, 2. Egocentric Instrumental Relativism and 1. Obedience. The T-Group's social vacuum *deprives members of the ability to use Stages 5, 4, and 3,* thereby offering a stark choice between 2 and the exercise of Stage 6 capacities.

2) *The small group climate*

There seem to be special characteristics of small groups which make them potential developmental vehicles. A group of nine to twelve persons can achieve an effective balance of depth with breadth. There are few enough members, meeting over a long enough period to permit deep insight (segment a) and intensity of investment (segment d). On the other hand there are not *too* few persons, a contingency which often leads to a collusion to deny cultural realities and to create private fantasies, ill suited to dissemination beyond the group.

The small group which meets on a regular basis also develops *as a group.* In the early sessions perceptions are poor for lack of familiarity, identities feel weak for lack of investment and confirmation, and there cannot be much experienced competence since feedback is scarce. Most small groups make the transition from near total alienation at first to progressive strengthening and warming of relationships. This development refers to the three week life of the group and should not be confused with any *permanent* learning which members take away with them to use in other situations.

But the experience of group development teaches the members that fear can be turned into knowledge and affection, that a vacuum is a tense opportunity and not a mortal danger, and that persons who appear hostile, sullen, or ambiguous can be transformed in the intimacy of a face to face group. The development of a group is the experience of victory over seemingly insoluble human dilemmas. It especially builds up the sense of competence (segment c), and it constitutes an arena for a dialectical confrontation leading to synergy (segment h).

Small groups of around twelve persons have historically great significance. There were twelve disciples, later twelve apostles. The number in a communist cell varies around twelve. Twelve sit on a jury. Work groups in industry and committee structures are seldom much larger than twelve – which is widely regarded as the maximum for informal cohesion and self-control. Ideas that have changed the world have been incubated and elaborated in small group settings.

3) *The enforced confrontation*

A most important stimulant to various segments of the cycle is the fact of prolonged confrontation between participants. This is especially potent in enhancing a) powers of perception, the investment of identity and competence (segments b, c, and d), the capacity to struggle through dialectic to achieve synergy (segment h) and the acceptance of feedback and responsibility (segment i).

We saw in Chapter V that it is much harder to hurt others in experimental situations, as well as in Vietnam if we must look them in the face and stay with them while they burn. The vast majority of risk reducing strategies involve moving away from and/or moving against others to coerce or repress their response. But in prolonged confrontation in a closed room, my hostility will not drive people away and it is difficult for me to leave the room, hence I must perceive the injuries I cause others and have my nose rubbed in the responsibility, while my victim explains to all assembled *exactly* how he feels.

Jean Paul Sartre conceived of Hell as a place for anomic men wherein their techniques for risk reduction could not work. He called his play *No Exit* and indeed the three characters are trapped in face to face confrontation – a whore, a male coward and an authoritarian lesbian. The three are totally incompatible. They cannot physically injure or eliminate each other since they are already dead and they cannot get out of the room. The point Sartre is trying to make is that in prolonged confrontation, *those that cannot persuade others to confirm and respect them are entirely at the others' mercy.* They exist only in the savage eye of those who despise them.

At one point in the play, Garcin, the coward, suggests that they can move away from each other and that mutual relationships are not necessary.

> No I shall never be your torturer. I wish neither of you any harm, and I've no concern with you. . . None at all. We must look at the floor and each must try to forget that the other is there.[8]

There is a desperate silence but they cannot escape from the reality that in silence they exist for others (being-in-itself) *without in any way existing for themselves* (being-for-itself). Transfixed by the other's gaze they are lifeless, impotent objects. Inez, one of the women, breaks the silence angrily.

> To forget about the others? How utterly absurd. I *feel* you there in every pore. Your silence clamors in my ears... Can you stop your thoughts? I can hear them ticking away... and I am certain you hear mine. It's all very well skulking on your sofa, but you're everywhere, and every sound comes to me soiled, because you intercepted it on the way. Why you've even stolen my face; you know it and I don't!... It's what one does and nothing else, that shows the stuff one is made of... you are a coward, Garcin, because I wish it. I wish it – do you hear? I wish it. And yet, just look at me, see how weak I am, a mere breath on the air, a gaze observing you, a formless thought that thinks you... you have no choice, you must convince me and you're at my mercy...[9]

By the same argument a T-Group confrontation blocks the usual avenues of escape for anomic man. If he remains silent he will be unilaterally defined by others and his "face" will be stolen from him to become a property of the group culture. In silent confrontation we are delivered into the power of those from whom we are estranged.

Hence confrontation presents each individual with a dilemma similar to the social vacuum. In the vacuum he was nothing until he declared himself and passed into a shared existence. In confrontation he is impotent and infinitely malleable by others unless he invests himself authentically and intensely in others, to recapture control of his own identity. Fortunately for most T-Group members, they are neither as corrupt nor as incompatible as Sartre's three characters. There is no exit for them either, but there is an *entry* into each other's consciousness and shared existence.

The enforced confrontation makes an excellent arena for a dialectic leading to synergy. The habit of breaking off discussions when disagreement provokes intolerable anxiety is prevented by enclosure within the group and prior agreement to see it through. In such close proximity dissatisfaction becomes visible if only through lack of participation, and even the more cautious members may eventually state an antithesis to the group's current thesis.

With theses and antitheses out in the open, reconciling them becomes almost a necessity. Unlike the wider culture there are no social sewers, slums and prisons to which deviant persons can be expelled when disagreement becomes too distressing. Rather than having a resentful, hurting member right in front of one's eyes, testifying to the group's incapacity to understand, it becomes less painful to attempt to reconcile his needs with those of other participants. Hence confrontation pressures participants into the practice of reconciling opposites and creating synergy.

The emergence of synergy (segment h) is vitally dependent upon the authentic expression of human needs (segment d) and "opening up" of identity (segment b). A major block to synergy is the declaration of rigid, unsuspended, moralistic goals and abstractions (see segment (e) of the anomic cycle). One T-Group theorist puts it well.

> On the other hand, if needs could be stated, it would appear that not a single goal, but a range of goals would be potentially satisfying to member(s)... (who) would be able to design activities to yield more widespread satisfaction...[10]

Confrontation and synergy also permit a balancing and "justice" among the segments of interacting cycles. Here there is much *less* danger that pieces of abstract, moral advice will unbalance the cycle of individuals. The condition of close proximity and continual feedback permits each person to get insights from the group which are tailored to his style and his needs. Unlike the over-pugnacious person hearing pulpit monologues on the armour of righteousness, he gets loud and clear signals that he is unpleasant to others. The advice to be more assertive is *not* directed at him but at the people he has been dominating. Outside group confrontation people can often manage to expose themselves only to those messages they want to hear. The authoritarian Klansman goes to meetings which he knows will confirm his distorted cycle. The drum majorette throws her bottom and baton around in predictable sequence with predictable whistles and applause. But in confrontation the opinions of eleven strangers cannot be "managed." It is the moment of truth.

> For now we see through a glass, darkly; but then face to face; now I know in part; but then shall I know even as also I am known.[11]

*4) The moratorium*

The moratorium provided by T-Groups can have the effect of freeing my existence. It allows me time in which to remake my identity (segment b), to increase the intensity of my investments (segment d), to suspend the assumptions of the everyday world (segment e), and when the moratorium is over, to make my learning count in the real world.

Much of our capacity to experiment with new ideas and life styles is constrained in the external world by the daily responsibility of work and the cultural emphasis upon efficiency and "smooth working relationships." If a "new me" appears at work, in the lodge, or at the club, all those who have a stake in the regularity of my working and consuming behavior are likely to kick.

Moreover, in many areas of my life the die is cast. I have chosen the kind of person I wish to be and those I encounter regularly claim the right to expect my consistency. Upon such consistency my job, mortgage, credit, and the food of my children may depend.

But in a T-Group I can reassess some of the decisions I have made and test out a new identity before showing it to the world. If my experimentation fails I have suffered loss, but nothing compared to the losses incurred by disrupting the external environment without convincing it that I have changed for the better.

Because the group will come to an end, its relationships have the same flavor as a shipboard romance. People will often feel free to engage each other with additional depth and intensity where time is limited and attachments can always be detached by the preordained parting of the ways.

The moratorium can also have the flavor of a "re-run" of one's past life. Because a T-Group starts in alienation, uncertainty, and anxiety, it is reminiscent of early adolescence. It is an enforced unsocialization followed by a resocialization. Arthur Koestler has referred to this process as ***reculer** pour mieux sauter* – literally pulling back to make a new leap at a familiar obstacle.[12] In this rerun of old mistakes that have persisted and plagued one's life can be corrected, not just in memory but in new activity.

*5) The rebellion against authority*

It is at least doubtful whether the presence of the Trainer in the T-Group assists the process of development. He has traditionally been there so that some experienced person could learn and observe the processes. He also makes "interventions" of varying skill.

Among the disadvantages of his presence is that he reduces the sense of absurdity and vacuum. Instead of rebellion against nothingness, members often turn to the Trainer and beg him to "explain-it-all," tell them who they are, and lead them out of the wilderness. We saw in Chapter IV that in periods of disintegration and severe anomie men long for authoritarian control as an alternative to making lonely and perilous decisions.

The anti-developmental influence of the Trainer's presence is solved by arranging for him to abdicate the task of leading and generally bungle that role. This is not easy at first, since the group will impute to him almost magical powers. When he scratches his nose he is warning them. The way he sits denotes displeasure. His face is scrutinized for the smallest "sign from Heaven" that members are not forsaken and cast out from Eden to suffer and choose for themselves. Eagerly they tell each other that there is a "Plan" for the group which He has worked out. Soone will come the Revelation. In the meantime, all suggestions are *not* the choice of individual participants for which *they* are responsible; on the contrary, the suggestions are divinations of His Will, foretold in his Master Plan.[13]

Some participants imitate the priestly caste. They dig up any articles the Trainer has written and spout to the group fundamentalist assertions from the scripture. But as the God continues to fail, there comes the rebellion. Some trainers like the Deans at several universities find the room occupied and themselves locked in or out. There is frequently talk of "revolution" and "taking over." One Trainer found a large cigar in his mailbox, presumably signifying bossism. Another, finding the door shut in his face, reported the following:

> Going around a side door he entered, amid great uproar and hilarity, to find Paul and Jim seated in his normal place at the end of the table. There was a great deal of clowning by the two usurpers, largely in the form of parodistic interpretations uttered in a deep and pompous voice, to the great enjoyment of the other members... Jim then began an elaborate burlesque, calling Paul taboo and shrinking away from him... At this there was some joking about the Trinity, and having concluded that Laura, being female, must represent the Magna Mater, the Holy Ghost must obviously be represented by the deposed group leader.[14]

These descriptions remind one irresistibly of recent campus disturbances, students sitting in the president's chairs and publicly ridiculing the pomposity of deposed leaders.

What does such rebellion accomplish? It would seem to be an existential theme in the process of development which involves a revolt against the external definition by authority figures. No sooner do developing group participants find the courage to define themselves than they also find themselves saddled and bridled by the same paternalism they once clung to so gratefully. Even where the authority figure has been trying to abdicate continually, he is not forgiven by those who first imputed authority to him and must now wrench it away, burning not only the effigy of their ex-leader but the effigies of their own psycho-social infancy.

Leaderless T-Groups do not usually go through this stage. The initial vacuum is like the *tabula rasa* on the morning after a revolution. Leaders are vanquished along with all the structures of society – and a new age begins.

*Research evaluations of T-Group outcomes*

I have argued that five principles of growth – the encounter with existential nothingness, the small group climate, the enforced confrontation, the moratorium, and the rebellion against authority – stimulate major parts of the double helix so that psycho-social development is induced. Is there research evidence that growth does, in fact, result? The remainder of this chapter will present some positive evidence and suggest some reasons for the occasional failures, and a brief account of induced regression.

A major study of unmodified T-Groups was undertaken by Douglas Bunker. He evaluated four conferences of educators and school administrators who met in a total of 60 T-Groups at Bethel, in the summers of 1961 and 1962. To evaluate the lasting effects on individuals each participant was matched with a "control member" of similar age, background, and occupation. Then both participants and controls nominated three "describers" in their occupational environment. Some ten months after training when any short-lived enthusiasms had worn off, questionnaires were mailed to describers. Bunker developed a "verified change score" by counting only those reported changes in which at least two describers concurred.

Using this conservative estimate 76.9% of those attending the three-week laboratories were described as having made developmental changes while 58.4% of those in the two-week laboratories were so described. (Only the three-week laboratories included training in how to reconcile new learning with the expectations of the external environment.) Bunker's methodology and findings were later replicated in a second study with substantially similar results.[15]

The verified changes, *i.e.,* those measures on which participants *significantly exceeded* the changes reported in matched controls (who improved slightly) are set out in Table 15. Here we see that *every* segment of the cycle showed substantial and significant gains from the three-week T-Groups. In the shorter groups without "application training" lesser gains were recorded, some of which might have been due to chance.

There are a few slight differences between the learning profile emerging here and the profiles of radical man in earlier chapters. The participants in T-Groups reported more ease and less anxiety in their outside relationships, while radical man in Chapters III and V pushed his anxiety tolerance to the limit. The participants were also described as more tactful and poised – a bit reminiscent of the conformers in Chapter V.

But these discrepancies are not difficult to account for. While the *skill* of participants went up, the demands made upon them by their bureaucratic environments were probably much the same. (Those who had been promoted were eliminated from the sample to avoid biasing reporting from "describers.") Hence a more skilled man in the same spot might well appear to accomplish his work with more ease and poise.

While these particular T-Groups encouraged rebellion *within* the group, they do less to encourage subsequent rebellion, because the trained individual returns to an environment where almost none of the persons he encounters

**Table 15**

**REPORTED CHANGES IN THE BEHAVIOR OF PARTICIPANTS IN T-GROUPS**

| *Segments of the Cycle* | In general and on average participants *increased* over controls in their capacities to......... |
|---|---|
| *Existence* | Express new ideas<br>Experiment with new behaviors |
| a) PERCEPTION | Show sensitivity for others feelings |
| b) IDENTITY | Show awareness of own behavior<br>Show insight into self and others |
| c) COMPETENCE | Reflect self-confidence<br>Control Manifest Anxiety |
| d) INVESTMENT<br>*authentic*<br>& *Intense* | Communicate and "send behavior" in general<br>(no data)<br>Express stronger feelings with less inhibition |
| e) SUSPENSION<br>& RISK | Exhibit greater flexibility<br>Take bigger risks |
| f) BRIDGING THE DISTANCE | Accept and tolerate greater shortcomings in others |
| g) SELF-CONFIRMING<br>SELF-TRANSCENDING<br>IMPACT | Relate successfully to others<br>Involve others |
| h) *Dialectic* leading to<br>SYNERGY | Take a stand on an issue<br>Encourage participation, create interdependence with others. |
| i) INTEGRATION of<br>FEEDBACK &<br>COMPLEXITY | Tolerate new information<br>Receive communications<br>(no data on complexity) |

N.B. A few of these measures narrowly missed significance at the .05 level when 2-week and 3-week T-Groups were combined. All measures were significant at .01 level for members of the 3-week groups.

*Sources:* Douglas R. Bunker. "Individual Applications of Laboratory Training". *The Journal of Applied Behavioral Science.* vol. no. 2. 1965

Douglas R. Bunker and Eric S. Knowles "Comparison of Behavioral Changes Resulting from Human Relations Training Laboratories of Different Lengths." mimeo.

have shared his experience. While he may be able to charm his colleagues into somewhat more developed styles of behavior, he is unlikely to have the same political and reforming impact as a whole group acting in concert to recreate in the wider society the relationships they enjoyed within their caucus.

The problem of T-Group learning losing its impetus as the participant moves into "unfriendly territory" has been partially solved by the "Managerial Grid Seminars" (modified T-Groups) designed by Robert R. Blake and Jane S. Mouton. Here participants are taken from the same company but are grouped with relative strangers from different departments. But when the training is over they return to an environment which has *shared* a similar experience and *has* learned to value more developed styles of behavior. This seems to make a considerable difference as we shall see.

An extremely thorough and detailed evaluation of "Grid Training" at a large plant in Texas was undertaken by Louis B. Barnes and Larry Greiner of the Harvard Business School. Using a large variety of measures, they found very substantial changes which correspond almost perfectly to the segments of the cycle. These are detailed in Table 16.

A number of these measures deserve comment and provide additional insight into the dynamics of psycho-social development. The Grid Seminar contains a specific device to "shake up" and disconfirm its participants, so that those who do not habitually suspend their assumptions and risk themselves (segment e) will have their assumptions pried from their grasp. This is done by making participants rate themselves on the "Grid Instrument," which measures dimensions of "concern with people" and "concern with production." The self-ratings are then compared with the ratings which *other* participants give the manager, and he often finds that the discrepancy is alarming. An interesting finding was that the degree of "shaking-up" had a curvilinear relationship with overall improvement around the cycle. The "moderately shaken up" improved the most, then the "severely shaken up," while those who succeeded in surviving the experience without any pain *hardly improved at all.*

Another point of note is that controllable costs fell sharply and a rise of $60 million in profits was traceable to the improved relationships between executives. To those who urge "practicality" and decry "soft data" on opinions, norms and attitudes, I must point out that improvement among these ambiguous intangibles has very "hard" results. I doubt if the American economy will collapse before any advance of humanism. On the contrary these results show that a greater "concern with people" among those overly concerned with "hard" productivity *will actually increase productivity,* so that psycho-social development – or the lack of it – may be at the root of the numerous things we grab for but which seem to evade our grasp.

Before the seminars began, the Texas groups saw a film, "Twelve Angry Men." This recounts how a jury, angrily impatient to send to the electric

**Table 16**

**INDIVIDUAL AND CORPORATE DEVELOPMENT FOLLOWING "MANAGERIAL GRID SEMINARS"**

**Designed by Robert R. Blake and Jane S. Mouton**
**Evaluated by, Louis B. Barnes and Larry E. Greiner**

| *Segments of the Cycle* | Questionnaires to 600 managers and analysis of cost indices revealed the following changes 10 months after training, compared with before training. |
|---|---|
| *Existence* | 26% increase in number of managers reporting "high quality decisions".<br>12% increase in no. of managers reporting support for novel suggestions. Increased support for self-expression and 11% decline in support of those remaining silent until others show their hand. |
| a) PERCEPTION | 55% of participants report clearer understanding of other's viewpoints.<br>12% increase in no. of managers describing boss as "aware of others". |
| b) IDENTITY | 9% increase in no. of managers describing boss as "aware of himself". |
| c) COMPETENCE | 6% increase in no. of managers describing boss as "self-confident". |
| d) INVESTMENT | 17% increase in no. of managers describing boss as "keeps me informed". |
| *authentic* | 22% increase in no. of managers describing boss "levelling with group members". |
| & | 22% increase in no. of managers describing work group as "laying their cards on the table". |
| *intense* | 24% increase in no. of managers reporting higher group effort.<br>26% increase in no. of managers reporting lively group discussion. |
| e) SUSPENSION & RISK | 30% increase in top managment conviction that "tension is necessary to solve problems".<br>Managers "shaken up" by training experience make largest overall improvement. |
| f) BRIDGING THE DISTANCE | 20% increase in top managment support for racial integration.<br>12% increase in low level managers receiving official top managment recognition. |

**Table 16 (Continued)**

| | |
|---|---|
| | Scholarships set up by employees for Black children.<br>Managers urge implementation of Civil Rights Act in local communities.<br>Relationships between plant and parent company substantially improved.<br>Union is so impressed by new managment attitudes, that they asked for and received Grid Training. |
| g) SELF CONFIRMING SELF-TRANSCENDING IMPACT | 12% increase in no. of managers reporting "my suggestions are encouraged".<br>11% increase in no. reporting clear communications from boss.<br>11% increase in no. reporting being "inspired to high goals" by boss.<br>11% increase in no. reporting being "listened to carefully" by boss.<br>The "most improved" managers (throughout the cycle) have *smallest* discrepancy between identity and impact on others.<br>*Indices of Good Management.*<br>Controllable costs fall from index fig. 94.1 to 86.2, results in $60 million dollars addition to profits. Productivity-per-man-hour rises from index fig. 104 to 131. |
| h) *Dialectic*<br><br>leading<br>to<br>SYNERGY | 25% increase in strong polarized positions over weak polarized positions.<br>31% increase in no. of meetings held.<br>12% increase in team problem solving.<br>49% of all managers report more effective relationships with boss.<br>55% of all managers report better in-group relationships.<br>11% increase in no. of managers reporting *joint* goal setting with boss.<br>17% *decrease* in support for compromised solutions. |
| i) INTEGRATION of FEEDBACK & COMPLEXITY | 26% increase in "integrated norms" over "polarized norms" (with simultaneous toughening of remaining polarized positions).<br>Substantial increases in *optimization and balancing* of "concern with people" and "concern with productivity".<br>30% increase in no. of managers reporting their work teams "conscious of profit and loss". |

Source: *Breakthrough in Organization Development* by Robert R. Blake, Jane S. Mouton; Louis B. Barnes, and Larry E. Greiner. *Harvard Business Review,* November-December, 1964.

chair an "obviously guilty" Puerto Rican boy, are stayed from reaching a unanimous verdict by the dissent of a single juror. At first furious at being trapped together in awkward confrontation on a very hot day, the jurors berate the single dissenter. But as relations develop between them, a human concern for the boy develops also, as well as the intellectual resources to re-examine the prosecution's case. One by one the jurors change their verdict. The lone dissenter has rebelled, waged a relentless dialectic, and overcoming prejudice and stereotyped thinking, has gradually won the synergistic support of increasing numbers. "I rebel, therefore we exist."

Perhaps it was the influence of this model that led the seminar members to spread their new behaviors beyond their business roles into Texas politics. Several of them started to implement the Civil Rights Act in their local communities, others set up scholarships for Black children and began to support integration in general.

Another interesting development was the increase in integrated norms and synthesized mental structures (see segment (i) of Table 16). But this was accompanied by a *hardening* of the remaining polar positions and toughening of conviction of certain values. This illustrates that thesis and antithesis can only be integrated where a convinced thesis is first stated, later to be qualified, *but not compromised,* by the antithesis. This study found that acceptance of mere compromise decreased substantially.

Although the research findings in Table 16 are not strictly comparable to those in Table 15, the former would appear more widespread and significant. Some additional research by Larry Greiner[16] indicates that these more substantial changes *are* due in part to the mutual support among trained persons *after* the training was over. The "most improved" managers back on their jobs enjoyed a ratio of support of 2.24 to 0.5 between "most" and "least improved" managers. But the "least improved" were surrounded by many others as little improved as they were. The ratio was 1 to 1. It seems, then, that synergistic relationships with other recently developed persons solidify one's own recent development and perhaps continue it.

In a number of reported cases trained groups have been returned to their bureaucratic environment only to have their new styles of behavior stamped out by higher management, afraid of the new freedom and informality. In one case the entire training staff were fired.[17] In another, the company President stormed into a T-Group session of his employees after hearing that members were "taking off their clothes." He took it literally. But the verbal self-exposure he found also disgusted his conservative soul. In a twenty--minute monologue he extolled the virtues of hard work and unquestioned obedience. He criticized the T-Group trainer for his abdication when competition was so strong. Later he explained privately,

> I do not think that this kind of discussion (of feelings) was crucial to management training. Matter of fact, some of it seemed like

communism to me; they've gone too far for me, too revolutionary![18]

The comment was revealing. If T-Group theorists are reluctant to admit their their methods produce political radicalization, at least conservatives have no doubt. T-Groups have joined Mental Health on the blacklists of the American Right.

Evidence that T-Group training reduces race prejudice, stereotypes, and anomie, while increasing "human heartedness," self-acceptance, and acceptance of others was found in another recent study.[19] An interesting sidelight was the inverse relationship between development and talking *about* "the race question" in mixed T-Groups. Those who intellectualized the loudest about race in general failed to move towards the *specific* Black Americans within the group, and thereby failed to develop themselves. "Liberal talk" was a substitute for action and for growth.

A series of T-Groups conducted and evaluated by William G. Schutz and Vernon Allen provides further confirmation of developmental gains and throws a useful light upon the gains and losses made during and after training. 22% of participants reported that the gains they had made faded promptly or soon after they had left the group. 35% reported gains which held constant, 30% reported gains which increased or only became evident after training, while the remainder reported no change or regression. Hence more than two thirds ceased to develop after the end of training and many slipped back again. Despite the substantial gains reported in Table 17, the maintenance of developmental climates outside training continues to be a problem.

Another interesting feature of Schutz's research is his concept and measurement of balance.[20] In order to develop, over-dominant persons must be less dominant, the over-submissive more assertive. Those wanting synergy and affection at *any* cost must learn that these ultimately depend upon greater independence, self-suspension, and perceptual powers. The developmental process described in Chapter III required such balance. The anomie described in Chapter IV was obsessively unbalanced and unjust. This study found that balance was indeed related to improvement and to gains throughout the cycle.

What kind of person develops in the T-Group climate and who remains unimproved? Current research points to the conclusion that there is a hard core of persons high in anomie who are exceedingly difficult to budge.[21] The social vacuum at the beginning of the T-Group is usually filled by the more developed and less anomic persons, and those afraid to make decisions have not very long to wait before structures and norms emerge to which they can conform. One antidote to this would be to assemble groups of highly and equally anomic persons so that at least *some* of them would have to break the silence and choose.[22]

**Table 17**

**EFFECTS OF A T-GROUP LABORATORY ON INTERPERSONAL BEHAVIOR**

| *Segments of the Cycle* | Content analyses of reports made by participants 6 months after training revealed the following % of responses. |
|---|---|
| *Existence* | (no data) |
| a) PERCEPTION | 35% report increased intellectual understanding; awareness and insight about other people. |
| b) IDENTITY | 40% report more tolerance, acceptance and more liking for self; a less critical view of self. |
| c) COMPETENCE | 23% report friendlier, easier to get along with, improved behavior with people. |
| d) INVESTMENT *authentic and intense* | 18% reported more aggressive, outgoing behavior and more honesty, confidence and willingness to reveal themselves. |
| e) SUSPENSION & RISK | 23% reported being more relaxed, at ease, less tension, more flexibility towards self and others. |
| f) BRIDGING THE DISTANCE | 31% reported being better able to solve differences between people. |
| g) SELF CONFIRMING SELF TRANSCENDING IMPACT | 41% reported either that others became more friendly, sympathetic and supportive to them, or that in general people reacted more positively towards them. |
| h) *Dialectic* leading to SYNERGY | 31% reported success in solving the human relations problems (also reported under bridging the distance).<br>60% reported at least one of the following: – more appreciation, interest, acceptance, warmth, and closeness to others.<br>Greater *balance* in behavior styles found through F.I.R.O. questionnaire. |
| i) INTEGRATION of FEEDBACK into COMPLEXITY | 29% report that in various ways they receive more personal and confidential information from people.<br>Increased intellectual awareness also reported: (see segment a). |

Source: "The Effect of a T-Group Laboratory on Interpersonal Behavior" by William C. Schutz and Vernon L. Allen. *The Journal of Applied Behavioral Science.* Vol. 2, No. 3, 1966.

Another class of persons who seem to respond sluggishly to T-Group training includes scientifically and technically trained staff experts. Their habits of mind are totally averse to making decisions before all the hard data are assembled. They regard as "unscientific" the intrusion of personality and identity into statements of fact. Since their staff role is advisory they generally restrict themselves to communicating scientific and technical statements, investments which require little self-suspension and almost no risk, since the facts are highly precise and verified. Insofar as these experts think of human affairs at all – theirs would be the vision of Conservative Man, as outlined in Chapter I.

Whatever the merits of this argument, the research on attempts to humanize technocrats speaks for itself. The evaluation of "Grid Seminars," detailed in Table 16, also found that staff engineers made little more than half the progress recorded by administrators and line managers.[23]

In another study, researchers attempted to identify the quality of perception and kind of visual field that characterized the most successful T-Group participants. One measure that discriminated strongly was the Sensation-Intuition Scale on the Myers-Briggs Type Indicator. This scale contrasts the preference for two kinds of perceptual processes. These are *Sensation,* which focuses upon discrete, factual stimuli, with attention to detail, practicality, and thorough retention of the "objective" images. This orientation is typical of bureaucratically organized science wherein the detached observer, separating subject from object, brings none of his personal feelings or needs to the understanding of the environment. The second mode of perception is *Intuition,* a process of *holistic* perception wherein the observer uses the humanity he shares with the other to comprehend him. This end of the scale includes insight, originality, and ingenuity.

Table 18 demonstrates that the intuitive perceiver is, indeed, the superior T-Group participant as rated by both his peers and the Trainer. He contributes more to the group, brings superior resources to the development of others, and changes more himself in a positive direction. On all indices and segments of the cycle, those passive perceivers of discrete, analyzed and unemotive facts made, on the average, less progress and showed poorer development before, during, and after the T-Group.

In view of these findings, and others which show engineering and business students substantially lower in civil libertarianism than those in the humanities and "soft" social sciences,[24] with engineering students in one study becoming less and less liberal as their education progressed,[25] the post-Sputnik emphasis on science and technology may be mass-producing anomic men. Have we become a nation of mechanical tinkerers with shrivelled self-hoods, each in his corporate cubicle, constructing a tiny piece of the largest military-technical complex the world has known? Are we like

**Table 18**

**T-GROUP PERFORMANCE AND INTUITIVE PERCEPTION**

| *Segments of the Cycle* | Ratings of participants by their fellow participants and Trainers, correlated as follows with the Intuition Scale (Product-moment correlation) |
|---|---|
| *Existence* | .40 with creative behavior |
| a) PERCEPTION | (Intuition Scale)<br>.40 with interest in group's activities |
| b) IDENTITY | .41 with awareness of, and sharing of relevant feelings |
| c) COMPETENCE | .38 with overall effectiveness in the group |
| d) INVESTMENT *authentic & intense* | .48 with strong effort to influence others to his point of view |
| e) SUSPENSION & RISK | .30 with values high trust. |
| f) BRIDGING THE DISTANCE | .49 with superior capacity to make understandable group events |
| g) SELF CONFIRMING SELF TRANSCENDING IMPACT | .49 with significant contribution to the group's development<br>.26 with development during T-Group |
| h) *Dialectic* leading to SYNERGY | .39 with willingness to disagree and criticize<br>.38 with valuation of shared control<br>.21 with warmth and supportiveness. |
| i) INTEGRATION of FEEDBACK & COMPLEXITY | .32 with values receiving new information<br>.23 learns and understands from the reactions of others.<br>(no data on complexity) |

Source: "Personality and 'Laboratory Style'." by Fred I. Steele
*The Journal of Applied Behaviorial Science.* Vol. 4. No. 1, 1968

the obedient minions of the electric chair in Chapter V, 90% of whom were willing to play a subsidiary part in senseless torture?

Science and technology play a considerable part in cold and hot wars. If technocratic vision impedes psycho-social development, what might happen when "win-lose" psychology is added to this situation? A series of small group experiments by Robert Blake and Jane Mouton vividly exemplifies the highly regressive impact of "win-lose" strategic thinking.

The researchers conducted a series of experiments in which two laboratory groups are placed in a situation where *synergy between the two groups is impossible.* Each group will work to produce a product and one product will be adjudged "the winner" over the other. Note that there are seldom any protests about this arrangement. On the contrary participants enter it with competitive gusto and *esprit de corps.* It is essentially a re-creation of many national pastimes and folklores, business competition, football and other team games, the Cold War, Junior Achievement Award competitions as run by local chambers of commerce – all predicated on the same basic principles.

The researchers measured from time to time, the attitudes, behaviors, and judgment of the competing members. What happened to the relations between the two groups can easily be predicted from the dynamics of the cycle. If synergy (segment h) becomes impossible and domination/submission is the only outcome, then all the other segments with which synergy is interdependent will crumble also. For example, why focus upon the needs of the other (segment a), or risk (segment e) bridging the distance to the other group (segment f) if by satisfying them, you harm yourself? Why reveal your inner identity (b), stake your competence (c), and invest it (d), when the other group is obviously going to *dis*confirm you (g)?

In Table 19 we see this rather obvious prediction come true, all the segments of the *intergroup* cycle show immediate and substantial disintegration. But less immediately obvious and far more ominous are the details in Table 19 of the deteriorating interpersonal relationships *within* the competing groups. Here we find a severe imbalance and substantial regression to a friendly, *low*-level synergy, with seriously impaired human resources. Creative thinking is sharply reduced, pressures for conformity arise, and there is a strong tendency for perceptual misjudgment with prominent members of one's own group seen through rose colored spectacles. There is a ludicrous sense of *over*-confidence, an incapacity to suspend favorable assumptions about the in-group, a shortening of the distance between members with purges of deviants, a much more structured and hierarchical system of relationships, and a decline in intellectual functioning.

This is not, at first, accompanied by any decline in pleasure or excitement. Indeed the situation is similar in some ways to intoxication because the group is congratulating itself on almost certain victory, and everyone can win easy confirmation from each other by "patriotic" agreement. There is no need for

Table 19

**DECLINE IN JUDGMENT AND INTERPERSONAL COMPETENCE IN WIN-LOSE CONDITIONS**

**(A total of 1,000 executives were run through these group conditions over a period of years.)**

| *Segments of the Cycle* | *Inter*group Phenomena | *Intra*group Phenomena |
|---|---|---|
| Existence | Pressures for conformity in group's behavior to rival group. | Creative thinking declines generally, across the board conformity demanded. |
| a) PERCEPTION | Highly stereotyped view of enemy. Concentration on his supposed weakness. Rapid loss of empathy. | Failure to appraise ingroup personalities realistically "Halo effect" in perception of leaders. |
| b) IDENTITY | Group identity greatly strengthened in short run. | Identity of individuals merged and overcome by group identity. |
| c) COMPETENCE | Surface confidence with repressed fear of defeat. | Serious overestimation and over confidence concerning group's product and chances of victory. |
| d) INVESTMENT *authentic and intense* | Reduced capacity to communicate to other group. Misgivings not revealed. High premium on "strategy" and rehearsed performances. | High effort and enthusiasm but personal feelings submerged for public good. |
| e) SUSPENSION & RISK | Rigid and righteous goals proclaimed. High cynicism and distrust of enemy. | Severe loss in the capacity to detach oneself or reconsider goals. |
| f) BRIDGING THE DISTANCE | Exaggerated sense of distance and disagreement between the two groups. Points of similarity and agreement not recognized. | Closing of ranks with increasing cohesion over shorter distances. Deviation and "treason" is punished. General ethnocentric trends. |
| g) SELF CONFIRMING SELF TRANSCENDING IMPACT | Total deadlock and frustration. | Vigorous agreement and esprit de corps concerning immanence of victory. |
| h) *Dialectic* leading to SYNERGY | Failure of dialectic. Constant belittlement of opponents and determination to vanquish them. Failure to create synergy even *when possibility is restored.* | More combative persons rise to leadership positions, tend to dominate other members, low level of synergy |
| i) INTEGRATION of FEEDBACK & COMPLEXITY | Messages from other group seriously distorted. Black and white dichotomous thinking. | Capacity to think and understand shows severe deterioration. |

Source: *Managing Intergroup Conflict in Industry,* by Robert R. Blake, Herbert A. Shepard and Jane S. Mouton. Houston: Gulf Publishing, 1964 the long anxious struggle to understand the perspectives of others, for the members have one perspective only – moronic in its simplicity: they must WIN. In this situation the truth, which is that they have a 50% chance of total defeat, is entirely separated from the means of becoming popular which is to predict victory. The "hangover" is very likely to follow. Within the losing group there is bitter criticism of those "wonderful" leaders of a short moment ago, and "revolutions" often depose the leaders. Within the winning group *there is a continuation of smug overconfidence, hierarchical relationships and the conformity that brought victory.* From a developmental point of view win-lose competitive conflict has *no* successful outcome for *anyone.* It corrupts "winners" and "losers" alike.

As a final twist to their experiments the researchers reintroduced the opportunity to create synergy between the groups. Now each can contribute to the others development, but win-lose psychology has eroded their capacities. *The opportunities for synergy, though present, are neither perceived nor acted upon by winning or losing groups.* Their empathy for each other is gone. It is the end of dialogue, in the laboratory and perhaps in history too. Camus looked at warring Europe and noted:

> Mankind's long dialogue has come to an end – a vast conspiracy of silence has spread all about us, a conspiracy accepted by those who are frightened and rationalize their fears in order to hide them from themselves... "You shouldn't talk about the Russian cultural purge – it helps reaction." "Don't mention the Anglo-American support of Franco – it encourages communism." Fear is certainly a technique...
>
> We live in terror because persuasion is no longer possible, because man ... can no longer tap that part of his nature... which he recaptures in contemplating the beauty of nature of human faces; because we live in a world of abstractions, of bureaus and machines, of absolute ideas and crude messianism ... And for all who can live only in an atmosphere of human dialogue, and sociability, this silence is the end of the world.[26]

The reader may have noticed a number of interesting parallels between the dynamics of growth in T-Groups and what students have been trying to do, albeit clumsily, in campus rebellions.

1) If producing a social vacuum in a T-Group is growth enhancing, could not the same be said for stopping dead the bureaucracy of the university, stripping away the formal status of administrators, declaring a moratorium on routine busy-work, and re-examining every policy in the light of *human* criteria?

2) If confrontation in a T-Group develops the human resources of

participants by preventing the numerous forms of evasion, and by thrusting problems into the center of consciousness where they cannot be ignored, then might not the confrontation tactics of students achieve the same ends? We have already seen how difficult it becomes to torture people if you must continually look at them. The tactic of bringing every victim into close, prolonged confrontation with those who have let him suffer is potentially a good one.

3) If new ideas are hatched in small, informal, face-to-face groups, and if new levels of human insight and sympathy are attained therein, might not such groupings have much that is valuable to contribute to their universities?

4) Should the phenomenon of student rebellion be regarded as a reproach to the "good university" considering that it is a natural stage in the development of a successful T-Group? Can *any* group of authorities, however well endowed, know better than developing persons themselves the psycho-social climate that best facilitiates development? Perhaps the education of the young involves the process of relinquishing authority over them in tune with their growing needs for freedom.

5) The T-Group phenomena suggest that there may be no growth without some periodic anguish and initial regression. Hence a degree of disintegration in a college community may be a necessary prelude to higher integration, and creative disorder may be the necessary means to a superior order. If this is so the "calm detachment" sought by many academics is the dignified death of psycho-social development. The price of creative self-renewal is a periodic return to basic, "low status," human needs and visceral reactions.

6) I shall present evidence in later chapters to show that student rebels study the more "intuitive" subjects, the liberal arts, philosophy, and the "softer" social sciences, while the "empirical" and conservative students are more often in science and engineering. We saw in Table 18 that intuitive students did much better in T-Groups than the practical ones who needed some concrete data to observe before they could act. Perhaps, then, campus rebellion creates an atmosphere *in which the creatively and intuitively perceiving student thrives and the practically-minded are relatively handicapped.*

7) The success of the whole enterprise of higher learning must depend upon the adequate representation of human needs in the rapidly growing complex of abstract thought and knowledge. So long as socio-psychological disciplines remain such infant sciences the very process of abstraction, systemization, and computerized thinking will tend to swamp our meagre knowledge of humanity beneath a mass of hard, non-human, data from the developed sciences. Our intuitive needs and feelings are still the best psychology we have. That is why men must periodically strip themselves of technological, economic and scientific pre-calculations and say to each other, "what as mere human beings do we need and desire?" Only *after* these desires are expressed and agreed upon is it once more possible to reassemble the vast

technological and bureaucratic apparatus upon reordered human preferences, so that this apparatus is our servant instead of our master. This is the lesson of T-Groups. Is it also what rebel students have been trying to tell us?

8) But what happens when students, rebelling like T-Group participants, find themselves trapped in prolonged win-lose conflict with representatives of the *status quo*? Table 19 suggests quite clearly what happens and how revolutions are betrayed. It has the makings of a recurring tragedy for radical man.

I shall pursue these issues in Chapters VIII to IX.

## NOTES FOR CHAPTER VII

1. For an exposition of the more traditional T-Group see *T-Group Theory and Laboratory Method* by Leland P. Bradford, Jack R. Gibb and Kenneth D. Benne. "Far out" elaborations of the method are explained in *Joy* by William Schutz, New York: Grove, 1968 and *Ways of Growth*, John Mann and Herbert A. Otto (eds.), New York: Grossman, 1968.

2. *The Brothers Karamazov* by Fyodor Dostoevsky, trans. by Constance Garnett, New York: The Modern Library, 1943, p. 299.

3. The novel by Albert Camus, trans. by Stuart Gilbert, New York: Alfred A. Knopf, 1961.

4. Also by Albert Camus, trans. by Stuart Gilbert, New York: Vintage, 1958.

5. *Ibid.*, last page.

6. *The Trauma of Birth*, New York: Harcourt, Brace and World, 1929.

7. "Little Gidding" in *Four Quartets*, New York: Harcourt, Brace and World, 1943.

8. *No Exit and Other Plays*, by Jean-Paul Sartre, New York: Vintage, 1955, p. 18.

9. *Ibid.*, p. 23.

10. "Training in Conflict Resolution" by Murray Horwitz in *T-Group Theory and Laboratory Method, op. cit.*, p. 372.

11. Paul's First Epistle to the Corinthians, XIII, 12.

12. *The Act of Creation, op. cit.*, pp. 455-66. "Regression in the service of the ego" is a similar concept in psychiatric parlance. It may be necessary to undo faulty integrations to permit re-integration. The theory of "crisis intervention" associated with Gerald Caplan, 1961, also assumes that in the crisis, old integrations may have been pried apart so that new ones can be formed.

13. For a good account of early stages in T-Group growth and its similarity to primitive, tribal beliefs and customs see *Microcosm* by Philip E. Slater, New York: Wiley, 1966, especially Chapter I, "Deification as an antidote to Deprivation."

14. *Microcosm, op. cit.*, p. 67.

15. "Contribution to the evaluation of a management training program" by Michael Valiquet, unpublished doctoral dissertation, Mass. Institute of Technology, 1964.

16. "Organization Change and Development," unpublished doctoral dissertation, Harvard University, 1965.

17. For three examples of disaster which befell laboratory training at the hands of the wider culture, see *Personal and Organizational Change Through Group Methods*, H. E. Schein and Warren Bennis (eds.), New York: Wiley, 1965, pp. 221-32.

18. *Ibid.*, p. 227.

19. "The Reduction of Prejudice Through Laboratory Training" by Irwin Rubin, *Journal of Applied Behavioral Science*, Vol. 3, No. 1, 1967, pp. 29-51.

20. Schutz uses his F.I.R.O.-B. questionnaire (Fundamental Interpersonal Relations Orientation – Behavior) to measure the behavior an individual expresses, and the behavior he wants to be expressed, by others towards himself. The hypothesis is that T-Group training will bring these halves into balance, so that persons who wish either to control or to be controlled will reconcile or "synergise" these opposites.

21. See "Personality and Laboratory Style," Figure 4 in this chapter.

22. This has been tried with some success, see "Working with an 'Impersonal' T-Group" by Thomas C. Greening and Hubert S. Coffey, *Journal of Applied Behavioral Science*, Vol. 2, No. 4, 1966, pp. 401-11.

23. "Breakthrough in Organization Development," *op. cit.*

24. "Determinants of Support for Civil Liverties" in *The Berkeley Student Revolt, op. cit.*, p. 512.

25. "Personality Changes in College Students" by H. Webster, M. Freeman and P. Heist in *The American College*, Nevitt Sanford (ed.), New York: Wiley, 1962.

26. "Neither Victims nor Executioners" in *The Human Dialogue, op. cit.*, p. 301.

# Chapter VIII

## Corporate Radicalism

To use a term like "corporate radicalism" is to risk encountering the objections leveled by Herbert Marcuse against "clean bombs" and "luxury fall-out shelters." But the fact remains that studies of change in business organizations are among the very few records, adequately researched, of the processes of psycho-social development.

We saw in Chapter VI that such development could discriminate the more successful and creative companies from the less in all cases where the overall task demanded behaviors and interactions which were sufficiently complex. We also saw in the last chapter that executives trained in groups to improve their interpersonal skills will subsequently interact more effectively at work to the greater profit of their company.

The fact that radicalization of human relationships can increase economic profitability does not mean that most American corporations appreciate this fact or that they are any less conservative than other segments of the culture. Nor does it follow, as I mentioned in Chapter VI, that because higher profits are realizable from greater concern with human development, that human development will be realized from a greater concern for business and profits. Many goals and values in society are *potentially* synergistic, but in practice conflict, because of an excessive, "unjust" emphasis upon one goal at the expense of another.

Moreover profitability may be a good *description* of a creative system but a poor *prescription.* We have seen in earlier chapters that developing man progressively increases his sense of competence and self-fulfillment, but he does this by the capacity to suspend his own concern with immediate fulfillment and accruing competence and to focus more on concerns external to himself. What is true of the individual is probably true also of the modern corporation – a narrow concern with self-aggrandizement is an infantile disorder. Today as thousands of the most talented students are turning their backs on business, these corporations are confronted by the withered fruits of their own niggardly spirit.

Occasionally, however, the obsession with self-interest has been relaxed sufficiently to permit considerable growth. In this chapter, I shall examine one accidental and two deliberate programs of change in organizations, brought about by change-agents in the form of experimenters, consultants, and managers. The three examples are as follows.

1. The bungled experiment – Hawthorne revisited.
2. Existentialism for workers – The Scanlon Plan.
3. The manager as a healer of anomie – a study of an automobile plant.

In each case interventions were made in key segments of the cycles concerned, which induced an "upward spiral" of development. In each case I shall describe the nature and effect of these interventions before conceptualizing the results.

1. *The bungled experiment – Hawthorne revisited.*

The Hawthorne Experiment is an oft-told tale. Here I will summarize it as briefly as possible. Some investigators from the Harvard Business School under the supervision of Elton Mayo conducted a series of experiments in the Hawthorne works of Western Electric, beginning in the Spring of 1927 and continuing for several years. Although there were a number of different experiments the one that will concern us here is the Relay Assembly Test Room Experiment.

For this experiment two girls were chosen and asked to pick four other girls to work with them in the experimental room, where their job was to assemble telephone relays. The researchers planned to alter systematically such conditions of work as the number and duration of rest periods, improved diet, shorter work days and work weeks, and the effect of wage incentives. Each of these "independent variables" was expected to influence the productivity of the workers. Hence this was a "classic" form of experiment with cause and effect hypotheses. During the course of the experiment production was observed to rise steadily whether or not the "independent variables" were present. When towards the close of the experiment all rest periods, modified wage incentives, and the shorter working week were withdrawn, production remained substantially higher than it had been at the beginning of the experiment before the introduction of the variables. Whatever caused the rise from an average of forty-nine relays an hour to sixty-eight, it was not the experimental variables.

There are a number of standard reactions to the Hawthorne findings which tell us much about the commentators even if they leave us in the dark about the actual experiment.

One common reaction is "Beware-the-Hawthorne-effect." This is typical of those experimental psychologists with a mechanistic model of man. Much of their energies are directed to exorcising the ghost from the machine. For them the Hawthorne findings deserve not to be explained as much as to be explained *away*. One authority tells us it was a "bad experiment" and that this is the kind of distressing epiphenomenon which periodically haunts the unwary researcher who fails to sterilize his instruments.[1]

Even those working in therapy have warned "of the ever present danger of the Hawthorne effect."[2] For another commentator the real danger is that sympathy might break out between the experimenter and his subjects. The Hawthorne experiment fell right into this horrendous trap:

> The researchers discovered that the subjects were reacting not to the experimental manipulations of their physical environment, but to what they believed the researchers were interested in – higher production. The more aware the subjects are of the interests of the experimenter, the more likely to contaminate the results is this desire to give the experimenter what he wants.[3]

The insidious germs of human cooperation are likely at any moment to infect experimental purity. What some of us might suppose to be the Ascent of Man is revealed as a contamination of the scientific method! The "Hawthorne effect" is an unexpected and vulgar intrusion of human enthusiasms upon formal logic. It all comes from letting one's feelings be known instead of displaying ascetic detachment and iron self-control.

A second general reaction is the paternalistic one. Doctors hasten to remind us that such is the charisma of the healer and the learned man that they arouse the hope of sick and dependent persons. In this explanation the "Hawthorne effect" joins the "placebo-effect" as a touching tribute by the Common Man to his superiors. Even those patients in hospitals who for research purposes act as "controls" and receive inert substances are really fortunate to be in the healing presence of the medical profession.

Winston Churchill once remarked, "People often stumble over the truth but they pick themselves up and hurry along as if nothing had happened." The phenomenon of psycho-social development frequently bestirs itself, and just as frequently, social scientists will sniff disapprovingly and pass it by. One is reminded of a Maiden Aunt who having stumbled over lovers in the grass, mutters, "lack of control – total lack of control" and pulls the strings of her poke bonnet more narrowly around her grim little visage.

One of the reasons why the principles of dialogue, emotional intensity, and social development are rarely used to explain the Hawthorne findings, is that many social scientists would find these principles difficult to follow and rather unprofessional. Jerome Bruner recently chided his colleagues:

> Yet because our profession is young and because we feel insecure, we do not like to admit our humanity . . .we are not satisfied to forge distinctive methods of our own. We must reject whoever has been successful in the task of understanding Man – if he is not one of us. . . our articles. . . have about them an asceptic quality designed to proclaim the intellectual purity of our scientific enterprise.[4]

I would argue that, indeed, the Hawthorne Experiment was a developmental, if accidental, phenomenon and that the small group of experimenters and girls developed as "intellectual purity," and human insecurity collapsed.

In Chapter VII, I argued that five characteristics of a T-Group encouraged psycho-social development: the encounter with the absurd, the small group climate, the enforced confrontation, the moratorium, and the rebellion against authority. To what extent were these features also present in the Relay Test Room experiment?

In the first place, the girls had been withdrawn from the factory floor and were assembled together in quite unprecedented circumstances, in a small group confronting one another in a social vacuum largely bereft of formal structures. There was a moratorium on what constituted "good" or "productive" conditions and behaviors, since these were yet to be discovered. In addition, and this is seldom noted, when the "independent variables" failed entirely to account for the substantial increase in production, all concerned were plunged into an encounter with absurdity, with an enforced suspension of prior assumptions.

What about the rebellion against authority? Here is another feature of the Hawthorne Experiment which is frequently omitted from popular accounts. We are seldom reminded that the girls became so boisterous that the foreman from the shop floor who periodically visited in the early weeks threatened to replace them. The researchers, noting that the *foreman was upsetting the girls* and was not part of the experiment, arranged for him not to have access to the room. ("What a deadly blow to discipline" – as Captain Vere would say.)

With the foreman removed the girls became *so* "cheeky" that even the academics became miffed. Eventually two ringleaders were returned to the shop floor. But later in the experiment there was no longer any question of discipline. The "independent variables" were discredited. It was the girls who had the power now. They knew why they were working more effectively and the researchers were asking them for the reasons. "We have no bosses here!" cried the girls, sounding not unlike the Wobblies, and they were correct. The researchers, eager to discover any scrap of evidence that would explain the climbing productivity, hung on the girls' words, and immediately relented when the girls demanded veto power over any feature of the experiment they did not like.

One wonders how often, before or since, a group of young, immigrant, working class girls have demanded and been granted so much "Polish Power." *Nearly every conclusion the investigators finally came to was first voiced by these young girls.* They defined and created the new reality themselves, and the more they defined, the more their production improved.

But there were other reasons for the dramatic improvements in morale and productivity. Among these were the *kinds* of hypotheses being tested. Nearly all of these were such that, had they been upheld, they would have improved the conditions of the workers by giving them longer rest periods, shorter working hours, earlier lunch periods, better nourishment, more money, better health care, etc. The common theme behind nearly all the hypotheses being tested was the assumption that if workers were benefited *directly,* management would benefit *indirectly,* via the improved morale of the workers. Thus the hypotheses were essentially synergistic in nature, and were intended to discover whether the needs of managers and workers could be optimally combined. Moreover, the synergistic theme of the hypotheses was combined with the temporary suspension of managerial concern with raising production at the least possible cost. On the face of it, the hypotheses being tested would cost *more* and leave *less* time for productive work. A worker cannot turn out high production while resting, eating, and being doctored. Nor are costs held down by paying bonus wages.

At an implicit level Mayo was testing the supposition that persons who receive benefits from others, where the giver is genuinely risking permanent loss, will reciprocate in like style and perpetuate a mutually profitable exchange. What the girls responded to, then, was not the supposed differences in the independent variables but the self evident intention of Elton Mayo to seek an economic excuse for improving their conditions of work.

The experimental situation also changed the identities of the girls (segment b), their level of experienced competence (segment c), and the frequency with which they were confirmed (segment g). When they moved into the experimental setting they ceased being just workers and became co-experimenters. When the official hypotheses failed they became not just consultants but the sources of novel truth. Such rapid upgrading of their roles must surely have increased their sense of competence and fulfillment. Seldom has such a distinguished audience of visitors paid court to girls officially designated as semi-skilled assemblers. We are told that, not only were top management frequent visitors, but also "there was an intermittent stream of other visitors or consultants: industrialists, industrial relations experts, industrial psychologists, and university professors."

Another most important change was introduced into the relationships of the girls with the experimenters. For the first time in their working lives they could consistently believe that what authorities told them was authentic. It says much about the anomic conditions of factory life at Western Electric when we hear that the girls were terrified of their medical examinations, believing them to have a sinister purpose, and that they were surprised and overjoyed to receive the wage incentive for higher production which they had been promised. *It had proved almost impossible to convince them that management's promises would be kept.* In the past any improved effort on their part had been entirely swallowed up by the organization, which would promptly raise minimum acceptable standards.

One final point needs to be added upon the concept of an experiment. While I have earlier cast doubt upon the carefully controlled, unilaterally manipulated experiment with causes and effects, my reservations do not extend to the *idea of experimentation.* That two or more persons should regard their relationships as improvable through experimentation aimed at the mutual discovery of fresh experience is a *sine qua non* of psycho-social development. This concept was present in the Hawthorne Experiment and is absent in many of those experiments where the norms of good methodology are borrowed from the physical sciences.

The extensive improvement in productivity and psycho-social development between the early weeks of the experiment and its later stages is set out in Table 20. There is narrative evidence of growth in every segment of the cycle, and productivity rose by close on 40%. There is, however, *no* evidence, as there was in T-Group studies, that the skills and morale of the girls survived the completion of the experiment and the break-up of the group. This aspect was never studied.

There is a sad sequel to the Hawthorne studies. The findings were co-opted into the dominant mode of corporate thinking, and their radical implications were lost. So long as the experiments continued, the perspectives of the workers themselves greatly influenced the new emerging synthesis, but once the experiments were over, the researchers joined management in trying to institutionalize the findings. From this point on, the workers lost any control of the interpretation or the use to which the findings were put. Not surprisingly, the counselling program proposed by the researchers and installed with management's approval was an aborted brain-child. No management-worker dialogue went into its creation and it institutionalized only a pseudo-dialogue, with female counsellors trained to reflect sympathetically feelings expressed by the workers.

The conclusion which the academics drew was that kindness and attention to the needs, feelings, and troubles of the workers were profitable investments. Managers were willing to assent to this interpretation, but they obviously did not feel that *they* should spend their precious and busy time being tender towards workers. Like everything else these findings could be turned into a technique. If "kindness works," then hire kind, motherly females and plug them into the circuit.

Like the "luxury fallout shelter" and the "clean bomb" mentioned at the opening of this chapter, the solution attempted here was not a modification of managerial Tough Mindedness but the grafting on to it of a tender minded appendage. The division of labor could take care of the contradiction. The Puritan Ethic went about its business as usual with a department of "Corporate Momism" hitched incongruously to its rear.

The Counselling Program transgressed nearly all the dynamics of the cycle. Low status female counsellors were available as soft appendices into which

**Table 20**

**HOW CONDITIONS CHANGED IN THE COURSE OF THE HAWTHORNE EXPERIMENT**

| *Segments of Cycle* | *Pre-change Conditions* (before and in the early stage of the experiment) | *Post-change Conditions* (the later stages of the experiment) |
|---|---|---|
| Man exists freely | Company has concerted plan to instill Thrift into employees. Insurance firms encouraged by W.E. solicit employees and urge them through lectures and programs to protect their dependents.<br>Arrangements are made between W.E. and local savings banks to "save" employees wages which are withheld for this purpose. | Company rules intended to promote and maintain efficiency are abrogated in order to take "psychological factors" *out* of the experiment room. |
| | All employees join the Hawthorne Club which sponsors lectures, classes athletics, social activities etc. | Girls in the experimental room design their own recreational activities. |
| | Girls (chosen for experiment) are severely reprimanded for arguing with their foreman and researchers.<br>Researchers expel two girls from experimental room for "gross insubordination". Girls say, "There are too many bosses in the department". | Girls rejoice at "greater freedom ... absence of bosses" ... "opportunity to set ones own pace" ... "less supervision" ... "You can scream and have a good time in the test room". They say of researcher "He's no boss!" "Look at the way she tells her boss to shut up!"<br>When girls complain, the foreman and his discipline are barred from the room.<br>Verbal threats by researchers are ignored.<br>Girls take time off without asking permission of each other or researchers.<br>Girls get veto power over any features of the experiment they do not like. |

**Table 20 (Continued)**

| *Segments of Cycle* | *Pre-change Conditions* | *Post-change Conditions* |
|---|---|---|
| a) through the quality of his PERCEPTION.. | Girls refuse to believe that they will get higher pay and rewards for higher output | "The observer in his daily association with the girls grew to be very much interested in them. He displayed almost too great a sympathetic identification with the girls feelings and sentiments". |
| b) the strength of his IDENTITY | Girls are terrified of exposing themselves for periodic medical examinations. | Girls enjoy medical examinations. |
| c) and the synthesis of these into his anticipated and experienced COMPETENCE | Girls are afraid that the object of the experiment is to discover maximum possible output which will then be demanded of them and all other employees. | Girls realize that they can only benefit by experimenting. They are convinced that they can improve conditions and wages. |
| d) he INVESTS this with ...... *intensity* and *authenticity* in his human environment | "Definite promises were not the rule in supervisor-employee relationships." "Employees were very hesitant to answer questions frankly". "The girls laughed and talked 75% more than usual – were reprimanded by the foreman." | Girls are at last convinced after repeated promises that researchers have put all their cards on the table. Girls laugh with researchers, banter and tease them and become "often boisterous". Researchers persuade the girls that only "whole hearted" cooperation is experimentally meaningful. They should not pretend. |
| e) by periodically SUSPENDING his cognitive structures and RISKING himself | General and widespread distrust of management's sincerity. "Suspicious and apprehensive of authority is general". | Researchers confess themselves puzzled by results – seek the girls help. Girls learn to trust each other, help each other out in sickness, and do not question absences, assuming them to be necessary. |

**Table 20 (Continued)**

| *Segments of Cycle* | *Pre-change Conditions* | *Post-change Conditions* |
|---|---|---|
| f) in trying to BRIDGE THE DISTANCE to others | Reports are given of alienation unhappiness, and mutual exploitation on the main floor of the department | A new friendly spirit had developed – "by Period XIII apprehension of authority had almost entirely disappeared". |
| g) he seeks to make a SELF-CONFIRMING<br><br>SELF - TRANSCENDING IMPACT upon the other | Researchers discover that when the results from the experimental room are evaluated by officials from the larger department (from which the girls come) there is a continual tendency to underestimate and belittle the production figures.<br>Reprimands by the foreman to the girls are sullenly resented | Researchers carefully record "the opinions, fears, qualms, and anxieties of the girls" Their spontaneous remarks are given very careful attention. A constant stream of distinguished visitors come to see increasingly successful experiment. |
| h) and through a *dialectic* achieve a higher SYNERGY | Attempts are made by girls to control each other unilaterally, by larger department to control girls in the test room, by researchers to insist on cooperation from the girls while telling them to behave "naturally" | Girls use the researchers' statements against the researchers "but I don't *feel* like working ... You want us to be natural ..."<br><br>Girls strongly attack certain features of the experiment. They demand and secure changes.<br>A strong spirit of mutual assistance arises. Votes are taken on preferred conditions and then implemented.<br>The rest of the plant becomes proud of the test room and its results. |
| i) Each will attempt to INTEGRATE the FEEDBACK from this process into mental matrices of developing COMPLEXITY | Girls say that they never see any of the results from their hard work.<br>Bosses or other workers get all the benefit from what they produce. | Daily history sheets carefully record the output, statements, answers, and feelings of the girls, who can see the record and see its influence upon the researchers. Girls are also taught to calculate their own earnings and progress. |

Source: Chapters I to VIII, dealing with the Relay Test Room Experiment, in *Management and the Worker* by Fritz J. Roethlisberger and William J. Dickson. Harvard Univ. Press. Cambridge, Mass. 1943.

employees could discharge their grievances. In this way management would not be bothered by the blatherings of inarticulate and undistinguished persons, while the workers would of course be happy. No synergy was created between managers and workers, or between toughness and tenderness, feeling and intellect, distance and relationship, competence seeking and suspension. On the contrary, workers, tenderness, feeling, relationship, suspension and femininity would all be in *one* department: and management, toughness, intellect, distance, competence and masculinity would be all in the *other*. The latter would, of course, dominate the former. So much for the Hawthorne findings. Conservatism emerged unscathed.

How this was accomplished is illustrated in the second half of *Management and the Worker*. A worker who complained to his counsellor that "wages are too low" had his complaint therapeutically reinterpreted. What he "really" meant, only the sweet simple fellow did not get it right, was that owing to illness in his family his wages could not stretch far enough. The solution? Lend him the money.

Now that worker's original perspective about the inadequacy of his wages just happened to be an issue upon which ten million American working men had recently organized themselves. The most obvious analogy to the Relay Test Room Experiment was the massive unionization of American industry occurring between the time of the experiment (1927) and the publication of *Management and the Worker* (1939). But this analogy has never to my knowledge been drawn. The rebelliousness of the girls, their rejection of bosses, their veto over experimental conditions, their increased earnings, and their major contribution in providing the answers which made the researchers famous – these were "somehow" forgotten.

The behavior of Western Electric over the publication of the book *Management and the Worker* is illustrative of the extent to which the Hawthorne findings modified management's attitudes. The book became a best seller, being translated into several languages. Western Electric demanded and received half the royalties on the grounds that it had hosted the experiment. It then remembered that while Dickson, the junior author, had been working on the book, Western Electric had paid his salary, so it pocketed *his* share as well. (After all, why be generous? There's a special department for that.) Roethlisberger was so upset that he sent half of his quarter-share of the royalties to Dickson. So the company got three quarters and the two authors one eighth of the royalties each. As for the girls, who had told everyone the answers, they got nothing. The moral is that you can lead a horse to water, but you can't stop it drinking your share, and then fouling the water hole.[5]

A few years ago the whole counselling program was quietly abandoned.

2. *Existentialism for workers – the Scanlon Plan.*

The Scanlon Plan is a formula for management-worker cooperation, named after its creator, the late Joseph Scanlon. The plan also requires for its operation a social philosophy of management which is known as "Theory Y."

The Scanlon plan is a means of sharing the economic gains from improvements in economic performance. This is done by calculating a ratio between total manpower costs and units of output or sales. The reduction in this ratio through cost savings is partly or wholly distributed to employees in the form of a bonus. It is important that this bonus be directly related to the efforts of employees to improve economic performance and reduce per unit costs.

The plan operates through a series of worker cells on the shop floor and larger departmental meetings which integrate the plans and suggestions of the cells. The larger planning groups attempt to implement the creative ideas and proposals which emanate from employees, carefully noting what effect each of these innovations has in reducing the cost ratios for the whole plant, for the particular department concerned, and for other departments which may be affected. A previously agreed upon percentage of the total savings, ranging from 50% to 100%, is distributed equally among the workers in the form of a bonus. It is often possible to give workers the entire proceeds from the reduction of direct costs while the company profits from better use of its fixed assets and the lowering of indirect and overhead costs.

But this plan would be nothing but an empty formula without the social philosophy which guides its implementation. The late Douglas McGregor, a professor and industrial consultant at M.I.T., named this philosophy "Theory Y."[6] It is essentially a set of operating assumptions or perceptions of the other (segment a). Managers who adopt these assumptions and attempt to invest and actualise them (segments d and g) can learn to develop themselves and others, through the dynamic of the "self-fulfilling prophecy."

Just how powerful expectations and assumptions can be was revealed in a recent study of school children in grades one to four.[7] Certain children were picked completely at random, and their teachers were made to believe that psychological tests had revealed that these children would "spurt" in the coming year. The children were not told. A comparison of gains in I.Q. at the end of the school year showed that in most grades and especially the earlier ones, the children whose improvement was expected by the teacher had an average gain in I.Q. 50% to 100% greater than the other children. Interpersonal expectation is communicated in subtle ways by smiles, respectful listening, and nods of the head. Perhaps the children shared the pleasure of the teacher that her expectations were being confirmed. "This child is about to grow and respond to my help" is an assumption of amazing potency.

Theory Y is a similar attempt, without the deceit, to persuade managers that they can *will* the autonomous development of others – though not its precise manifestation. The assumptions are as follows:

I. The expenditure of physical and mental effort is as natural as play or rest.

II. The capacity to exercise a relatively high degree of imagination, ingenuity and creativity in the solution of organizational problems is widely, not narrowly distributed in the population. (Principles 1 and 2 are basic statements of the existential nature of psycho-social development as a self-generating, natural phenomenon, which seeks competence in relation to its environment through the reconciliation of "is" and "ought.")

III. Man will exercise self-direction and self-control in the service of objectives to which he is committed. (In other words, once the requirements of the organization can be harnessed to the inner needs of employees, then the cyclical process of human development will be discovered to have its own authenticity and self-regulating dynamics.)

IV. Commitment to objectives is a function of rewards associated with achievement. (*i.e.* The confirmation of an employee's investment will increase the risk and intensity of his subsequent investments.)

V. The average human being learns, under proper conditions, not only to accept but also to seek responsibility. (*i.e.* Where competence is increased through investment, a natural corollary is to accept and seek to understand the feedback from investment).

VI. Under conditions of modern industrial life, the intellectual potentialities of the average human being are only partially utilized: (*i.e.* It is the responsibility of managers to confirm and to call forth the unrealized potential among employees for psycho-social development and complex intellectual integration).

In short, the principles of Theory Y either stimulate directly or draw attention to segments (a) (c) (d) (h) and (i) of the cycle, along with their creative, existential qualities.

To return to the Plan itself. Since it consists of a network of small groups or cells, whose predominant task is to create, incubate, and implement novel ideas, such groups have obvious similarities to the T-Groups discussed in Chapter VII. The shop-floor cells experience the absurdity of meeting with an agenda that says simply "create." They have a small group climate, a moratorium from busy-work, a mutual confrontation, and rebellions against the *status quo* which they regard as something to be periodically dismantled and resynthesized.

But there is more to the Scanlon Plan than small group dynamics. Let us proceed "around the cycle" to see how every one of the segments is stimulated by the Plan and by its style of implementation.[8]

*The Plan and man's free existence*

It is a very rare company which announces that the prime duty of the ordinary worker is to render himself extraordinary by the creation of productive ideas. Of course suggestion boxes are nothing new but these are for idle moments when the worker is resting from the obedient discharge of orders from above.

But the Scanlon Plan is a "revolution" in the sense that initiative can now come from the very lowest levels in the organization, and each man is first and foremost a creator (if he wishes to be) and second one who implements the flow of ideas. Mind is valued far above muscle, and it is assumed that once men and groups have generated ideas, the requirement for the strenuous, even repetitive work needed to translate those ideas into practice, will be forthcoming as a natural consequence of their need to give their ideas birth.

It is not possible to have creativity without rebellion against old ideas. Every constructive act must also be an act of negation to that which preceded it. A basic principle in implementing the Plan is that *management must learn to take the gaff.* There are repeated warnings by consultants and researchers that the Plan cannot succeed if managers stand on their dignity. "The men will invest him with the dignity he deserves – no more, but no less." There are frequent shouting matches, since the participants care deeply wherever personal ideas are at stake.

*a) The impact of the Plan on the PERCEPTION of employees.*

In the traditional plant the division of labor typically reduces the worker's contribution to a small, repetitive piece of the overall plan. The programmed harmony of individual techniques makes strong demands for the precision, the punctuality and the subordination of each mechanical part and sub-assembly to the overall process of convergence and final assembly of completed products. The entire process is governed by *non*-dialectical, formal logic of which P.E.R.T. (program, evaluation and review technique) is an example. Given the dollar cost and estimated time for each component in the productive process, a "critical path" can be worked out mathematically and programmed on computers. Obedience to the logic of the computer is then required of each worker along with a minimization of those "human relations problems" which might disturb the pre-established harmony of a mechanical universe.

Despite the logical beauty of these computer programs in which every circuit pleases and only man is vile, their wide vision of things economic, and mechanical, including Conservative Man outlined in Chapter I, is very narrowly shared. It is of little psychological benefit to the worker himself that he is a part of a more inclusive whole perceived by Operations Research, if this whole is totally beyond his comprehension, and if he himself feels like a box car in a marshalling yard, shunted from place to place.

Undoubtedly the master plan creates economic and mechanical synergies which enrich employees and which lower costs for consumers. But the master plan could hardly create *psychological* synergy because only the less ennobling aspects of men – their needs for rest, money, food, and elimination are programmed into the computer. The capacity of the human being to create and constantly reshuffle his preferences is not a phenomenon with which the computer can deal.

No wonder, then, that surveys taken prior to the installation of the Scanlon Plan have found workers with little perception of how their action ramifies upon anyone, especially other departments. They are part of a system whose operations are largely mysterious to them and of which they have a worm's eye view. The worker knows his bench and his mates and "the rest is propaganda."[10] That blue collar factory workers tend to be isolationist and segregationist as we saw in Chapter VI, is then hardly surprising. People beyond the range of the worker's perception have been confounding him all his life. What more can he expect from black men and foreigners?

The Scanlon Plan works with a set of simple ratios which are explainable to all. The department has a ratio of controllable costs to output. Hence higher output for the same costs, or the same output for lower costs will improve the ratio, and all or most of the money from that improvement is directly contributed by the innovative members to others in the department. Perhaps for the first time in his life the worker can comprehend that his brains and effort "register" in the workings of the company, show up on its indices and make friends for him among his associates.

He will also discover that the ingenuity of others – with whose existence he has previously been unconcerned – is periodically padding his earnings. He is likely to thank them and ask them how he can help. Where once he may have rushed through his work, risking and ignoring a high rate of defective pieces and regarding work inspectors as his natural enemies, he now sees that his carelessness is making other people's work difficult, and that his failure may show up in analyses with which everyone has become extremely interested. He is now part of a community, wherein relative contributions and interdependence are highly visible. This is a system he can understand and begin to control.

b) *The impact of the Plan upon the IDENTITIES of employees.*

In Chapter VI, I argued that the role a man plays in an organization fixes and constrains his identity. Only in the companies with low degrees of structure could a technician, for instance, become an engineer. Those who clutch hold of the system, to ensure that their official role shores up their identity, may find themselves "prisoners of deadly forms," commanded by the system to commit conscienceless acts. In contrast, we saw that T-Groups, by breaking the structural mould, freed their members to redefine themselves in radical ways.

In a plan where the worker's primary role is to create he can become anything he dares so long as he can persuade others to accept and confirm him. If he wants to change his job or create a better fit between man and machine, he has *carte blanche* to discover where his greatest talents lie. If he makes successive contributions worthy of an engineer, so that all members – including the engineers – take home several dollars traceable to his efforts, who would *stop* this man from becoming an engineer? Those who earlier pocketed the fruits of his intelligence could hardly now oppose him, even though the word "janitor" were printed on his file. In a creative department, each man's identity is under his control.

c) *The impact of the Plan upon anticipated and experienced COMPETENCE.*

A man's competence, it will be recalled, is his personal synthesis of talents and resources which he chooses to bring to the solution of problems. Such competence may include equal or unequal parts of ingenuity, muscular strength, concentration, critical capacity, manual dexterity, social skills, patience and an eye for exactitude, etc. The crucial question is what brings these catalogues of virtues into active relationship with the overall task?

The traditional approach has been for management to "set standards" of various kinds and reward each worker via incentives for his approximation to management's ideal. There are many problems in this approach. The high producing, uncomplaining, hyper-active, and management-oriented worker has little time or inclination to contribute social rewards to his fellow workers. Not only does he threaten them by a high performance which compares invidiously with their own, but his efforts also can lead to a raising of minimum acceptable standards and hence to more work for commensurately less pay. The "rate-buster," through his *lack* of rebellious existence, contributes nothing to the shared existence of workers.

Everything we learned in Chapter V about those conforming persons who respond to the commands of authority, in preference to the needs and even the pain of their peers, would lead us to shudder at the kind of man which management typically seeks to reward and promote. Technically efficient, he yet spreads anomie like a plague through the system.

So long as managers do not recognize that the right to create, rebel and resynthesize is fundamental to human growth, then the antagonism between managers and workers, the social ostracism by peers of those workers who obey the pressures of authority, and the repression by management of those rebellious workers whose *potential* contribution is by far the greatest, will continue to cripple the system.

The Scanlon Plan obviates this crippling condition by starting from totally different premises. Instead of assuming that "good standards" are something *external* to workers, which can be derived from Holy Writ, the Puritan Ethic, or Scientific Management, and to which workers should then aspire worshipfully, the Plan assumes that good standards are *within* workers and managers and are discoverable through processes of personal expression.

Allow men to create and communicate and all that catalogue of virtues which comprise overall competence will look after itself. Men will develop patience, exactitude, and manual dexterity in order to prove that their own ideas – or those of their group – are viable. They will learn to play the roles of exacting critics because their own creativity demands it. A recent study of creative persons was surprised to discover "the brief-case syndrome." Highly creative persons often imposed disciplined habits upon themselves as the necessary concommitant of their work. Their rebellions flirt with chaos to achieve a higher order.[11]

*d) The impact of the Plan upon INVESTMENTS, authentic and intense.*

To those who have wrought their own novel synthesis, it is a matter of deep commitment to expose these ideas to others for confirmation and feedback. It would also be singularly useless to create and then fail to communicate one's competence authentically. With inauthenticity neither confirmation nor feedback is really meaningful.

Managers have long complained that workers restrict output, fudge records, collude in "goldbricking" and "featherbedding" and in various ways defeat managerial purposes. The reason is simple. "Managerial purposes" preclude the developmental competence of workers. Where obedience to external standards is demanded the only path to growth and self-expression is to sabotage external standards. Had workers ever been permitted to communicate ideas which were personally valuable and meaningful, then intense investments, authentically expressed, would have been a natural outcome. This is precisely what happens when the Scanlon Plan is put into operation.

e) *The impact of the Plan upon the capacity of employees for SELF-SUSPENSION and RISK-taking.*

In the usual management-worker relationship there are several deterrents from taking personal risks. With the suggestion box system a man who shares his idea risks having it stolen and thrust into the box by others. There is seldom any incentive to develop ideas in concert. Suggestions are usually received by some remote committee, and raw ideas are evaluated in the worker's absence. Small payments are often made merely to keep ideas coming, and when genuinely useful ideas are presented there are insufficient funds to reward them and too much development work still to be done before anyone can be sure that the ideas are viable. Under these circumstances workers feel at best patronized and at worst exploited. Since the same idea may have occurred to several people and theoretical possibilities can exist long before their economic application, it is not unusual to find workers who have received ten dollars for what they are convinced was a "million dollar" idea.

So long as managers insist on holding the initiative over workers, the latter will tend to regard any new methods as a threat or a nuisance. Every fresh initiative by management will call forth some countervailing move by workers to thwart it and restore the antagonistic balance of powers. Far better, then, not to give management any ideas. They will only re-time the jobs, re-evaluate the standards and oblige the work force to search for new loopholes. Why invent trouble?

Where workers *do* invent new methods they often hide these from their supervisors, do the standard work in less time than expected and create discretionary time for their own use. This simple need for dignity and freedom from external pressure is then seen by management as proof positive of mendacity and laziness. Management reflects on the High Standards they set, the sparkling symmetry of their grand design, and the unworthiness of the swinish multitude who desecrate these ideals.

In one reported case an engineer discovered that a worker had invented a new tool but was hiding it. The engineer crept into the shop at night, borrowed the tool, copied it, and replaced it. But the worker had baited the trap with an unworkable substitute. Much money and managerial dignity were wasted in producing useless tools![12]

The Scanlon Plan greatly increases the willingness of workers to risk themselves in efforts on behalf of each other and the company. This is much easier to do when exploitation is rendered very unlikely through the agreement, *in advance,* that a certain percentage of cost savings will go to employees, and that the credit for the idea will belong to its inventor. The anxieties of creativity are high enough, without the fear that one's ingenuity will be lost in a morass of red tape, or will be exploited by strangers, only to bring dislocation to one's friends at work.

Risk also entails the temporary, "unselfish" suspension of one's own perspectives in favor of others. This is extremely important not only for the rebellious person searching for new attachments, but also for those who must learn to tolerate and comprehend the novel imputs of others and reward creativity. By installing a *group* bonus, the Plan teaches employees that the creativity of one is the shared existence of the many, and that the risk and anxiety inherent in suspension are very much worth it. Creativity is too often experienced not only as disorder but as selfish disorder to boot. Creative minorities like the Jews have been persecuted because their deviance was seen as threatening reliable communication. Temporary self-suspension is the crucial dynamism that renders false the dichotomy between selfishness and unselfishness, individual and the group, rebellion and confirmation. In so doing it lays the basis for synergy within and between cycles. The Scanlon group bonus skillfully leads the lonely creator back into harmony with his environment, while making a further break (and reconciliation) with that environment a good risk.

f) *Impact of the Plan on the capacity to BRIDGE THE DISTANCE.*

Some of the principal exponents of the Scanlon Plan are trades unionists,[13] and many are the Scanlon companies in which ancient enemies have combined to increase output and ingenuity.

Workers come to understand that managers are not just parasites sucking their blood and that the coordination of work is an extremely valuable skill. In some Scanlon Plans there are plant-wide ratios in addition to departmental ones, so that workers discover that a good manager in department A has wrought changes that considerably improve (or reduce) the ratio in their own department. In any event they no longer remain indifferent to persons previously remote. They learn to make sensitive adjustments for the benefit of distant persons and in so doing learn to share their perspectives.

Since creative persons are, by definition, widely differentiated from others, the capacity to tolerate and reward originality develops hand in hand with the capacity to understand persons in differentiated roles and activities in remote parts of the company.

g) *Impact of the Plan on the capacity of employees to achieve SELF-CONFIRMING, SELF-TRANSCENDING IMPACTS.*

To encourage creative efforts but to fail in providing confirmation and transcendance would be an invitation to disaster. The Scanlon Plan must rely heavily, therefore, upon the skilled acceptance of potentially productive ideas.

The innovator is encouraged to share his ideas with his immediate circle who form a nucleus for screening, communicating, modifying and implementing the idea. The idea is then presented, in as finished or practical form as the group's resources permit, to a departmental committee. Depending on its scope, the idea may go to a committee at the plant level. In any event and in all instances, the sponsoring group will receive the fullest hearing.

The greatest care of all is taken with those few ideas which are finally rejected. It is absolutely essential that the idea's contributor understands exactly why it could not be implemented. The least his colleagues owe him is a detailed explanation which will prevent his repeating a mistake and which will enable him to take better aim the next time.

Where ideas are successful, the all-important ratio between costs and productivity acts as a public signal which confirms and publicizes the creative success of individuals. It is frequently possible to trace the distribution of, say, $1,000 dollars to the creativity, advocacy, and receptivity of specific men. It would be a mistake to assume that the Plan stimulates only the technically creative person. Rather, the organization comes to appreciate the critic, the interpreter and the patron of creative enterprise, along with those able to turn ideas into concrete applications.

The capacity of a Scanlon plant to appraise and implement ideas was exemplified by the Lapointe Company, a pioneer of the Plan. Here 513 innovative plans were brought before the plant-wide committee during the first year of operation. By the year's end, 380 had been successfully implemented, 28 were about to start, 65 had been rejected, and the rest were pending a final decision. If we exclude this last category the implementation of ideas is running about 85%.[14]

h) *The impact of the Plan on a dialectic leading to SYNERGY.*

We have already noted that the informal shop floor cells, the departmental committees, and in some Plans, the plant-wide committee, all provide arenas for mutual confrontation and the clash of dialectic. Each stage involves a greater "distance" and higher risks, but motivation to go to the next stage comes from accruing confirmation and evolving competence.

The necessity for dialectic is widely recognized by exponents of the plan. If plants are unionized it is axiomatic that the union should be intelligent and aggressive. What is needed are representatives who are determined that full justice will be done to the ingenuity of their members and who engage in vigorous advocacy of their client's ideas.

The same cost/productivity ratio that signals the contribution of "distant" persons and publicly confirms them, is also and primarily a symbol of synergistic processes. The ratio dramatizes for all to see, *that there is always enough to go around when human minds in active relationship can create surplus.* It is this realization that enables men to suspend simultaneously their self-concerns, trusting in their mutual capacity to retrieve more than they hazarded.

The Plan also illustrates the reconciliation of potential opposites within the cycle. Distance and relationship, rebellion and confirmation, self enrichment and the enrichment of others, suspension and reintegration, risk and reward, all can be unified when the ratio signals a gain.

i) *Impact of the Plan upon the INTEGRATION of FEEDBACK and COMPLEXITY.*

Finally the cost/productivity ratio – among its many functions – also performs as a "feedback loop." By investing their ideas in the environment employees learn more and more about the operations and possibilities of that environment, and many lessons come with popularity and money attached.

This feedback loop is far more useful and meaningful than its counterparts in the more traditional profit sharing plans. The overall profits of a company may be boosted or eclipsed by factors way beyond the control of the work force. The world price of raw material may rise, a competitor may go into liquidation. During such periods the work force may be unusually inventive or slack, and yet find their inventiveness punished or their slackness rewarded by coincidental events. In these circumstances it becomes extremely difficult to learn by experience or to feel in control of one's own destiny. Cost saving calculated on the basis of controllable costs is a means of instruction, while profit sharing is by comparison a lottery.

Workers discover that the figures put out by the controller's office are actually there to *help* them. Through joint meetings they discuss which cost figures should be available to them, at what intervals and in what form. Instead of control figures being a mysterious rationale for *ex post facto* blame and punishment, they are used to alert employees at all levels to unfavorable or favorable trends. An important principle of the Plan is *equal* access to that information which is used in judging joint performance. Managers are not permitted to keep "cards up their sleeves" with which to confound employees during arguments.

In one important respect the Plan differs from the rhetoric of many radical reformers and trades union leaders. It has often been fashionable to stress the dirty, back breaking toil which workers must do, and via theories of value to state that this is "real" work while the function of the entrepreneur and manager is but to exploit the labor of others. While some reformers romanticized "real work," others have described it as so degrading that minimum work and maximum leisure have been made the substance of demands.

The Scanlon Plan is among the few radical solutions which treat the worker as capable of *complex thought and learning* on the job and which regard his muscles as mere adjuncts to a lively mind capable of infinite expansion.

In Table 21 we see that the installation of the Scanlon Plan in a number of plants has immediate impacts on all segments of the cycle, stimulating them into development. All the descriptions in Table 21 are taken directly from the writings of researchers who have observed the Plan at work.

Social scientists often scoff at such idealistic descriptions. They point out, with some justice, that employees, consultants and researchers, all tend to become imbued with humanistic enthusiasm for the New Dawn. In this mood they run the danger of describing, not any permanent changes in the level and capacity of human functioning, but a "honeymoon period" of inflated expectations. This criticism is given added potency by various theories of cognitive dissonance or cognitive consistency. For instance a person committing himself deeply to a cause will tend to "see" improvement, because failure is cognitively dissonant with his expectations and hence difficult to accept. A patient who has spent $10,000 and two years in psychotherapy will tend to regard himself as improved – since the alternative is distressing to say the least.

Enough has been said in this volume so that no apologies are required for human enthusiasm, even ecstasy. They are concomitants of development and the fact that they create methodological problems is small excuse for ignoring

**Table 21**

**THE ORGANIZATIONAL CLIMATE BEFORE AND AFTER THE INSTALLATION OF THE SCANLON PLAN**

| *Segments of the Cycle* | *Before the Plan* | *After the Plan* |
|---|---|---|
| Man exists freely | There exist only very circumscribed opportunities for workers to think or to create. Obedience to overall organizational plans is required. The "good" worker conforms to standards set by management. | Every worker is a potential cretor. He can do anything, be anything, or create anything which he can persuade others to confirm as useful to the joint enterprise. The "good" worker creates the standards which he then fulfills. |
| a) PERCEPTION | Worker's vision is confined to his own small section of the plant. | Workers understand the needs of one another and the contribution to their own function of the many different roles and persons in the organization. |
| b) IDENTITY | Workers are confined by their externally designated roles and their often narrow and repetitive tasks. | A worker can attempt to improve any existing function or propose a new function in any part of the company, thereby creating for his own future a new identity and role. |
| c) COMPETENCE | Workers are saddled with low status jobs and can seldom shake off the conviction of management that they are only fit to take orders and obediently discharge them. | Workers can, through their own innovative ideas render themselves valuable and irreplaceable to all concerned. |
| d) INVESTMENT *authentic & intense* | Restriction of output, "featherbedding" "goldbricking" and many other ingenious methods of defeating managerial purposes are noted. | 513 innovative plans are received in the first year at Lapointe Company. Workers are excited and make strenous efforts to advocate and demonstrate the superiority of their own ideas. |
| e) SELF-SUSPENSION & RISK | Workers are fearful of offering or implementing new ideas in case management grabs the profits and reorganizes their schedules with more trouble for relatively less pay. | Workers take temporary pay cut to improve company's competitive position and get higher wages in the end when new contracts are won. |

**Table 21 (Continued)**

| *Segments of the Cycle* | *Before the Plan* | *After the Plan* |
|---|---|---|
| e) (continued) SELF SUSPENSION & RISK | Suggestion box system makes workers hide ideas from each other. With no suggestion system workers hide ideas from management but implement them secretly to get more time off. | Engineers cancel their own vacations to complete a new design. The product is a great success and engineers become heroes of the company.<br>Opportunities for progressive increases in risk and self exposure as new ideas are shared with wider and wider environment. |
| f) BRIDGING THE DISTANCE | Cold War exists between management and workers, with no real confrontation and a widespread feeling of isolation and alienation. | Groups who have nurtured creative ideas, confront the screening committees face to face. |
| g) SELF-CONFIRMING SELF-TRANSCENDING | Workers efforts and ideas are swallowed up in the vastness and impersonality of the plant. There is little proof of their existence.<br>Ideas are often rejected for no understandable cause | Successful new ideas are publicly confirmed and distributed in the form of a shared bonus. The most creative persons become the most valued.<br>85% of new ideas actually transcend the mind of their creators to become reality. Reasons for rejection are very carefully explained. |
| h) *Dialectic* leading to a higher SYNERGY | Unilateral punishments, dismissals and arbitrary commands are answered with walk-outs, strikes, go slows and sabotage. Attempts to bargain deadlock.<br>High producing workers are often ostracized. Workers must choose between productivity and mutual affection | There is often stormy, always animated dialectic as union and workers insist on the validity of their new ideas. Managers respond likewise. Highests producers help to train other men and become popular instead of socially ostracized. Money and affection become synergistic. |
| i) INTEGRATION of FEEDBACK and COMPLEXITY | There is no way for workers to discover a departmental or plant-wide trace of their previous efforts. Little possibility exists of learning from their working experience of anything but the mechanical routine of their job. | The indices and ratios record for all to see the significance of their several contributions, and provide them with clues for new opportunities. They also receive much verbal feedback from those who stand to benefit from their ideas. |

Source: *The Scanlon Plan ... A Frontier in Labor Management Cooperation.* by Frederick G. Lesieur. (ed) Cambridge: M.I.T. Press, 1958 their importance to the human psyche. But it must be acknowledged that the deliberate arousal of hope, followed by variations upon the question "are things improving?" may not provide meaningful evaluation.

It therefore becomes important to ask whether reported changes were more than temporary and whether changes also occurred in non-experiental indices. Note the use to which humanistic psychology can put so-called "hard data." They are used to establish consistency between "inner" experiential and "outer" environmental phenomena. An experience of development is validated *if it has the expected and desired impact upon the environment.* We do not fall into the anti-humanist trap of the "methodolators" who claim that only non-experiential data are measurable and hence meaningful, and we avoid the snare of the "psychedelic Left" which regards transcendent and oceanic feelings as sufficient ends in themselves, which it is futile to symbolize, measure, or submit to intellectual discipline.

There is substantial evidence that the enthusiasms engendered by the Scanlon Plan do manifest themselves as anticipated in higher productivity, lower costs, and increased bonuses. Table 22 shows the average gain in efficiency, over and above the base rate, for ten typical Scanlon companies, chosen from more than fifty because they were set up with very similar control indices. Efficiency was measured by comparing the volume of saleable production with total payroll costs, excluding the bonus. The figures were adjusted for changes in prices, wages, and product mix occurring after the base period.

We can see that on average the annual increase in efficiency is 23.1%, and that improvement continues many months after the installment of the plan for the entire two years of the survey. In five of the ten plants improvement accelerated in the second year well beyond any honeymoon period. In two plants the second year's improvement was over 40%.

Compare this situation with the plight of Detroit automobile workers described in Chapter VI, Table 13. Many of the latter were anomic, alienated, tense, neurotic, frustrated, and bigoted. They were increasingly so where the simplicity, repetitiveness, and machine timed nature of work were greatest, and least so where the work was skilled and complex.

Now few if any of the Scanlon companies had an overall productive task which was *more* complex than the manufacture of automobiles. Hence the degree of overall simplicity or complexity is unlikely to be the crucial determinant in this comparison. The more probable explanation is that while the Detroit companies had the usual pattern of complexity at the top of the hierarchy with increasing degrees of simplicity towards the bottom, the Scanlon plants *shared* the available complexity with all employees.

There are, of course, numerous difficulties, anxieties, and resistances to the installation of the Plan. It is no more guaranteed to succeed than the process of development itself, which involves irreducible elements of risk and

**Table 22**

**AVERAGE INCREASES IN PRODUCTIVE EFFICIENCY IN TEN PLANTS FOLLOWING THE INTRODUCTION OF SCANLON PLANS**

*% Increase in Productivity Ratings*

| *Company* | *First Year Relative Efficiency* | *Second Year Relative Efficiency* | *Two-Year Avg. Relative Efficiency* |
|---|---|---|---|
| A | 14.9 | 10.9 | 12.9 |
| B | 21.9 | 12.7 | 17.3 |
| C | 16.7 | 13.2 | 15.0 |
| D | 36.7 | 29.3 | 33.0 |
| E | 28.9 | 49.4 | 39.2 |
| F | 32.9 | 42.9 | 37.9 |
| G | 38.7 | 25.1 | 31.9 |
| H | 14.1 | 16.5 | 15.3 |
| I | 12.9 | 23.2 | 18.1 |
| J | 6.8 | 13.7 | 10.3 |
| Avg. (unweighted) | 22.5 | 23.7 | 23.1 |

Source: *The Scanlon Plan. op. cit.* Table 21.

existential anxiety. Trouble often occurs with the low level supervisors, who feel stripped of their authority. They can be as reactionary as the petite bourgeoisie in wider political communities. Some trades union leaders have been in opposition so long that doing anything that will help management seems a betrayal. Some top managers regard the role of listening and reacting to initiatives from below as an abdication of authority.

But the fact remains that the Plan had succeeded in over fifty companies by 1958 and more have been added since. It has succeeded in large plants and small ones, with complex technologies and relatively simple ones, in unionized and nonunion plants.

3. *The Manager as a healer of Anomie – a study of Plant Y.*

In 1963 "Plant Y" of a large automobile company was on the verge of total breakdown. Losing money at an accelerating rate, it was the worst in its division in indices of productivity, absenteeism, labor grievances, safety, and turnover among others. It had recently suffered walk-outs and a series of wild-cat strikes. The manager was close to nervous exhaustion and would tape record all his instructions to subordinates in an attempt to prove later that he had given them! The social system was a nest of hatreds, frustration, and despair. The description given by researchers fits almost perfectly into the Anomic Cycle outlined in Chapter IV. Table 23 summarizes the grave situation which faced the new manager, Matthew Cooley, when he arrived to take over the plant in 1953.[15]

I will first detail the action taken by Cooley to heal the anomic system, and show that it was equivalent to stimulating key segments of the cycle into growth. Second, I shall conceptualize the changes which the researchers noted three years later. Cooley's strategy may be considered under the following heads:

Breaking out of the vicious cycle
Instituting lateral transfers
Promoting anxiety tolerance, dialectic, and synergy
Restoring initiative to the various supervisory levels
Repairing the feedback loop

*Breaking out of the vicious cycle.*

Cooley's very arrival resulted from the dismissal of the previous manager, whose growing panic and exhaustion were doubtless exacerbated by the increasing imminence of his own demise. The parent company had leant heavily on this manager to account for his poor performance and he had exerted unrelenting pressure on *his* subordinates all the way to the bottom of the hierarchy, where the union fought back and the men sought alternative employment in record numbers. The entire system was gripped by authoritarian and hysterical spasms.

In this atmosphere no one hazarded an original thought. Each superior assuming that his subordinate was malevolently unenterprising, would proceed to fulfill his own assumption by his threatening and uncompromising manner of issuing orders. With no one daring to question foolish orders, they were implemented with increasingly disastrous consequences, which only confirmed the suspicion of superiors that their subordinates while outwardly compliant were secretly saboteurs.

As can be seen from Table 23, column one, it was a *regressive spiral* feeding on itself. Top management at the corporate headquarters had seemingly forgotten nothing and learned nothing. They gave Cooley a *carte blanche* to follow the dismissal of the previous manager with a Great Purge – to "clear out the dead wood." The previous manager had *himself* followed this advice when he was first appointed and over sixty heads had rolled – and now his own.

Luckily Cooley knew better. As a first step he moved to cut the fear out of the system, halt the Gadarene Rush, and restore to employees the capacity to risk, suspend, and control their fate. He called everyone together and announced, "I don't believe in firing a lot of people and using threats and fear." He told them frankly that the plant had a bad reputation – but not with him. He was assuming that everyone was capable of productive and skilful work until the opposite was proved. He was not interested in catching people out – only in helping them do a good job.

By the end of the first year only three supervisors had been asked to leave – a "purge" of one twentieth of the size of the previous one.

*Instituting lateral transfers*

Since Cooley had found the plant in a state of "clan warfare" with nearly every department and sub-department locked in mutual recrimination, he decided to set up a wide system of lateral transfers. Combatants would learn at first hand about the experience of "the enemy." Later they could be switched back to their former positions. At the very first meeting he rearranged all the seating so that the cliques were broken up and people found themselves uncomfortably close to former enemies.

*Promoting anxiety tolerance, dialectic and SYNERGY*

The relaxation of fear and pressure and the breaking up of cliques did something to deter the old and unsuccessful habits of anxiety reduction, by which risk and suspension were evaded, but it was not enough.

Departments in conflict would control their anxiety in at least two very dysfunctional ways. They would fail to reveal authentically the full extent of the information in their possession, hiding anything that might be used to criticize them. Where disputes broke out between low echelon supervisors

**Table 23**

**THE ORGANIZATIONAL CLIMATE AT PLANT Y BEFORE THE ARRIVAL OF MATHEW COOLEY AND TWO YEARS LATER**

| *Segments of the Cycle* | *Before* | *Two Years Later* |
|---|---|---|
| Man exists freely | "Fear, that's the trouble. No one questions an order. In the meetings we have, they just give us hell." "It's not just the foremen, some of the department heads yell at us and the men." "You can't change the system." | "I can make innovations off my own hook." "We got the green light to go ahead and do something." 21 out of 25 foremen report a substantial decrease in the number of direct orders |
| a) PERCEPTION | Each person and subgroup wears "departmental blinders" and is in a state of private obsession with their own troubles. | "One of the big changes ... is the way foremen and inspection people view each other ... Inspection will always tell you when something is wrong but they understand the foreman's problems ..." More "global perspectives" were achieved. |
| b) IDENTITY | "You can't be a good foreman at the same time that you're scared .." "They are scared and they hide behind their authority which is pretty shaky .." | "This plant now recognizes the worth of the individual." "We broke through the wall of secrecy and suspicion." |
| c) COMPETENCE | "I roll with the punches...... get butterflies in my stomach.." | "The way I look at it is this. Before it was push, push, push, all the time. Now it's go, go, go." "Fear was no longer the motivating force ..." |
| d) INVESTMENT *authentic & intense* | "The foremen under me don't make any decisions. They're scared to. I've had my boss come in and say, "Get this done", but he never suggested how it should be done or asked me how I thought it should be done." Very low scores registered on index of Shared Information. Refusal to disclose evidence on which others were being judged and punished. | Ratio of "downward" to "upward" initiation shifts from 5 to 1, to 2 to 1. Cooley levels with all and asks departments to do so with each other. There is a large increase in index of Shared Information. |

**Table 23 (Continued)**

| *Segments of the Cycle* | *Before* | *Two Years Later* |
|---|---|---|
| e) SELF - SUSPENSION & RISK | Many Games are played like "pulling rank" "going through correct channels", "following the book" and "getting backing from the top" in order to force the other's compliance. "He puts on the heat and we can't talk back." Impersonal mechanisms like quality control are used to punish persons and departments. | Cooley goes around plant "in old beat up jacket" and "never acts superior". Large increase occurs in informality, mutual trust and give and take, with much less rule orientation. |
| f) BRIDGING THE DISTANCE | "They just don't know in the Central Office what we have to face ... how to get down to our level." No communication exists between controllers office and plant. Norms against "getting too friendly with other departments" indicates the narrow range of interaction. | "We are in contact with each other a lot more ... we tip .. (the other department) off to keep an eye out for things." An index of Daily Interaction scores shows supervisors at all levels interacting much more widely than before |
| g) SELF-CONFIRMING SELF-TRANSCENDING | "There's no recognition of the the foremen ........" "I need a little decent treatment *(but)* ...... I have to jump on them to keep them in line." | "My boss listens to my ideas." "Management expects me to run my own section but I can get help when I ask for it." "The foreman knows ... he's going to be recognized and promoted." |
| h) *Dialectic* leading to SYNERGY | Quality v Quantity conflict, and interdepartmental conflict with "flooded" union grievance procedures are evident. Supervisor in chassis department calls for the dismissal of his entire work force. 60 executives were fired after present manager was installed. | " ... management shows respect for the men and the men respect management for it too." "My boss treats me better because he gets treated better" "There was a high degree of convergence between the values of the manager and those of the subordinate managerial group." |

**Table 23 (Continued)**

| *Segments of the Cycle* | *Before* | *Two Years Later* |
|---|---|---|
| i) INTEGRATION OF FEEDBACK and COMPLEXITY | Feedback and indices from various departments are seen as devices to punish or lay blame when it is too late to correct matters. "Each action or set of events .... tended to make it increasingly difficult, if not impossible for the organization to improve performance." | Feedback from staff departments seen as useful for productivity and capable of being used for timely corrective action. "There was *a spiraling effect in precisely the opposite direction.* Now each action ... made it increasingly possible for the organization to improve..." (my emphasis). |

Source: *Organizational Change: The Effect of Successful Leadership.* By Robert H. Guest. Homewood, Ill.: The Dorsey Press, 1962.

they would not even try to reconcile the differences. Each would rush to the telephone and "call down the heavy artillery," hoping that the senior man in his department could somehow force the other department to comply. Senior managers were often besieged by requests to make an arbitrary judgment in favor of one disputant or the other. Dispute after dispute had to travel up departmental hierarchies to be laboriously settled at the top by persons who had to rely on the distorted information filtered upward through their departments. Few of the solutions were satisfactory.

Cooley approached the departments most often in dispute and told them that disagreements would no longer be settled by intervention from above. In each case the sharing of all information was essential. Then those persons most concerned with the dispute must arrive at a mutual resolution. This joint resolution would then be submitted to a planning committee of senior managers from all concerned departments.

This procedure not only split up the cliques, it prevented the systematic avoidance of "distant" persons and prescribed the settling of disputes by domination or submission. Employees, even at the lower levels, were to learn how to reconcile opposites by tolerating the anxiety of dialectic until synergy was found.

Cooley joined warring departments into a series of bi-partisan "planning groups." These groups could recommend widespread revision of the procedures for, say, inspection and quality control. There was no obligation to adhere to existing structures. There was an obligation to create a system to provide better cooperation and optimal satisfaction to both parties and to convince the bi-partisan group of higher managers that the new proposals would work.

Having moved to heal the "vertical divisions" between departments, Cooley knew better than to promote clashes between the "horizontal levels" of the hierarchy. He informed managers that from now on they would be promoted and rewarded according to the progress made *by their subordinates.* Each must train understudies. This had the function of encouraging the nurturance of juniors by seniors and promoting synergistic goals. When the joint proposals of junior planning groups were presented to senior planning groups each superior would be motivated to hope that his subordinate would acquit himself well. He would "see" the good sense of his subordinate and draw public attention to it.

*Restoring initiative to the various supervisory levels*

The planning meetings between departments not only promoted the dialectic, confrontation, and synergy which have characterised every developmental program examined so far, it also helped to restore to each hierarchical level some captaincy of its fate. Each could, via joint resolutions, invest on the basis of its perception and have a reasonable expectation of obtaining the anticipated outcome. Note that Cooley was especially anxious to stimulate *upward* initiation. The capacity of superiors to influence subordinates is seldom in doubt – even in a "sick" system – but the upward flow of information from subordinate to superior is a sensitive indicator of "health." This is especially true in highly technical and complex organizations where vital skills and access to knowledge are widely distributed among relatively junior persons. In such circumstances decisions coming down can only be as good as data, suggestions, and proposals flowing up.

Cooley surprised nearly everyone by making few initial decisions, but he did a lot of listening, permitting a wide spectrum of groups to influence him. From those who made complaints he would at once ask for proposals. Typical of his approach was an early visit he paid to a Union meeting. The men, expecting the usual exhortation and pressures, anticipated attack by attacking themselves. They confronted Cooley with a massive backlog of grievances. He replied bluntly that he was not going to concern himself with past dissatisfactions. He was, however, very interested in receiving the union's plans on how all such grievances could be avoided in the future. The union was staggered. For years they had used the grievance machinery as a way of forcing management to acknowledge their existence. Their leader recalled:

> This was a completely new approach to the committee, and although some of the boys were skeptical, most of us felt that this man meant what he said. What a change!

When definite requests were made Cooley would as far as possible accede to them. He had the washrooms repainted on request, and the plumbing was overhauled. Despite the fact that these initial requests were probably symbolic of more basic dissatisfaction with the general climate of relationships, Cooley took everyone at his word. When "trial balloons" proved successful, then the deeper needs would be voiced.

One can only marvel at Cooley's tolerance for anxiety. Plant Y was already the graveyard of scores of managerial careers. Funds poured through it as through a sieve. Few persons whose opinions were canvassed seemed primarily interested in production or in helping Cooley with *his* urgent problems. He constantly acceded to requests which would directly increase only costs, not production. He constantly stressed the need for people to meet and plan for the future, where a man with less nerve would have screamed about short-term neglected production and tomorrow's deadline. He restored initiative and the capacity to invest to numerous groups by temporarily suspending his own desperate needs in order to stimulate theirs.

*Repairing the feedback loop*

If there was one department which was regarded as little better than a vulture, signaling impending death, it was the controller's department. The figures it periodically published functioned only as a dreadful reproach to all concerned. They were not broken down in ways useful to supervisors. They were received too late for corrective action and were comprehensible only to the accusers and not to the accused.

Cooley took the controller from department to department, asking in each case how meaningful the existing figures were, what breakdowns *would* be useful to the supervisor and at what intervals. In this way a new set of indices was set up and in the weeks that followed supervisors would actually visit the controller's department to seek information.

The condition of Plant Y three years after Cooley became manager is set out on the right side of Table 23. There are clear gains in every segment of the cycle and the rampant anomie detailed on the left side has disappeared. For those wary of optimistic mass delusion, the indices of efficiency speak for themselves. Direct costs were at an index figure of 116 in 1953, the worst in the division which consisted of six plants. By 1956 they had fallen to 102, the best record in the division. Annual savings from this reduction were around $2 million. In indirect costs Plant Y had also moved from last to first place in the division. In records of quality it shared the lead throughout 1956, and moved from last to first place in safety records. Once highest in union grievances it was now lowest. Absenteeism and labor turnover were also well down. Indeed there was no record kept by corporate headquarters on which Plant Y had not improved substantially.

This study and this chapter will conclude my survey of the induction of developmental change by a series of deliberate interventions in the social system. Further studies tell the same story with comparable statistics. I have reviewed developmental dynamics in six settings, three involving Training Groups, four involving heightened capacities to communicate and increase productivity in corporations. In all six the natural processes of development were nurtured and facilitated. In all cases, participants changed from those conditions noted in Chapter VI as characterizing less creative systems, to conditions typical of the more creative systems.

Besides the dynamics of the cycle itself, what additional themes are common to our six examples of psycho-social development? What tentative conclusions can we draw concerning the necessary pre-conditions and accompaniments of facilitated developmental change? Here are some tentative conclusions:

1. In none of the examples studied did development ensue without a strong, almost paralyzing shock to the existing system. T-Groups are designed to administer such shocks and provide a "post-revolutionary vacuum." In the study of the Texas plant (Figure 2, Chapter VII) only those managers severely or moderately shaken up subsequently developed. The Hawthorne Experiment went completely off the rails. Joseph Scanlon discovered his plan when his company was literally desperate,

and subsequent installations of the Plan have always involved a total break with the past. The plant to which Mathew Cooley came was completely demoralized.

2. By the same token, no developmental gains have been recorded without the suspension and extensive modification of social structures. New levels of development require new or modified structures created by the participants themselves, who can be trusted not to tolerate excessive simplicity at the lower levels.
3. In all cases developmental change brought into more active participation persons or groups previously regarded as peripheral to the system. Increased "upward" influence and egalitarianism were concomitants of the development of a more inclusive whole.
4. At least four of the successes contained reports of verbal violence directed towards persons against whom aggression had earlier been inhibited.
5. All the corporate change studies contained at least four of the five dynamics characterizing T-Groups: - an encounter with the absurd, the small group climate, the enforced confrontation, the moratorium, and the rebellion against authority.

These points will assume great importance in the next chapters, in which I will discuss political forms of radical development.

## NOTES FOR CHAPTER VIII

1. *The Scientific Study of Behavior,* by Michael Argyle, London: Methuen, 1954.

2. D. L. Johnson, *et. al.,* in *Personal and Organizational Change Through Group Methods, op. cit.,* p. 152.

3. *Small Groups and Political Behavior* by Sidney Verba, Princeton University Press, 1961, p. 75. See also Abraham Zaleznik and David Moment, *The Dynamics of Interpersonal Behavior,* New York: Wiley, 1964. They refer to the "primitive efforts of early researchers. . . grasped with a cult-like zeal." p. 406.

4. *On Knowing: Essays for The Left Hand,* Cambridge: Harvard Univ. Press, p. 5.

5. Fritz Roethlisberger has since informed me that W. E. made a contribution to the Harvard Division of Research.

6. See *The Human Side of the Enterprise,* New York: McGraw-Hill, 1960.

7. "Teacher Expectations for the Disadvantaged" by Robert Rosenthal and Lenore F. Jacobson in *Scientific American,* Vol. 218, No. 4, 1968, pp. 19-24.

8. The Plan is discussed by McGregor in *The Human Side of the Enterprise, op. cit.*, pp. 110-124, and by a number of contributors in *The Scanlon Plan. . . A Frontier in Labor Management Cooperation,* Frederick A. Lesieur (ed.), Cambridge: M.I.T. Press, 1959.

9. *Ibid.*, p. 33.

10. The slogan of Brian Seaton, a factory worker in *Saturday Night and Sunday Morning* by Alan Sillitoe, New York: Signet Books, 1960.

11. "The Highly Effective Individual" by Donald W. MacKinnon in *Teachers College Record,* April, 1960. Also in *Explorations in Creativity,* Ross Mooney and Taher Razik (eds.), New York: Harper and Row, 1967, p. 65.

12. See "Work Group Ownership of an Improved Tool" in *Organizational Behavior and Administration: Cases, Concepts, and Research Findings,* Paul R. Lawrence, *et. al.*, Homewood: Irwin and Dorsey, 1961, pp. 260-266.

13. Notably Frederick Lesieur, union president of local at Lapointe Machine Tool Company and Clint Golden, former Vice President of the United Steelworkers.

14. *The Scanlon Plan. . . op. cit.*, p. 25.

15. *Organizational Change: The Effect of Successful Leadership* by Robert H. Guest, Homewood: Irwin – Dorsey, 1962, p. 42.

# *Chapter IX*

## The Radical – Conservative Dimension in American Politics

One of the most consistent failings of the social sciences has been their inability to produce a comprehensive and plausible theory of political allegiance. Especially unsatisfactory are the expositions of what constitutes conservative and extreme liberal or radical orientations; however, these descriptive terms persist in everyday political discourse and appear useful in discriminating persons of different views and behavior within the same political party. Various scales for the identification of liberals, conservatives, and radicals have been constructed, and while they remain reasonably true to "common sense" descriptions of such persons, the theory behind their construction remains largely obscure.

In this chapter I hope to illustrate that high levels of psycho-social development correspond to *certain kinds* of political radicalism – though by no means all kinds – and that most who call themselves conservative and some of those on the left manifest attitudes and behaviors designed to prescribe lower levels of development and to proscribe the anxiety and struggle necessary for growth. My argument will proceed in the following stages.

1. The inadequacy of conventional explanations.
2. Problems in defining developmental radicalism.
3. The Dogmatic Left, the Dogmatic Right and the New Left.
4. Legitimacy and the battle against Anomie or Repression.
5. Basic polarities in ideology and psycho-social development: How the New Left, Moderates, and Conservatives score on the segments of the cycle.

### 1. *The inadequacy of conventional explanations*

The most emphasized dichotomy in political allegiance is between the "haves" and the "have nots." The wealthy are supposedly conservative in order to conserve their privileges, and the poor and excluded are radical because they have little stake in the existing system. In America successive immigrant and minority groups have made overtures to one of the two political parties and, depending on the response, have formed traditional ties of allegiance.

Another divisive issue between Left and Right which frequently occurs in political rhetoric is the proper role to be played by the Federal Government. The Right insists that the "Free Enterprise System" is the economic manifestation of democracy with an "Invisible Hand" which regulates far more effectively the interests of all citizens, than do the meddling hands of federal officials. The Left has complained of much abuse and domination by "economic royalists" and that deliberate intervention in the economy, under the supervision of elected representatives, makes for a system more responsive to pluralistic demands. As a result of the clash between pro-government and anti-government forces, we have a mixed economy which is welcomed by "moderates" and "liberals." Only "extremists" of the Right wish to return to an economy dominated by private enterprise, and only "extremists" of the Left seek a totally "socialized" state.

This popular vision of the political arena celebrates moderation. Wisdom and, of course, power lie with those who occupy "the vital center" where they forge consensus between the pressures of pluralism, pragmatic to the last! No romantic ideologies or wishful thinking tarnishes their business-like deliberations and their technical solution of problems. They are, in the title words of a recent book, "Beyond Right and Left."[1] Towering above the partisan excitements of lesser men, they speak the neutral language of rational calculation.

The inadequacies of this concept of the political arena are too many to detail here. I shall merely content myself by mentioning a little of what it fails to explain. The New Left, for instance, consists of mostly privileged young men with affluent backgrounds, whose views on the Federal Government are scarcely printable. Yet they are not conservative. Indeed they have largely turned their backs on economic and status rewards – a fact which pulls the rug from under all those political theories with a primary stress on economics.

A glance at the voting records of the Dixiecrat-Republican conservative coalition in the Congress will show that they have supported a fantastic increase in the size of the Federal Government and the scope of its intervention in the economy – the bulk of it in defense related work, road building, and space exploration.[2] Moreover, the notion that conservatives are concerned above all with the conservation of their wealth stumbles upon the historic fact that the vast majority of American Conservative movements have risen to prominence in times of economic boom,[3] and, as compared with their educational peers, conservatives tend, during such periods, to increase their wealth.[4]

There is also reason to suppose that economic motivation, as such, may be declining. For example, a major study of the economic achievement motive in the American culture, which used the device of scoring literature and children's readers for "achievement imagery," found that this motif has been declining slowly yet inexorably since early in the century.[5]

But even if greater access to money remains a prominent political goal for most Americans, this still tells us little of their psychological motivation. Money, like the Federal bureaucracy, is for most persons the means to an end, and not the end itself. Money may mean status to one person, security to another, survival to a third, and power, nurture, education, luxury, or leisure, etc. to others. If it is too much to assume that everyone wants more money, it is also too little and too meager an explanation of those who *do* seek more money, to rest an analysis of their motivation with that conclusion. Beneath economics and beneath the shifting alliances with centralized or decentralized power, there lies the psycho-social theme of development. Politics is not a game in which all persons can safely expose their innermost needs, and so naturally we find developmental and regressive motivations glossed over by layer upon layer of economic and moral camouflage, with many highly symbolic appeals such as Prohibition, Law and Order and the Communist Conspiracy, appeals which voice implicitly what their followers do not care to make explicit.[7]

2. *Problems in defining developmental radicalism*

It would be a serious mistake to assume that all those persons labeled as "radical" in their political leanings were exponents or examples of psycho-social development. In order to distinguish genuine talent for social creativity from mere frustration and disgruntlement with the system, it is necessary to make several important distinctions among those generally regarded as radical. Four useful distinctions are between investors and receivers, between those who experience the social system at its relatively unstructured top and those who experience it near its highly structured bottom, between those who rebel freely and "obedient rebels," and finally between the content of a communication and its style.

If we measure the characteristics of those supporting or opposing certain radical *issues* like the guaranteed annual income or disbursements to the disadvantaged, then those *investing* these funds and this concern may be motivated quite differently from those who also support the measure because they are to *receive* help. Those making successful efforts to help the disadvantaged require keen PERCEPTION, high INVESTMENT, and a considerable tolerance for anxiety, RISK and stormy dialectic. Those receiving help, whether or not it is skilfully rendered, require only an acquisitive impulse in order to vote their support. As measured by the cycle model, the relative maturity of successful helpers is likely to be outweighed by the narrow desperation and anomie of those most in need of help.[8] So we shall find few consistent psychological themes by lumping together the helpers and helped around issues of compassion.

An early study of democratic socialists in Great Britain illustrated this point. Among the middle class, degrees of socialism predicted tender minded and compassionate attitudes, while conservatism correlated with tough mindedness. But the opposite trend was found in the working class. Middle class compassion provided an opportunity for working class militance and the same issues led different groups of supporters into quite different styles of behavior.[9]

We shall fare no better by defining as more radical and hence more developed, those expressing anger and rebellion against the system. The problem lies in the very wide variation between the upper and lower levels of the same social system. The "liberal" near the top of the system may have opportunities for creativity, which the "radical" near the bottom of the system could only match by insistent demands and defiance of authority, yet the two may seek very similar goals and consummate similar values. In Chapter XII we shall review some research that shows a very high level of agreement in the values of radical sons with their liberal fathers. The contrast is in the means of realization and in the structural obstacles to realization encountered by differently situated persons.

But even if persons similarly situated in a highly structured and oppressively simple system were to exhibit identical amounts of rebellion we must still be cautious in assuming that they rebel for *less* structure and *more* freedom, since it often happens that a system too structured for A, is experienced by B as insufficiently structured and requiring of him so much discretionary behavior that he is plunged into indecision and anomie. Under these circumstances A is likely to become a creative, development-seeking rebel, while B may become an "obedient rebel," attacking the system because it demands and legitimizes more strength in the segments of the cycle than he can command. Hence when the Supreme Court strikes down local segregation laws, then white citizens discover that the exclusion of Negroes in order to keep psychological distances short, and the resolution of black/white conflict by the enforced submission of black perspectives, are styles of interaction no longer sanctioned by the formal system, and they may rebel against the maturity demanded of them.

Even when we have made sure that those defined as radicals are investors of help and concern, and creative rebels against the constraint of social structure, there is still the necessity of ensuring that their *style* of interaction and communication is consistent with the *content* communicated. Ever since I was struck on the head by a demonstrator against the Franco-British invasion of Suez, who floored me with a sign labeled "DON'T USE FORCE," it has concerned me that the content of a message may be contradicted by its style of delivery. It is not uncommon to extol brotherhood and tolerance while persecuting as unbrotherly those who dispute the details of the policy for furthering brotherhood.

While content and style are obviously related among those who reflect upon the impact of their own behavior, it is possible to maintain a remarkable degree of divorce. Indeed, one definition of anomie and general underdevelopment of the cycle is a state of poor integration, which would include moral sentiments delivered in ways and contexts which vitiated their aims.

### 3. *The Dogmatic Left, the Dogmatic Right and the New Left*

Most research upon the personality functioning of liberals and conservatives has failed to evaluate the style and structure of the communication apart from its content. The result has been that Right-wing persons have had much of their thought and attitudes labeled as authoritarian, while Communist authoritarianism failed to register at all upon the well-known California F-Scale, a standard measure of authoritarianism. On this instrument it is not possible to discriminate between Communists and Peace Corps volunteers.[10]

To correct this situation Milton Rokeach designed a scale to measure dogmatic thought structures, as independent as possible from political doctrines. He obtained high scores from communists, fascists and religious fundamentalists alike, despite wide differences in their dogmas. His long, complex 40-item scale is of especial interest since it covers almost every segment of the cycle and reveals a consistent pattern of weakness and underdevelopment in the psycho-social relationships of dogmatic persons.

In the left hand column of Table 24 are listed the subscales of the dogmatism scale, and in the right hand column are some of the experimental tests and situations, most of which are totally apolitical in character, in which dogmatic people fail, as the scale predicts they will. The right hand column also reveals that dogmatic persons are capable of high levels of Right-wing or Left-wing *opinionation* – i.e., delivering their opinions with a belligerence that deters disconfirmation and disparages in advance those who might disagree. Both Right and Left can be singularly uncreative, while compulsively repeating the same arguments and ideas. Both can be blind to the flaws and discrepancies within their own beliefs while rejecting the subtleties of the other's argument. Both, by defining all non-believers as enemies, dupes, or apathetics can cut themselves off from the receipt of novel ideas.

However, the relationship between extremes of Right and Left and the degree of dogmatism is not the simple U-shaped curve that is commonly anticipated. It all depends whether we are referring to the "Old Left" based on communist rhetoric and concerned principally with economics and the victory of the proletariat, or whether we are referring to the "New Left" of middle class student activists, civil rights groups, and Vietnam protestors.

That this distinction between the old and new Left has become crucial is illustrated by Box 1, which compares the scores on Rokeach's dogmatism scale of a small group of pro-communist English students in 1955 with four groups of American students at Boston University in 1967. Here we see that the relationship between the *New* Left and the Right is *linear,* with *least dogmatism on the Left, moderate dogmatism in the Center, and highest dogmatism on the Right.* Whereas the communist students virtually burst out of the top of the scale, Left activists are almost out of sight near the bottom. The communist score of 165 means that on average these students agreed with over half the items indicating dogmatism. The New Left activists scoring 128, on average disagreed with four out of every five statements indicating

**Table 24**

**DOGMATISM, THE "OPEN" AND "CLOSED" STRUCTURES OF THOUGHT**

| *Segments of the Anomic Cycle* | *Characteristics measured by The Dogmatism Scale* | *Characteristics found to correlate with High Dogmatism* |
|---|---|---|
| Anomic failure to exist ... | Tendency to follow party line<br>Conformity to group<br>Compulsive repetition of arguments and ideas | Capacity for analysis but not for novel synthesis<br>Incapacity to tolerate novel belief systems<br>Acceptance of Roman Catholic dogma or Communist dogma |
| a) PERCEPTION, narrow and impoverished | Unwillingness to differentiate among the beliefs of others<br>Belief in the explanatory power of Great Philosophy<br>Narrowness of perception | Incapacity to accept pieces of information discrepant with held beliefs<br>Glorified and ideal descriptions of parents<br>Very low levels of ambivalence in description of parents |
| b) IDENTITY "locked in" and stagnant | —— | Poor capacity to detect flaws within own belief system |
| c) InCOMPETENCE and anticipated loss | Unsureness about future<br>Self-depreciation<br>Concern with achieving status and power | Feelings of Personal Threat |
| d) Fails to INVEST authentically or intensely | —— | —— |
| e) Non-SUSPENDING RISK-reducing strategies | Fails to listen because of of self-absorbtion<br>Advocacy of self-interest<br>Rejection of others' foolishness and ignorance | Rigidity *or* total abandonment of one set of beliefs in favor of of another set.<br>High Manifest anxiety<br>High anxiety in childhood |

**Table 24 (Continued)**

| *Segments of the Anomic Cycle* | *Characteristics measured by The Dogmatism Scale* | *Characteristics found to correlate with High Dogmatism* |
|---|---|---|
| f) Avoidance of BRIDGING the (wider) DISTANCES | Chooses as friends only those with similar beliefs<br>Accentuates differences in belief.<br>Rejects those who deviate from his beliefs | Reports being uninfluenced by outsiders<br>Rejection of others is a function of their perceived dissimilarity. |
| g) Inability to make SELF-CONFIRMING, SELF TRANSCENDING IMPACT | — | Opinionated Left-wing or Right-wing statements.<br>(i.e. belligerence designed to ward off disagreement) |
| h) Domination of, or submission to, others perspectives, in a *non-dialectic,* negantropic failure of SYNERGY | Authoritarianism<br>Unreconciled opposites within belief system which are isolated not solved.<br>Fears and proscribes arguments within his group.<br>Dreads the prospect of compromising with outsiders rather than conquering them. | — |
| i) No responsibility for FEEDBACK, hence DIS-INTEGRATION | Internal conflict and non-communication between different elements within the belief system | Incapacity to recall novel ideas<br>Incapacity to synthesise new ideas into existing belief system |

Notes: Scales and Tests correlating with Dogmatism Scale

1. Rokeach Doodle Bug Test
2. Gough-Sanford Rigidity Scale
3. Anxiety items from M.M.P.I.
4. Rokeach Left-Opinionation
5. Rokeach Right-Opinionation.

Source: - *The Open and Closed Mind* by Milton Rokeach. New York: Basic Books, 1960.

**Box 1**

Degrees of Dogmatism in University Students on the Left, Center and Right

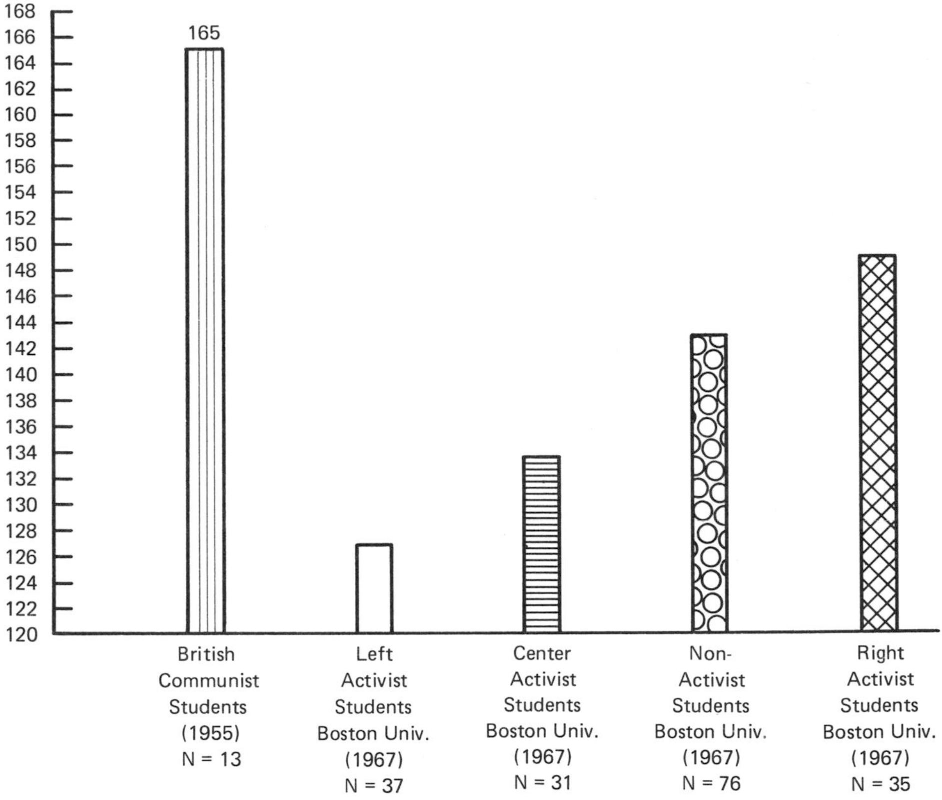


Source: — "A Study of a Sampling of Boston University Student Activists," Unpubl. Doctoral Dissertation by Irvin Doress. Boston Univ. 1968.

dogmatism. In the style and structure of their thought and in development of the segments of the cycle, the New and Old Left *are further apart than any of the other groups measured.*

This is not so surprising when we reflect that the New Left comes close to our definition of developmental radicalism, as opposed to radicalism in general. Activist Left students on campus are not the deprived receivers of federal aid but the would-be investors of help. They are saddled with much social structure against which they rebel in order to attain the kind of rights and representation long enjoyed by trades unionists who have a fraction of their education and political knowledge.

4. *Legitimacy and the battle against anomie*

In Chapter IV, I described the underdevelopment of the cycle as being characterized by anomie, alienation, cynicism, futility and despair.

If dogmatism is a measure of underdevelopment and adherents of the Right and the Old Left are more dogmatic, then are they also more anomic and alienated? Table 25 details the results of a nation-wide sample of over a thousand persons. Those subscribing to a Right Wing Ideology and Left Wing Ideology are much more likely than the average respondent to be anomic, alienated, anxious, pessimistic, authoritarian, less educated and afraid to reveal their true feelings.

The Right-wing scale expresses distaste for "do-gooders," "bleeding hearts," socialism, and collectivism and praises anti-communism. It laments the disappearance of the "true American" and the contemporary honoring of traitors instead of patriots, and advocates that peace and order be achieved through commanding strength.

The Old Left Scale attacks private ownership, considers Russian communism superior to "dog eat dog," advocates that Labor should opt out of the two party system, and offers the Soviet Union as an appropriate model for America to follow. Military spending is seen as a device for saving private enterprise from collapse and profit making as the chief barrier to peace. There is no hope for critics to be heard, and all progressive forces are systematically hounded by the two parties. Here again we find a curvilinear relationship between the Right, Moderates and the Old Left with Moderates showing the least anomie and rigidity.

But if less-developed persons are so burdened by alienation, futility, miscommunication, and guilt, how can I account for the skilful takeovers by communist movements or the way in which the Goldwater Conservatives wrested control of the Republican Party from the moderates in 1964? If, as indicated in chapters VI to VIII, lower levels of development characterize the less successful corporations, how could authoritarian forces ever compete?

The answer to this is that the Right and Old Left are not *necessarily* more anomic and socially frustrated at all. They are only so *under the formal*

**Table 25**

**THE CORRELATES OF RIGHT-WING AND OLD LEFT IDEOLOGY**

| *Segments of the Cycle* | *Scales Measuring* | *Correlations with ... Right Wing Ideology* | *Old Left Ideology* |
|---|---|---|---|
| Anomic failure to exist.................. | Anomy | .70 | .64 |
| | Conventionality | .43 | .38 |
| | Conservatism | .60 | .59 |
| | Religiosity | .40 | .24 |
| a) PERCEPTION, narrow and impoverished ........................ | Intolerance for Ambiguity | .58 | .47 |
| | Political Indifference | .30 | .40 |
| | Political & Moral Indulgence | .45 | .45 |
| b) IDENTITY, "locked in" and stagnant ............................... | Need Inviolacy | .53 | .49 |
| c) INCOMPETENCE and anticipated loss .................... | Political Impotence | .48 | .49 |
| | Guilt | .42 | .38 |
| | Pessimism | .44 | .43 |
| d) Fails to INVEST authentically or intensely ................. | Acquiescence | .63 | .59 |
| | Political Cynicism | .60 | .61 |
| | Obsessive (compulsive) | .37 | .26 |
| e) Non-SUSPENDING RISK-reducing strategies ................ | Elitism | .36 | .32 |
| | Political Suspicion | .56 | .54 |
| | Chauvinism | .69 | .50 |
| | Rigidity | .44 | .33 |
| f) Avoidance of BRIDGING THE (wider) DISTANCES ........... | Isolationism | .67 | .53 |
| | Contempt for Fraility | .49 | .41 |
| | Calvinism | .36 | .20 |
| | Ethnocentrism | .65 | .50 |
| | Anti-Semitism | .40 | .31 |
| | Segregation | .32 | .17 |
| | Toleration (negative) | –.41 | –.35 |
| g) Inability to make SELF CONFIRMING SELF TRANSCENDING IMPACT | Alienation | .46 | .50 |
| | Status Frustration | .38 | .41 |
| | Life Satisfaction (negative) | –.30 | –.35 |

**Table 25 (Continued)**

| | | | |
|---|---|---|---|
| h) Domination of, or submission to, others perspectives, in a non-dialectic, negantropic, failure of SYNERGY ............ | Contempt of Human Weakness | .42 | .41 |
| | Paranoid Tendencies | .63 | .64 |
| | Authoritarianism | .69 | .55 |
| | Hostility | .52 | .45 |
| | Populism | .71 | .66 |
| i) No responsibility for FEED-BACK, Hence DisINTEGRA-TION and lack of COMPLEXITY | Social Responsibility (negative) | –.48 | –.52 |
| | Intellectuality (negative) | –.48 | –.42 |
| | Education (negative) | .41 | –.35 |
| | Totalatarianism | .64 | .61 |

Source: Herbert McClosky & John H. Schaar **Op. cit.** Table 3 *system, laws and social structures imposed upon them by the dominant forces in society.* What these dominant forces do is legitimize and institutionalize their own preferred styles of interaction and levels of development. They sanction the extent of allowable rebellion and creativity, they decree how widely differentiated various groups or persons can become, what distances must be bridged and which distances may be avoided, and how much coercion may be used to bring deviant persons into line. In many ways they set the conditions under which persons may interact and these conditions may be hostile to or favorable to the levels of psycho-social development which certain groups have attained or to which they aspire.

I believe we can characterize much political strife as *a struggle against anomie by the underdeveloped and a struggle against repression by the highly developed.* The formal system of legitimacy usually supports the *average* level of development somewhere in between the principal combatants. The developmental radicals struggle to raise the legal and social requirements for developed behavior, and the dogmatic Right and dogmatic Left struggle to conserve or lower them. The underdeveloped cry with pain because the system forces more choice upon them than they can handle – which is the definition of anomie I have been using. The highly developed cry with pain for all those who are suffering and will continue to do so because the system will not legitimize their emancipation, and represses individual efforts to help. The system of legitimacy sets the norm, so that those who feel more than the norm, bridge wider distances than the norm, and create more than the norm, are regarded as "over emotional," "far out" and "reckless" while those who bridge lesser distances than the norm are "ethnocentric," those who manipulate more than norm are "authoritarian," and those who suspend themselves less than the norm are "prejudiced." The struggle to set the norm decides *who will successfully label whom, what, when and how.*[11]

Now underdeveloped persons would *not* be so labeled and would not suffer so much frustration, anomie, guilt, and incipient disintegration if they won the power to set the norm at *their* comfortable level and then repress or purge others until they regressed to the same or lower levels. In order to do this, the underdeveloped group first withdraws into a cabal where it can set its *own* norms and hence minimize its suffering, and then it will strike at the larger culture and attempt to "take over" the norm-making functions in a quick coup. This explains the relative efficiency and speed of *organized* groups on the Radical Right and the communist Left. The obvious misery and anomie we see in Table 25 is the result of being mostly unorganized politically and trapped in a system which expects too much, and by whose standards the individual is falling short. This would also help to explain why those political movements appealing to underdeveloped persons have such zeal, such desperate hopes and so chiliastic a flavor. If the members of the group can capture the "commanding heights of the economy" they will no longer be alienated, frustrated and deprived of self-esteem. Society will thenceforth be structured to applaud what they can do and condemn what they cannot.

5. *Basic polarities in ideology and psycho-social development: How the New Left, Moderates and Conservatives Score upon the segments of the cycle*

A single philosophical polarity provides us with the nexus of a whole series of disagreements between radical and conservative man. Silvan Tomkins in his seminal essay *Left and Right* states the polarity as follows.

> Is man the measure, an end in himself, an active thinking, desiring, loving force in nature? Or must man realize himself, attain his full stature only through a struggle toward, participation in, conformity to, a norm, a measure, an ideal essence basically independent of man?[12]

Tomkins traces the ramifications of this dispute from discipline to discipline. In mathematics there is Henry Poincare on the Left regarding mathematics as the finest type of human play and exercise of the imagination, and there are two authors of a textbook who extol mathematics as "the discipline of responsibility," constraining the caprice of the individual. "Only guided by intrinsic necessity can the free mind achieve results of scientific value."[13]

In the philosophy of science, Tomkins quotes the Right as insisting that science is the correspondence of reality with facts. Measurement is the most direct route to physical reality. In contrast, Einstein on the Left is quoted as stating,

> The formulation of a problem is often more essential than its solution, which may be merely a matter of mathematical or experimental skill. . . Physical concepts are free creations of the human mind, and are not, however it may seem, uniquely determined by the external world.[14]

This same issue is argued in metaphysics between the idealistic and realistic conception of the relation of man to reality.

In politics there is the Right-wing view of law and tradition as superordinate and the Left-wing emphasis upon change in all structures guided by the feelings and needs of people. "The laws of God and of Nature have no dateline," was one of Senator Goldwater's favorite pronouncements. As he saw it the Constitution was *not* subject to periodic reinterpretation, but had a fixed meaning over and above the willful caprice of men.

An interesting Radical/Conservative controversy convulsed the Church of England in the early sixties with the publication of John Robinson's book

"Honest to God."[15] The Bishop argued that we should think of God in terms of depth rather than height, as dwelling in the depth of our being and not as an "old man in the sky." This change has considerable developmental significance. If God is within us, each must first act and exist, spontaneously and intensely, and risk being mistaken, in order to uncover the depth within. In this case obedience, innocence and virginity, become not virtues but forms of spiritual and moral cowardice – the failure to live fully and to "let God speak" from inside us. Conservative critics rushed to rebuke Robinson.

> The clear implication is that God's laws have something in common with a political program and should be restated when they are felt no longer to command the support of the majority.[16]

The Bishop had sounded an "uncertain trumpet" and "bewildered the flock." From now on every slave of passion would regard his case as exceptional and moral landmarks would be swept aside.

This basic polarity underlined by Silvan Tomkins is, of course, the same issue that I addressed in Chapters I to III. The first three words of the cycle read, *Man exists freely.* This is the radical position. The conservative position is that *man is the product of known or knowable scientific or moral forces which exist prior to and independently of man.*

From this initial dichotomy are derived a series of dichotomies which apply to *each segment of the cycle* and result either in the development of the segments (Radical) or in their remaining in a relatively undeveloped state (Conservative).

These dichotomies are as follows:

| | *Radical* | *Conservative* |
|---|---|---|
| Segment (a) | The PERCEPTION of human needs as guiding behavior | The knowledge of external values and facts as guiding and shaping human behavior |
| Segment (b) | Comprehension of, and sensitivity to, one's own inner IDENTITY and feelings | The disciplined subordination of inner feelings to internalized or external morality |
| Segment (c) | Man as morally COMPETENT through his own experiental resources | Man as morally incompetent, or competent only as an agent of a superior moral purpose |

| | | |
|---|---|---|
| Segment (d) | INVESTMENT as an authentic and intense expression of a unique personality | Human action as the attempt to attain the accomplishment or extension of some norm or value |
| Segment (e) | Acceptance of the vulnerability, doubt and despair inherent in SELF-SUSPENSION and RISK | Praise for self-control, "masculinity," and a dignified appearance. Use of economic analogies to reduce psychological risk-taking. |
| Segment (f) | Encouragement and idealization of BRIDGING the wider DISTANCES between those who personify equally legitimate yet discrepant human needs | Idealization of the shortest possible DISTANCE between persons, whose interaction is mediated by, and should approximate to, those Supreme Values around which the faithful are exhorted to assemble. |
| Segment (g) | Emphasis upon the experience of SELF-CONFIRMATION and TRANSCENDENCE as a test of acting rightly towards others. | Emphasis upon the achievement of external norms and just rewards for the accomplishment of goals, previously sanctioned by responsible authorities. |
| Segment (h) | An egalitarian *dialectic* leading to a SYNERGISTIC and "just" reconcilation of formerly discrepant needs. | The victory in any conflict of those Supreme Values relevant to the dispute, which should be imposed if necessary, upon the undisciplined and unreliable feelings of men. |
| Segment (i) | The INTEGRATION of human affect and reason into a belief system of intercommunicating thought-matrixes of developing COMPLEXITY | The permanent separation of reprehensible desires, appetites and hasty reasoning, from those Superior Values and Great Wisdoms which have stood the test of time. |

This clear split between radical and conservative ideology helps to explain why the representative groups of radicals to be discussed in this chapter score higher on the segments of the cycle than do conservatives. Simply stated, radicals value psycho-social development as I defined it, and conservatives value it appreciably less, if at all. Moreover each radical/conservative polarity is directly derived from the original dispute between the notion of man's free existence, and man as a product of natural and moral forces, external to himself, so that both conservative and radical views are internally consistent, and not irrational as is so often claimed by the opposing side. Our opponents *appear* irrational because we assume that they perceive and value what we do.

Notice also, that radical and conservative are being defined in a very special sense. Given our definitions, *Soviet communism would be regarded as conservative.* Orthodox communist doctrine believes in an external, historical force of which men are the mere agents, who can choose only to facilitate the inevitable triumph of the proletariat. Bridging the distance to the doomed perspectives of bourgeois decadents is neither enlightening nor necessary. Self-suspension is hardly required, for the historical process unfolds despite our personal feelings, so that steadfastness, certainty, and participation in the inevitable triumph of socialism are the chief requirements of the faithful. In any dispute, the principles of Marxist-Leninism will prevail and if necessary crush, reactionary and revisionist stirrings in the souls of mistaken comrades. Thus the real distinction between developmental radicals and conservatives is not "pro-change" v. "anti-change" but a rigid and fearful certainty that change will bring triumph *or* disaster v. an exploratory and flexible orientation to "change-as-learning." A recent book by the Marxist intellectual, Leszek Kolakowski, describes his radical opposition to communist orthodoxy in Poland, in words essentially similar to my model.[17]

I now propose to discuss the ten dichotomies between radical and conservatives and to illustrate with research findings that the New Left, or developmental radicals, score better on every segment of the cycle in accord with their higher evaluation of that segment. The research findings come from a study of student activism at Boston University by Irvin Doress[18] (see also Box 1). Although it is dangerous to generalize from these small and selective samples to conservatism and developmental radicalism in general, much additional evidence is available in later chapters to suggest that these findings are indeed representative. What is especially valuable about the Boston University research is the number of instruments used and the fact that the students were of approximately the same age, educational attainment, and class, differing chiefly in their *active* political allegiance and membership; whereas most conservative/radical comparisons discover that conservatives are less educated, a fact which then makes it difficult to attribute differences to ideology alone.

Included in some of the diagrams are the scores of a very small sample of British communist students tested a decade earlier by Milton Rokeach upon some of the same instruments.[19] We shall see that communist students score closest to Boston Student Right activists, as my theory would predict, while the Left activists are at the opposite ends of the various scales. Radical man rejects conservatism in all its guises.

*Man exists freely (Radical) v. Man should be (or is) the product of moral values (or scientific forces) which are prior to and independent of the individual's existence* (Conservative)

Among Boston University students, the degree of rebellious existence characterising members of the Left, Center, and Right political groups, including a sample of politically non-affiliated non-activists, can be estimated from the three scales in Box 2. The "Moral Freedom" Scale (actually the Reiss Moral Acceptability Scale) is an index of sexual permissiveness in interpersonal relationships. High scorers would condone even adultery where the circumstances were experienced as appropriate, as well as petting, kissing, pre- marital relationships, etc. Low scorers would follow the rule despite the particular circumstances which might tempt them to make an exception.

The "Existentiality Scale" measures the same tendency to deal with the environment situationally, only here the situations go beyond male/female intimacy. On both scales the Left activists are least constrained by conventional codes and are the most likely to choose for themselves according to the particular circumstances. On both scales the student Right scores substantially and significantly below the Left.

But is this any more than adolescent revolt? Are Left students merely conforming with one another, fearful of *not* having a mistress or an affair? A third scale (actually a subscale of the 40-item Dogmatism Scale presented in Table 24) measured "Party Lining" or conformity-to-group motivation. Here we see that the British communist students have the strongest tendency to imitate each other, but from there on the tendency declines linearly from Right to Non-Activist, to Center, to Left: The latter group are free from moral codes *and* each other's opinion. They *ex-ist,* that is stand out, more than the others.

These findings are consistent with the nationwide samples detailed in Table 25 where we saw that *both* the Right-wing ideologists *and* the Old Left are higher in anomie, conventionality, and "classical Conservatism" in the sense of rejection of human needs in favor of moral imperatives. This latter scale which I shall call "Conservative Rejection of Existence" is the subject of Table 26. Here we see that those who most reject existence, and claim "Duties are more important than rights"; "Most people don't know what's good for them"; "People will become soft if they are babied or coddled," etc., are extremely anomic when it comes to letting go of their duties and exercising their rights. They feel unable to choose in direct proportion to their rejection of existence. The relationship is clearly linear from extreme conservative to moderate, to radical positions.

**Table 26 (Continued)**

| Segments of the Cycle | Name of the Scale | Position on Scale Top 1/3 = High Bottom 1/3 = Low | Radical Extreme Liberal | Moderate Liberal | Moderate Conservative | Conservative Extreme Conservative |
|---|---|---|---|---|---|---|
| f) Avoidance of BRIDGING THE (wider, DISTANCES .. | Contempt & Intolerance for Human Fraility | High | 8 | 16 | 23 | 54 |
| | | Low | 52 | 30 | 17 | 6 |
| g) Inability to make SELF CONFIRMING SELF TRANS-CENDING IMPACT | Alienation | High | 4 | 20 | 27 | 59 |
| | | Low | 57 | 47 | 35 | 10 |
| h) Domination of, or submission to, others perspectives, in a non-dialectic, negantropic, failure of SYNERGY ..... | Hostility | High | 18 | 37 | 46 | 71 |
| | | Low | 59 | 38 | 26 | 9 |
| | Paranoid Tendencies | High | 16 | 27 | 37 | 62 |
| | | Low | 56 | 42 | 28 | 13 |
| i) No responsibility for FEED-BACK, hence DISINTEGRA-TION and lack of COMPLEX-ITY .... | Social Responsibility | High | 47 | 31 | 23 | 8 |
| | | Low | 12 | 25 | 36 | 62 |
| | Intellectuality | High | 62 | 43 | 26 | 11 |
| | | Low | 7 | 20 | 34 | 56 |

Source: Herbert McClosky "Conservatism and Personality", *American Political Science Review 1958, 42.*

Table 26

CHARACTERISTICS AND ATTITUDES OF CONSERVATIVE REJECTORS OF FREE EXISTENCE

| | | *Position on Scale* Top 1/3 = High Bottom 1/3 = Low | *Radical* | | | *Conservative* |
|---|---|---|---|---|---|---|
| *Segments of the Cycle* | *Name of the Scale* | | Extreme Liberal | Moderate Liberal | Moderate Conservative | Extreme Conservative |
| Anomic failure to exist. | Anomy | High | 4 | 16 | 30 | 59 |
| | | Low | 71 | 48 | 32 | 10 |
| a) PERCEPTION, narrow and impoverished .. | Political and Social awareness | High | 54 | 32 | 21 | 9 |
| | | Low | 9 | 25 | 45 | 66 |
| b) IDENTITY, "locked in" and stagnant .. | Need Inviolacy | High | 11 | 20 | 38 | 60 |
| | | Low | 68 | 58 | 36 | 17 |
| c) InCOMPETENCE and anticipated loss .. | Guilt | High | 16 | 18 | 28 | 47 |
| | | Low | 62 | 42 | 36 | 18 |
| | Self Confidence | High | 46 | 38 | 24 | 20 |
| | | Low | 18 | 23 | 32 | 35 |
| d) Fails to INVEST authentically or intensely ..... | Social Dominance | High | 72 | 50 | 29 | 14 |
| | | Low | 9 | 19 | 37 | 51 |
| e) Non-SUSPENDING RISK-reducing strategies | Rigidity | High | 18 | 32 | 41 | 60 |
| | | Low | 28 | 43 | 29 | 14 |

**Box 2**

"Moral Freedom Scale"

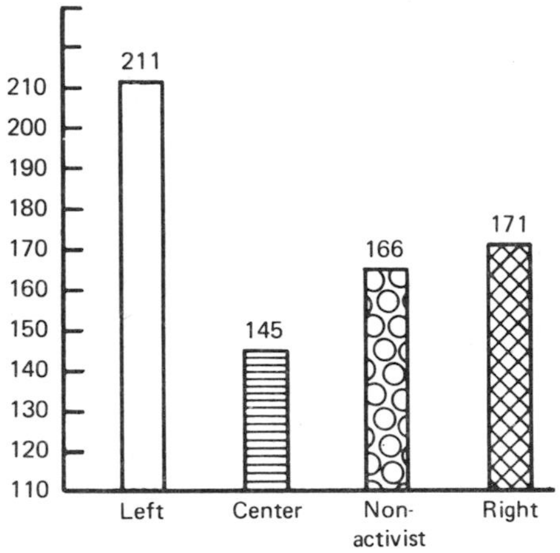


Existentiality Scale (P.O.I.)

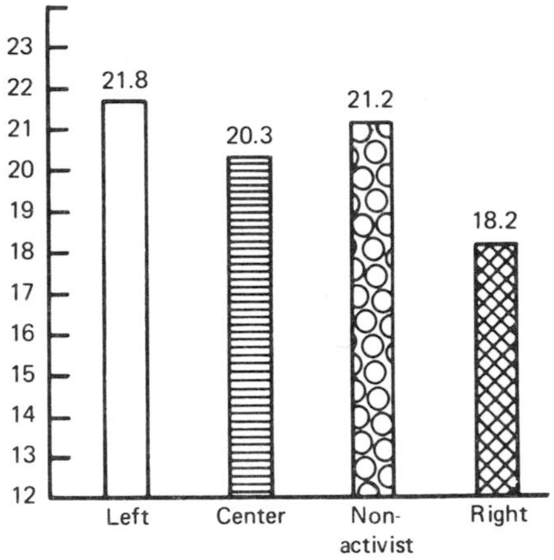


"Party Lining"
Subscale of Rokeach Dogmatism Scale

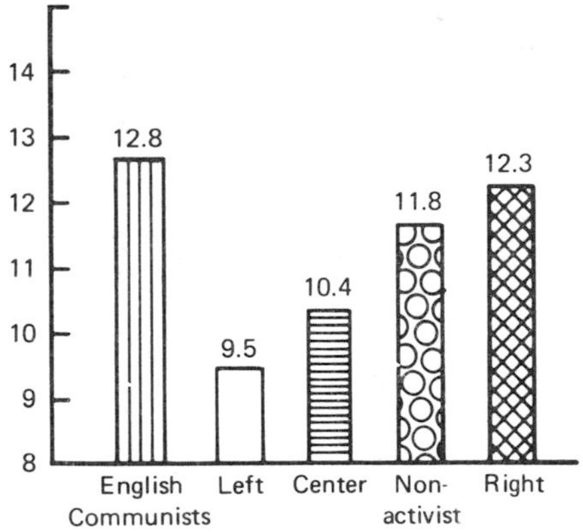


Source: — "A Study of a Sampling of Boston University Student Activists," Unpubl. Doctoral Dissertation by Irvin Doress. Boston Univ. 1968.

*Segment (a) The PERCEPTION of human needs as guiding behavior (Radical) V. The knowledge of external values and facts as guiding and shaping human behavior* (Conservative).

In the Boston University Study we can see from Box A (each box letter corresponds to a segment of the cycle) that the activist Right has significantly greater perceptual narrowness than the activist Left, but that British student communists (a decade earlier) were even narrower than the current American Student Right. Once again, the relationship between the Old Left, and the liberal Center and the Right is curvilinear with the moderates least narrow, but the relationship between the Right and the New Left is *linear,* with the so-called extremists on the Left less narrow than even the Center.

The increasing narrowness on the Right is, of course, justified by a philosophy that regards eternal verities, of which there are a limited number, as most important, but human proclivities, of which the spectrum is extremely wide, as of secondary importance. Senator Goldwater would periodically insist while running for the Presidency that he was not aiming to satisfy individual wants.

> I have gone into the heart of Appalachia. . . and there I have *deliberately* attacked this administration's phony war on poverty. I have gone into the heart of Florida's retirement community and there I have *deliberately* warned against the outright hoax of this administration's medicare scheme. . .
>
> I have done all these things deliberately. . . for a reason that is clear in my own mind. . . and I want to make it clear to you tonight. . . I will not treat any of you as just so many special interests. . . I will not appeal to you as if you were simply pocketbooks. . . surrounded on all sides by self-serving concerns.[20]

Clearly Goldwater regarded the perception of, and investment in, the needs of others as a doubtful road to virtue or moral success. There is little value in perceiving human feelings if these feelings are not a reliable guide to appropriate behavior. Which brings us to the next segment of the cycle.

*Segment (b) Comprehension of and sensitivity to one's own inner IDENTITY and feelings (Radical) V. The disciplined subordination of inner feelings to internalized or external morality* (Conservative).

In Box B we can see the results of testing our student samples on their Feeling Reactivity, a standard scale in the Personal Orientation Inventory.

**Box A**

"Perceptual Narrowing"
Subscale of Rokeach's Dogmatism Scale

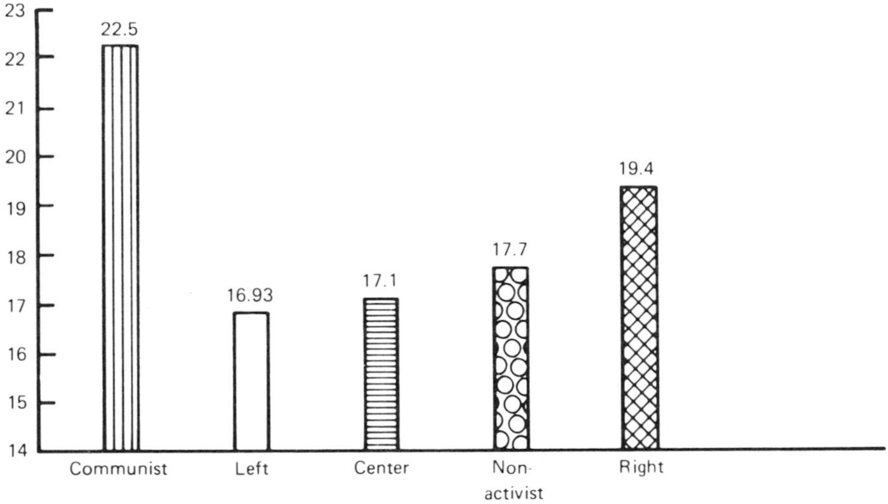


**Box B**

"Sensitivity to Own Feelings"
(Feeling Reactivity –
P.O.I. Scale)

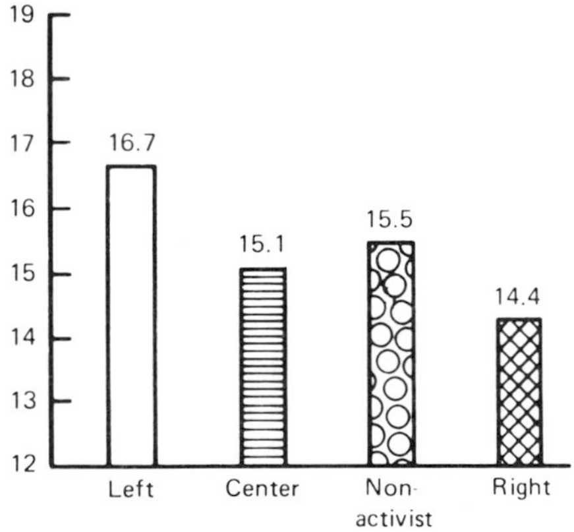


**Box C**

Social Dominance (C.P.I.)

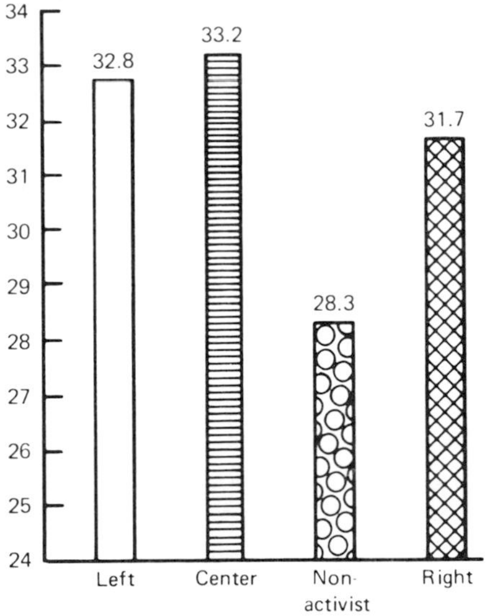

Left activists are significantly more responsive to their inner feelings. If they are disgusted and sickened by the Vietnam War, they trust their feelings sufficiently to say so, loudly and rudely. Less constrained by external authority, they regard patriotism or support for prior Presidential commitments as a poor excuse for condoning acts which turn their stomachs.

On the Right we see that inner feelings are less respected. Evidence will be cited shortly to show that such feelings are less exposed and examined. An early study using a scale of Political and Economic Conservatism showed that conservatives were more "anti-intraceptive" – unwilling to explore their own motivations and feelings.[21] Jim Lucier, an intellectual of the far Right, and a regular contributor to *American Opinion,* the house organ of the John Birch Society, put his attitude to human feelings succinctly.

> Now this question of absolute moral values is pretty much the test of what is meant by *conservative*. . . a conservative doesn't really trust anyone, much less himself. He doesn't make himself a judge in his own case because he doesn't want a prejudiced judge. His experience teaches him that man is always falling short of his aspirations because some lowly desire often appears to be the illimitable good. Therefore he is always struggling to submit his bodily desires to the regimen of some external permanent standard of conduct.[22]

Conservatives advocate the suppression of inner feelings in many ways. Young men are urged to prepare themselves for a specific career and "plan your job campaign," which entails deliberately fashioning one's personality to fit a pre-ordained slot in some organization several years hence. A study of Right-wing counter pickets who were ridiculing a Left peace march found the former students were mostly preparing for careers in business, law and the foreign service, while the Left had few such definite plans. While the peace marchers referred to their fear of nuclear weapons, their belief in the possibilities of international trust, and their indignation at the Government's insensitivity to the evils of radioactivity, the Right regarded this expression of feelings as appalling weakness, if not cowardice, a failing of which the communists would almost certainly take advantage.[23]

The counter-pickets of the Right were of conventional, clean-cut, and "American" in appearance, while the Peace marchers were extremely diverse. Of the latter, several were unshaved and few of the girls wore make-up or curled their hair – much to the disgust of local police officers. The researchers inferred through interviews with these young people that they were seeking a less "commercial," a more "pure and uncontaminated" image of themselves. Just as they trusted their feelings, they wanted to show their real unvarnished selves, and to accept and be accepted as they really were.

These findings are consistent with those in Table 26 where we see that degrees of Conservatism and Rejection of Existence are directly related to Need Inviolacy, the fear and disinclination to let one's inner needs be known. In Table 25 *both* the Old Left and the Right have this same fear of exposure. Finally a recent study of activist conservative youth on several campuses found that they scored significantly higher than liberals on a scale of Impulse Repression.[24]

*Segment (c) Man as morally COMPETENT through his own experiential resources (Radical) V. Man as morally incompetent, or competent only as an agent of a superior moral purpose* (Conservative).

In Box C we see that the trends are mixed with no statistically significant differences among the three activist groups, all of which appear as more Socially Dominant than non- activists.

In fact, the scale itself falls short of what I have defined as competence. It fails to discriminate power *through* people from power *over* them.

But even if this distinction had been made we might still expect the Right to feel as competent as the Left *where both are organized with a group of like minded persons.* As explained earlier, the less developed may start to hurt and disintegrate only when forced to dance to the tune of the more developed. Part of the objectives of organizing may be to increase feelings of competence in areas of common interest by creating norms suitable to the developmental level of the members and urging these norms upon the larger environment.

The most unorganized (politically) nation-wide samples in Tables 25 and 26 do, however, show the expected feelings of Guilt, Pessimism, and Political Impotence, according to their degree of non-existential conservatism, while the Extreme Liberals in Table 26 show the highest Self Confidence and the least Guilt.

There are limits on the extent to which conservatives can permit one another to feel competent, for no man must be so "proud" as to challenge eternal verities or regard himself as qualified to suspend them. In any dispute or scandal it is the standards which must be upheld and the weak and sinful human beings who have disgraced the "honor code" who are singled out for punishment.

The workings of this conservative morality were recently exemplified in the cheating scandals at the Air Force Academy, where the issue was treated entirely as a series of individual derelictions from a glorious code, in the General Electric Price Fixing scandal where the company publicly regretted the unauthorized deviation of their top executives from "company policy," and in the Television Quiz scandals where leaders vied with one another to moralize about individual responsibility.

Critics on the Left asked, in effect, what else could be expected from a commercial system of entertainment which had long since discovered that only unreality will move soap and that truth was insufficiently profitable. But the industry knew how to save itself. One coached contestant, who had wrinkled his brow in simulated effort to "remember" answers fed to him before each show, had one last scene to play – "The Scapegoat's Confession." A contemporary account ran as follows:

> The record remained perfect to the end. Charles Van Doren was a superb quiz contestant; a staunch, believable defense witness; and when it came time for him to deliver his confession, a nonpareil repenter. He had given the producers what they wanted, the reporters what they wanted, and now he told the Congressmen and the nation what nearly everybody, trained by the Hollywood Code, thirsted to hear. "I've learned a lot in those three years," he told them, "especially in the last three weeks. I've learned a lot about myself, and about the responsibilities any man has to his fellow men. I've learned a lot about good and evil." He spoke of the millions of friends whom he had deceived; of his "intense moral struggle" of his relief ("Thank God") when he was able to leave the program with his $129,000; of his feeling that he was carrying "the whole burden and honor of my profession"; of his final realization "that the truth is always the best way"; of a letter from an unknown woman admirer, which convinced him to make his public confession – "Whatever the personal consequences, and I knew they would be severe, this was the only way"; and of his attorney's happiness that he had "found courage at last." The Congressmen were moved to near-unanimous bipartisan praise. Committee chairman Oren Harris, echoing the attorney, said, *"God bless you,"* and Representative Rogers, who had been so disappointed in other contestants, lit up like a despairing missionary presented in the nick of time with a docile heathen: "I know it makes you feel cleaner inside." The spectators applauded, and Dave Garroway broke down and sobbed while taping his show.[25]

Thus is the individual sacrified to the "standards" of the larger commercial system, *in the name of individualism!* The dissonance between an image fostered for commercial gain and the reality behind the image is the fault of one or two sinners. Long live the image of our values – only men are unworthy of it! Charles Van Doren has passed into obscurity but his sponsor, Revlon, lives on, pasting over the reality of the human condition.

In the conservative view, man must always be prepared to bend his knee to values he has failed to live up to. In the Radical view the failings of men are more likely to stem from the inadequacies of a system which has warped and repressed the moral competence that lies dormant or active in every man, and which should be employed to reform the system.

*Segment (d) INVESTMENT as an authentic and intense expression of a unique personality (Radical) V. Human action as the attempt to attain the accomplishment or extension of some norm or value,* (Conservative).

Mere action alone would not differentiate the Right from the New Left. What concerns us in distinguishing developmental radicalism from conservatism is the degree of personal choice and expression within the act. Accordingly we would expect the B.U. Left activists to score higher on an Inner Directed Scale, and as Box D shows, they do. Once again, there is an almost perfect linear relationship from Right to Left, and again the Center liberals and Non-activists show less development than the Left. Another test of radical as opposed to conservative action is whether it expresses independence or is merely an active striving toward previously sanctioned goals, like scoring a touchdown in a game of football. The Achievement via Independence Scale of the California Psychological Inventory tests just this capacity for radical investment and again the Left scores significantly higher and scores drop as we move rightwards.

That this independence and inner-direction is not shared by the Old Left is made quite clear in Table 25. The communist-leaning Left represented on McClosky's scale score high in Acquiescence, Political Cynicism, and Obsessive and repetitious behavior, as do Right-wing Ideologists. The study of Right-wing students on several campuses mentioned earlier found them to be significantly higher than liberals on a scale that measured conformity to authoritarian demands. They would strive energetically to fulfill goals set by superior authority.[26]

Both radicals and conservatives extol freedom in their political rhetoric but for conservatives freedom is more often a physical act or task like building a business or winning a prize. Less often do they conceive of freedom as being present in relationships. Indeed, conservative economic theory would hold that the free man need not concern himself directly with the welfare of the citizenry, since the market mechanism harnesses his own self interest to the public good.

Conservatives tend to regard freedom as best represented by self-sufficiency, financial independence, and *not* relying on others to help. If Conservatives are less psycho-socially developed as our data seem to show, their reluctance to enter relationships of interdependence and complex communication is very understandable. They often tend to assume that

**Box D**

Inner-Directed Scale (P.O.I.)

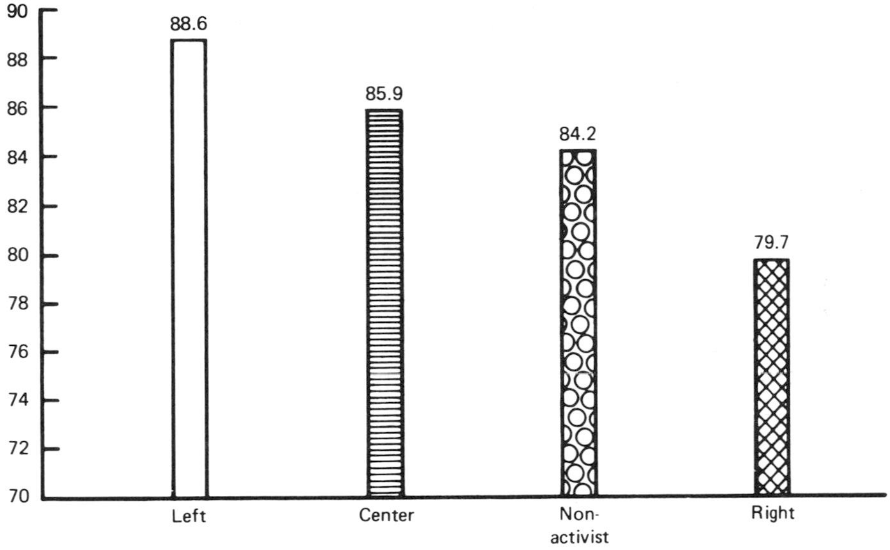


Achievement via Independence (C.P.I.)

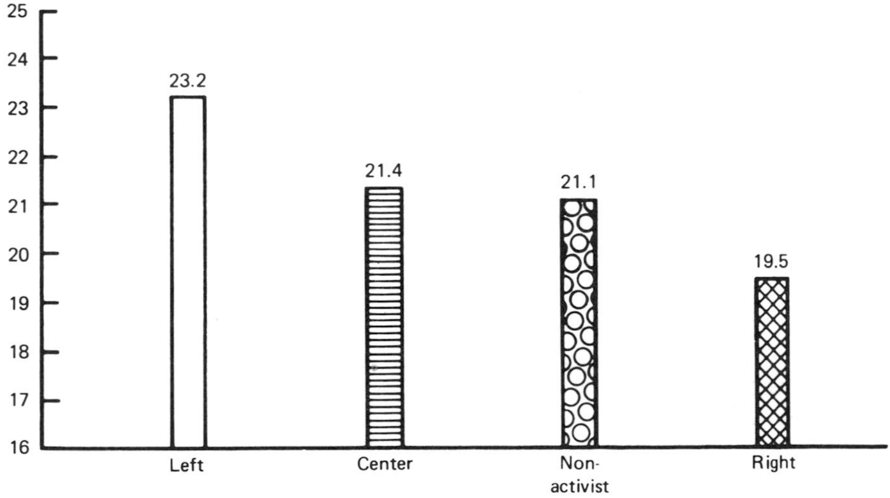

people who receive help must lose their freedom as a consequence, instead of being emancipated through help. Senator Goldwater typified this view.

> I do not undertake to promote welfare, for I propose to extend freedom. . . And if I should later be attacked for neglecting my constituents' 'interests,' I shall reply that I was informed their main interest is liberty and in that cause I am doing the very best I can.[27]

*Segment (e) Acceptance of the vulnerability, doubt and despair inherent in SELF-SUSPENSION and RISK (Radical) V. Praise for self- control, "masculinity" and a dignified composure. Use of economic analogies to reduce psychological risk-taking.*

In the Boston University samples we can see in Box E that the Left activists are overwhelmingly more flexible and more willing to suspend their perspectives to admit new data. Every step to the Right brings a reduction in Flexibility Scale.

I argued in Chapter III that Radical man permitted human suffering and the knowledge of death, isolation, and man's finiteness to flood periodically over his consciousness. Self-suspension is a minor intimation of death, a flirtation with the void, and acknowledgment of the nothingness in spite of which man exists. Here we see some support for this theory. The Left activists are the most conscious of man's aloneness and isolation, yet the most determined to face it alone. In the realization of being outcast they scored the highest, but in hoping that someone *else* would rescue them from this dilemma they scored *lowest* (and the Right highest). Note especially the stark contrast between the developmental radicals of the Left and the Communist students. The latter overwhelmingly rejected the slightest sign of hesitation or despair, expressing total confidence in their historical band-wagon.

However despair about the human condition *is* found among the unorganized, less educated conservatives of the Right and Left, but here it serves a different function. Man is so wretched and exasperating that he is *deservedly* abandoned and has no right to succor.

The failure of self-suspension is found in Table 25 to characterize both the Right and old Left ideologists, whom we see to be high in Rigidity, Suspicion, Elitism and Chauvinism. Table 26 shows that the degree of conservative rejection of existential values is directly proportional to the degree of Rigidity.

A partly discrepant finding was reported by Rokeach in *The Open and Closed Mind.* He found that while his rightist samples were mostly rigid in their thinking – e.g., they declined to suspend any of their assumptions in the face of contradictory evidence – the leftist samples were *not* rigid. They

**Box E**

Flexibility Scale (C.P.I.)

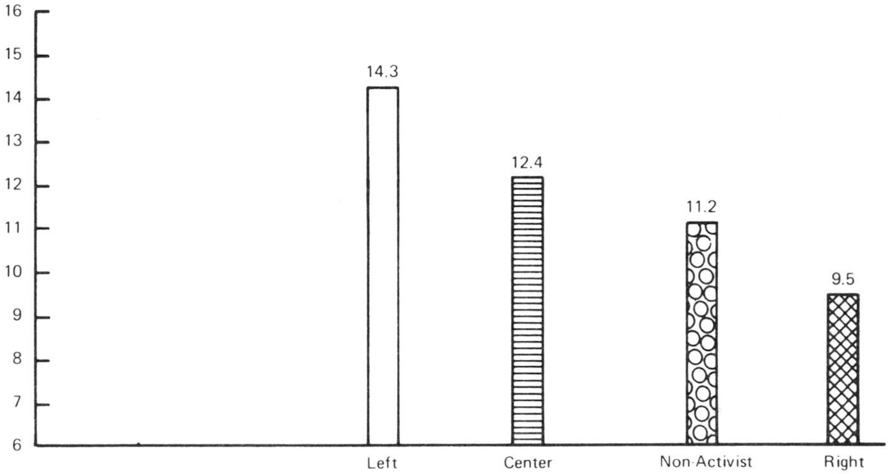


"Belief in the Aloneness and Isolation of Man"
(Subscale of Rokeach Dogmatism Scale)

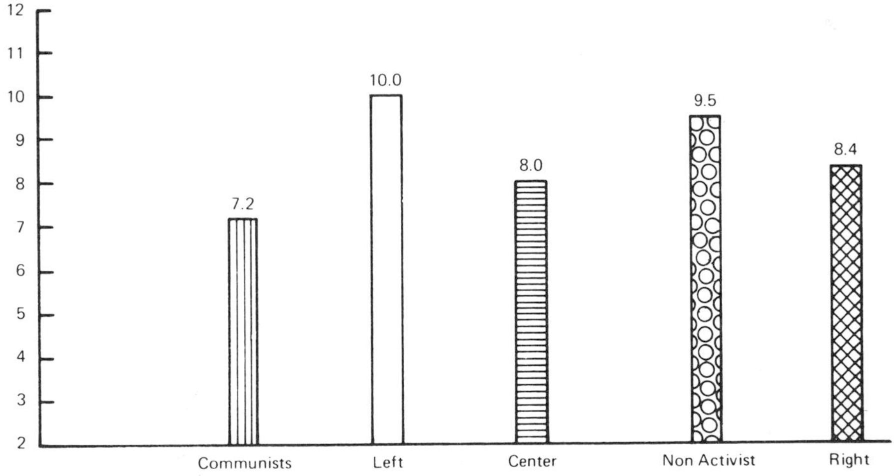

could abandon their assumptions and accept a new set, but they were often *dogmatic*, e.g., they would refuse to integrate single pieces of data which interfered with their current set. Rightists were both rigid *and* dogmatic and on average somewhat more dogmatic than Leftists.

The cross-campus study of right-wing students already referred to found that these young men romanticized risk-taking and spoke respectfully of the dountless courage of entrepreneurs and pioneers which had made America great. Yet almost without exception their career choices were low-risk, banking, business, insurance, and membership of large corporations. In addition they scored much higher than a control group of liberals on a scale of Ego Control v. Manifest Anxiety; that is, they used rigid self-control to lessen their experience of anxiety. They were not about to be discouraged in the totalism of their beliefs.

Of course, the conservative finds himself with less ideological reason for self-suspension and cognitive risk taking. Verities are verities, and his own secret doubts are irrelevant to their truth. Indeed he would logically regard inner-doubt and despair as a personal failing, a temptation corroding his faith during the dark hours.

> Lead kindly light amid encircling doom
> Lead thou me on. . .
> Keep thou my feet: I do not ask to see
> The distant scene; one step enough for me.[28]

If, on the other hand, every act is a personal, perilous and creative choice, rather than obedience to God's Light, then the interval between action and impact is one of genuine risk and self-suspension and comprehension of the distant scene is essential to developing skill.

Conservatives frequently refer to radicals as lacking "back-bone," being "dupes and suckers," "squishy-soft" and behaving like "a bunch of Eleanors." Among less educated and populist style conservatives the deliberate vulnerability of the Left towards dangerous minority groups is regarded with considerable disgust "Jew-kisser," "nigger-lover" and "bleeding heart" are epithets all aimed at discrediting the process of intimate surrender to the perspectives of the distant other.

More educated and image-conscious conservatives have devised a large number of codewords and economic analogies designed to make lower levels of psychological risk-taking sound praiseworthy. I am not saying that *all* economic arguments are disguised pleas for non-suspension (obviously some are *bona fide* statements addressed to tax payers and knowledgeable persons) but many are analogies and economics is especially useful, since profligate spending of money is bad, while the greatest possible investment of emotional energy in helping others is widely regarded as good. It is more effective to accuse the Left of wasting national resources and *other* people's money than wasting their *own* idealism and affection in trying to help the incorrigible. Below is a list of economic images and my estimate of their implicit psychological referents.

| | |
|---|---|
| Fiscal responsibility, the "sound dollar" and fiscal integrity | Don't over spend your emotional energy or suspend your integration of beliefs to let in subversive ideas |
| Balance the budget and avoid deficit financing | Don't unstabilize yourself by giving others more than you are sure you can get back. |
| Honorable settlement of the National Debt | Any loss or frustration in our attempt to communicate with the distant or disadvantaged is unacceptable. We should concentrate more narrowly in preserving, not risking, our competences. |
| Cut waste out of Government spending | Self-suspension only leads to loss through the ingratitude and failure of the other to confirm you |
| Keep American sovereignty unimpaired | Suspending and risking ourselves in overly-intimate relationships with alien persons will lead to the *permanent,* not temporary, disintegration of our belief system. |

Only occasionally does the underlying issue of emotional risk-taking emerge. According to a conservative bard in *American Opinion,* the liberal Left is like a moth flying into a lighted candle, oblivious of danger.

> Yet, ancient folly still the same,
> Out of the trees, the dark wet grass
> Flutters the moth to kiss the light
> Oh fragile fool of silken dust,
> In your small kind what oversight
> Allowed this fatal love and trust!
> Not all the tiny wings that flew
> In lamps and died since lamps were made
> Have left the fear of fire in you;

Only the longing they obeyed
Remains to draw you from the dark,
And you the fugitive from sun
Go mad in presence of a spark
And beating on it are undone.

Another way of avoiding the "fatal love and trust" of individual self-suspension is to act as the moral agent of Supreme Values. Whoever heard of Americanism, Patriotism, Christian Anti-Communism, or Morality itself being suspended for one moment except by traitors? As agents of these values, conservatives can claim to know *before* they interact with others precisely what is right and what is wrong. Nor are the feelings and remonstrances of the listener very relevant, for a value independent of and superior to human wishes cannot be judged by its impact on those wishes. The value of "Americanism" brandished by the House Un-American Activities Committee cannot be suspended because of the protests of "Un-Americans." Indeed *either* their protests *or* their cooperation go to "prove" the value of "Americanism."

This brings us to the final strategy of risk reduction and non-suspension. If the Communist Enemy is at the gates – nay subverting us from within by his insidious doctrines of brotherhood – then dare we trust others, or leave ourselves for one moment, undefended and vulnerable? A moment's indecision, the smallest doubt cast upon our moral purpose, will give the Enemy his chance to undermine and destroy us. It follows *that all who ask us to suspend our assumptions are either in league with the Enemy or are the unwitting dupes of his conspiracy.* Thus do the besieged justify rigidity, and the rigid claim they are besieged.

*Segment (f) Encouragement and idealization of BRIDGING the wider DISTANCES between those who express equally legitimate yet discrepant human needs (Radical) V. Idealization of the shortest possible DISTANCE between persons, whose interaction is mediated by, and should approximate to, those Supreme Values around which the faithful are exhorted to assemble (Conservative).*

Rokeach found that the dogmatic Left and Right have different styles in the way they refuse to BRIDGE the DISTANCE to others. The Right was often ethnocentric, believing that certain groups are so unworthy and deviant that their skin color or their ethnicity is proof enough of the dangers of investing oneself in them. The dogmatic Left which, for strategic reasons, wishes to make the greatest possible contrast between itself and "colonialists," officially deprecates ethnocentrism *but instead discriminates on the basis of belief.*

In fact there is some research which suggests that the distance between beliefs is the real test of open-mindedness. If white persons, prejudiced against Negroes, are told *in advance* that a particular Negro agrees strongly with them, they will prefer his company to that of a white person critical of them. Color differences seem to symbolize distance but only in the absence of more precise information.[30]

The best educated conservatives are generally similar to the dogmatic Left in that they do not reject on the basis of ethnicity but on the basis of how different the other's beliefs are from their own. Campus conservatives expressed strong preferences and admiration for respectable middle class circles, an attitude which would perpetuate their avoidance of minority groups, but only indirectly.

Box F shows that communist students show the most intolerance towards the "renegade, disbeliever and deviant," followed interestingly enough by Non Activists, then the Right, Center, and Left. Perhaps political groups are particularly sensitive to the value of tolerance, since the Right scored very slightly below Non-activists. (However, the difference was not statistically significant.) Once again the sharpest contrast of all is between the New Left and the communists, who occupy opposite poles on the tolerance-intolerance continuum.

In Table 25 the Right Wing Ideologists and the Old Left, a sample much less educated on average than the Boston students, are distinctly Isolationist, Ethnocentric and Intolerant, with a lesser but still significant proportion of anti-Semitic and pro-Segregation respondents. McClosky found astonishingly high *positive* correlations between Right-wing and Old Left Ideologists. Both scales correlated strongly with Populism. Among the highly anomic there seems a general tendency to endorse bellicose and dire predictions about the imminent collapse of everything and the disloyalty of public figures, with little concern for ideological consistency.

In Table 26 we see that conservative rejectors of existential values have the greatest contempt for Human Frailty. The more they deny existence the more salient becomes the intolerance.

While radicals praise international cooperation, the voluntary integration of equals from different races, and confrontation even with enemies, conservatives have a number of strategies designed to shorten distances or to avoid the wider ones. These include toughminded attitudes towards those with distant beliefs, warm praise and celebration of short distances, the use of objects to symbolize the unity of shared values, and the call to close ranks against the Enemy. Below is a sample of statements from books written or introduced by Barry Goldwater.

> (Conservatives believe in). . . the necessity and inevitability of social and economic classes. . .[31]

**Box F**

"Intolerance towards the renegade, the disbeliever and the deviant." (Subscale of Rokeach Dogmatism Scale)

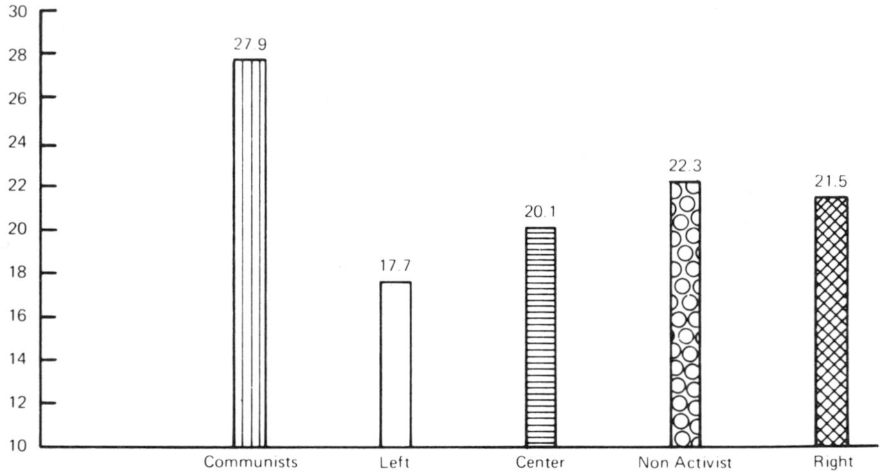


**Box G**

Self – Actualization Scale (P.O.I.)

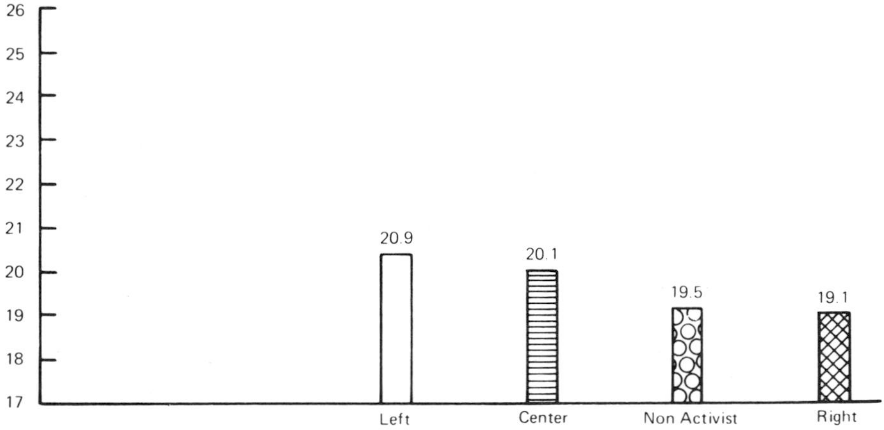

> (Conservatives can win by)... LIMITING FOREIGN AID ONLY TO OUR ALLIES... and distinguish between allies and those practicing a questionable form of neutralism.[32]
>
> The Negro has increased his own chances for complete acceptance through self-improvement and patient effort toward social equality.[33]
>
> The result is a Leviathan, a vast national authority out of touch with the people, and out of their control.[34]
>
> I am firmly convinced – not only that integrated schools are not required – but that the Constitution does not permit any interference...[35]
>
> And so if we would improve education in America... we will not rush to the federal treasury with requests for money. We will focus attention on our local community...[36]
>
> We should declare the world Communist movement an outlaw in the community of civilized nations. Accordingly, we should withdraw diplomatic recognition from all Communist governments...[37]

The constant theme of these statements is that the distances between social classes, between America and neutralists, between black and white, between government and people, and between communists and capitalists are too wide and dangerous to bridge and that anyway it is not necessary to do so.

In direct contrast and perhaps to compensate for the uncharitable nature of the above statements, conservatives have nothing but affection and kind words for the family, the local community, the church, the squad of army buddies, the Elks, the college fraternity, Southern Hospitality, the community chest, the football team, the local Chamber of Commerce, the American Legion post, and the Boy Scouts. Here distances are short and interaction is safe, structured, and predictable.

Conservatives will tend to alter their attitude to certain relationships depending on which of any two is shorter in distance. Hence relationships of dialogue with the Federal Government are to be minimized if the alternative is States' Rights and local control, but can be maximized if the object is to arm ourselves and avoid the wider distance to the Soviet Union or neutralists. In the thirties and forties anti-Semitism was endemic in Conservative circles but was quite unacceptable when two Jewish aides joined Joe McCarthy to expose leftists. Similarly Vietnam "hawks" take great pride in the fact that black and white Americans have integrated to kill communists.

A third conservative device for keeping distances short is to assemble persons in highly structured situations for the purpose of acclaiming an object which symbolizes shared values. Objects can receive the tears and tribute which it is dangerous and "soft" to invest in other human beings. After all, a cross, a flag, or a graven image cannot reject you, and if five hundred persons acclaim the object on cue and in unison, one achieves the sensation of unity with negligible risk – or learning.

As I found in the British Army, it is completely acceptable to weep as the regimental colors are unfurled for the last time, but effeminate and distasteful to weep for a friend who shot himself during the rigors and hazing of officer training. The rallying around flags is a perfectly logical extension of the belief that values are independent of men's needs. In this view communication is best achieved when persons assemble with prior agreement to revere the Superordinate Good. In such ceremonies it is seldom even necessary to *look* at another human being. It is a dignified, rehearsed, shoulder to shoulder relationship, with all eyes on the Object.

Hence a very recent study of American Protestant churches found that regular attendance, giving money to the Church and the degree of spiritual rather than secular concern were all *inversely* related to an ethical concern to help and succour one's fellow man. Despite innumerable songs and sermons on love, those who assembled with like minded persons to bend the common knee were usually less willing to engage other human beings face to face in a helping relationship.[38]

These correlations were considerably strengthened when conservative and fundamentalist churches were taken alone, but tended to disappear in the liberal and secular churches. The crucial distinction is not whether persons assemble in church groups, but whether these groups are exclusive, inward and upward looking to Heaven, or whether they are inclusive and outward looking to man or to God *in* man.

A very successful conservative strategy has been to accentuate the "communist menace" so that people will close ranks and shorten distances. Deviant persons of many kinds are labeled communist, including those selling pornography, experts in Mental Health, advocates of gun control and police review boards, and of course, homosexuals, who are allegedly attracted to the Left by easy pickings among proletariat youth.[39] Many anti-communist writings and speeches show far less interest in Russia than in the control of domestic deviations.

The ingenuity of anti-communism lies in its strategy of taking the widest and most feared psychological distance, that between America and Communist countries, and substituting it for the medium long but still anxious distances between Washington and local authorities, black and white Americans, the sexually conventional and the sexually deviant, and the intellectuals and laymen. If difficulties in communication over these *medium* distances can be attributed to *widest gulf of all,* so that professors, homosexuals, and federal officials are seen as "communist inspired," then even these medium distances can be avoided, and patriotic, vigilant Americans can huddle together in the tight, safe formations demanded by such an emergency.

*Segment (g) Emphasis upon SELF-CONFIRMATION and SELF-TRANSCENDENCE as a test of acting rightly towards others (Radical) V. Emphasis upon the achievement of external norms and just rewards for the accomplishment of goals, previously sanctioned by responsible authorities. (Conservative)*

If the Left is more oriented to self-actualization we would expect Left activists in our Boston Sample to score the highest on instruments measuring this. In Box G we see that this is so. Despite a rather poorly constructed scale, the difference between Left and Right is statistically significant, and the relationship is again linear. These findings are important because they provide the first pieces of evidence that the Left does not rebel for nothing, but in fact achieves higher levels of fulfillment via rebellion.

The impression that the Right pursues external incentives and more public goals was strengthened by an analysis of the various subjects in which students of different political leanings specialized. The Right and Non-Activist students had a strong tendency to specialize in career oriented applied fields, which would win them a coveted place in recognized professional or business institutions. These fields included accounting, pharmacy, law, engineering, agriculture, business administration, medicine, dentistry, and for women, subjects like home economics. In contrast the Left and Center activists were located in basic disciplines, such as history, philosophy, economics, social science, etc., subjects less immediately saleable on the market, but which might satisfy a search for meaning in life, and provide knowledge for the expansion of awareness. The percentages of various groups in basic disciplines show an unmistakable trend.

| | |
|---|---|
| Left Activists | 88.9 |
| Center Activists | 67.7 |
| Right Activists | 45.7 |
| Non-Activists | 35.1 |

Similar differences were found at the University of California, at Berkeley, where students in the top half of a "libertarianism" Scale were much more likely to study the humanities, social sciences, etc., while the business, education, and engineering students were, on average, considerably lower in "libertarianism."[40] The study of Right-wing counter-pickets found that they mostly studied business and law at Catholic universities.[41]

The effect of pursuing goals which are less one's own but which constitute public symbols of success seems to lower the amount of self-actualization experienced (see Box G). In the national samples in Table 26, the conservative rejectors of existential values were the highest in Alienation, while the acceptors were the lowest. In Table 25 Right-wing and Old Left ideologists are much more likely to report Bewilderment, Status Frustration, Alienation, and poor Life Satisfaction.

It is not difficult to see why. The best hope of obtaining self-fulfillment is to ensure that one's own personality and predilections are put foremost in an activity. Even in cases where "everyone agrees that plastics are the coming thing," they may no longer agree ten years hence. The conservative's seeming desperation with maintaining a consensus about values reveals his fear that the prize he seeks will cease to be regarded as a prize after a lifetime's struggle to attain it. It is as if a football team, having marched 80 yards from its own goal-line, finally scored a brilliant touchdown, only to find that the bored spectators had drifted from the stadium to watch a peace demonstration. Those who regard norms as independent of man must insist on wide-spread allegiance to these norms, over long periods of time. The "rules of the game" *must* be respected and conserved or the lives of game players cease to be meaningful.

Developmental radicals are far less concerned with a dwindling consensus because they are convinced that so long as their personal expression is authentically true to the human condition, which they share with all men, then somehow and somewhere will be found others who appreciate its basic humanity. The most "far out" rebellion will find a response, provided always that it is genuinely experienced.

Many conservatives who worked long, late hours to sell the equivalent of an extra ten-gross of plastic bottle caps must have been nagged at times by the same feeling of ultimate meaninglessness which causes students to rebel. But conservative philosophy tends to disparage these inner doubts and to regard rebellion of the spirit as a manifestation of willful laziness and an obstacle to glowing prize of a vice-presidency. When, therefore, a conservative sees hairy Hippies or rampaging students mocking these golden symbols of success, it must seem to him that these devils on the outside have formed a secret alliance with the devils *inside himself.* What these kids are shouting about is precisely what his own "natural laziness" whispered to him when the fiftieth buyer closed the door in his face. Rebels must be crushed along with his own doubts. They *will* learn to respect that for which he has slaved all these years.

The forgoing scenario is not without foundation in research. The conservative and populist supporters of Joe McCarthy came preponderantly from the *higher* income groups within each educational bracket, although education itself was negatively related to support for the Senator, as was social status.[42] Hence a man with a high school education, earning several times more than the average high school graduate, would be significantly more likely to support McCarthy than the rest of his class. The pursuit of money or "success" during a period in which respect for business achievement is declining seems to induce in its "successful victims" a reactionary ire against those "comsymps" in high places who change the rules in ways that rob the newly rich of the respect due to them. No wonder these McCarthyists reported acute dissonance between their wealth and their status.[43]

There are many ways in which conservatives reveal their failing powers of communication, and the consequent lack of meaningful rapport with others. Even their own literature complains of the shortage of conservative communicators.

> (Liberals have) flooded the book shelves, the magazine stands. . . One of Conservatism's glaring deficiencies has been its shortage of articulate spokesmen.[44]

One sign that persuasion is failing is the constant conservative emphasis on forcing the compliance of others without confronting them. While developmental radicals may use force in gaining access to authorities who previously ignored them, the access, once assured, must be used for moral suasion. But the conservative statements which follow share the theme of avoiding dialogue all together.

> . . . all mothers of illegitimate children should be advised that, should they have any more children out of wedlock, the mothers would be denied relief.[45]
>
> The United States has great power, and it must use that power firmly and effectively against the Communist menace. No course we may pursue will please all our world neighbors, and we should not be unduly concerned about whether the course we choose pleases or displeases them.[46]
>
> It would not be America really if it did not produce men who suddenly tire of palaver and reach for the rifle on the wall. . .[47]

Conservatives find themselves obliged to employ coercive measures for another good reason. Their rhetoric is characteristically conventional and repetitive (See Table 25). Why *should* a proponent of eternal verities change his message? But, as we have seen in earlier chapters, confirmation and self-transcendence comes to those who say something *different,* who resynthesize sense data into novel patterns. The endless repeater of conventional wisdom encounters the serious problem of boring his listeners with eulogies to motherhood and country. Only if motherhood and country are in serious danger from pubescent black men and agents of the communist conspiracy will the values he proclaims appear vital or important. Clichés or truisms which we usually take for granted can only electrify us *if we believe them to be endangered,* so that we are hearing precious truths for the last time from a defender of the faith. The anti-communist crusaders are locked in a never ending battle with their own atrophying resources. The devil they fight is boredom incarnate and the beast of their own nothingness.

*Segment (h) An egalitarian dialectic leading to a SYNERGISTIC and "just" reconciliation of opposites (Radical) V. The victorious imposition upon any conflict of the relevant Superior Values (Conservative).*

Do we have any evidence which suggests that the New Left is more likely to form nurturant and synergistic relationships with significant others? Box H shows the Left student activists at Boston University are significantly less afraid of being compromised and short-changed in a face to face dialectic with those of differing views. In a Fear of Compromise Scale the relationship is again linear with increasing fear from Left to Right, with non-activists most similar to the Right, and with communist students slightly more fearful than the Right.

These findings closely resemble a study of three hundred and fifty students at a mid-western university.[48] They were given a questionnaire covering current issues on social problems, civil rights, foreign policy, economics, etc. and according to their responses were divided into four categories stretching from Extreme Liberal to Extreme Conservative. They were then questioned about their willingness to engage persons of discrepant political views along the radical conservative dimension. The results were as follows. The greater the distance, the greater on average was the disinclination to engage or befriend the deviant. The further to the Left the more willing was the individual to engage others in general. The further to the Left, the wider was the distance which the individual was willing to bridge before expressing fears and reservations.

But it is not enough merely to enter relationship, any more than it is enough to rebel and deviate. If a *balance* between "I rebel – we exist" has been attained, then the same Left Activists who ignored sexual taboos should also have found higher levels of SYNERGY with their chosen partners, thereby justifying the rebellion. In Box H we see that the Left does indeed show superior capacities for Intimate Contact despite their preoccupations with politics. The Right sample had the lowest score of all, and in subsequent group interviews several reported sexual "hang-ups" and problems.

In no sense could the Left-activists be called promiscuous or irresponsible. More than any other group they showed in interviews a deep concern for the integrity of their personal relationships with sexual partners. They sought and usually found a depth of rapport, yet demanded no long term commitment from the other.

The evidence for higher levels of synergy on the New Left is by no means conclusive, since "intimate contact" is usually over *short* distances. The reconciliation of widely discrepant opinions would provide more satisfactory evidence.

However the problem can be attacked from the other way around. The opposite to synergy is either the authoritarian domination of the one

**Box H**

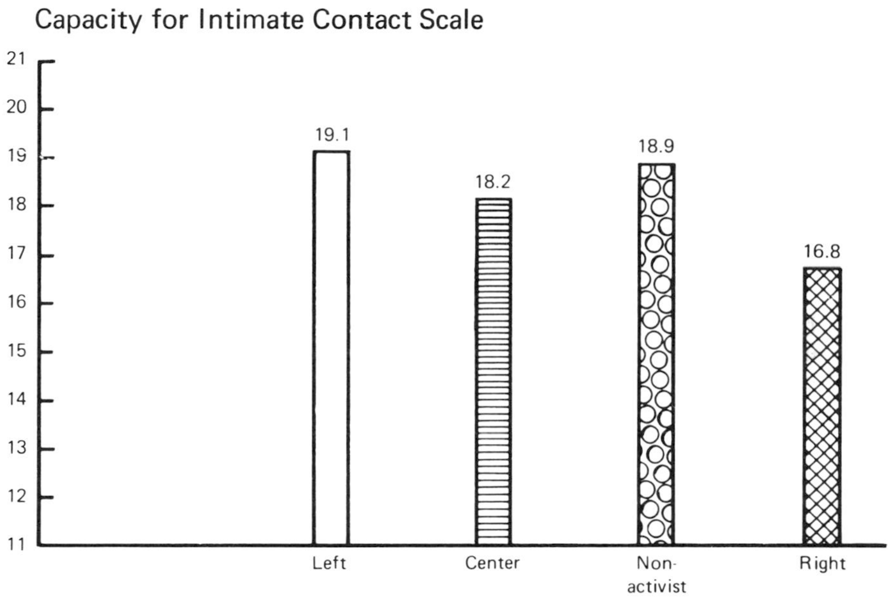
Capacity for Intimate Contact Scale
21
20
19
18
17
16
15
14
13
12
11
19.1
18.2
18.9
16.8
Left
Center
Non-activist
Right

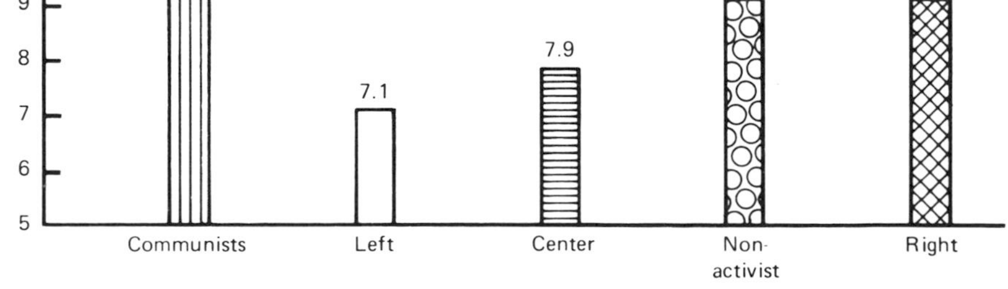
"Fear of Compromise" (Subscale of Rokeach's Dogmatism Scale)
12
11
10
9
8
7
6
5
9.9
7.1
7.9
9.2
9.2
Communists
Left
Center
Non-activist
Right

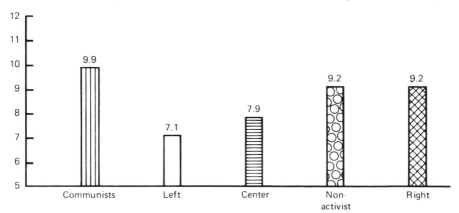

Box H (Continued)

"Authoritarian Belief in Great Cause"
(Subscale of Rokeach Dogmatism Scale)

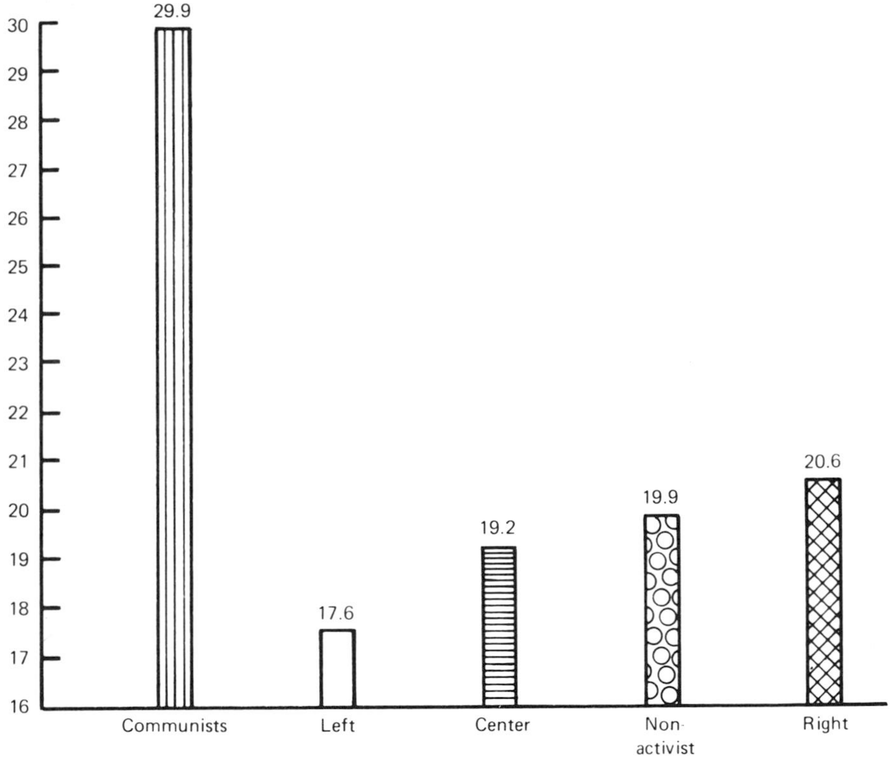


Source: — "A Study of a Sampling of Boston University Student Activists," Unpubl. Doctoral Dissertation by Irvin Doress. Boston Univ. 1968.

perspective by another, a mutually frustrating compromise between the two, or the destruction of both perspectives brought about by repeated attempts by either party to subordinate the other. We would therefore expect that the Right would be more authoritarian, and in Box H we see that except for British communist students, the Right is the most authoritarian (on a scale deliberately designed to attract communists) and the Left is, as usual, the least authoritarian. In fact the scale items measured Authoritarian Belief in a Great Cause, and *all* the American samples rejected the "great cause" items, which accounts for the extent to which the communists outdistanced the Right on this subscale.

When we look at McClosky's national samples, we find somewhat higher authoritarianism among Right-wing ideologists than Old Left Ideologists in Table 25, and authoritarianism declining with each degree of increased radicalism in Table 26. The cross-campus study of right-wing students, already cited, found that they were higher in Authoritarian Conformance than a sample of liberals.[49] In fact the greater authoritarianism of conservatives has been extensively documented.[50]

Authoritarianism is the logical outcome of conservative philosophy. If the Good is apart from man and man can only approach it by keeping to the straight and narrow path to virtue, then deviation from the path is as wrong as the path itself is right. Compromise between man's devious ways and the "right path" is therefore *less* satisfactory than the total victory of "rightness."

Authoritarianism is also the logical outcome of the functioning of conservatives on segments of the cycle already discussed. If X has narrow PERCEPTION (segment a) so that he cannot perceive the needs of Y, yet knows the values to which he himself adheres, then the settlement of conflict between X and Y is likely to involve the submission of one to the values of the other.

Similarly if X keeps his inner needs inviolate within his IDENTITY (Segment b) as does Y, then clearly these needs cannot be synergised. To obtain need fulfillment one must subordinate the other to his strictly private satisfaction. Where private needs are expressed as moral goals these will almost inevitably produce a clash of rigid abstractions which neither party can SUSPEND so that they "mesh" with others. Again the necessity for the "victory" of one morality over the other follows logically.

When X finds himself too DISTANT (Segment f) from Y, mutuality is impeded. For a period of time X (or Y) may implore the other to shorten the distance by embracing X's value and acknowledging its superiority over Y's willful and disobedient spirit. Y is likely to make the same appeal. After a period of talking past each other, both will regretfully announce that their patience is exhausted. The "flexible" manner in which each has offered five alternate plans for dominating the other has led to mutual rejection. There is now a state of emergency brought about by the enemy's bad faith and deviation from virtue. Force is required to "restore morality." As I have already argued, authoritarianism and force are also precipitated by the incapacity to achieve a SELF-CONFIRMING IMPACT (Segment g).

The foregoing argument suggests that well meaning groups may virtually stumble into authoritarian behavior by encountering problems of communication too great for their level of development. But groups are also lured into authoritarianism by a number of secret satisfactions which act as substitutes for the pleasures inherent in development.

The attack upon the enemy produces a "counterfeit-contrast," which injects into the weak and disintegrating segments of the cycle a temporary and euphoric strength, which has probably killed and maimed more people than all the addictive drugs in the world. Most of our sensations are sharpened by contrast. A person with inadequate PERCEPTION can buy the sensation of sharp vision by etching his gestalt in black and white. We form our IDENTITY, not only by what we are, but by what we are *not.* The fuzzy delineation of a weak ego can be strengthened by merging it with the "mission of America" and regarding "Un-Americanism" as the blackest night. Serious doubts about the DISTANCES which can and cannot be bridged are resolved by splitting the world into good and bad parts, only the first of which can be reached.

As explained in Chapter IV the mutually defensive alliance against the powers of darkness permits easy, cheap confirmation between ethnocentric comrades-at-arms, with no grey cliche unapplauded since it now shines gossamer white against the lowering darkness. But more than this, authoritarian militance *substitutes for the contrast between reconciled polarities within the cycle.*

To make clearer what I mean, let us recall how radical man sharpens his experience of contrast. He "tastes death" every time he suspends himself in creative endeavor or leaps the hitherto unbridgeable chasms between highly differentiated groups. In his eventual confirmation and self-transcendence he finds a reconciliation contrasted with aloneness, an acceptance contrasted with rejection, a closeness contrasted with distance, and an intense joyfulness contrasted with prior despair, what A. H. Maslow has called a "peak experience,"[51] the ascent into Heaven after three days in Hell. With each successful revolution of the cycle, radical man overcomes the contrast between rebellion and confirmation, distance and relationship, differentiation and integration. But uncreative persons fail to risk and suspend themselves and so fail to taste the sheer exhilaration and ecstasy of reconciled opposites. Their only hope of "tasting contrast" *is to operate under siege conditions.*

The siege condition puts back the missing contrasts. It replaces existential anxiety by physical fear and danger. It replaces the existential leap by the "heroic" leap into oblivion. Thousands of little men with undistinguished and indistinguishable identities experience the relative value of their lives only as death beckons. One thinks of Mersault on the eve of his execution for one triumphant moment made alive by the imminent prospect of death and the execration of the crowd.

In the contrast of siege conditions it is possible to achieve self-transcendence with utterances and acts so banal and destructive that in peaceful conditions such behavior would cause only boredom or anger. As it is, the most underdeveloped member of the squad can save his buddies by falling on a grenade, and so live for years in their memories and in the honor rolls of his country. Every general and president associated with the war policy will eulogize him, desperately grateful that his sacrifice has ennobled their crass mistakes. Who will now dare to say he died in vain during an unjust and grossly misconceived campaign? One American judge sentencing a twenty year old father to five years in jail for draft resistance specifically stated that he must do this for those who died.[52] Thus does authoritarianism feed upon itself as we gather around war memorials ostensibly to consecrate the dead, in fact to consecrate the mistakes of our leaders, and to lay the solemn foundation for the next war.

This capacity for armed struggle to produce counterfeits of creativity leads me to the tentative conclusion that authoritarian militarism acts like a cancerous growth that imitates yet devours the processes of life.

How do conservatives reveal their greater authoritarianism and militance? Apart from incessant demands for a "win policy" and victory over communism, which I regard as self-evident, their rhetoric is full of unreconciled dichotomies, and the implication that one dichotomy must conquer the other.

Consider the following statements:

> We cannot delude ourselves with the expectation that we may go a little way further and then stop in the belief that we can combine socialism and capitalism, and preserve the best features of each. The very first hard and cold fact that we must face is that these two systems cannot live together in the same society. . .[53]

> . . .leaders of both the Liberal and Conservative points of view are sincere, intelligent, loyal Americans. But somebody is *right* and somebody is *wrong* in this debate.[54]

> Conservatives believe in: *The superiority of liberty over security. The rights of men as something earned and not given.*[55]

> True independence can never be enjoyed by those who must rely on other persons or agencies – especially government – for

> food, shelter, and material comforts.[56]
>
> (Liberals) place what we need above what we can afford.[57]
>
> Even if a government *could* regulate as effectively as does the free market, the freedom of the people must be decreased as the degree of government planning increases.[58]
>
> Peace is a worthy objective, but if we must choose between peace and keeping the Communists out of Berlin, then we must fight. Freedom, in the sense of self-determination is a worthy objective; but if granting self-determination to Algerian rebels entails sweeping that area into the Sino-Soviet orbit, then Algerian freedom must be postponed. . .[59]

For those able to synergize and reconcile opposites between persons and within themselves these statements are puzzling.

It is not necessary to choose *either* liberty or security for to increase the other's security can set him free, or vice versa. It is precisely by bestowing *rights* on others that they can *earn* for themselves more than was bestowed. In disputes between these false dichotomies one side is not right and the other wrong, rather both have part of the truth and need each other. Only those who invest and *fail* to find confirmation are placing what they need above what they afford and only in authoritarian relationships would government planning decrease the freedom of the governed, or Algerian self-determination decrease American self-determination.

The incapacity of conservatives to combine these dichotomies into "just" synergies leads to a "see-saw effect" with conservatives in different moods extolling one dichotomy and then suddenly switching over. The self-interest of the entrepreneur is admired along with saintliness of the nun or the self-sacrifice of the missionary. We are exhorted to march to war with a perfect obedience that will uphold our perfect freedom. Admiration for pure and sacred womanhood and lifelong married fidelity rides double harness with the exploitive sexuality of fraternity brothers and evening visits to the whore. Righteous indignation is bracketed with a personal sense of sin, and domination must stand ready to let submission take its place at a moment's notice.

This see-saw mechanism is a very crude and rudimentary substitute for flexibility and the need to combine the segments of the cycle in different combinations of strength, depending upon the circumstances and the human needs for fulfillment. While the concept of synergy allows for very sensitive, moment by moment adjustments, the hierarchical ordering of values necessitates a succession of sharp bends, like a ship laboriously tacking against the wind, as one value after the other struggles for ascendency. First Selfishness is subordinated to Self-Sacrifice until the whole society is so repressed that selfishness breaks out of its cage like an animal to the applause of Social Darwinists and mystical references to an Invisible Hand that makes everything right again despite appearances. Puritannical reformers struggle to return Selfishness to its cage, and set Self-Sacrifice to guard the culprit. Selfishness then proclaims that Self-Sacrifice is in fact in league with a foreign, godless power that preaches just this doctrine. And so it goes on, the battle between dogmatic Right and dogmatic Left, the confusion between internal and external conflict.

One final point about authoritarianism. This negation of synergy is a relative phenomenon which ebbs and flows in the character of an individual depending upon the difficulty and distance of his various relationships. A man may be simultaneously synergistic with his family and destructive to outsiders, understanding one moment and blind the next. He may destroy the Vietnamese culture in his mornings and dandle a Vietnamese orphan in his afternoons. He may even desire passionately integration with American Negroes while passionately desiring the everlasting destruction of the Viet Cong. We nearly *all* become authoritarian in situations of sufficient danger and perplexity, like being locked up in a ward with paranoid schizophrenics.

*Segment (i) The INTEGRATION of human affect with reason into a belief system of inter-communicating thought-matrices of developing COMPLEXITY (Radical) V. The permanent separation of reprehensible desires, appetites and hasty reasoning, from Superior Values and Wisdoms which have stood the test of time (Conservative)*

Since it proved impossible to discuss relationships between persons without simultaneously mentioning the relationship of ideas within each person, much of the argument in Segment (i) has been anticipated. It follows that where synergistic relationships are formed, each party can carry away with him the integrative thought processes by which formerly discrepant views were reconciled. X can fit Y's views into his own and enjoy an expanded awareness. As we have seen a mind with poor internal communications is both the result and in turn the product of poor external communications.

One difficulty, then, from which conservatives might be expected to suffer would be a poor integration of their thought structures. If Chastity is to overcome Lust, then by definition Lust must not be heard, nor given a chance to break loose. Moreover a philosophy which separates value from human need is in that respect dichotomous and unintegrated.

In Box I we see that, as expected, there are marked differences between the Left and Right on a subscale measuring "Isolation, contradiction and non-integration of ideas *within* belief systems." Here the Right scores even

**Box I**

Intellectual Efficiency Scale

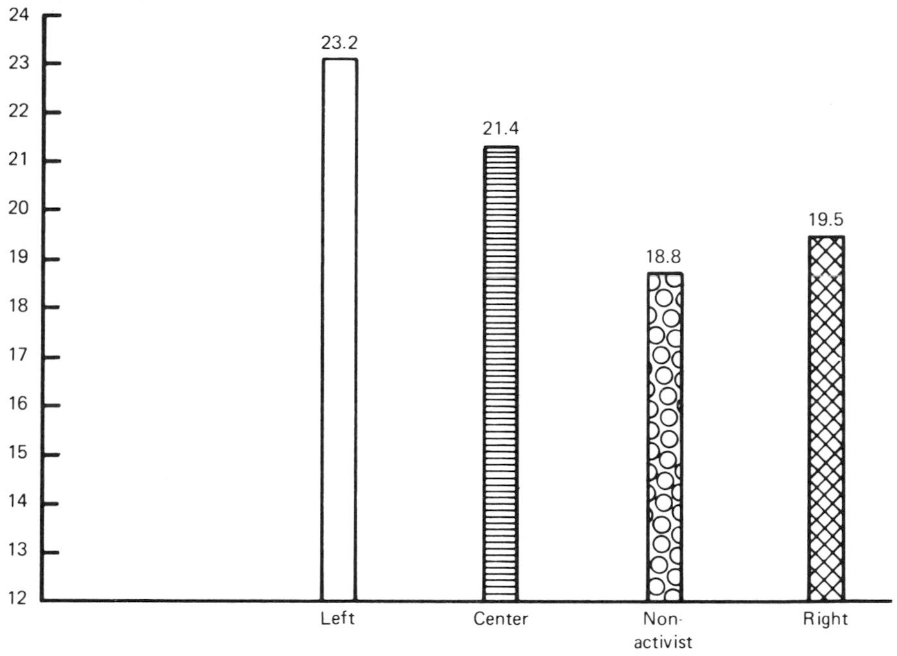


"Isolation, contradiction, and non-integration of ideas within belief system." (Rokeach subscale)

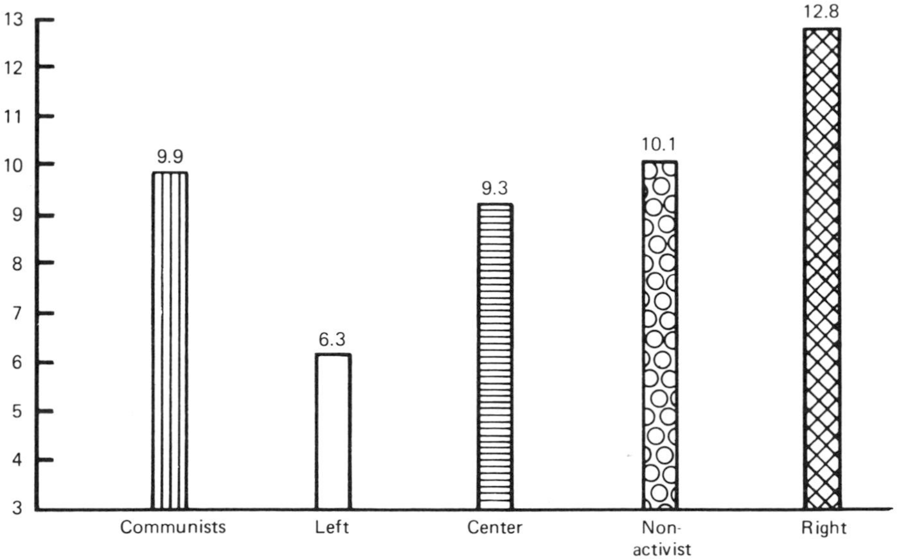

higher than the communist students, tested a decade earlier. The differences are substantial and the Left scores lower than other groups to an extent which is statistically significant in every case. Their higher scores on Intellectual Efficiency scale would seem to be a natural consequence. (However no differences could be found in grade point averages, perhaps because basic disciplines where the leftists were located, attract better scholars overall than the applied subjects studied by right-wing students, so that a B in English and a B in pharmacy would not be really comparable.)

In the national samples in Table 25 Right and Old Left Ideologists are overwhelmingly anti-intellectual. Their lack of Social Responsibility indicates a refusal to pick up the feedback from their action or inaction. Finally their belief systems are Totalistic and petrified so that the elements cannot "move" and modify each other and cannot "loosen" to let in novel matrices. Both Intellectuality and Social Responsibility increase in Table 26, as the degree of conservatism and rejection of existence decrease. The totalistic nature of right-wing thought was also found in the cross-campus study of Young Americans for Freedom.[60]

A more subtle form of conservative rhetoric pretends that the irreconcilables have been reconciled. What in fact is domination by a single dimension of thought is presented as a "pseudo-synergy." Herbert Marcuse is especially perceptive on this issue. The "clean bomb," the "luxury fallout shelter," "harmless fallout," "father of the H-bomb," "*your* favorite drugstore," "science-military meeting," "Labor Seeking Missile Harmony" are all his examples, but there are many more. Television commercials show us innumerable demonstrators "protesting" in favor of mouthwash or spaghetti. We are urged to show our "individuality" by joining thousands in the choice of a new cigarette, and bouncy teen-agers urge us to "rebel" in favor of a mass produced automobile. In a contemporary film by Jean Luc Goddard, *Les Carbinieres* return from a bloody war without the promised booty and cheated of glory, but with a pile of incongruously jumbled picture postcards, images strung togeher in a pathetic imitation of experience. In reality all these pseudo-synergies are hierarchies, with the fall-out shelter and the H-bomb threatening to extinguish forever all luxury, all cleanliness, and all life. Within each contradiction the stronger holds the weaker captive, and democratic window dressing disguises the total domination of one idea by the other and the non-communication between them.

This completes the preliminary discussion of the Radical-Conservative dichotomy and its implications for psycho-social development. The issues leave many questions unanswered, which will be pursued in the three remaining chapters.

## NOTES FOR CHAPTER IX

1. *Beyond Right and Left* by Richard Kostelanetz (ed.). New York: Morrow, 1968.

2. See the *ADA World,* Washington, D.C., which gives liberal and conservative voting records. Those high on conservatism vote consistently for certain Federal expenditures. See also *The Congressional Record.*

3. See various essays in *The Radical Right,* Daniel Bell (ed.), New York: Anchor, 1964, especially "Three Decades of the Radical Right" by S. M. Lipset, "The Pseudo-Conservative Revolt" by Richard Hofstadter, who also develops this theme in *The Paranoid Style in American Politics,* New York: Alfred Knopf, 1965.

4. *The Radical Right, op. cit.,* p. 402.

5. *The Achieving Society* by David McClelland, *op. cit.,* p. 150.

6. An excellent exposition of the different meanings which Prohibition had for diverse groups who found the issue useful to them is contained in *Symbolic Crusade* by Joseph R. Gusfield, Urbana: University of Illinois Press, 1963. For the way in which the British Labor Party used the issue of "The Bomb" see *Middle Class Radicalism* by Frank Parkin, New York: Praeger, 1968.

7. Murray Horwitz observes "Now characteristically in public discussion, persons will be more inclined to talk about the goal they would like to pursue than about the needs they are trying to meet. For goals are more impersonal, less revealing of "weakness" . . .although the goal statement contains information about needs. The information is quite incomplete. . . Given a need, it is clear that many goals can be potentially satisfying. . . But each person states a particular goal. The discrepancies among various goals produce an impression of incompatibility. . ." See *T-Group Theory and Laboratory Method, op. cit.,* pp. 371-2.

8. "Interrelations of Opinion" by V. O. Key Jr. in *Readings in American Political Behavior,* R. E. Wolfinger (ed.), Englewood Cliffs: Prentice Hall, 1966, p. 291f.

9. See *The Psychology of Politics* by H. J. Eysenck, London: Routledge and Kegan Paul. However his scales have been very seriously questioned by R. Christie, "Some Abuses of Psychology," *Psychol. Bull.,* 53: 1956, pp. 439-451, also pp. 411-430 of same issue.

10. For example, Milton Rokeach reports that Communists rate very low on the F-Scale; see *The Open and Closed Mind, op. cit.,* p. 119. Yet the F-Scale is still used in predicting the success of Peace Corps volunteers and it does so better than peer-group and teacher assessments during training. See W. Mischel in *Pers. and Soc. Psychol.,* May, 1965, pp. 510-16.

11. This, of course, is an indirect reference to Harold Lasswell's *Politics: Who Gets What, When, How,* New York: Meridian Books, 1958.

12. "Left and Right: A Basic Dimension of Ideology and Personality" by Silvan Tomkins, in *The Study of Lives,* Robert W. White (ed.), New York: Atherton, 1963, pp. 391-2.

13. *What is Mathematics?* by R. Courant and H. Robbins, New York: Oxford University Press, 1941, p. 321, also quoted by Tomkins in *Study of Lives, Supra,* p. 392.

14. *The Evolution of Physics* by A. Einstein and L. Infield, New York: Simon and Schuster, 1942, p. 313, also quoted by Tomkins in *Study of Lives, Supra,* p. 393.

15. Published in London by the Student Christian Movement in March 1963.

16. *The New Morality* by Arnold Lunn and Garth Lean, London: The Blanford Press, 1964, p. 74.

17. *Towards a Marxist Humanism* by Leszek Kolakowski, New York: Grove Press, 1968.

18. "A Study of a Sampling of Boston Student Activists," unpublished doctoral dissertation, Boston University, 1968.

19. See *The Open and Closed Mind* by Milton Rokeach, *op. cit.*, pp. 413-15.

20. Nationally televised broadcast on Oct. 9, 1964, quoted by Richard Hofstadter in *The Paranoid Style in American Politics, op. cit.*, p. 120.

21. *The Authoritarian Personality* by Adorno, *et al., op. cit.*

22. "For Morality" by Jim Lucier, *American Opinion,* January, 1965, p. 25.

23. "Youth and Peace: A Psychosocial Study of Student Peace Demonstrators in Washington, D.C.," by Frederic Solomon and Jacob R. Fishman, *Journal of Social Issues,* Vol. 20, No. 4, 1964.

24. "The Obedient Rebels: A Study of College Conversions to Conservatism" by L. E. Schiff, *Journal of Social Issues,* Vol. 20, No. 4, 1964.

25. *All Honorable Men* by Walter Goodman, Boston: Little, Brown, 1963, 306-7.

26. "The Obedient Rebels. . ." by L. E. Schiff, *op. cit.*

27. *The Conscience of a Conservative,* New York: MacFadden Books, 1960, p. 23.

28. "The Pillar and the Cloud" by Cardinal Newman, Stanza 1.

29. "Moth (A Warning to Liberals)" by Elizabeth Bohm, *American Opinion,* June, 1965, p. 104.

30. See *The Open and Closed Mind, op. cit.*, pp. 132-170. However there is reason to suppose that discriminating on the basis of skin color and ethnicity may show less tolerance for "distance" than discriminating on the basis of belief. In order to reject someone for their beliefs one must often encounter them first and at least risk discovering their disagreement. To reject on the basis of skin color and ethnicity is to avoid ever engaging the other, and to insist that their superficial appearance reveals all the necessary facts about their beliefs and behavior.

31. *Conservatism: A Guide to its Past, Present, and Future,* Dean Smith, Introduction by Barry Goldwater, p. 34.

32. *Ibid.*, p. 193.

33. *Ibid.*, p. 208.

34. *The Conscience of a Conservative, op. cit.*, p. 20.

35. *Ibid.*, p. 61.

36. *Ibid.*, p. 87.

37. *Ibid.*, p. 123.

38. "Will Ethics be the Death of Christianity" by Rodney Stark and Charles Y. Glock, *Transaction,* June 1968, pp. 7-15.

39. R. G. Waldeck in *Human Events,* April 16, 1952, frequently restated. See, for instance, *Britain and The Beast,* by Peter Howard, London: Heinemann, p. 48.

40. *The Berkeley Student Revolt,* S. M. Lipset and Sheldon S. Wolin, (eds), *op. cit.*, p. 496f.

41. "Youth and Peace. . ." by Frederic Solomon and Jacob S. Fishman, *op. cit.*

42. See "Three Decades of the Radical Right" by S. M. Lipset in *The Radical Right, op. cit.*, p. 401-2.

43. *Ibid.*, p. 403.

44. *Conservatism: A Guide to its Past, Present and Future* by Dean Smith, *op. cit.*, p. 18.

45. *Ibid.*, p. 120.

46. *Ibid.*, p. 197.

47. Karl Hess (Goldwater's speechwriter) in *The American Mercury,* May 1954. Quoted by Murray Kempton in *Portrait of Goldwater,* New Republic Special, 1964.

48. "Tolerance for Divergent Attitudes" by J. L. Simmons in *Social Forces* Vol. 43, No. 3, 1965, pp. 347-52.

49. "The Obedient Rebels" by Lawrence Schiff, *op. cit.*

50. See *The Authoritarian Personality* by Adorno *et al, op. cit., The Open and Closed Mind* by Milton Rokeach, *op. cit.*, "Authoritarian Personality and Foreign Policy" by Daniel J. Levinson in *War*, L. Bramson and G. W. Goethals (eds.), New York: Basic Books, 1964, pp. 133-50.

51. See *Towards a Psychology of Being,* New York: Van Nostrand, 1962, pp. 67-109.

52. *We Won't Go* by Alice Lynd, Boston: Beacon, 1968.

53. From *The Road Ahead* by John T. Flynn, quoted by Dean Smith in *Conservatism: A Guide. . . . op. cit.*, p. 18.

54. *Conservatism: A Guide. . ., op. cit.*, p. 20.

55. *Ibid.*, p. 34.

56. *Ibid.*, p. 76.

57. *Ibid.*, p. 36.

58. *Ibid.*, p. 150.

59. *Ibid.*, p. 181.

60. "The Obedient Rebels" by Lawrence Schiff, *op. cit.*

*Chapter X*

## Conservative and Radical Issues

In this chapter, I shall pursue just a few of the innumerable questions raised by my discussion of the radical-conservative dichotomy in Chapter IX. Is conservative philosophy *so* pathological as to lack all merit? Are there different kinds of conservatism, including some crucial to development? How can we recognize the themes of psycho-social development in issues before Congress? Are the views of developmental radicals more supportive to those qualities which distinguish democratic countries from less democratic ones? I shall try to answer some of these questions in the following sequence.

1) Conservatism as an antidote to the pathologies of the Left
2) The "situational conservative" and his contribution to psycho-social development.
3) The need for a radical-conservative dialogue.
4) Problems in the use of violence by Radical Man.
5) Radical-conservative issues in Congress, an analysis of voting patterns.
6) The humanists and the custodians – two styles of liberalism in Congress.
7) Democracy and psycho-social development.

1) *Conservatism as an antidote to the pathologies of the Left*

At the end of Chapter I, I warned the reader that neither the "scientific" model of conservative man, nor my radical model, would by itself do full justice to the whole man, beset as he is by a variety of conditions. I argued that focusing upon "one side of the coin" could lead to obscuring or distorting the other side.

In order to understand some of the functions of conservative belief which my model fails to stress, let us return to Kohlberg's model of the growth in Moral Judgment. The stages, described in full in Chapter V, are abbreviated below in the left-hand column with some very preliminary research findings on the characteristics of persons at different stages in the right hand column.[1]

| | |
|---|---|
| 6. Conscience and principle orientation | Bay Area radical students, who are very likely to be "Free Speech" protestors. |
| 5. Social Contract Orientation to shared values | Liberal-radical Bay Area students, quite likely to be Free Speech protestors.[2] |

| | |
|---|---|
| 4. Law and Order Authority maintaining orientation | Most American males, especially older ones.[3] Conservative Bay Area students, very few protestors. |
| 3. Personal Concordance, with cultural stereotypes, "good boy" orientation | Most American females; Conservative Bay Area students, very few protestors. |
| 2. Instrumental Relativism, Egotistic orientation to self-gratification | Radical Bay Area students, quite likely to be Free Speech protestors, very likely to approve the protest. |
| 1. Obedience and punishment avoidance orientation | Small children |

This model illustrates, with added perspective, why radical students came off better than conservative ones in the last chapter. Essentially I was comparing Stage 6 and Stage 5 students with Stage 3's and Stage 4's, and the lower group of radicals at Stage 2 were obscured in the gross averages. In fact a closer look at the Boston University activists detailed in Chapter IX reveals that nearly 20% of those on the Left are more dogmatic, narrow and authoritarian than the average conservative student, so that radicalism does have a seamy side. Hence those conservatives who see in every radical protest the Four Horsemen of the Apocolypse emblazoned on a Red Cloud, cannot be dismissed out of hand. The actual degree of risk posed by radicalism is exaggerated by conservatives because few Stage 4's and 3's can comprehend more than one stage of moral judgment above their own,[4] so for many conservatives radicalism is *all Stage 2.* Acts of conscience by radicals will often appear to conservatives at Stage 3 or 4 as incomprehensible anarchy. Now one of Kohlberg's most central findings is that children and young adults in the process of socialization and moral growth *learn each stage in sequence.* If he is correct, then "conservative truths" at Stages 3 and 4 can be a kind of heuristic device by which the developing person learns to "home in" upon the needs of the other. It is like learning to swim with a pair of water-wings. Later these are discarded, for they actually impede the good swimmer, but without them the task of learning might be considerably harder.

Hence if we reject all conservative values out of hand and flood the mass media with the philosophy of radical man as expounded in Chapter IX, there could be some unintended side effects. We might greatly increase not only the numbers of those who move beyond Stages 3 and 4 but also the numbers of those "stuck" at Stage 2, and we may cut the middle rungs out of the developmental ladder.

Consider one major aspect of socializing a child. In order for the child to develop, some approximate synergy or balance must be maintained between his own needs which he experiences directly and the needs of the environment which *at first he perceives only dimly.* The conservative could plausibly argue that balance would require that the dimly perceived environment be sacrilized and infused with authority and mystique until it weighs as heavily with the child as his own clamorous needs and directly experienced impulses.

Fortunately we have some research findings on Stage 6 and Stage 2 student radicals in Bay Area Schools,[5] which not only helps us discriminate between "the two radicalisms" but permits us to infer how a radical or conservative philosophy might impinge upon each group with developmental or regressive impact.

The following traits characterized students at *both* stages: Interrupted college careers, independent living arrangements, support for the "Free Speech Movement," high political involvement, high evaluation of creativity, artistic tastes, rebelliousness, curiosity and individualism. But the following crucial differences were noted.

| *Stage 6* | *Stage 2* |
|---|---|
| High self-ideal congruence | Low self-ideal congruence |
| Moderate differences with parents | Widest differences with parents |
| Some agreement with parents on major issues | Highest level of disagreement with parents |
| Highest occupational focus | Low occupational focus |
| Describes self as responsive, perceptive, altruistic, guilty, idealistic | Describes self as reserved, aloof, stubborn, uncompromising and less altruistic or responsive than other groups |
| Idealizes sensitivity, empathy | Idealizes playfulness, foresight |

The similarity and the cleavage between these two groups of radicals is most clearly seen if we distinguish the self-*differentiating* capacities of the cycle from the self-*integrating* ones. Both groups can rebel, widen the distance between themselves and others, and suspend personal and cultural beliefs, but Stage 2 radicals *cannot put the pieces together again.* They leap the abyss and *fail* to reach the other's side. Their low self-ideal congruence suggests a failure of self-confirmation and self-transcendence. Their coldness, aloofness, stubbornness, and relative unconcern for sensitivity and responsiveness to others suggests that *no* higher synergy follows rebellion and no complex integration follows suspension. Their cycles are seriously unbalanced.

Compare the Stage 6 radicals. They can protest and overthrow but into the resulting vacuum pours their empathy, sensitivity, idealism, sympathy and altruism. With them there is a good chance for a better society, for a shared existence follows their rebellion and their communicated ideals are generally confirmed by others and fulfilled.

When a conservative denounces rebellion as anarchistic and destructive, demanding that students or ghetto residents obey laws (Stage 4) and keep to their proper roles (Stage 3) he may be rightly insisting that for *certain* radicals these stages of development have never been attained and cannot be omitted. However, it is more complicated than this, for while "good laws" and "proper roles" may be precisely what some rebelling students and ghetto residents need, the particular laws and roles prescribed for their concrete situation may be neither good nor proper for moral development.

In a certain sense the Stage 6 "radicals of conscience" have *transcended the dichotomy between radicalism and conservatism.* Their act of conscience ideally should be capable of becoming a shared contract (Stage 5), a good law (Stage 4), an appropriate role (Stage 3), an occasion for personal satisfaction (Stage 2), and a reward or punishment appropriate to circumstances (Stage 1). Only the individual conscience, comprehending as it does all the lower stages, can keep the "radical" and "conservative" aspects of the social and personal systems in an active unity, providing each person and group with that which it most lacks. But notice that conscience achieves this reconciliation by what can only be considered as *radical acts.*

There is another way of thinking of conservative versus radical philosophies of human socialization. The former is a low-risk alternative and the latter a high-risk one. It is within the limited power of most parents and schools to wean a child out of "Stage 2 egotism" into a response-set which defers to rules, laws and role expectations (Stages 3 and 4). But it takes much more human love and interpersonal competence to teach him the principles of conscience and how to integrate his own needs with those of his environment. The high risk which schools and parents take when they attempt this is that the young person will achieve Stage 6 *or* Stage 2. Hence the superiority of a radical philosophy can never be absolute, but must depend for its efficacy upon the existing and potential psycho-social skills of the actors involved. The higher the risk, the greater is the possible accomplishment *and* the possible failure. Conservatism is an attempt to hedge one's bets.

This brings me on to the real limits of radicalism. *Man can only be as radical as his developing psycho-social skills will permit.* This does not mean that radical man will not periodically over-reach himself. It does mean that if he perpetually over-reaches himself, this will spell disaster for his movement and his philosophy. Perhaps nothing is so fatal to radical movements as the facile formula "Left good – Right bad, the further Left the better." Radicals will literally burn themselves out with anxiety and frustration when they employ this formula.

2. *The "situational conservative" and his contribution to psycho-social development.*

Up to now a conservative has been defined as one who regards values as external to men and largely independent of his wishes. But it is also possible to comprehend, value, and seek the development of every segment of the double helix, to be a humanist first and foremost, and still play upon appropriate occasions a conservative *role.* We must differentiate between the person who is overwhelmingly committed to propositions like "don't think unhappy, disloyal thoughts," "reports of starvation are typically exaggerated," "you will only be exploited or rebuffed if you try to help Them," etc., and persons who, in a specific situation, warn that this particular idea will not be successfully communicated and will not have the anticipated impact. Every radical man should in appropriate circumstances be a "situational conservative."

This is necessary because the cause of psycho-social development is considerably damaged by the more avoidable miscalculations. If radical man proposes a giant effort against poverty, while conservative man warns that the plan is misconceived, that the money will be embezzled, and that rival grass-roots leaders will disable one another to control so much money, then conservative man could, in foreseeable conditions, be the better prophet. He only becomes the enemy of human progress if he uses these arguments to combat the very principles of social emancipation contained in every conceivable plan. But even if C is determined to oppose development *per se* the arguments he uses in any particular case might still serve as a valid warning to R that his plans could be improved.

3. *The need for a radical-conservative dialogue.*

This brings us to the need for a radical-conservative dialogue, preferably with "situational conservatives," but including all conservatives who wish to participate. For conservatives of any stripe, even if they organize their experience in anti-developmental ways, may have truths and opinions that, taken singly, could help to rebalance the cycle and add extra dimensions to consciousness of men. Conservatives may supply valuable antitheses which contribute to a higher synergy. The capacity for risk taking in radical man is not complete without knowledge of the perils of risk, and attention to developmental capacities in man is ludicrously inadequate without knowledge of his regressive capacities. We need to remember the investments which failed, just as we need to remember those that succeeded.

The conservative role in any relationship can be valuable because human capacities and resources are, in the short run, limited. It is quite true that unless we first try to bridge the distance to those of different pigmentation and perspectives, we can never ultimately succeed, and that falling on our faces and being exploited is part of the learning process. But *how much* humiliation and initial set back an electorate will tolerate before becoming reactionary is still a question of judgment. It is better not to give foreign aid in a particular instance if the probable misuse of that aid angers the giver so much that he bombs the ungrateful recipient back into the Stone Age. It *is* possible to be too radical for one's own personality resources and to set back one's own vision by sheer inexperience and incompetence.

The conservative position on any issue deserves consideration for other reasons, whether more synergistic relationships between people can be created depends not only on the skill of radical men and the dedication of leaders and negotiators, but on whether ordinary citizens of less education and with fewer advantages can live with the new system and the expectations it imposes. Radicals may fall into the trap of abstraction if they assume that their ideals or their moral sentiments have so great a value in themselves that lesser men must be forced, if necessary, to live by them. It is not enough that values *originate* within radical man, it is also necessary that they enter the minds and enhance the lives of other men, including conservatives. Hence we can never afford to ignore the protests of conservatives that our proclaimed values do not work for them. It may well be true in theory or on average that more developed persons make more decisions, but forcing twice the number of decisions upon an already anomic man may make him worse. In such an event, the developmental idea has failed to become a psycho-social reality. There is much to be said for Karl Jaspers' concept of truth as communicability.[6]

Unless the value and usefulness of the conservative role and the "situational conservative" is fully realized by radical groups, they will have a tendency to escalate leftwards in their expectations and then starve themselves of the success and confirmation required to maintain morale. When a radical group discusses tactics, there is a tendency for anyone who sounds remotely like the conservative opponent to feel uncomfortable. In group interaction it becomes easy to make ever more radical proposals, but difficult to "sound like a conservative" in opposing them. The longer a group interacts with itself the higher its radical aspirations may soar and the more explosive is its subsequent confrontation with authority.

Another, more obvious, reason for taking a conservative role in a radical-conservative dialectic is the periodic presence of a dogmatic Left. The dogmatic Left can occasionally be very destructive towards the developmental Left. The latter has norms of trust and openness which make exploitation relatively easy. The dogmatists will also take advantage of the natural phenomenon of the "leftward escalation" in group interaction, and by proposing the highest risk alternatives exert a disproportionate influence on other group members, who are unwilling to play a conservative role.

In a certain sense dogmatic leftists are counterfeit radicals. They urge major risks upon the group without *feeling* the attendant anxiety within themselves, since the principal function of dogmatic thought is to avoid the anxiety inherent in self-suspension. We know from research that a flexible, self-suspending person suffers severe anxiety in conflict situations. We saw in Chapter IX that the undogmatic New Leftists at Boston University were severely pained by their struggles as compared with dogmatic communists in England who neither doubted nor suffered in any appreciable degree. The developmental radical has a built in stabilizer. He enters a conflict, his anxiety soars. He considers, as he must, that he may be mistaken and that his investment could be meaningless and irretrievably lost. The degree of conflict is controlled by this knowledge, by the anxiety of it, and by his own estimate of just how much anxiety he can tolerate before cracking. But the rigid or dogmatic person, while suffering more anxiety in ordinary life through his interpersonal incompetence, *does not substantially increase his anxiety in severe conflict situations because his dogmatism protects him.* Consequently he is relatively more comfortable in siege conditions than the genuine radical.

In Figure 3 we see this phenomenon diagrammed. The increase in the degree of conflict in an organizational setting produces a "cross-over" effect with the rigid person suffering *more* than the flexible person in low conflict conditions but *less* than the flexible person in a high conflict situation. This phenomenon suggests a reason why the dogmatic Right and Left stoke up the fires of group enmity. Besides the many reasons discussed in Chapter IX, we see here an additional one. *In severe and prolonged conflict situations the anxiety of flexible and developed persons can be driven so high that they eventually become disabled vis-a-vis the dogmatic elements within their groups, who may then assume leadership.* If dogmatists can lure genuine radicals into a sufficiently traumatic revolution they can often take over while those with genuine feeling and humanity are paralyzed by agonies of the mind. This is how revolutions are betrayed as they so often are, for only men with a gross insensitivity to human misery can exploit the revolutionary situation with the disciplined precision of automata.

Of course, conservatives have long been saying that communists form fronts consisting of liberal dupes, and like most scares it has a kernel of truth, hugely magnified for political ends, but still deserving study. It also illustrates the need for continual dialogue between radicals and conservatives. It takes a political opponent to pinpoint the weakness in your own cause.

In summary, developmental radicals need the insights of all their political opponents in order to develop. If, as our data suggest, radical man is more skilled at communicating and integrates a greater wealth of ideas, then his is the larger stake in the dialogues by which such ideas reach him. He needs to listen to "conservatives" – in the broadest sense of the term, since his own

**Figure 3**

The Experienced Level of Anxiety in Flexible and Rigid Persons Under Different Degrees of Conflict

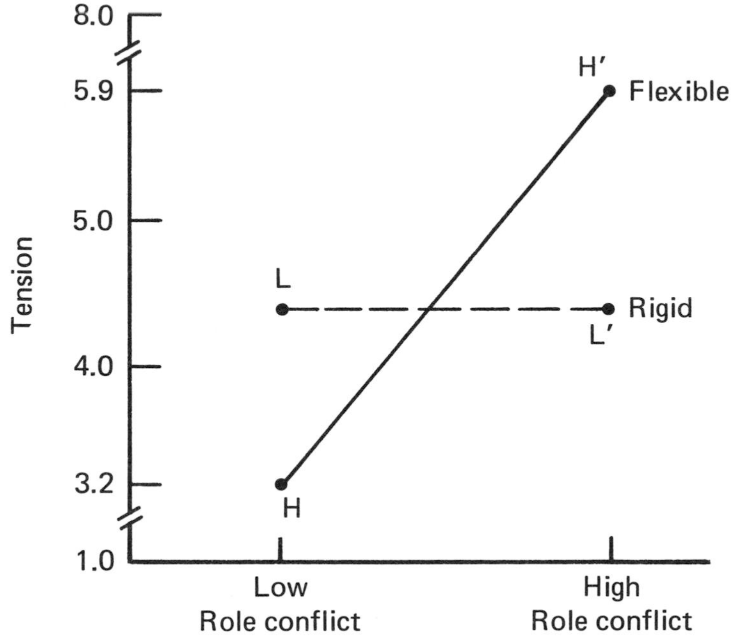


Mean tension in relation to role conflict and flexibility-rigidity (from the intensive study). N: H = 8; H′ = 11; L = 15; L′ = 15. *Comparison*–H (3.1) vs. H′ (5.9): $p < 0.001$; L (4.4) vs. L′ (4.4): n.s.

Source: *Organizational Stress: Studies in Role Conflict and Ambiguity.* Robert L. Kahn *et al.* New York: John Wiley, 1964, p. 3000.

exploration depends upon his capacity to *conserve* the basic processes of psycho-social development. He can no more close his mind against a particular political advocate than against any human creature with some experience of life. Nor is the meaning of the word conservative an unchanging one; rather it is always relative to some level of anticipated competence which may be attainable or unattainable, well or badly conceived.

4. *Problems in the Use of Violence by Radical Man*

How violent and disruptive can developmental radicals become without corrupting themselves and causing their opponents to destroy the creative minority? Superficially, the case against any kind of sustained violence is a strong one. No sooner do I start to force my decision upon another than *his* freedom, which is also *my* feedback, is destroyed. When I begin to harm him, I must avert my eyes from the perception of his humanity. If I cause him agony, I will soon cease to accept the responsibility, and the rot will spread through my cycle.

But we need to distinguish that which is corrupting for middle-class radicals from that which is corrupting for the poor and disadvantaged. In Table 19, Chapter VII, I traced the breakdown in cooperation between two groups of middle-class executives, who regressed into a win-lose conflict. Each group and its members became more narrow-minded, rigid, hierarchical, conforming and chauvinistic. The least interpersonally skilled and least democratic members rose to leadership positions.

But if this predicament was unfortunate for the members concerned, can the same be said for the hopelessly impoverished and apathetic street-corner Negro who then joins the Black Panthers? For him the militant group is a step *up* on the road to emancipation. He may harass white society now, but before he joined the group he had failed to make *any* impact on his environment. His existence may be a modest and conforming one, but before joining the group he had been virtually non-existent.

Violence is indeed a threat to the middle class who face the prospect of prolonged siege conditions which impoverish them psycho-socially. But for those trying to climb out of destitution, militant and guerrilla organizations are the dawn of their existence. Herein lies the bargaining strength of the poor and the vulnerability of the affluent. It is not only that the poor have nothing to lose by violence; they may actually have much to gain.

But what of the middle-class radical? Is it not the height of bourgeois sentimentalism and liberal fastidiousness to insist upon a minimum of personal corruption, while The People struggle? I do not believe it is. Freedom does not reside in an abstract system, but in the human personality. Even in the unlikely event that a bloody revolution ushered in a "Better System," this intellectual abstraction would be betrayed for the lack of free and compassionate men capable of personifying the system. All that we have to give to others is ourselves. And human culture is itself diminished when we become small-minded and embittered through weary years of struggle so that we have nothing left to give.

One of the most encouraging features of much of the New Left is its capacity to combat its enemies without imitating them and become frozen into para-military forms. Spies and informers have difficulty in discovering the plans of the New Left because it has very few secrets to steal. It is a simple matter to infiltrate the New Left, and strangers at meetings are rarely challenged, but so flexible and mercurial are these meetings that by the time an informer reaches the telephone, the plan has been changed twice, and anyway something quite different is liable to happen in the actual situation.

To an astounding extent these groups can thwart their enemies and *still* remain free individuals, rather than a disciplined army. What maddens the police and local authorities is precisely the kaleidoscopic variety of the New Left, which "blows the mind" of persons intolerant of ambiguity and human deviance. Yippies will give daffodils, chicken pies, insults, and ordure to the police in quite random sequences. You "fight" your enemy with what he cannot comprehend, a creativity which transcends the "machine-mind." How can a computer respond to an unforeseen contingency, or bureaucracy deal with a problem for which no department exists? In such situations authorities respond with a ferocity that shocks and often radicalizes spectators. It is seen as an over-reaction to provocation. In fact, we are watching the helpless fury and brutality of the conceptually simple as they confront the conceptually complex.

But even if middle class radicals survive the rush towards militarization as the struggle intensifies, they are still very much prone to the tragedy of Billy Budd, described in Chapter VI. As anxiety grew and grew in the conflict between the crew and Claggart, there arrived the inevitable point where communication broke down. Billy could no longer communicate and in desperation lashed out at Claggart. In this crisis those in charge of the social system fell back upon *earlier communications* in the shape of Law and Order. They ceased to ask "who is right?" and asked instead "what is legal?" Legality decreed the murder of Billy Budd.

Now just as Billy was on the side of life against an oppressive system, so too are many radical students more "alive" in every segment of the cycle than were their liberal and conservative opponents (See Chapters IX and XII). Yet this fact did not save Billy and will not save the New Left, once the Claggarts and Veres of this world are let loose. Billy died because he was flawed, because when the crisis came he was too overcome by anxiety to communicate his fundamental goodness and convince others.

Student radicals need to ask themselves, "How much anxiety can *I* take before my powers of communication disintegrate into rhythmic chanting or mindless violence?" "Have I the courage to hope desperately and risk greatly and still suffer the accompanying disappointments?" It seems clear on at least some campuses that certain students cannot afford their own radicalism.

They match their considerable abilities against such overwhelming odds that they are reduced to a kind of frenzy in which they are easily discredited. Or else, withdrawing into tight groups of like-minded persons, they indulge in what Orwell called "the masturbatory fantasies of the Left," outdoing one another in the imagination of impossible victories.

But to say that violence is inherently corrupting to the educated mind is by no means entirely true. There is experimental evidence which indicates that violence breeds further violence only in certain circumstances, and that a certain kind of violence breeds *less* subsequent violence.

In one series of experiments,[7] two groups of subjects watched a film clip from the closing minutes of *The Champ,* in which the hero receives a ferocious beating in the boxing ring from his opponent. Although the two groups watched the identical film, they had been separately briefed on the *context* in which the action occurred. The first group was told a story in which the beating appeared as a thoroughly justified retribution for suffering caused to others. The second group was told a story in which the beating seemed appallingly unfair and disproportionate. A third group saw no film and heard no story.

Members of all three groups were next invited one by one to judge and to punish a very incompetent draftsman who had designed a hypothetical apartment for each member's use. Displeasure and punishment could be registered by pressing a button for a certain duration which would give the draftsman a mild yet painful electric shock. As usual, the punishment was contrived, the real intention being to measure (a) the individual's propensity to punish, and (b) whether this propensity was increased or decreased by the film and its context.

As might be expected, the *justified* violence evoked considerably greater motivation to punish than did the *unjust* violence. Indeed the unjust violence *reduced* the desire to punish so that it was less than the punishment inflicted by the group members who had seen no film at all.

The tentative conclusions we can draw from this are as follows. The New Left probably *decreases* the amount of violence in the world in the longer run, whenever it succeeds in placing violence in the context of a sickening injustice and "over-reaction." It has succeeded in placing Vietnam violence in such a context. At Harvard, Columbia, the Chicago National Convention and elsewhere, many onlookers have been "radicalized" by official reactions which were so violent as to be grossly disproportionate to the offense. Where war protestors have been beaten, the violence of foreign policy has been skillfully attached to the domestic suppression of dissent, thus re-enacting a "minor Vietnam" in the hallowed halls of the academy or near the Democratic Convention.

It seems to me that New Left radicals are extremely unlikely to fall in love with violence as an instrument policy so long as they remain the *physical* victims of official violence and thereby the *moral and political* victors over those who ordered the disproportionate response. The entire strategy is to disgrace those practicing the *greater* violence and to appeal to the growing constituency of those disgusted by Vietnam. When students, bareheaded and unarmed in an occupied building, wait for the police to break in and club them into unconsciousness, then clearly they are seeking a *strength through vulnerability.* Their appeal to our consciences could not work in a totally brutal society. Their appeal is an act of faith in our capacity as onlookers to feel shame and disgust at official violence and to withdraw allegiance from the authorities who sanctioned that violence. "The whole world is watching," students cry as the authorities lose control.

By continually associating the greater violence with *in*justice in the public mind, radicals actually create a climate of opinion that would condemn their *own* use of brutal violence to overwhelm those weaker than themselves. For example, if radical students were to put on helmets and club the administrators to the ground, then such students would bring down upon themselves the same obloquy which they earlier directed at American oppression. They could be isolated quite quickly. A few of them, overwhelmed by their own anxiety, show ominous signs of making this kind of mistake.

Of course, we live in a society where television and other media spawn brutalities nightly, like mushrooms popping out of hot manure. In tens of thousands of TV programs our tensions are slightly aroused by the deviant doings of stereotyped villains. But the hero bursts onto the scene forty seconds from the end to administer a well-deserved beating or killing. Again and again we are trained to associate victorious violence *with the solution of our problems and the reduction of our anxiety.* We broadcast the myth that muscular Christianity and red-blooded Americanism will always win and that when deviants are beaten or killed, this is generally appropriate.

To associate violence with *in*justice and *dis*equilibrium would leave the television audience with tight, constricted throats unable to swallow the latest merchandized pap, and with minds too concerned with human suffering to remember commercial trivia. Once advertisers began to disturb our equilibrium, why, we might even *act* to insure justice and to put things right ourselves, instead of passively consuming while the police thrash the daylights out of deviants, on and off the screen.

There is an intimate connection between commercially-oriented communications and the promotion of a self-indulgent, familial privatism in which distressing social truths are suppressed. When a whole culture screens out mentally disturbing phenomena, the better to suck on the latest taste sensation, then discontent will boil among the poor. Violent suppression of this discontent is encouraged by mass media which say, in effect, "Eat up. The police or the Marines will take care of it."

Only if our media showed us what violence was *really* like, that it corrupts those who use it, that it is usually misdirected so that the innocent suffer, only then would we seriously begin a search for alternatives. The world's finest film-makers consistently portray the banality and evil of violence. Ingmar Bergman in *Shame* showed war inexorably destroying human love and meaning. Goddard repeatedly portrays beautiful young girls tortured to death. It is just such appalling absurdity that acts upon the audience like the social vacuum in a T-Group (see Chapter VII). One is impelled to action by despair. One leaves the cinema vowing never to rest until such injustices are made just.

The young radicals along with the world's greatest film-makers are offering us a final opportunity to comprehend the true nature of violence. We have a simple, urgent choice of being mentally disgusted and ashamed now, or of suffering prolonged physical violence at the hands of our victims.

5. *Radical-Conservative Issues in Congress, an Analysis of Voting Patterns*

I now wish to consider a number of political issues which have come before the two Houses of Congress between 1965 and 1968. I shall argue that these issues have considerable relevance to key segments of the cycle, and that support for the issues is indicative of various levels of psycho-social development. Later I shall demonstrate that the votes of more or less radical members can be predicted from the developmental themes characterizing the political issues.

*Voting to Disclose Personal Assets*

On a number of occasions the U.S. Senate has had an opportunity to vote on whether Senators and Senate employees should make a total disclosure of their financial assets, including capital gains, private interests and holdings, market values of their property, details of business and professional associations, etc.

This issue is primarily a test of the willingness of the Senator to "open up" his personal IDENTITY (segment b) and INVEST himself *authentically* and completely in the public he represents.

Less developed persons, it will be recalled, tend to be anti-intraceptive and to regard their personal needs as inviolate. Anyone wishing to dominate and manipulate his social environment would take care to know more about his constituents than he revealed about himself. Anyone serving special interests and lobbies and receiving financial rewards for so doing would naturally wish to perpetuate the secrecy which makes his inauthenticity possible.

This willingness to reveal oneself is especially indicative of development when a powerful person does so voluntarily. It would not, of course, indicate development where a humble supplicant was increasing his dependence upon a superior confessor.

*Open Housing Votes*

Votes for Open Housing are an important test of development. Those who advocate it are likely to have the radical PERCEPTION (segment a) to comprehend the anger and pain of the excluded group. In the relaxed atmosphere of their homes, a place of trust and SELF-SUSPENSION (segment e), they must stand prepared to BRIDGE the (wide) DISTANCE (segment f) to previously remote black persons, and as neighbors must form SYNERGISTIC relationships (segment h) with them.

The less developed person and his constituents would have the greatest difficulty in living up to this requirement, even were they to support it.

*Arms Control and Disarmament Agency*

Wide though the distance between the perspectives of black and white Americans may be, that between Russian and American belief-systems is probably wider.

Hence support for the continued deliberations of the Arms Control and Disarmament Agency involves a belief that this widest of DISTANCES can and should be BRIDGED, that mutual SELF-CONFIRMATION (segment g) with the Russians must be attempted, so that the domination/submission strategies behind the arms race can give way to joint dialectic and eventual SYNERGY. Any agreement reached would, of course, entail a measure of RISK (segment e) arising from the SUSPENSION and subsequent INTEGRATION of perspectives (segment i), with a continued need for understanding and trust.

Less developed persons would tend to regard negotiations as a snare and delusion (in reality as intolerable strain on their capacities). Poverty of PERCEPTION, dogmatically and hierarchically ordered belief systems, and the incapacity to remain "open" in arenas of social conflict would predispose them to avoid what is for them the futile and frustrating process of negotiation.

*Construction of an Anti-Ballistic Missile System*

In a world where "long distance" communication has broken down, the only alternative is to accumulate, endlessly, vast defenses against anticipated attack by those we have learnt to fear, through our continued ignorance of their more human propensities, and our narrow concentration upon the possibilities of injury. Indeed our own fear and "defensive" precautions render the enemy more dangerous and prone to similar "defensive" precautions, an example of the self-fulfilling prophecy.

If I am correct in this "anomic" interpretation of defense strategy then those who most strongly urge armaments upon us also seek to banish humane dimensions from their PERCEPTION of the Enemy in the name of "strong posture." They seek to bottle up human IDENTITY in the name of security, and INVEST *in*authentically in the cause of espionage. Dogmatic failure to SUSPEND is called "never doubting our national mission." Keeping DISTANCES short is "supporting our boys." The subjugation of others is "victory" or "containment," and isolating from our own belief system any trace of the social ethics contained in the Enemy's belief system is "being loyal to ideas Americans have died for." Votes for superior armaments with which to deter a brutish foe will be regarded as indicative of low psycho-social development and should therefore be *inversely* correlated with support for Open Housing, Asset Disclosure, and the Arms Control and Disarmament Agency.

*Ordering Strikers back to Work*

We saw in Chapter VIII that an important dimension of development was the capacity to "stand the gaff" of heated dialogue and prolonged dialectic. In Chapter IX we saw that as the DISTANCE between persons becomes wider first conservatives, then moderates, then extreme liberals will seek to escape confrontation. Developmental radicals have a greater tolerance for conflict, dialectic, and ambiguity in general.

A good test of the tolerance for social and verbal conflict is whether a Senator will vote for a compulsory return to work by strikers, in this instance Airline machinists, where a national emergency has *not* been announced and vital services are being maintained. Such an order seems indicative of an *anti*-SYNERGISTIC suppression of the strikers' perspectives, intolerance of confrontation, and a rather dogmatic interpretation of the "national interest" as exclusive of the needs of disaffected groups. Since such strikers cause a disequilibrium and disturbance in social life generally, the most intolerant of the consequent ambiguity and anxiety might be expected to move against the most immediate cause of the disturbance.

*The Constitutional Amendment seeking to restore Prayers in Public Schools*

In Chapters IV and V and IX we saw that the following traits characterize the anomic, those nice, acquiescent persons who would regretfully torture others rather than create a scene, and those on the Right and dogmatic Left.

- Hierarchical relationships
- Ritualized and repetitive statements of conformity
- The belief that words and dogmas *in themselves* have some holy or authoritive meaning which is greater than the intentionality of the person uttering them; that these Great Truths need not therefore be suspended
- A preference for one-way over two-way communication
- Use of object symbols e.g., Flag, cross, shrine, etc. as "iron lungs" for impoverished investors, who can acclaim the object unanimously without risk of rejection and over short psychological distances.

School prayers help to perpetuate all these blocks to development. The acclamation of an external "Almighty Being" functions to maintain the hierarchy with God at the top, and schoolmasters, priests, and senators as His intermediaries and interpreters. This ritualized one-way obeisance generalizes to all authority figures and assigns to a sacred compartment of the mind, isolated from political dialogue, a large number of conservative strategies, as well as fostering a questionable connection between Church and State.

We would expect positive correlations among support for the Prayer Amendment, support for strike breaking, and support for increased defense expenditures. In contrast the advocacy of Open Housing, negotiations with Russia, and disclosure of personal assets would all be negatively correlated with the urge to pray publicly.

*Outlawing Poll Taxes*

The poll tax is a straightforward device for excluding from participation in one's own cycle those persons regarded as too distant for SYNERGY to be achieved. The argument is similar to that under Open Housing.

*Stronger Gun Control*

The issue is similar to that of the Arms Control and Disarmament Agency except that distances are relatively short and concern relationships between Americans. This does not prevent widespread distrust of Federal Arms Control, or the assumption that freedom may necessitate the defense of one's home from federal agents conspiring with or infected by subversive elements. Even the registration of guns is seen as providing unspecified enemies with a way of locating and disarming loyal Americans. Guns are also seen as a last protection during an anticipated breakdown of law and order. This self-fulfilling defensiveness is a domestic version of the international arms race and a further indication of poor psycho-social development.

In contrast those who support a limitation on firearms seem prepared to risk their COMPETENCE in reconciling conflict without resort to weapons.

*Three Rebellion Issues*

Three votes in the House of Representatives tapped the capacity of members for existential rebellion against overwhelming yet absurd limitations on human development. These were:

1. The vote against a resolution authorizing the government to intervene, unilaterally and by force in any area of the Western Hemisphere where "Communism threatened."
2. The vote to cut off federal loans or scholarships to any student demonstrator identified by officials at his university as a threat to orderly education.
3. A motion to resubmit the annual defence appropriation for the Vietnam War, and thereby protest government policy.

All three votes were destined for defeat and were overwhelmingly defeated. All votes included an obvious SUSPENSION of self-interest and a strong RISK of repudiation by constituents. What could be more dangerous than suggesting that "our boys" be left without arms? What "pragmatic" man would plead for voteless persons, overwhelmingly rejected in opinion polls?

Such a vote is likely to emanate from one's conscience, from the conviction that superior physical force is inherently corrupting in the settlement of disputes. The rebel congressmen must also have resisted strong social pressures for patriotic conformity.

Yet without people willing to voice lonely and passionate dissents, how would the Practical Politician know that the time had come to hop on the progressive bandwagon? When the five thousandth civil rights worker has been beaten bloody in a Southern jail, *then* the Practical Politician may sense the wind of change and piously intone "We shall overcome," as he clambers upwards to power and fame over the bruised bodies of the constituency of conscience. If politics is the art of the possible, it is only because enough radical men once dared advocate the impossible. As George Bernard Shaw wrote – long before Bobby Kennedy began to misquote him,

> I hear you say 'Why?' always 'Why?' You see things; and you say 'Why?' But I dream things that never were; and I say 'Why not?'[8]

These three votes were all "impossible dreams" of an America which may one day come to abhor the pulverizing of political opponents in the name of national interest, and can comprehend why students scream with vicarious pain and rage at official inhumanity.

If all the foregoing issues share the underlying theme of more or less psycho-social development, then we should expect members who vote "developmentally" on one issue to vote for this same underlying dynamic on other issues. We expect this *despite* the "situational conservatism" of members who may agree with the spirit of the proposed law but object to its letter. Primers in political science are always telling us of the competing special interests. Thus the anti-ballistic missile opponent may be concerned with the government's choice of land in his state. Congressman X may be a trustee of a university where rebellion is imminent and the contributors of campaign funds may be interested in defense contracts or the sale of firearms to sportsmen. If we really face the end of ideology and the arrival of pragmatic, technical decision making on the basis of pluralistic and economic pressures, then developmental themes would be virtually smothered beneath an overlay of special circumstances, and students of politics must despair of finding anything but the weakest themes of idealism and conscience in the minds of national representatives.

Yet Table 27 demonstrates that on psycho-social issues, contrasting levels of development are extremely salient and consistent. If we know that a member of Congress has a Liberal Voting Quotient of 50% or higher (using an intuitive judgment of "liberalism" provided by Americans for Democratic Action – who seek ends which are close enough to my developmental helix for present purposes) then it is considerably more probable that he will vote "developmentally" on a variety of other issues.

**Table 27 (Continued)**

| *Votes in U.S. Senate (continued)* | *% of* Senate Members with High Liberal Quotient | % of Senate Members with Low Liberal Quotient |
|---|---|---|
| **Vote** *against* Prayer Ammendment | 86 | 14 |
| Vote *for* Prayer Ammendment (Sept. 21, 1966) | 18 | 82 |
| Vote *against* Poll Taxes | 88 | 12 |
| Vote *for* Poll Taxes (May 11, 1965) | 16 | 84 |
| Vote *for* stronger Gun Control | 61.5 | 38.5 |
| Vote *against* stronger G.C. (May 16, 1968) | 24 | 76 |

*Votes in the House of Representatives*

Table 27

**THEMES OF CONSISTENT LIBERALISM IN SELECTED VOTES IN BOTH HOUSES OF CONGRESS**

| *Votes in U.S. Senate* | % of Senate Members with High Liberal Quotient | % of Senate Members with Low Liberal Quotient |
|---|---|---|
| Vote *for* Asset Disclosure | 69 | 31 |
| Vote *against* Asset Disclosure (March 20th 1968 | 13 | 87 |
| Vote *for* Open Housing | 93 | 7 |
| Vote *against* Open Housing (March 5, 1968) | 26 | 74 |
| Vote *for* Arms Control & Disarmament Agency | 92 | 8 |
| Vote *against* A.C.D.A. (April 22, 1968) | 25 | 75 |
| Vote to *delay* Anti-Ballistic Missile System | 61 | 39 |
| Vote *against* delay in A.B.M. (June 26, 1968) | 18 | 82 |
| Vote *against* ordering Airline Strikers back to work | 88 | 12 |
| Vote *for* compulsory return to work (August 4, 1968) | 32 | 68 |

**Table 27 (Continued)**

| *Votes in the House of Representatives* | % of House Members with High Liberal Quotient | % of House Members with Low Liberal Quotient |
|---|---|---|
| Vote *against* unilateral intervention by U.S. in Western Hemisphere | 96 | 4 |
| Vote *for* unilateral intervention (Sept. 20, 1965) | 34 | 66 |
| Vote *against* cutting off federal grants to demonstrating students | 98 | 2 |
| Vote *for* cutting off federal grants (May 9, 1968) | 27 | 73 |
| Vote *to* resubmit defense appropriations for Vietnam | 100 | 0 |
| Vote *against* resubmission (March 2, 1967) | 35 | 65 |

Source: - The Congressional Record. A.D.A. World. Jan. 1968, November 1968, November 1966 and November 1965.

N.B. The Liberal Quotient is calculated on the basis of the votes cast by members on approximately 15 issues a year, which are selected by A.D.A. as indicative of "liberalism". Senators receive term ratings (4 years) and so do congressmen (2 years). A "high liberal quotient" is defined as 50% or better support for liberal issues. "Low" = 49% or less. Where votes listed above were themselves used in defining "high" or "low", I have substracted them from the total and recalculated.

For instance, a Senator voting to continue the Arms Control and Disarmament Agency is eleven and one half times more likely to have a "liberal" than a "conservative" voting record. One who refuses to break the airline machinists' strike is over seven times more likely to have a liberal record. A Senator who supports the constitutional amendment to allow public prayers in schools is nearly five times more likely to have a conservative voting record than a liberal one. A House member who opposes cutting off economic lifelines to demonstrating students is forty-nine times more likely to have a liberal record, and so on.

We can see from the figures that the three "rebellion issues" pre-select the most radical men whose liberalism is stronger and more consistent across all the other issues. The Vietnam rebels, the sympathizers with student demonstrations, and those who refuse to encourage American intervention abroad are 96 to 100% "liberal" in their records.

We might also expect that those willing to try to BRIDGE the *widest* DISTANCES of all, in this case between America and Russia, would also vote developmentally on issues involving the relatively shorter distances between Americans. Yet the reverse tendency would *not* be so marked. Those favoring domestic confrontations over short distances might well balk at the wider, international distances, since these are more risky and lack the immediate advantage of adding voters to the rolls of one's party.

Table 28 shows that these predictions are accurate. If we take just those Senators, 25%, who voted for the continuation of the Arms Control and Disarmament Agency, we find that their willingness to BRIDGE the widest DISTANCE to the Russians is part and parcel of a general propensity to vote for open housing, delay the Anti-Ballistic Missile construction, oppose the Prayer Amendment, and advocate Gun Control at home as well as internationally, etc. The average support of the whole Senate for the seven issues set out in Table 28 is 43%, yet the average support for the seven issues among the "international arms-control senators" is 81.6% – a most substantial difference.

If we select out of the total Senate only those who voted for the Emergency Job Program, thereby showing their willingness to bridge the *shorter* distance to ghetto youth and potential voters, then we find once again that this group of senators is more likely to support all seven issues, but the tendency is significantly weaker. Their average support of the seven issues is 71.4%.

Similar variations are also found if we select out the total Senate, a predominantly conservative group voting for a conservative issue. Take for example the group which voted for immediate construction of an Anti-Ballistic Missile System (see Table 29) and compare this with the remaining 40% who voted against immediate construction. The pro-missile group are overwhelmingly against self-disclosure (72%), against Disarmament negotiations (91%), in favor of ordering strikers back to work (81%), against

Table 28

**ESTIMATING GREATER OR LESSER LIBERALISM BY THE DEGREE OF PSYCHOLOGICAL DISTANCE INVOLVED IN THE PROPOSAL**

| *Issues before Senate* | *All Senators (100%)* | *Senators voting for International Arms Control Agency (April 22, 1968) (25%)* | *Senators voting for Emergency Job Program (Oct. 4th 1967) (47%)* |
|---|---|---|---|
| | % | % | % |
| Vote for Asset Disclosure | 48 | 83 | 76 |
| Vote for Open Housing | 52 | 92 | 89 |
| Vote for Gun Control | 34 | 69 | 58 |
| Vote *against* Anti-ballistic Missile Screen | 40 | 85 | 69 |
| Vote *against* ending Airline Strike | 38 | 64 | 55 |
| Vote *against* Prayer Amendment | 43 | 80 | 73 |
| Vote *against* Poll Tax | 48 | 88 | 80 |
| Average Support for 7 issues | 43.3% | 81.6% | 71.4% |

Source: see Figure 27

**Table 29**

**"DEFENDING AGAINST THE ENEMY" AS A GENERAL TREND IN CONSERVATIVE VOTING**

| *Issues before Senate* | All Senators (100%) | Senators voting *for* A.B.M. (60%) | Senators voting to delay A.B.M. (40%) |
|---|---|---|---|
| | % | % | % |
| Vote *against* Asset Disclosure | 52 | 72 | 32 |
| Vote *against* Open Housing | 48 | 69 | 23 |
| Vote *against* Arms Control and Disarmament Agency | 74 | 91 | 40 |
| Vote *against* Stronger Gun Control | 65 | 81 | 47 |
| Vote *against* Emergency Jobs for ghettos | 52 | 78 | 26 |
| Vote *for* Compulsory end of Airline Strike | 62 | 81 | 47 |
| Vote *for* Prayer Amendment | 57 | 74 | 37 |
| Vote *for* Poll Tax | 52 | 67 | 31 |
| Average for 8 votes | 57.7% | 75.8% | 34% |

Source: see Figure 27

domestic Gun Control (81%), and against supplying Emergency Jobs to unemployed ghetto youth (78%). The eagerness to arm oneself against communists seems to be part of a generalized tendency to arm domestically, hide information about oneself, subordinate workers and avoid negotiations. (So much for "negotiation from strength" – a pseudo-synergy if there ever was one, with strength substituting for, not increasing, the willingness to negotiate.)

On the eight issues, the group seeking to delay the anti-ballistic missile system are almost diametrically opposite. Only 32% prefer not to disclose their assets, compared with 72% of the "missile-men." Only 37% of those against the missile system would restore public praying in schools, while 74% of "missile-men" seek to pray-as-they-arm. Opposition to missiles accompanies the inclusion of Negroes in voting and in working, while arming correlates with exclusion and subordination of Negroes in both these areas. On the eight conservative issues the "missile-men" average 75.8% support. Those opposed to additional armaments average 34%. Senators as a whole average 57.7%.

6. *The humanists and the custodians – two styles of liberalism in Congress.*

Among so-called liberals in the House of Representatives two partially distinct groups emerge from an analysis of voting. The Committee for a More Effective Congress recently dubbed these *humanistic liberals* (rebels) and *custodial liberals.*

Table 30 illustrates the contrast. If we select from all House members just that small group which stood alone in protest against the Vietnam War and voted to resubmit the defense appropriations, despite accusations of treason, then we see that these rebels for humanity have a 100% voting record on six out of nine issues, all with strong developmental themes.

If, by way of contrast, we take an issue of compassion which is not an issue of rebellion, for example, the vote in the House against deleting rent supplements for poor people, then a clear division appears between those whose compassion is rebellious (sometimes called the constituency of conscience) and those whose compassion is custodial.

Compare the voting patterns of the rent-supplement group (humanistic and custodial) with the voting pattern of the anti-Vietnam war group (humanistic only). On five issues, the Civil Rights Bill (open housing), the Food Stamp Program to combat malnutrition, the disbursement of non-military Foreign Aid to underdeveloped countries, and the Gun Control and Rat Control bills, the average support by "rent-supplementarians" is 91%, compared with 98% by the Vietnam dissenters. The differences are scarcely significant.

There is little in these five votes which would risk the custodial status of a liberal Establishment. Someone intent on maximizing his custodial power might logically propose a large increase in the grateful recipients of food stamps, rat control, and desegregated housing, while taking away from recipients as many guns as possible. While it required courage and rebellion to

Table 30

**CUSTODIAL LIBERALISM AND HUMANISTIC-REBELLION PATTERNS OF SUPPORT IN THE HOUSE OF REPRESENTATIVES**

| *Issues of Compassion in the House* | All House Members (100%) | Rent Supplementarians (42%) | Vietnam Dissenters (4.5%) |
|---|---|---|---|
| Vote *for* Food Stamp Program (June 8, 1967) | 57 | 98 | 100 |
| Vote *for* Rat Control Program (July 20, 1967 | 46 | 95 | 100 |
| Vote *for* Civil Rights (open housing) (April 10, 1968 | 56 | 89 | 100 |
| Vote *for* Non-Military Foreign Aid (July 18, 1968) | 36 | 84 | 89 |
| Vote *for* Stronger Gun Control (July 24, 1968) | 48 | 78 | 100 |
| Average level of support for 5 "compassion issues" | 48.6% | 91% | 98% |
| *Issues of Compassion* and *Rebellion* | % | % | % |
| Vote *against* House UnAmerican Activities Committee (April 5, 1967) | 25 | 51 | 100 |
| Vote *against* Cutting off Federal Aid to Demonstrating students (May 9, 1968) | 15 | 30 | 89 |
| Vote *against* "Intent to Riot" bill (July 19, 1967) | 17 | 37 | 94 |
| Vote *for* Seating of Adam Clayton Powell (Jan. 10, 1967) | 24 | 71 | 100 |
| Average level of support for issues of "compassionate rebellion" | 20% | 47% | 96% |

Source: See Figure 27

set up New Deal reforms originally, an increase in this institutionalized welfare in 1967 was comparatively safe and routine. It falls short of a developmental compassion, which risks one's own competence and status in an attempt to create new ways to help others. Whether the majority of custodial liberals genuinely desire the self-assertion of the disaffected and downtrodden is at least problematic.

How problematic can be seen from the sharp division between custodians and rebels on the remaining four issues involving support for dissent and self-assertion: opposition to cutting off federal aid to campus demonstrators, opposition to the House Un-American Activities Committee, the seating of a defiant and uncontrite Negro congressman, Adam Clayton Powell, and the "Intent to Riot" bill. This bill sought to infer from the statements of traveling radicals whether a subsequent riot had been provoked by their agitation, and then punished their use of interstate travel facilities to reach the riot area. The logic is wholly ethnocentric, in blaming riots not on the ghetto conditions for which local politicians are responsible, but on alien influences creeping across state lines to mislead and inflame the otherwise happy but suggestible ghetto resident.

On these four issues the "Vietnam dissenters" maintain an average support of 96%, but a large block of the "rent-supplement liberals" vote against any sign of ingratitude or displeasure by the disaffected. 53% of this block joined conservatives to maintain law and order. Only an average of 47% supported the four "rebellion issues," a fall of forty-four percentage points from their level of support for "custodial issues."

This split between custodial and rebel-humanistic liberals is also regional. The rebel-humanists are largely absent from such democratic bastions as Chicago-Cook County, West Virginia, parts of Texas, Tennessee, Washington, and Boston, Mass. The rebel-humanists, though few in numbers anywhere, are strongest in the cosmopolitan cities, New York City, urban districts of California, Philadelphia City, and parts of Wisconsin. Custodial liberalism seems to have an affinity with ethnic blocks and trade unions. The rebel humanists include the highly educated, urban and suburban youth, intellectuals, and professionals.

The custodial-humanistic split was nowhere better personified than by the Johnson-Humphrey administration and its own Democratic dissenters. What are we to say of the much vaunted Presidential "compassion" that led to progress in Civil Rights, yet did not balk at the fire bombing of thousands of Asian peasants, restless under American custody? What kind of humane impulse is this which can be turned on or off like a tap, that flows copiously if briefly for potential Democrats with black skins, but closes like a precision valve for the pulverized people of Vietnam? The moist-eyed sincerity of Hubert Humphrey who publicly kisses the television screen on which his wife appears would be bearable, if the *same* expression and the *same* enthusiasm had not tirelessly extolled the war policy.

For rebel humanists, in touch with their inner feelings, and convinced that the humanitarian impulse is the moral compass of man, there is a sickening horror in the realization that long-time allies can manipulate moral impulses in themselves and others, as if man's most precious gift was a handy instrument for occasional use. The anger of dissenters was based on a well-known psychological principle. A sudden breaking of norms by a person who is regarded as a friend, and as one least likely to turn renegade, provokes much more anger and frustration than the misbehavior of an identified enemy and opponent.[9] The former friend is then disliked with far greater intensity than the consistent opponent.

7. *Democracy and psycho-social development.*

Is there evidence that radical man, as defined in the last ten chapters is also democratic man, and that he upholds in his behavior, feelings, and thoughts the neccessary conditions of a democratic society?

There are at least two approaches to what constitutes a democratic citizen. The first holds that democracy is a function of public loyalty to certain institutions of problem-solving. Political authority rest with elected representatives and in duly constituted authorities, nominally if not always effectively answerable to these representatives. In this version democracy becomes identified with due process and the systematic operation of administrative machinery, whose regularity and impersonality – as personified by "blind" justice – is the guarantor that we shall all be treated equally, if with equal coldness. Theories of this kind I call "mechanistic." Virtue is alleged to rest in predictability, legality, consensus, equilibrium between competing powers who check and balance one another, and proper procedure.[10] It is rare for social scientists to describe democracy in terms of realizing ideals. The proper *empirical* procedure is to examine what is being done "out there" at the time of observation, and to label this "democracy." Needless to say such habits of mind are "one-dimensional," anti-idealistic, and have a strong bias towards the more formal aspects of the *status quo.*[11]

A second approach to democracy, the one favored here, is to regard it, first and foremost, as *a developed state of mind and a climate of relationships between citizens.* If democracy consists of interpersonal relationships which exemplify and nurture creative self-expression, then the various institutional forms which democracy takes are but temporary structures designed to legitimize and facilitate certain degrees of participation. Social structures, as I argued in Chapter VI, are the implements and tools of our development, useful at one stage, but often redundant at the next. The "democratic mind" which forged the old tool must be regarded as capable of forging new ones in dialogue with others.

The major research study on mental attitudes in democracies is by Gabriel Almond and Sidney Verba, who questioned one thousand citizens in each of five countries, a total of five thousand respondents. The countries included two "stable democracies" which I have called Developed Democracies, the United States and Great Britain, and three "unstable democracies" Germany, Italy, and Mexico. In the lifetimes of most respondents in the undeveloped democracies, major allegiance was given by the citizens to various totalitarian forms.

Table 31 shows the results of the international survey, and what we see, in effect, is that the citizens of the United States and Great Britain are considerably closer to the profile of radical man than the citizens of the three other countries.

Citizens of the two Anglo-Saxon democracies protested more as children, they express more political opinions spontaneously to strangers. They feel more competent to influence their national and local environments. They are much more likely to discuss politics with *excitement, pleasure and anger,* to believe in the unselfishness of certain people, to value generosity above all and to feel that others can usually be trusted.

What comes clearly out of this research is the impulsiveness of democratic man. There was no substantial difference between the degree of knowledge in the U.S. and West Germany. Neither intelligence nor calculation seems to make the difference. Germans with the same degree of knowledge hazarded fewer opinions, fewer protest, and fewer individual or organized representations, and reported significantly *less* emotional investment in political affairs. Such emotion as they did feel was overwhelmingly on the side of anger and distaste. Despite all their political knowledge, Germans were substantially less willing to confront those of different perspectives in "open partisanship."

The reader may object that German and Italian fascism were orgies of political excitement, mass protest, and positive and negative affect. Quite true, but periods of dull apathy and resignation are the harbingers of romanticist explosions. It is because citizens do not care sufficiently and soon enough that crises come in which only hysteria reigns. Pure reason and pure affect war with each other and thus promote total revolutionary ascendancy of one absolute and then the other.

In both Italy and Germany the researchers found crucial failure to INTEGRATE concern, trust, and affection for people with reason and intelligence. In the United States and Great Britain the university-educated were, on the whole, more concerned with fostering democratic norms and humanitarianism than were the less educated. Here the inculcation of knowledge and psycho-social development seem positively intercorrelated. In Italy there was no such relationship and in West Germany *there was a reverse correlation.* The most highly educated Germans are disdainful of partisan excitements. They become more angry than other groups with political fighting. They are the most detached from humane concerns generally. It is not difficult to imagine their deserting democracy a second time.

Unfortunately this research, although a great deal better than nothing, is seriously flawed in a number of respects. All the questions about trust, "open partisanship," and competence to influence those of opposing viewpoints was presented to the American sample in the .context of Democratic v. Republican, while these same questions appeared to the European and Mexican samples in the context of much more widely polarized political parties. It is not too useful to show higher levels of integration in a country if this appears in a less differentiated context. America is actually more polarized than the names of the two parties suggest. To have used the terms conservative and radical (or liberal) might have introduced into *all* the subsequent questions an enmity productive of less bland and optimistic answers and more comparable to polarities implied by the same questions in the other national settings.

This brings me to the second flaw – a too constant use of truisms and questions to which the "good" answer was obvious to persons trained in schools to memorize democratic norms, as American children are. No real effort was made in this research to uncover discrepancies between image and reality. No mention was made of the many phobias from which Americans suffer anti-communism, belief in Hell fire and the Devil, fallout shelter panic, racism, the warfare state, and a crime rate in which New Yorkers murder more people annually than are murdered in the whole of Great-Britain. Just a single mention of one or two of these topics could have pulled the American sample out of a "copy-book" response-set and offset the peculiarly American habit of moralizing.

For example, a much larger proportion of American respondents insisted that it was the citizen's duty to vote. But the *World Handbook of Social and Political Indicators* gives the following proportions of the electorates actually *going* to the polls: Italy 92.9%, West Germany 86.9%, Great Britain 78%, the United States 64%, and Mexico 34.6%. Moral sentiments, especially the more conventional ones, can be poor guides to performance.

This research was written up in the "Camelot years" of President Kennedy at a time when the arrival of the good society had been proclaimed by academics. It reflects a consummate skill in asking Americans tactful questions from which comforting replies could be reliably predicted. The glowing picture it presents of trustful Americans always ready to talk to outsiders stands in curious contrast to our subsequent ghetto riots, the rash of political assassinations, and the carnage in Vietnam. It serves us as a warning of how shallow is the gaze of the uncritical and how ever-present is the danger of the "Polyanna Syndrome" among investigators and their respondents.

**Table 31 (Continued)**

| Segments of The Cycle | Norms, attitudes & behaviors of cross-section of adult citizens | *Proportion of Citizens subscribing to norm, attitude, or behavior* in *Developed Democracies* *United States* % | *Great Britain* % | in *Underdeveloped Democracies* *Germany* % | *Italy* % | *Mexico* % | Average Developed % | Average Under-Developed % |
|---|---|---|---|---|---|---|---|---|
| d) INVESTMENT *authentic & intense* | Discuss politics at least sometimes | 76 | 70 | 60 | 32 | 38 | 73 | 43 |
| | Reports excitement pleasure and enjoyment during election campaigns | 66 | 52 | 28 | 18 | 34 | 59 | 27 |
| | Reports angry feelings during election campaigns | 57 | 41 | 46 | 20 | 26 | 49 | 31 |
| e) SUSPENSION & RISK | Do *not* feel free to discuss my political concerns with anyone | 18 | 12 | 32 | 34 | 21 | 15 | 29 |
| | Most people can be trusted | 55 | 49 | 19 | 9 | 30 | 52 | 19 |
| | Many people will help others rather than think of themselves first | 31 | 28 | 15 | 5 | 15 | 29 | 12 |
| | Generosity and consideration as most admired characteristics | 59 | 65 | 42 | 25 | 36 | 62 | 34 |

**Table 31**

**A COMPARISON OF NORMS, ATTITUDES AND BEHAVIORS IN TWO DEVELOPED DEMOCRACIES AND THREE UNDERDEVELOPED DEMOCRACIES**

| *Segments of The Cycle* | *Norms, attitudes & behaviors of cross-section of adult citizens* | *Proportion of Citizens subscribing to norm, attitude, or behavior* in *Developed Democracies* | | in *Underdeveloped Democracies* | | | | |
|---|---|---|---|---|---|---|---|---|
| | | *United States* % | *Great Britain* % | *Germany* % | *Italy* % | *Mexico* % | Average Developed % | Average Under-Developed % |
| Existence | Expressed opinions spontaneously to interviewer | 63 | 56 | 47 | 26 | 46 | 59.5 | 37 |
| | Reports having protested family decisions as a child | 66 | 62 | 45 | 53 | 41 | 64 | 46 |
| a) PERCEPTION | Pays at least some attention to political and government affairs | 80 | 68 | 72 | 37 | 55 | 74 | 55 |
| b) IDENTITY | no data | | no data | | no data | | | |
| c) COMPETENCE | Can do something about unjust *national* regulation | 75 | 62 | 38 | 28 | 38 | 68 | 35 |
| | Can do something about unjust *local* regulation | 77 | 78 | 62 | 51 | 52 | 77.5 | 55 |
| | Can organize informally to get their point across | 56 | 34 | 13 | 7 | 26 | 43 | 15 |
| | Can make individual representation to get point across | 20 | 45 | 15 | 15 | 12 | 33 | 14 |

**Table 31 (Continued)**

| | | *United States* % | *Great Britain* % | *Germany* % | *Italy* % | *Mexico* % | *Average Developed* % | *Average Under-Developed* % |
|---|---|---|---|---|---|---|---|---|
| h) *Dialectic* leading to SYNERGY | Persons reporting "open partisanships" i.e. willingness to confront those of opposed viewpoint. | 82 | 61 | 44 | 14 | 42 | 72 | 36 |
| | Persons reporting themselves enhanced by their relations with government. | 76 | 77 | 61 | 66 | 58 | 76.5 | 60 |
| | Persons reporting that they are consulted at work about decisions affecting their jobs. | 78 | 80 | 68 | 59 | 61 | 79 | 63 |
| | Persons reporting influence on family decisions as a child. | 73 | 69 | 54 | 48 | 57 | 71 | 53 |
| i) INTEGRATION of FEEDBACK and COMPLEXITY | | (relative balance in cycle) | see text | (relative imbalance in cycle) | | | | |

Source: *The Civic Culture: Political Attitudes and Democracy in Five Nations.* by Gabriel A. Almond and Sydney Verba. Princeton Univ. Press. 1963.

**Table 31 (Continued)**

| *Segments of The Cycle* | *Norms, attitudes & behaviors of cross-section of adult citizens* | *Proportion of Citizens subscribing to norm, attitude, or behavior* in *Developed Democrasies* | | in *Underdeveloped Democracies* | | | Average Developed | Average Under-Developed |
|---|---|---|---|---|---|---|---|---|
| | | *United States* % | *Great Britain* % | *Germany* % | *Italy* % | *Mexico* % | % | % |
| f) BRIDGING (wide) DISTANCES | Proportion of intense and parochial partisans i.e. those *unwilling* to discuss their differences with distant others | 10 | 13 | 38 | 56 | 34 | 13 | 41 |
| | Proportion who feel able to influence *local* regulations but feel unable to influence *national* ones | 2 | 16 | 24 | 23 | 14 | 9 | 20 |
| g) SELF CONFIRMING, SELF TRANSCENDING IMPACT | Reports that "no one really cares what happens to me" | 38 | 45 | 72 | 61 | 78 | 41.5 | 70 |
| | Police would give serious consideration to my point of view | 56 | 74 | 59 | 35 | 12 | 65 | 35 |
| | Govt. Bureaucracy would give serious consideration to my point of view. | 48 | 59 | 59 | 53 | 14 | 53.5 | 42 |

## NOTES ON CHAPTER X

1. These findings are summarized in "Stage and Sequence: The Cognitive Development Approach," Kohlberg (1969), *op. cit.*

2. See "Moral Reasoning of Young Adults," Haan *et al,* 1968, *op cit.*

3. Kohlberg (1969), *op. cit.*

4. *Developmental Hierarchies of Comprehension. . .* by James R. Rest (1969), *op. cit.*

5. "Moral Reasoning of Young Adults," *op. cit.*

6. *Reason and Existence,* by Karl Jaspers, New York: The Noonday Press, 1955, p. 77f.

7. "The Effects of Observing Violence" by Leonard Berkowitz in *Scientific American,* Vol. 210, No. 2, 1964.

8. *Back to Methusulah* by G. B. Shaw, Harmondsworth: Penguin Books, 1961.

9. See *Attraction and Hostility* by Albert Pepitone, *op. cit.*

10. *Political Behavior:* H. Eulau, S. J. Eldersveld and M. Janowitz (eds.), Glencoe: Free Press, 1956, p. 275f.

11. See Herbert Marcuse's discussion of this in "The Closing of the University of Discourse," *One Dimensional Man, op. cit.,* pp. 114-116.

*Chapter XI*

## The Crypto-Conservatism of Technological Thinking

We have already seen that much of the conservative opposition to psycho-social development is hidden behind symbols of nationalism, morality, spirituality and commerce, and that economic appeals for thrift are often disguised attempts to inhibit the social conscience of the electorate.

But there are far more modern and streamlined versions of crypto-conservatism. In this chapter there is only space to discuss one major impediment to our political development. So serious that I believe it threatens the open society itself is the growth of strategic thinking and "technotronic" futurology, in a culture increasingly dominated by technical forms.

We have been conditioned into believing that technology is neutral as to value and potentially useful for ends good or bad. The oldest cliché in Western movies has a nervous female exclaim: "This valley would be better if there were no guns – no killing." To which the hero replies: "Pardon me, m'am, but a gun is as good or bad as the man who uses it." This argument overlooks the fact that men will attempt to solve problems and conflicts by the use of their most sophisticated and developed resources. Only now we are told that the decision to bomb North Vietnam was taken because this is what America was best equipped to do. Any culture that spends several thousand times as much on weapons acquisition as upon the psychology of negotiation and mutual understanding has *already* chosen to bomb and blast its way out of a dilemma.

The first thing to notice about rapid technological development is that the most repressive persons and regimes are heartily in favor of it, along with the less repressive. Hitler, Stalin, and Mussolini, whatever they feared about human freedom, were strong advocates of technological advance. The "gothic politicians" of the Deep South are gothic only about people, not about new industry. The government of East Germany elaborately celebrates technology while freezing social forms. Persons identifying themselves as conservative ideologically, and opposed to "federal interference" will vote millions for the latest armaments, for space exploration, and for road building. The Federal Government seems to lose its sinister and subversive character, in the eyes of conservatives, the moment it serves the needs of technology, rather than the needs of the people. Senator Barry Goldwater was accused by many of a retarded comprehension of human needs. None could accuse him of a similar backwardness in electronics by which he raised and lowered the American flag outside his house. He flew his own aeroplane and was an enthusiastic ham radio operator.

We saw in the last chapter that pro-change and anti-change attitudes failed by themselves to discriminate developed from under-developed persons. What was crucial was the attitude towards change. The open and undogmatic saw change as an opportunity for creating the future, discovering, choosing, suspending that choice, and choosing again. The dogmatists of the Right and Left saw change as the extension and triumph of present tendencies and external values.

Could it be, then, that our much-vaunted experts on the "Technotronic Age" who pronounce with great assurance the extension and acceleration of existing technologies, have in reality succumbed to a kind of Higher Dogmatism? This will be my argument through most of this chapter.

Let us run through the ten Radical-Conservative dichotomies presented in Chapter IX and ask on what side of each dichotomy the Technotronic Age, as described by its prophets, comes down.

*Man exists freely (Radical) V. Man is (or should be) the product of known or knowable scientific (or moral) forces which exist prior to and independently of man (Conservative).*

I argued in Chapters I and II that a large proportion of the social sciences were working with a toolbox, borrowed from the physical sciences, and totally unsuited to the discovery of the developmental capacities in man. This philosophy, typified by behaviorism, regards man as shaped by a combination of stimuli, reinforcements and intervening variables. In much of sociology man is likewise regarded as the product of his class, income, role, culture, occupation, ethnic group, status, etc. The moment we start to frame our hypotheses in this manner, we have already chosen to regard man from the conservative end of the above dichotomy. Thereafter we can only get conservative answers. Just as the traditional conservatives, discussed in the last chapter, insisted that man *should be* subject to external values which properly limit, control, and direct his behavior, so many social scientists, without even discussing this proposition, assume that man *is* shaped and controlled in this way. The topic is not even raised for discussion, it is already closed and decided. As years and years of work are piled high upon this closed issue, it becomes increasingly difficult to reopen it. To do so would cause the stack of learned papers to slide off the sealed chest onto the floor.

An almost identical situation is occurring among scholars engaged in the task of predicting our futures. Buoyed up by the prestige of the physical sciences and the unbroken, accelerating march of technology into the future, they regard a very high degree of technological impact upon man as a forgone conclusion. We will be "shaped culturally, psychologically, socially, and economically by the impact of technology and electronics, particularly computers and communications." In a perfect example of how to frame a conservative question in order to get a conservative answer, Zbigniew Brzezinski goes on to "ask": "Can the individual and science coexist or will the dynamic momentum of the latter fundamentally alter the former?"[1] One envisages a robot labelled "Science," stumping around the countryside like the Jolly Green Giant, demanding changes of product and behavior from his childlike and servile employees.

It is of some interest that these futurologists are an amalgam of ex-RAND employees and other deterrent theorists such as Herman Kahn, William Gorham, Emmanuel Mesthene, Don K. Price, and Robert Strausz-Hupe, cold war experts on communism and defense like Zbigniew Brzezinski, Robert Bowie, Samuel P. Huntington, and Ithiel de Sola Pool, and end-of-ideology theorists like Daniel Bell.

They all share a similar style, that of the "value free" empiricist who notes what is going on "out there" with scholarly detachment. A new technique has been developed and *that technique,* rather than the persons controlling it, will decree the shape and style of our future.

However, the scene is not one of unrelieved determinism, we are not *completely* at the mercy of our tools. Emmanuel Mesthene of the Harvard Program on Technology and Society holds that the process is one of "soft determinism."[2] While being conveyed into the future by our techniques it is still within the power of scholars like himself to project existing trends, anticipate problems and give the government the time and the information with which to make key decisions at some later date. If by 1980 we have the means to determine the sex of our children, what social problems and issues will this raise? What new institutions and values will spring up to exploit the opportunity? How will man be changed as a consequence?

This line of questioning seems eminently reasonable. What objections could one have?

The first objection is that the projection of present trends into the future represents a vote of temporary approval for such trends. Yet the trends themselves are the consequence of thousands of individual *human* decisions. Here I regard the decision not to change direction as a decision. By concentrating upon the technical and material aspects of the trends, the impression is fostered that these things "are," like stars and planets around us, so that "realistic" men must humbly subordinate their minds to these physical "facts" which exist prior to and independent of man and are little influenced by his wishful thinking.

But these projections of existing trends are quite *unlike* the physical universe of dead objects. They are *cultural, political, and social choices.* Men have the capacity to rebel against any trend at any time, in any place, by deciding to stop it, or alter its direction, or persuade others to do so. The argument that if we do not fulfill some technical possibility, then the

Russians will, is merely a derivative of our choice to compete in celestial races while fellow Americans go hungry. Such competition proves only how similar we are to the Russians, how incapable of rebelling against the unwritten "rules of the game," and how man delivers himself into the power of those from whom he is estranged. We fear the Russians and so we have to conform to a mutual orgy of waste and weaponry.

Even if the political possibilities of redirecting these trends in the next few months are infinitesimal, the strongest possible rejection of certain trends *now* can start to mobilize opinion, and the shared expectation that the trend whose direction you oppose will *not* be continued into the future may be politically essential to any success in halting or redirecting it.

The obverse is also true. The acceptance of a trend which is implicit in projecting it into the future, the gathering together of technical statistics, scholarly opinions, and humanistic concerns about what this trend will mean by the year 2000, has the *inevitable effect of strengthening that trend and making it more certain to occur.* Much of the efforts of these scholars would be wasted if by the year 1975 a major social rebellion against certain trends were to succeed.

Now there is no scholar alive who, having spent a major portion of his life in assembling data which depend for their validity upon the continuance of certain normative premises, does not by his very efforts become deeply attached to these underlying norms and their conservation. The entire value of the work of certain strategic thinkers ultimately depends upon their premises being accepted as applicable to the real world. If I have labored for ten years to simulate the cold war as a zero sum game or as a Prisoner's Dilemma game, then the growth of synergistic relationships between America and Russia vitiates every last calculation I have made. I will no longer have access to large research grants or to the ears of Presidential advisers. Being human and wishing to protect my status I am likely to "see" in the international situation a continuation of the dangerous conflicts which make my simulations appear relevant.

By the same process those who now amass data on the assumed continuance of certain trends must inevitably become concerned, privately if not publicly, with conserving such trends. Their own personal competence and status as human beings is maximized only if the trends continue in a way which confirms them as prophets and qualifies them as the scholars who are best prepared to comprehend the very dilemma they predicted.

But it remains to be asked, how does technology become a value and a force in itself, apart from man and his needs? This was partly answered in Chapter I, where we saw that research technique is capable of detachment from its inventor and dissemination to other investigators, where it is validated, modified, applied and often combined with other techniques to become a sub-system in a vast network of technology.

Once separated from their creators, systems merge to take on characteristics of their own. Jacques Ellul has pointed out that technological systems have an "autonomy," a tendency to self-augmentation, and a monism. Let us consider these terms.

Technology has a tendency to make automatic technical "choices" based upon its own logical progression.

> "The one best way" so runs the formula to which our technique corresponds. When everything has been measured and calculated mathematically so that the method which has been decided upon is satisfactory from the practical point of view, the method is manifestly the most efficient of all those hitherto employed or those in competition with it, then the technical movement becomes self-directing. I call this process *automatism.*
>
> There is no personal choice, in respect to magnitude, between, say, 3 and 4; 4 is greater than 3; this is a fact which has no personal reference... Technique itself, *ipso facto* and without indulgence or possible discussion selects among the means to be employed. The human being is no longer in a sense the agent of choice.[3]

This capacity of technology to point towards its own maximal utilization is also the basis of its self-augmentation. The combination of two techniques in a form which maximises energy output also creates the feasibility of adding a third technique and so on. Each each case the existing "nest" of techniques helps to "choose" and control the direction of the augmentation. In this way technical progress becomes irreversible. To whatever abysmal depths of anomie and mutual destructiveness men have sunk, the whole arsenal of techniques was at their disposal.

The monism of technology refers to the order imposed by the total design upon its parts. Although the parts can be separated from the whole their meaning resides in their function in the total operation. No antagonistic forces, or loose screws, are to be tolerated. They are an offense against the logic of the machine with its emphasis on minimal friction, smooth operation, and the maximum ratio of input to output of energy. Sophisticated cybernetic systems even have principles of self-regulation so that a missile deflected from its course by uncontrolled variables or stratagems of the enemy will "restore order" within itself and home in upon its predetermined target.

Hence technology may legitimately be regarded as a force and a value separate from man. It seems destined to grow so long as there are enough men to serve it and it is *less* subject than man himself to any process of regression. There is something almost god-like about technology. We have long assumed that if God was worshipped humbly and prayerfully, He would distribute his gifts to His children. We should not attempt to direct or to question His mysterious ways. If we follow technology's inner wisdom it distributes to us the same kind of unexpected and "miraculous" gifts.

Should we have spent billions to go to the moon? We knew it was dead. Did it really matter who got there first? We did it because it was *possible* and if you follow the way Technology points, all kinds of exciting dividends drop into your lap. Satellite photographs reveal geological faults in the earth's crust. They help map ocean currents which assists the fishing industry, helps weather forecasters, and could save the lives of communities threatened by hurricanes. Space medicine will lead to breakthroughs in other medical fields.

Of course, similar "spin-offs" would probably occur if we directed technology at the most urgent human problems. It is, after all, our servant *if* we choose to regard it as such. To do something because the machine says "possible" is a choice to drop the reins and let technology run itself. It actually freezes certain human decisions made many years ago and lets technology elaborate endlessly upon them. Technologists are like the youth described by Sartre who asked his village priest whether he should fight for the Resistance or remain with his sick mother. The youth knew when he asked that the priest would tell him to stay with his mother. In the same way does the technologist know when he "asks the machine" about its possibilities, what range of answers the machine will give him. One man seeks the authority of the church. The second computes the maximum efficiency of a mechanism and pretends that he must dedicate his life to this impersonal calculation. Both men are trying to hide from themselves their failure to make a rebellious human choice which departs from rule and rote.

Where once the refinement of tools was intimately related to our housing, agriculture, hunting, and sheer survival, today our tools have become separated from basic human needs. As middle-class tool makers and users have risen to affluence, burgeoning technical means have displaced human ends to become ends in themselves, symbols of "development," "progress," and "science." Even those techniques ostensibly dedicated to the preservation of human life and healing are clearly considered of more intrinsic interest and merit than the human beings they are supposed to save. How else can America explain the fact that while she leads the world by an incredibly wide margin in medical research and technology, her infant mortality rate is 13th in the world, behind several European democracies? Similarly in maternity or from preventable diseases, the U.S. citizens pay more on the average and die more.[4]

The conclusion is unavoidable. There is more joy (and money) in elaborating a technique than in giving thousands of desperate people more life, health, and strength through the application of that technique.

Technological "progress" has been running further and further ahead of the people it is supposed to serve, who have died of neglect and malnutrition while a heedless profession ogled at the latest gadget. Medical costs climb out of sight in geometric progression partly because hospitals must be tooled up with the latest devices and people must be trained to use them. "The best way" must be employed even if the patients who receive the benefits are relatively few, and relatively rich or lucky. One gets the unpleasant feeling that the real function of the patient is to test the technique and be occasionally televised as a symbolic tribute to medical research.

It is no coincidence, then, that modern America produces techniques of staggering sophistication, side by side with unmet needs of equally staggering yet tragic proportions, for which there are no available techniques or resources. This inexorable divergence between what is feasible technically and what is needed humanly is the result of decades of grovelling before the God of Technique, of resolving what to do next by following meekly the direction in which the tool itself pointed, even though it pointed away from human needs towards the "opportunity" of a circus in space and other distractions.

This tragic and inhuman lopsidedness is being sanctified by futurologists and the self-styled prophets of progress. In the discussion that follows we find human beings themselves increasingly treated like billiard balls. And all the time it is alleged that novel techniques are "necessitating" this. We hear all too little about the men behind these techniques pulling the levers and acting as the agents of "progress."

Like most elites in history these scholars point to some authority beyond themselves to justify their rule. "God decreed that it should be so," intoned Oliver Cromwell, while burning fifty Irishmen in a Wexford church. Luckily for Cromwell, God did not choose to dispute the issue. "Technology makes certain changes in human behavior and values necessary and inevitable" our new masters tell us, and like Cromwell, they enjoy the benefits of a monologue with their deity. Just as Cromwell maintained his authority by explaining the mysteries of religion and interpreting the will of God, our new prophets are telling us what plans a Technetron has for the future of mankind. They will kindly preside over our adjustment to the coming "necessity." It seems we have little choice but to recognize the inevitable – but then I get this sneaking suspicion that someone, somewhere, behind all that machinery, *has* made a choice, if only to go along, and that this choice involves our subordination. Let us look closer at this mechanamorphosed entity.

a) *The PERCEPTION of human needs as guiding our behavior (Radical) V. The knowledge of external values or facts as guiding and shaping our behavior (Conservative).*

If for "external values and facts" we substitute "the latest techniques," then there can be little doubt that a dominant emphasis on such techniques would support a conservative and anti-developmental philosophy. The technique is interposed between the actor and its ostensible human beneficiary and gradually it comes to dominate the actor's vision and to concentrate his attention upon what the tool can perform until the human dimension is virtually eclipsed.

In the social sciences today "good methodology" is virtually a tyrant, while the urgency of human needs to which one's work is directed is very seldom given an equivalent weight. In doctoral theses "limited topics" and "manageable" research studies are the rule, and he who hopes for an invitation to join the faculty following the completion of his dissertation, knows quite well what that dissertation must do. It must elaborate and refine the concepts and research techniques of those who have the power to employ him. No professor says to a doctoral student, "Your function is to advance my career and do what I tell you." He does not have to put it so crudely. He has only to "help" the student "to see for himself" how "good methodology" is developed.

The most "valuable" part of the student's work will be that which the technique picks up the records. He is trained to distrust those events external to the technique which may arouse or excite him. These are reminders of his mere humanity. The technique is what renders him a special, superior, and scientific person, qualified to join the narrow and select band of academic colleagues.

This tendency towards a narrow and reductive perception is increased by technical insistence upon quantitative indices. In order to measure, compare, and compute the various aspects of a complex system it is often necessary to reduce qualitative characteristics to quantitative indices of grossly simplified dimensions. Here, for example, is a description of an "allocation model" for systems analysis.

> The process of reasoning in this model is very simple. One searches for a central quantitative measure of system performance, which has the characteristic: the more the quantity the better. For example, the more profit a firm makes, the better. The more qualified students a university graduates, the better. The more food we produce, the better. . . We take this desirable measure of performance and relate it to the feasible activities of the system. The activities may be the operations of various manufacturing plants, of schools and universities, of farms, and so on. Each significant activity contributes to the desirable quantity in some recognizable way. The contribution, in fact, can often be expressed in a mathematical function that maps the amount of

> the desirable quantity. The more sales of a certain product, the higher the profit of the firm. The more courses we teach, the more graduates we have. . .[5]

The "sophistication" of such models is only purchased at the price of the crudest stereotype. To think of all the activities of a university as increasing some central quantitative indices is the ultimate vulgarization of learning and experience. As for the assumption that the more we have of some crudely defined substance, the better, this would spell disaster to any finely balanced personality integration or attempts to orchestrate a rich variety of human values.

We saw in Chapter IX that traditional conservatives and communists also perceive narrowly, their vision screened by moral imperatives which denounce as illegitimate and immoral a wide spectrum of human needs and expressions that fall outside of the boundaries of "duty" and "convention" or "historical necessity." But these admitted conservatives and communists are infrequently regarded as the latest experts, possessed of the most up-to-date and saving knowledge. For this we turn to our technical specialists, many of whom may qualify as the most narrow-visioned persons that ever appeared in the garb of modernity.

Just as Senator Goldwater announced during his campaign that he was not going to appeal to individual human needs, since people ought to be guided by "the laws of God and of Nature," so our futurologists assure us that we *will* be shaped by our technology anyway. This being so, the comprehension of human needs becomes rather a waste of time. Would it not be quicker, easier, and more accurate to investigate Supreme Instruments, since they will ultimately shape our needs and behavior? Once we assume that technology is shaping our behavior and set up models which calculate technology's stimulus and reinforcement and human response, then the decision to abdicate our humanity, to avert our eyes from purely human initiatives *has already been made.*

We stick a jeweller's glass on each eye which vastly magnifies what originally interested us, while blurring all the rest. Through our distorting lenses we dimly perceive that everyone else has lenses clapped to his eyes too. What does this mean for humanity? It means we must use "better" lenses to examine the lenses themselves. Only thus can we discover "scientifically" the degree to which we are all being distorted by our lenses. But would not the use of additional lenses *itself lead to further distortion?* Oh no, because you see we *are* our lenses. They are an extension of the nervous system. Are you trying to turn back the clock, you Luddite, you anti-intellectual?

If I am right in my contention that technological perspectives are narrow and that they screen out the merely human and the integral wholeness of the human, then we might expect an intolerance towards humane dissent by the technological futurologists. After all, a dissenting and rebelling humanist is attacking the model itself, the model of the machine-shaped man. He is opening the sealed chest upon which the learned papers are being stacked.

Zbigniew Brzezinski's way of dealing with disagreement is to peer into his metaphorical microscope and announce that the intellectual is dying out.

> The largely humanistic-oriented, occasionally ideologically-minded intellectual-dissenter, who saw his role largely in terms of proferring social critiques, is rapidly being displaced either by experts and specialists, who become involved in special governmental undertakings, or by the generalist-integrators, who become in effect the house-ideologues for those in power. . ."[6]

There you see, everyone is becoming rhinoceros, why buck the trend? Rebels and dissenters of the New Left may be interested to hear what this "detached" and "objective" scholar sees for them. They are the Luddites of the technotronic age, the psychological offspring of "various disaffected groups in the early 19th century, reacting to the first strains of the industrial age. . . Not fully comprehending its meaning, not quite certain where it was heading. . . many Europeans strove desperately to adapt earlier, 18th century doctrines to the new reality."[7]

While Brezezinski sees humane dissent as an impotent struggle against technotronic historicism, Herman Kahn sees rebellion as a *possible* trend but one we could avoid. We have, according to Kahn, entered the Increasingly Sensate Trend, which is one of the branches of the Basic, Long-term, Multi-fold Trend. The probable Sensate Trend is

> . . .worldly, naturalistic, realistic, visual, illusionistic, everyday, amusing, interesting, erotic, satirical, novel, eclectic, syncretic, fashionable, technically superb, impressionistic, materialistic, commercial, and professional.[8]

It goes without saying (and Kahn is too scholarly to say it) that all these companion adjectives of the materialistic, the commercial, and the technically superb are desirable. Yet Kahn has a second vision, "The Late Sensate Stage." If your incipient rebellion has not already been crushed by Kahn's weirdly imposing nomenclature, then behold the Late Sensate Stage and confess the errors of rebellious youth.

> (It is) characterized as underworldly, expressing protest or revolt, overripe, extreme, sensation seeking, titillating, depraved, faddish, violently novel, exhibitionistic, debased, vulgar, ugly, debunking, nihilistic, pornographic, sarcastic or sadistic.[9]

So see what happens when you do not stick close to the technically superb, the materialistic, and the commercial! And do not say that futurologists offer us no choice. Here is a clear choice of being "worldly" and "fashionably" in agreement with Herman Kahn or being "depraved," "debased," and "vulgar" in rebelling against him, a clear case of "Herman's Choice."

If we have any objections to these futurologists and their work, it is not going to be easy to get it across, belonging as we do to doomed classes of irrelevant, unhelpful, pessimistic, and depraved persons, squealing impotently like field mice in the path of a threshing machine.

b) *Comprehension of, and sensitivity to, one's own inner IDENTITY and feelings (Radical) V. The disciplined subordination of inner feelings to internalized or external morality (Conservative).*

If we substitute for "morality" the word "technique" we have a perfect statement of the technocrat's crypto-conservative creed. Just as the conservatives I discussed in Chapter IX would display enthusiasm for flags, crosses, and shrines, but tended to inhibit their affect towards distant human beings who might reject this affection, so can the wielder of technique croon with delight over his research instruments, but he must not "bias his data" by extending this enthusiasm beyond the technique itself. To do so would confuse the impact of his personality with the impact of his technique, and this would hamper the detachment of the technique from his own personality and the replication of his work by others.

Hence when Herman Kahn declares that several million dead, dying, and poisoned Americans represent "acceptable" losses in a nuclear war, he is only following the scientific tradition of repressing "irrelevant" personal feelings. To discover what is an "acceptable" number of deaths you cannot ask over-emotional people themselves – least of all the "over-ripe extremists" of the Late Sensate Stage. To find out what is acceptable only another technical measurement will do, the estimated recovery of G.N.P. following a nuclear war.

But suppose a nuclear war leads to a variety of emotional problems? (It is amazing how human feeling keeps lousing up rational calculations.) For example, following a nuclear war, ignorant people may refuse to work hard believing that they have received a fatal dose of radiation. To our rescue comes *another* technique, a radiation meter, which will set our silly minds to right. Kahn explains:

> Assume now that a man gets sick from a cause other than radiation. Not believing this, his morale begins to drop. You look at his meter and say, "You have received only ten roentgens, why are you vomiting? Pull yourself together and get to work."[10]

However many millions of people nuclear bombs destroy it seems that the Puritan Ethic and conservative styles of supervision will survive.

The underlying issue beneath the whole tone and style of futurology and strategic thinking is whether the norms of scientific detachment and the suppression of personal feelings have any place in the study of social, political, and cultural events. When the human perceiver studies *socio*-technical systems do his own feelings provide important clues to these phenomena or do they betray his reason?

My own view, for which research evidence has been adduced in almost every chapter, is that personal feelings are nearly always salient in human affairs and that those who attempt to suppress them or pretend to be detached will on closer inspection be revealed as expressing their preferences in forms disguised by morality, historicism, or technique. I would like to offer as a general proposition, that we are able to detach ourselves temporarily from our own needs in order to understand the other, only to the extent that our needs are revealed to others as to ourselves. (Others must know so that they will periodically rescue us from self-delusion.) There is a derivative of this proposition, namely that those who deceive others as to their own emotional stake in certain events or alternatives, are likely also to delude themselves and to suffer a crippled sense of personal identity and awareness. Since awareness of one's own preferences is essential to distinguishing these from events in the external environment, a third proposition follows logically. Those who try to detach their feelings from their reason and attempt to explain events "out there" in neutral terms, are the *most* likely to finish up by confusing their inner state of mind with external events.

I take the assumptions of futurologists and "end-of-ideology" theorists about their own detachment no more seriously than I would take the statement of a Victorian schoolmaster who was flogging the buttocks of a small boy "in order to uphold sexual morality." I regard such public detachment and private relish as part of a single syndrome, disastrous for psycho-social development.

It seems to me much more likely that Daniel Bell is talking about himself and his own earlier Trotskyism when he announces the end of ideology and the separation of ethical impulse from pragmatic politics. When he heralds the arrival of the "good society" and the exhaustion of ideas, does this not refer to his ideas and his promotion to the higher reaches of the academy on Morningside Heights? (Not to be confused with neighboring Harlem where the arrival of the good society is not immediately visible to the untrained eye.)

When Brzezinski solemnly predicts that those who disagree with him are dying out, I think it makes more sense to treat him as a political advocate of their demise. His prediction is so obviously self-serving that no other treatment is possible. Is it *really* sheer chance and coincidence that Kahn's probable and possible Manifold Trends protect him so well from his critics and place protest against him in such an unflattering light?

On the issue of whether, and to what extent, human beings are shaped by their technology and their institutions, I regard the theorists who insist that this is so as talking chiefly about themselves. That Brzezinski is himself a part product of technological conditioning seems highly plausible given his views and his stated intention to adapt himself. His view on the decadence and doom of the humanist intellectuals is quite probably shaped by his earlier exposure to totalitarian communism which holds such "scientific" views about its own enemies.

But I also contend that the degree to which we are shaped by external forces is largely an inverse function of our capacity for creative resynthesis and rebellion and the intrusion of our own human identity into the environment. I, too, am talking about myself when I expound my theory of development. And however harsh is the criticism of my exposition, I doubt if anyone will read this book and say "This is shaped culturally, psychologically, socially, and economically by the Harvard Business School." Yet that is my origin and that is where I found the bits and pieces which I turned into this book.

The dangerous thing about crypto-conservative scholarship is its tendency to disguise its normative premises along with its humanity. These are literally buried beneath piles of statistics, projections, analyses, and technical words. Extremely doubtful normative premises – for example that the Russians would immediately exploit an American concession, that only the knowledge of sure retaliation will deter aggression, premises *which tell us much more about the strategists than they do about the Russians*, are almost never discussed and rarely reconsidered.

To meet a deterrent theorist is to comprehend the consistency of his policy. Like America herself, he is armed to the teeth, with every kind of statistic and projection. His strategic plan is presented as a triumph of reason, mathematically proven. What mere laymen could fail to be impressed?

And yet, if the normative premise is not worth a farthing, if the aggression attributed to Russia is mostly or partly in *his* mind and not "out there," then none of his projections is worth a farthing either. Unfortunately his technique is such effective character armor that finding the normative premise beneath the virtuoso display of formal logic is difficult.

It is not only difficult, it is *impolite.* It is hard to say, in effect, "You, not just the Russians, are planning to kill us" without reflecting upon his morality. As Anatol Rapoport explains, this is simply not done among gentlemen and scholars who are bound by "cherished academic standards." Rapoport describes how on hearing a lecture on "Defense and Strategy in the Nuclear Age" he was "engulfed in a wave of repugnance."

> Succumbing [sic] to my feelings, I asked the speaker whether he would agree to a definition of "genocide" as the deliberate

> slaughter of helpless populations for political ends... I then asked him whether he realized that in view of several precedents set at Nuremburg, Warsaw, Jerusalem, and elsewhere, genocide was a hanging offence, and, if so, how would he defend himself if at some future time he were co-defendent in a genocide trial.[11]

It was quickly made clear to Rapoport by his colleagues that questioning the basic norms and morals of a visiting scholar was not to be tolerated.

> I had violated the standards of academic discourse. These standards include the constraint of keeping the discussion within the mode of reasoned argument and within the sphere circumscribed by the subject of discussion. It was expected, therefore, that questions would be confined to matters pertaining to the accuracy of asserted facts, the consistency of stated assumptions, the validity of drawn inferences, and the like. Questions of morality, while possibly crucially important in themselves, should have been excluded, because they were not pertinent to the subject of discussion. Personal attacks on the speaker were altogether taboo... I could not but acknowledge the correctness of this criticism.[12]

To me this incident marks the nadir of academic liberalism. A group of social scientists cannot bring themselves to discuss the psychological assumptions of a psychologist! What if the truth lies *beneath* the surface of easy social intercourse? May we not dig or probe for fear of creating ripples of anxiety in the groves of academia? As we saw in Chapter V, men will torture each other or pull a switch which enables a second man to torture another, rather than create a nasty scene with an academic or violate his expectations.

Suppose war is perpetuated by the self-delusions and masked identities of strategic thinkers, and is abetted by the pusillanimity of academics who lack the impulse to unmask pretension. It takes little *intelligence* to perceive that strategists are attributing to communism much that is present in themselves – that insight has been around for some time. What it takes is *courage* to say it and make it stick. Somewhere along the line that courage was lost.

I am reminded of the nightmare story of Eichmann attending the meeting at which the Final Solution of the Jewish Question was proposed and agreed to. He was extremely anxious and flustered, not about the fate of the Jews, *but about the prospect of unpleasantness during the meeting.* He feared that so drastic a solution might involve distressing arguments.[13]

One reads Rapoport's account of "cherished academic standards," and in the light of Vietnam it reeks of death, of men insufficiently alive and trustful of their own humanity to be outraged and to communicate that outrage.

Before the mountain of disembodied reason and technique, the molehills of human identity shrivel into silence.

c) *Man as morally COMPETENT through his own experiential resources (Radical) V. Man as morally incompetent, or competent only as an agent of a superior moral purpose (Conservative).*

If we alter "competent only as an agent of a superior moral purpose" to "competent only as a wielder of the latest technical instruments" then we have a major principle of technocratic conservatism.

We only have to listen to the inspiring messages sent from outer space by astronauts to realize by what an incredible degree the medium dwarfs the human content of the message. The large majority of statements relate either to the space capsule's mechanism or the human mechanism. The sophistication of reported human experience is much on the level of "Gee it's real pretty up here" – and similar statements which hardly deserve to be sent by Pony Express.

Caught up in the grandeur of a technology so much wiser than themselves, astronauts also give tongue to religious utterances in a style reminiscent of William Jennings Bryan in the bible belt. The further technology advances into the twentiety century – the further our spiritual temper retreats into the nineteenth. We are small, frightened creatures totally unworthy of the grace of God and our own rockets. After returning from the moon we celebrate not so much the men who designed and made the technology, but loose-limbed, crew-cut, all-American astronauts, wafted aloft by forces so much greater than their own. Their amazement at the wonder of it all establishes rapport with the man in the street who is footing the bill, and will keep paying if the sentiments expressed are conventional enough and the astronauts sufficiently resemble Miss Teenage America's Daddy.

It is but a short step from here to claim that we, as mere human beings, are too incompetent to interfere with technology. This is precisely the contention of Robert Strausz-Hupé, the Director of the Foreign Policy Research Institute at the University of Pennsylvania.

> It would seem there are no practical ways to *guide* the further development of technology. If such methods existed they would create problems and dangers just as grave as those resulting from spontaneous technological growth. It cannot therefore be a question of controlling technology as a whole but rather guarding against concrete dangers.
>
> Throughout history attempts have been made to curtail technological development, military and civilian. These crude interventions against one or the other device were invariably

> unsuccessful. Technology tends to be integrated as a whole phenomenon. Therefore, selective interventions are counter-productive. . . In sum, the chances are that society retains only those tools which are really useful, at least on balance; rejects the harmful tools; and gradually masters the problems posed by the appearance of 'uninvited guests.' "[14]

Have we not heard this somewhere before? In slightly different guise it is the reincarnation of 19th century laissez-faire. Instead of the "survival of the fittest" and the "Invisible Hand of the Market Mechanism," we now have a mechanomorphosed and manifest destiny, the Spontaneous and Integral Growth of Technology. We who actually made it, *are not fit to guide it.* Its will must not be transgressed by pathetic human interventions, doomed to futility.

In the same way that the Market Mechanism was supposed to make us free, the Integral Growth of Technology interacts in some mystical way with "society" which "retains those tools which are really useful, at least on balance; (and) rejects the harmful tools. . ." It is not explained by Strausz-Hupé why men competent enough to retain useful tools and reject harmful ones, are not also competent to meet together and guide technology. The second task may be rather more complex but are we not doomed to permanent incompetence and subordination to our tools unless we at least try?

Strausz-Hupé seems to be giving us a modern variation of the American business creed. This holds that highly *organized* business (and technology) and *un*organized aggregate consumers, accepting in greater or lesser degree that which business offers them, constitute a "democratic system." In his scenario initiative belongs rightly to technology, and we, wearing dime store paper hats inscribed "The Consumer is King," may tune in and adjust to certain technologies in preference to others.

One of the main distinctions between the Radical and Conservative style was the concept of competence and power *over* things and persons (Conservative) versus power *through* people (Radical). The vision of Strausz-Hupé and the "soft determinism" of Mesthene leave little doubt about the kind of technical competence these thinkers have in mind. Brzezinski, as usual, has expressed it in the baldest terms of all.

> In the technetronic society, the trend would seem to be towards the aggregation of individual support of millions of uncoordinated citizens, easily within the reach of magnetic and attractive personalities effectively exploiting the latest communication techniques to manipulate emotions and control reason.[15]

In Brzezinski's prophecies the influence of Social Darwinsim and 19th century scientisms is quite undisguised.

> If the industrial society can be said to have developed through a struggle for survival of the fittest, the technotronic society – in order to prosper – requires the effective mobilization of the ablest. Objective and systematic criteria for the selection of those with greatest gifts will have to be developed. . .[16]

Like it or not, the age of manipulation is coming and the third world countries can only gnash their teeth in frustration for "the capacity to assert social and political control over the individual will vastly increase. . . Power will gravitate into the hands of those who control the information and can correlate it most rapidly." Man rigged out in instruments will be supreme. Man representing humanity alone will be incompetent and powerless.

d) *INVESTMENT as an authentic and intense expression of a unique personality (Radical) V. Human action as the attempt to accomplish or extend some external norm or value (Conservative).*

Technology is, of course, the "Compleat Game." It has its own internally consistent, non-human rules, by which its human users can "bowl a perfect score," through rigorous training and practice and years of dedication to the possibilities of a mechanism. In this way it gives strong support to the conservative end of the above dichotomy.

However we must not confuse the roles of the technician and those shaped by him, with the role of the scientist who creates the rules in the first place. The latter is generally radical and creative in the broader definition of my model. He lets into his mind much "useless" and "impractical" information which he associates in what appears at first to be vague and unreliable ways. He pays close attention to his inner excitement, natural curiosity, and the intuitive prompting of his subconscious mind.

Only *after* he has made a novel discovery does the technical game become detached from his own personality, to become a separate entity over and against him. The rule makers themselves are relatively self-fulfilled. It is the rest of us who live in their beautifully designed cages who suffer. As Abraham Kaplan has pointed out, there is a *logic of discovery* concerning which we know very little, and *reconstructed logic,* consisting mostly of the "things" allegedly "discovered." (I prefer to say, the concepts created.) These systems tend, through reconstruction, to be emptied of the feeling and imagining processes by which they were created, and they are passed on to us as if they were physical facts and objects quite neutral to human existence. (In fact the physical sciences are full of unobservable, human constructs.)

For those of us who must live with an increasing flood of reconstructed logic, the Good often appears in conservative guise, as the servant of pre-calculated reason, the "one best way." In contrast, opportunities to discover shared preferences through radical expression and exploration become fewer.

A typical product of reconstructed logic which cannot discover any meaning that transcends its own premises, is the simulation exercise – the game par excellence. I think the author of *Alumnus Football* would have loved it – given a requisite grasp of statistics:

> When the One Great Scorer comes to write against your name –
> He marks – not that you won or lost – but how you played the game.

The Simulation Game not only ensures relative conformity by all contestants, it is unserious, and in itself lacks ultimate meaning or significance. Simulations of nuclear war, for instance, in which several of our current crop of futurologists made their reputations, have none of the agony, horror, drama, and tragedy of a real holocaust – but then simulation experts seldom regard their feelings and humanity as in need of development, only their reason, and in this sense war can be reconstructed on a card table.

By treating war as a game to be played by external rules, "rationally" adhered to, the simulators ignore the fact that to create peace we must first break the rules of war; that is, we must act *irrationally* in the eyes of the person still playing the original games. They also ignore the fact that creative impulse and feeling may be the chief "irrational" motivation seeking to alter the rules by which "rationality" is now defined. By putting aside our personal feelings and calculating about war, we may have closed off the avenue by which an answer could come.

For the real failure of strategic and technological thinking is an inability to grasp that the human emotions are themselves lawful, that there is a logic of human ends, and of human needs, as well as a logic of means. The emotional outburst may not, after all, be the irrational utterance of the weak flesh, but a warning that the unexamined normative premises on which calculations have been mounted are ludicrously inadequate, and do violence to the *rational* laws of man's emotional and intellectual development.

But more than this, war is *by definition* a game, a conservative contest along previously defined parameters of win-lose. Yet the peaceful solution of conflict entails breaking out of games as such, into a non-game. A non-game is a dialogue of unique personal expressions wherein every radical statement transcends the internal consistency of the previous statement and by expanding it, *alters its rules.* In radical parlance "each does his own thing," and does not compete with the other because what he does cannot be compared on the same dimension. Without conformity to rules, without an implicit agreement to compete along dimensions imposed by hostility and available techniques, there could be no war. The opposite is also true. The decision to play a game, any game, locks you into a win-lose-compromise dilemma. "Suppose they gave a war and nobody came" reads a well known protest placard. It is an interesting thought.

Futurologists make great play with the notions of "freedom" and "technology creating opportunities" for us all and presenting us with a greater number of alternatives. Yet the meaning of freedom in the contexts which they use it is essentially a choice of a large number of games, or the choice in playing a particular game to reach a predetermined objective by interchangeable routes. Thus George A. Miller, a Harvard psychologist, and a prominent contributor to *Toward the Year 2000* envisages numerous children in communication with a central computer.

> Within the broad limits set by what materials have been prepared by the computer, the student is free to study those things that are of most interest to him.[17]

Leaving aside for a moment the question of whether the computer as opposed to the programmer can be said to have prepared anything, let us consider this use of the term "freedom." It is the freedom of a rat to run a maze by turning left or right on any of a hundred separate occasions. It is the freedom of a guided missile to reach a predetermined target by an infinite number of paths or the freedom of a quarterback to gain fifty yards by kicking, running, or passing in a myriad of ways. I can think of few marine commanders who would not endorse the kind of "initiative" by which recruits dropped in the wilderness find their way back to base by *any means they wish,* provided they cover three hundred miles in thirty six hours.

Freedom, of course, means more than the ability to explore a vast technological prison with new wings added yearly and play alternative technical games therein. Unless the paths chosen by the individual contain a *human* logic and meaning, then it makes little sense to regard the human being as investing himself freely, intensely, or authentically. Given a run-away technology, wherein "can" is repeatedly translated into "ought" as technical means become ends in themselves, the survival of human freedom and meaning and the confirmation of this meaning by others, becomes harder and harder to achieve.

Anyone reading Miller's essay on the year 2000 cannot help wondering whether he is setting students free as he claims or drilling soldier-technicians. He tells us that the major problem of the future will be "how to motivate students to study."

> As an advertising executive once said, there is only so much the public wants to know about toothpaste: the advertiser's job is to force his product into that small mental compartment, because he knows that he will thereby almost surely force some competitor's product out. . .
>
> If more and more technical competence will be required in order to earn a living, it means that more and more of man's precious cognitive capacity will have to be devoted to that. . .[18]

Miller comes over like a veritable Child Buyer: "we need every good brain we can train." The "packaging" of technical knowledge must be improved. "Obviously we must see to it. . . that the student, whether he realizes it or not, really needs to know it." According to Miller, "the central problem of education is to make the student want it."

> We know how to break up a unit into small steps and drill each step separately. . . but we do not know how to inject the urge to learn into a student's heart.[19]

Miller doubts if the students will actually want his kind of freedom. The answer is to instill the Need for Achievement into them by "a deliberate public program of personality modification."

Free investment in the radical sense I have used it in this book, means something quite different. It means that learners must themselves be free to design their own learning environment in dialogue with their teachers, a freedom which persons hooked up to a computer do *not* have. Nothing they say to the computer can alter its overall design. It has a very complex yet very closed mind that declines to be modified by any input not envisioned in its original program. Freedom in the existential, rule-transcending sense, does not seem to lie within the comprehension of many technocrats or social scientists. We have a whole generation of academics with a *trained incapacity to understand what freedom is,* since there is no room for it in their philosophy of science. For example, Miller does not regard creative resynthesis and its personal expression as among man's principal endowments. On the contrary, men are the supreme *rule followers* of the animal kingdom.

> More than anything else it is man's capacity to cope with large inter-related systems of habits and rules that sets him apart from other animals – that enables him to learn a linguistic system, to invent a system of mathematics, or to learn all he must know to be accepted as a member of society.[20]

So there we have it – the psychology of the ant-hill and the soldier ants.

> The sands of the desert are sodden red
> Red with the blood of the square that broke. . .
>
> And it's not for the sake of a ribboned coat,
> Or the selfish hope of a season's fame
> But his Captain's hand on his shoulder smote –
> "Play up! play up! and play the game!"[21]

e) *Acceptance of the vulnerability, doubt, and despair inherent in SELF-SUSPENSION and RISK (Radical) V. Praise for self-control, masculinity, and a dignified appearance. Use of economic (or strategic) terms that reduce psychological risk-taking (Conservative).*

As Rappaport has pointed out, the strategic thinker is not at all fazed by moral outbursts from his audience. According to *his* values, on the conservative end of the above dichotomy, the objector has merely underlined the greater need for rationality. If men protest shrilly when faced with the prospect of nuclear war, how blessed are they with calm courage to "think the unthinkable" and compute megadeaths without turning a hair. The screamers are clearly in "the camp of the scandalized defenders of obsolete prejudices, together with the anti-evolutionists and decency leaguers." A favorite rebuke by the prophets of the Year 2000, directed at potential opponents, is the term "over-emotional."

> Fears have been expressed that the computer represents an assembly-line approach to the educational process that will increase alienation, identity crises, *anomie,* and so forth. Such attitudes seem over-emotional.[22]

The problem with regarding emotion as the sure mark of a Nervous Nellie, is that we cannot "change gear" and suspend our prior assumptions without some degree of internal disintegration in which emotions of anxiety and *lack* of control play a vital part.

The act of suspension does not come easily to the technocratic thinker for a number of reasons we have touched upon already. Techniques piled high upon certain normative premises tend to freeze those premises and prevent their reopening and reconsideration. The formal logic of "policy science" can only begin *after* a process of dialectical logic has defined the actual policy. Reopening the dialectic threatens the foundation of numerous interlocking techniques, and the very rationale for a military-industrial complex. Moreover "cherished academic standards" deter one from cutting the psychological ground from beneath scholars.

My own view is that strategic thinking on nuclear deterrence and many other subjects is closely akin to a kind of international prejudice and racism. This seems a shocking accusation so let me document exactly what I mean.

Consider the literal meaning of the word "prejudice" – *pre-judicare* – to judge before the event and not suspend that judgment in the light of the concrete situation and encounter. Why is the racist prejudiced? Because encountering the black (or white) face of the "distant" person exposes the racist to unbearable anxiety, *but only if he suspends himself* and leaves himself open and vulnerable to experiencing *anything* that might happen. But anxiety, vulnerability, and suspension can be avoided if the person pre-judges the other and comes to the encounter with a ready-made "game" – *a strategic plan for every contingency he forsees.* (i.e., smile at the good nigger, slap down the sassy one, talk down to all of them – but don't change your overall style in response to any unforseen event). Armed with his strategy the racist hopes to manage the situation with dignity, aplomb, and the minimum of distasteful emotion.

Like the racist, the strategic thinker on national defense has prejudged the intentions of the other side prior to any encounter. He has done this for the same basic reason. When a confrontation comes it may be so full of violent, confused, and hysterical emotions, that only a total plan, a game automatically followed can preserve "rational" behavior. The strategist drills himself in simulations as the soldier drills for the battlefield. In the face of the enemy only tested routines enable both to survive. It is most important to the racist and strategist alike that mutual behavior is predictable. If communists and blacks can know for certain that they will be slapped down for acting "irrationally," outside the rules of the game, then they will not deviate from expectation and strategy itself need not be suspended. A more sophisticated racist might even plan a series of escalating slaps. It is a more humane way of controlling "nigras" and gives them time to get the message.

But is not race prejudice irrational? This is what we are constantly assured. On the contrary *within* the limitations of his perspective, I believe the racist to be rational. Most surveys have shown that black persons in ghettos commit more crimes per capita, have higher absenteeism at work, poorer health, less education, etc., etc. Accepting this as an "objective fact," "out there," it could also be demonstrated that hiring white persons was "objectively" more profitable. From an idealistic point of view, intimate knowledge of each employee would give you better information than the judging by his skin color, but that additional information can be time consuming, expensive, and even dangerous to obtain. We live in a world of imperfect information where again and again we must guess on the basis of limited impressions and where errors are costly. The majority of our relationships are impersonal so we rely on the few cues we have. From a purely rational point of view a black face *is* a fairly good predictor of poor education and similar conditions unprofitable to employers.

But communists are genuinely dangerous and aggressive, it might be argued. There is very real danger in encountering them without a strategic plan that maintains our deterrent and locks us both into the same "rational" perspective. I agree, there is danger. There is also genuine danger for the racist. Now he, of course, has helped to *make* the danger and perpetuate it, and so has America in the Cold War.

Suppose policeman A who patrols the ghetto never talks to a black resident without holding his night stick in the vicinity of his head, while policeman B relaxes, smiles, offers genuine friendship and thereby leaves himself open both to attack and to the discovery that some residents are friendly, humorous, and complex people. An experiment which assumed that a policeman must maximise his chance of survival could well discover that policeman A has a better chance of survival than B, *given the emotional climate created by many policemen with A's assumptions.* Whenever B relaxes and smiles a previous victim of A might say to himself "kill the pig while he's off his guard." Both the racist and the nuclear deterrent theorist have, in the name of group security and self-interest, helped to create a climate where their unsuspended assumptions about the villainy of the other are self-fulfilling. They dare not take the risk of discovering they are mistaken, and their strategic precautions repeatedly deter *not only attack but any chance of psycho-social development in themselves or the other.*

What is needed to break out of strategic games and racist games is a comprehension of the *heroism of vulnerability.* Instead of jeering at the "sucker," we must learn to admire those who leave themselves open to exploitation in a skilled and authentic attempt to communicate with others. The road to relative international and interracial security is by indirection, by a series of short term *in*securities. The way to avoid the run-away emotionality of war, is to feel and express *more* emotion in the short-run, not less. Suspension involves a flirtation with what you fear.

The Hero of Vulnerability would not be the super-technical policeman, squirting every kind of paralysing fluid from a hovercraft, but a single human volunteer. Perhaps a terminal cancer patient who looks death in the face with a fierce determination to snatch some meaning out of this terrifying absurdity. This vulnerable specimen of humanity walks slowly up to the armed suspect, pleading gently with him not to shoot, asking him to save both of them and to accept this one last chance to surprise and confound every dogmatist and disciplinarian. Such a volunteer might not live long, but then millions of human beings have already died for the *unsuspended* concept of national and group security. They have died for the premise that *either* their group *or* the enemy group must perish, which, when all is said and done, are pretty miserable alternatives. Might we not find new heroes in this anti-heroic age, men willing to risk death (not wanting to die) to create the possibility that *both* groups or cultures could survive?

The celebration of the conventional war hero does, as we have seen, lay the foundations for the next war by consecrating war policy. The saddest fact about the dead in wars is that they transcend themselves and enter into the memory of their nation in a way that lures the next generation to a similar death.

But the Hero of Vulnerability is a man who transcends himself in death to become a genuine developmental force in world society. When he dies it is for *all* men and the principle of reconciliation. Even assuming the very worst – that he is gunned down in cold blood at his very first attempt to help another, even this would make his slayer less of a hero within his own group than if that slayer had killed an armed and dangerous man. It is when we *cease* to create military heroes among rival groups, that we can genuinely claim that our Hero of Vulnerability died to make the sacrifice of additional lives less probable. We have only to comprehend this kind of valour and the valorous would, I believe, come forward. Already we have the example of young men going limp beneath ferocious beatings by the strategists of Southern racism and we have seen a nation turn with contempt upon the beaters.

f) *Encouragement and idealization of BRIDGING the wider DISTANCES between those who personify equally legitimate yet discrepant human needs (Radical) V. Idealization of the shortest possible DISTANCE between persons, whose interactions are mediated by, and should approximate to, those Supreme Values around which the faithful are exhorted to assemble (Conservative).*

There is something indelibly old-fashioned about congregating around a flag or sacred symbol. It is still done, of course, by millions, including a majority of Americans, but the scent of nostalgia is in the air at these gatherings. Yet the faithful can take heart, for now, streamlined "iron lungs" for impoverished investors are in plentiful supply. "Young moderns" can assemble as before around the latest technique and so long as they all interact in the terms and symbols demanded by the technique, and if they all accept those basic premises upon which the technique maximises its energy, agreeing in effect that "this thing is bigger than both of us," then they can safely huddle together as did the Elks and Shriners before them, with their secret, in-group language and safely predictable behavior, and an attitude of ethnocentric superiority towards mere laymen.

Given a few more years of technical education, Babbitt and his fellow Boosters would have rejoiced at this set-up. Those like-minded, like-speaking, jolly good fellows could band together to make *their* technique bigger and better and more profitable, year after year, in competition with the boosters of rival techniques, each rootin' and tootin' for his own team, while pausing at intervals to celebrate the entire game, and excoriate foreigners and critics. It's a very short step from Zenith in the Twenties to Dr. Harold Agnew, the current Director of the Los Alamos Laboratories Weapons Division:

> The basis of advanced technology is innovation, and nothing is more stifling to innovation than seeing one's product not used or ruled out of consideration on flimsy premises involving world opinion.[23]

There speaks, in more dignified idiom, the modern booster, or as Brzezinski has put it, one of "the house idealogues for those in power."

But perhaps it is too optimistic to conjure up such scenes of immature conviviality from the Twenties. Many techniques do not encourage so much face-to-face interaction or sharing of sentiments. A closer analogy might be my earlier one of a thousand worshippers on their knees, alienated from each other with their faces hidden, but each struggling to convince himself that he has a private line to some supreme entity who is the repository of wisdom.

Futurologists have a very similar prospect in mind for us. George A. Miller would advise us to adjust to the following scene:

> Imagine a classroom partitioned into semi-isolated booths. In each booth are a pair of headphones, a typewriter keyboard, a screen similar to a television set's, and a photosensitive "light gun." All these stations (and others in the classrooms) are in communication with a central computer. A student communicates with the computer by typing on the keyboard or by touching his light gun to designated spots on the screen. The computer communicates with the student by playing recorded speech through the student's earphones, or by writing or by drawing pictures on the cathode ray tube...
>
> A science fiction fantasy? Not at all. Such systems are already operating.[24]

Even Miller sees dangers in this vision. What if his "deliberate public program of personality modification" is abused? The answer, readily supplied, is to discover *better techniques for controlling the controllers.* "It will be necessary to develop and instil a code of professional ethics among scientists who use such data. . ." So the problems of unilateral power and its inherent capacity to corrupt is somehow to be cured by *more* "ethical" power – whatever that may be. If ethics are to be instilled into the elite, who will guarantee the ethics of the instillers? How would I discover that my "ethical technique" was harmful to the human condition if that technique is expected to modify personality rather than personality modifying the technique?

This is obviously a conservative vision of Ethics, not to be found in the pliable personality of human beings, but floating in the ether like some eternal code, and capable, one assumes of being programmed into a computer. What astonishing naivete is this, which assumes that any *human* code of ethical behavior could long survive the deliberate alteration of the human personality "necessitated" by electronic techniques.

One gains the impression that technotronic man is not going to be very skilled at bridging the widest distances to the "wretched of the earth." In fact, the rich and poor, the black and white, the "ins" and "outs" will become more alienated. Those who can play the game will progressively enrich themselves; those who cannot will peer out of their shrunken faces at us with envious eyes. All this is predicted by Brzezinski. Before humanistic dissenters die out their "disaffections" may become "linked with increasing bitterness of the deprived Negro masses." Scientific technological change may mean that "not only will the gap between the developed and the underdeveloped worlds become wider. . . but a *new* one may be developing *within* the industrial and urban world." The one hope for the underdeveloped peoples everywhere is to imitate America and join her in rallying around Technetron. Yet this is seen as unlikely.

> With the widening gap dooming any hope of imitation, the more likely development is a rejection of the developed world. Racial hatred could provide the necessary emotional force, exploited by xenophobic, romantic leaders. The writings of Frantz Fanon – violent and racist – are a good example. . . Indeed, one might ask at this point: who is the truer repository of that indefinable quality we call human. The technologically dominant and conditioned technetron, increasingly trained to adjust to leisure, or the more "natural" and backward agrarian, more and more dominated by racial passions, and continuously exhorted to work harder, even as his goal of the good life becomes more elusive.[25]

I believe the quality called human *is* definable, and I have been doing my best to define it. What are we to say of the "humanity" of the technetron who adjusts to leisure while millions starve? Is *this* the example which the rest of the world is to follow? As for the widening gap this is caused by Brzezinski himself, or by anyone else with the arrogance to say, "You should imitate me," as if the lives of other people had no integrity of their own. Perhaps violent words are too mild a rebuke for the "scenario" Brzezinski is asking us to accept. I am reminded of the opening night of a play which featured a live horse on the stage. Seconds before the final curtain the horse disgraced himself right in the middle of the grand finale. "Disgusting," remarked a member of the audience, "but what a critic!" Brzezinski deserves Frantz Fanon. The coldly detached intellectual helps to create in exaggerated form, that which is missing from his own personality.

g) *Emphasis upon the experience of SELF-CONFIRMATION and SELF-TRANSCENDENCE as a test of acting rightly towards others (Radical) V. Emphasis upon the achievement of external norms and just rewards for the accomplishment of goals, previously sanctioned by responsible authorities (Conservative).*

Most often, technological thinking leans to the Right on the above dichotomy. A technical system is usually envisaged as the extension of known laws and techniques. Its feasibility is calculated. Authorities give the "go ahead." Thereafter the performance of human beings in setting up the system, "debugging" it, and making it run efficiently, is measured against a precalculated norm of "good performance." Only where the success of a technical system is highly tentative, where it goes beyond known prescriptions and calculations, and where in itself it necessitates a change in the yardstick by which "success" is measured, only then does the situation begin to lean towards the radical end of dichotomy (g). I submit that such situations are relatively rare and are enjoyed mainly by those few who work on the frontiers of knowledge.

For the vast majority of people there is what Mario Savio called "the end of history." We make our impacts on teachers or bureaucrats along pre-calculated dimensions of "go" and "no-go" – soon to be computerized no doubt. Nothing we say can *surprise* them or cause them to suspend those categories by which they process us, or the dimensions along which we "compete" (in this context synonymous with "conform"). It is the end of self-transcendence, of the ability to leave some small evidence of one's potency in the womb of the menopausal institution.

Men are expected to trample each other to get an "A" or promotion, or $20,000, a process which keeps the competitors unorganized and divided and the system designers strong. When the individual is rewarded for success in a pre-designed game he begins to doubt whether *his* personality is being confirmed at all, or whether the system is not just celebrating itself in stamping "Grade A" on its more successful products. Really he is interchangeable with any other top product. When he makes a novel and creative investment for which the system has no prepared category or response, there is silence or perhaps a "no go" signal. At first creative individuals are perplexed, then angry, later perhaps they become cynical or resigned. Sometimes they demonstrate in open defiance to be answered only by the routine clanking of machinery. One leader explains.

> We sat around a police car and kept it immobilized for over thirty-two hours. At last the administrative bureaucracy agreed to negotiate. But instead, on the following Monday, we discovered

> that a committee had been appointed, in accordance with the usual regulations, to resolve the dispute. Our attempt to convince any of the administrators that an event had occurred, that something new had happened, failed. They saw this simply as something to be handled by normal university procedures.[26]

In a tragic miscomprehension of what "equality," "opportunity," and "freedom" means to a developing individual, the notion has grown up that the standardised criteria of meritocracy and universalism will best guarantee the rights of everyone. Greater universalism and less particularism is on the agenda of many futurologists. The best system is one clearly marked out like a playing field – with entrance requirements, grades, rules, and pre-defined dimensions of excellence. In such a system the race is to the swiftest, all competitors are equally treated and those who complain will be referred to published rules and can be shown their scores.

I suspect that those who run such a system are actually more concerned with justifying its operation and simplifying the verification of its "fairness," than with how the individual student actually feels about it. As Kenneth Keniston has noted:

> Our gods are accuracy, realism, verifiability, and objectivity: while intuition, fantasy, and private illumination are considered useful only insofar as they lead to "objective" achievements or help dissipate the tensions created by the "real" world.[27]

George A. Miller looks to the day when computers will automatically record students' efforts. In his scenario all additional evaluation then becomes unnecessary!

> A teacher can teach and leave the threatening duty of evaluation to the machine. . . and a computer treats all children alike, regardless of race, creed, and color.[28]

This vision of "opportunity," "equality," and "development" is so flawed, one scarcely knows where to start criticising it.

Firstly, and most fundamentally, if reward systems are standardized, the particular and creative personality is only confirmed, if at all, in its least original aspects. The race along simple numerical dimensions produces a hierarchy almost immediately, and persons therein build envious concepts of "better than," "worse than," "the more the better," etc. Such systems extol the docile "grind" and penalise the creative person, prompted by his curiosity and personal depth to diverge from the syllabus.

Secondly the system produces the grossest *in*equality between game-players and game-designers. The latter can easily train a whole generation of students to converge upon the opinions and facts held by the designers, so that the hierarchy of differential rewards may finish up by measuring degrees of youthful conformity or what Paul Goodman calls *Compulsory Mis-Education.*

Thirdly it is naive to regard the rules of the game as value-free and objective. What is programmed into the computer or posted on the notice board is no less prejudiced, white, middle class, and elitist in its content than is the mind of its programmer or author. To claim as Miller does, that a teacher is not evaluating students when he programs (or accepts from the programmer) what students "ought" to answer, is strange indeed. About the only statement with which I can agree, is that a teacher *can* reduce "the threatening duty of evaluation" by absenting himself from the presence of those he has prejudged. He can hide from anxiety *and any enlightenment* coming from his students whose novel ideas and protests transcend the design of his program.

Genuine equality and opportunity for psycho-social development can only come when trainees and subordinates are free to express themselves in ways that ensure that the history of man's development *never ends.* If education consists of learning to think, then the thinker must inevitably challenge and reconsider the adequacy of his own learning environment. The developing man continually transcends his condition and in so doing renders inapposite the present criteria for evaluating him. Those who struggle to understand creative persons must live with the vast uncertainty and ambiguity of human expressions and stop dreaming of time-saving, anxiety-reducing mechanisms, that promise to anaesthetize bureaucracy from its fear of the new and the unknown.

h) *An egalitarian dialectic leading to the SYNERGISTIC or just reconciliation of formerly discrepant needs (Radical) V. The victory in any conflict of those Supreme Values relevant to the dispute, which should be imposed if necessary, upon the undisciplined and unreliable feelings of men (Conservative).*

Technological thinking has the greatest difficulty in achieving a synergistic reconciliation of opposites for a number of reasons touched upon already.

There can be no inter-meshing of different perspectives without suspending the "rational rules" within each perspective. The rational means of attaining our own ends cease to be rational when the ends themselves shift to combine with ends sought by the other. There can be no synergy in the sense I have defined it, in a value-free and neutral science, since men must first value certain ends with passion, in order to discover that the passions of others can enlarge those ends.

There can be no dialogue concerning ultimate ends or policies with strategists who have assumed the rightness of ends sought by their respective departments of defense, and are intent only on demonstrating to us the most economic ways of achieving those ends. There can be no synergy when strategic thinkers on both sides are forced by one another to value the same ultimate ends, namely their own survival. Each side knows that if they stopped frightening the other, the other would start to develop and seek qualitatively different values. In the absence of dialogue, *how could we verify the rationality of means towards ends which elude our comprehension?* The theory of rational deterrence is a cage that imprisons us within a conformity of outlook and perpetuates a mutual obsession with survival. The loss of one must be the gain of the other upon an agreed dimension of rival self-interest. While cooperation is not impossible, this involves *not* synergy, but "splitting the difference" or compromise in the interest of survival.

Any system which evaluates persons or groups along universalistic, unidimensional, and quantitative indices, kills synergy and accelerates entropy. If businessman X and businessman Y both value their high salaries as symbols of their success, then X's $50,000 per annum tends to eclipse Y's $35,000. They are likely to be envious, alienated, and power oriented in their relationships. As W. S. Gilbert put it, "When everybody's somebody then no one's anybody."

Gilbert's maxim becomes inapposite *only* when X and Y value qualities which are quite incomparable, like good ballet and good music, yet quite capable of forming a creative synergy. In this situation the capacities and perspectives of both men are enlarged by their mutual enjoyment or composition of musical ballet.

In fact any creative effort leading to a final synthesis or synergy between previously discrepant or even opposed points of view, usually entails a number of offenses against the technical norms of efficiency, predictability, accuracy, parsimony, and practicality.

Technique usually demands a maximum energy output for a minimum input, yet research on creative persons shows that they produce a superabundance of raw material, whose relevance, much less efficiency, is only apparent *after* the creative synthesis has been made and understood. Before this happens the scene is one of waste and inefficiency. Besides, many creative efforts come to nothing and the process is most unpredictable. It is one full of disconfirmation and tragedy, dimensions quite alien to the optimistic, technological expansionism.

Technological thinking is repelled by snags and strains in the machinery, yet the synergy growing out of dialectic requires human systems to oppose each other in ways incredibly "inefficient," "irrational," and unpredictable until the pain, excitement, and learning inherent in this process teach them how to combine. This reconciliation of prior opposites seems to lack a mechanical analogue and remains beyond the grasp of formal logic.

Finally a synergistic resolution requires for its attainment all the resources of myth, metaphor, and idealism. A larger, more inclusive whole, be it a nation made up of previously warring states, or a world made up of previously warring nations, requires so hard a struggle to attain, that only people fired with imagination and sustained by their visions can build these Higher Synergies. Thus Edmund Leach has followed Marx in arguing that ideology is the imagined reconciliation of the existing contradictions within society.[29] Technocrats with their hostility to myth, dream, and imagination attempt to purge all the metaphors of human development from the minds of men by insisting on "empirical realities."

Not surprisingly, therefore futurologists offer us a future dominated by America and her technology, with the weakest going to the wall.

> To be sure, the most advanced states will possess ever more deadly means of destruction, possibly even capable of nullifying the consequences of the nuclear proliferation that appears increasingly inevitable. Chemical and biological weapons, death rays, neutron bombs, nerve gases and a host of other devices possessed in their sophisticated variety (as seems likely) only by the two super states, may impose on the world a measure of stability.[30]

Along with this sober prophecy of American domination, Brzezinski sees the likely destruction of more emotional nations.

> Some local wars between the weaker, nationalistically more aroused, poorer nations may occasionally erupt – resulting perhaps in the total nuclear extinction of one or several smaller nations? – before greater international control is imposed in the wake of the universal moral shock thereby generated.

As with most conservative and anti-synergistic styles of thought, we see here stark, unreconcilable alternatives, passionate war or universal and "rational" constraint. And everywhere there will be elites, corporate, intellectual, managerial.

> This could encourage tendencies during the next several decades towards a technocratic dictatorship, leaving less and less room for political procedures as we now know them.[31]

i) *The INTEGRATION of human affect and reason into a belief system of inter-communicating thought-matrices of developing complexity (Radical)*
*V. The permanent separation of reprehensible desires, appetites, and hasty*

> *reasoning from those Superior Values and Great Wisdoms that have stood the test of time (Conservative).*

The conservatism of technotronic thinking dethrones Superior Values and Great Wisdoms, promotes "hasty reasoning" from its subordinate position to the point of supreme control, and keeps "reprehensible" desires and appetites" in their former states of subjection. The motto of Goldwater conservatives, "In your heart you know he's right," gives way to its equally dogmatic opposite, "In your mind you calculate the answer." At least in Goldwater's scheme of things the human emotions could be trusted to recognize the "Laws of God and of Nature," and to combat man's overweening pride in his critical capacities. With the ascent of Technetron, emotions lose even this modest function. However, the rigid hierarchy of values within the mind remains, with Reason in iron control, and emotional objections of any kind identified as less than reasonable by definition.

Indeed Brzezinski seems to regard Reason as being insufficiently in control. At the moment we have only *post*-crisis institutions, which step in after conflict and all that nasty emotionality have broken out. What we need are *pre*-crisis institutions which will prevent open disputes from even occurring. Miller sees social systems and social conflicts simulated in advance on computers for ready-made solutions. (The "end-of-history" and the "exhaustion of ideas in our time" must presumably have occurred.)

Among the outstanding characteristics of conservative thought, noted in Chapter IX, were the contradictions within the belief system, the inability to reconcile democracy with authority, rights with duties, welfare with freedom, etc. We saw this was part of a more general failure to justly balance the segments of the cycle. In technological thought, there is the same contradiction between the determinism of statements made when "speaking as a scientist" and the freedom demanded when "speaking as a citizen." Many of the essays in *Toward the Year 2000* slip from one style into the other, occasionally recognizing but never reconciling the contradiction. Typical of this is Gardner C. Quarton's essay, "Controlling Human Behavior and Modifying Personality." When he has listed the techniques of the future, gene selection, modification of the genetic code, neurosurgical interventions, Skinnerarian conditioning, etc., he suggests that their use will be justified by "humanitarianism" and warns us against "puritanical avoidance of behavior control." At length he turns his attention to the issue of human freedom and we get the usual non-integration of ideas.

> The civil rights issues involved in behavior control are very difficult to state with clarity. Since society has been controlling the behavior of the individual throughout history by providing and preventing opportunities for action and by manipulation of

> reward-punishment systems, it does not make much sense to argue that the control of one individual by another is in itself unethical. . .
>
> One of the major effects of increased efficiency of some behavior control techniques will be a proportional growth of discussion of the problem in relation to civil rights. In the future, government officials and agencies will spend much more time about these matters than they do now. There are many problems lying ahead. . .[32]

Thank you, Dr. Quarton. Let us hope their discussions are more fruitful than yours.

Erich Fromm, in his passionate dissent against just this kind of unthinking, yet ever expanding technical expertise, refers to the writings of Kahn and Brzezinski as evidencing a form of "low grade chronic schizophrenia," with the typical schizophrenic isolation between intellect and emotional experience.

> The tendency to install technical progress as the highest value is linked up not only with our overemphasis on intellect but, most importantly, with a deep emotional attraction to the mechanical, to all that is not alive, to all that is man-made. . . Those who are attached to the non-alive are the people who prefer 'law and order' to living structure, bureaucratic to spontaneous methods, gadgets to living beings, repetition to originality, neatness to exuberance, hoarding to spending. They want to control life because they are afraid of its uncontrollable spontaneity. . .[33]

The isolation between intellect and emotion has the same pattern that we found in Chapter IX, with the isolation *inside* the mind corresponding to the (predicted) isolationism between groups, between races, and between the economically developed and less developed. Along with this failure of mental integration, we have the domination of man by technique, of the rest of the world by super-powers, and of controlled persons by a variety of expert controllers.

And last, but not least, there is the total failure of responsibility for what is predicted. The nuclear annihilation of smaller countries, the poor excluded from development, the increasing alientation of black Americans, the systematic modification of personality – all is laid at the doorstep of Technetron which allegedly makes it happen and calls upon us to adjust. So long as present technical attitudes prevail we shall fail to learn from human mistakes through the pretense that these were technological imperatives.

Are there any research findings that might support my critique of technological thinking and arbitrate between this view and those put forward by the advocates of Technotronic man? If Emmanuel Mesthene is right about technology acting as a prime creator of opportunities and new freedoms, then presumably students of engineering, physical and biological sciences, etc., would exhibit much of this autonomy in their personalities, along with a penchant for limitless horizons. If Herman Kahn and Brzezinski are correct in designating student rebels as nihilistic, vulgar, debased, bewildered and generally incompetent at grasping social and cultural realities, then presumably these incapacities would register on personality tests. The students in science-technology fields, the carriers of "the commercial, professional and technically superb" should by now be demonstrating those superior capacities which qualify them to rule over us in The Technotronic Age.

A summary of the personality attributes found among engineering students was made in 1958 by Martin Trow. Piecing together the consistent threads from half a dozen studies, he found that student engineers, as shown in Table 32, and as compared with other student groups were uncreative, unimaginative, narrow minded, materialistic, security seeking, prestige oriented, parochial, authoritarian, ultra-masculine, anti-intellectual, and unable or unwilling to play a part in university controversies and affairs. Part of this may result from the "blue-collar" social origins of many engineering students, but why, then, does engineering hold such attractions for the culturally deprived? In view of research findings that show engineering students becoming *more* conservative while at school,[34] the education itself can hardly claim to be emancipating the students in any sense except the material. Technology does seem to shape the minds of these students, but not in the beneficial manner which futurologists have supposed.

A study of the impact of occupations upon values found that engineers were 13th out of 16 other professions upon an index of Faith and Trust in People, 16th out of 18 in their Concern for People, and relatively high in desiring security, prestige, and extrinsic rewards for themselves.[35]

Some much more recent studies conducted at campuses of the University of California, following the Berkeley student rebellion, are set out in Table 33. Here we see that student radicals so far from being the lost, bewildered, anti-intellectuals that futurologists contend, are remarkably more competent upon a large number of psychological indices, used to measure the intellectual, emotional and creative development of personality, than are students in the "hard" sciences and in engineering.

In Thinking Introversion, a measure of intellectual curiosity, sensitivity and openness to new ideas, and the capacity to associate philosophical concepts, the Berkeley Free Speech Movement towers above its contemporaries, and especially above students of agriculture, engineering and the "hard" sciences who come at the tail of the field. This pattern is repeated for Estheticism, a measure of artistic and esthetic sophistication, and concern for beauty and form in the environment. A scale for Complexity measures tolerance for

**Table 32**

**A PROFILE OF THE ENGINEERING STUDENT**
**A SUMMARY OF RESEARCH FINDINGS**

| *Segments of the Anomic Cycle* | *Characteristics of Engineering Students* |
|---|---|
| Anomic failure to ex-ist. . . . | Failure to question received truths or information<br>Unconcern with fundamental issues<br>Unimaginative<br>Uncreative |
| a) PERCEPTION, narrow and impoverished | Courses in literature and history referred to as "bull".<br>Narrow "workmanlike" perspectives<br>Instrumental view of education<br>Hostility to art and culture |
| b) IDENTITY, "locked in" and stagnant | Anti-intraceptive |
| c) In COMPETENCE and anticipated loss | High concern with gaining prestige and assured status. (Many students lents have working class backgrounds.) |
| d) Fails to INVEST authentically | Overriding concern with "buying a union card" to well paying jobs |
| e) Non-SUSPENDING RISK-reducing strategies . . . . | Strong belief in efficiency and reliability of the machine<br>Refusal to be "distracted" by affairs not re0 lated to "getting ahead"<br>Oriented to "secure Middle Class position" with well known corporation |
| f) Avoidance of BRIDGING THE (wider) DISTANCES . . . . . | Parochial values and attitudes |
| g) Inability to make SELF-CONFIRMING, SELF-TRANSCENDING IMPACT | Very low participation by engineering students in current affairs, public discussions, or intellectual ferment within the school |
| h) Domination of, or Submission to, others perspectives, in a non-dialectic, negantropic failure of SYNERGY. | High in authoritarianism<br>Belief in tough competition<br>Severely socialized as children |

**Table 32 (Continued)**

| | |
|---|---|
| i) No responsibility for FEEDBACK. Hense disINTEGRATION and lack of COMPLEXITY | Poor performance in cultural subjects at school<br>Unconcerned with style of life<br>Anti-intellectual in attitudes (However very *high* scores of mathematical and engineering aptitude tests. High I.Q.) |

Source: "Some Implications of The Social Origins of Engineers", by Martin Trow. Paper read at the annual meetings of the American Association for the Advancement of Science, December 1958.

**Table 33**

**SCORES UPON THE OMNIBUS PERSONALITY INVENTORY OF VARIOUS STUDENT AND FACULTY GROUPS ON THE UNIVERSITY OF CALIFORNIA**

*Thinking Introversion*

| | | |
|---|---|---|
| 1. | Members of Free Speech Movement | 63 |
| 2. | Humanities Freshmen | 58 |
| 3. | Random Sample Berkeley Seniors | 55 |
| 4. | Creative Arts Freshmen | 53 |
| 5. | Engineering School Faculty | 52 |
| 6. | Social Science Freshmen | 50 |
| 7. | Physical Sciences Freshmen | 48 |
| 8. | Biological Sciences Freshmen | 47 |
| 9. | Engineering Freshmen | 45 |
| 10. | Argriculture Freshmen | 44 |

*Estheticism*

| | | |
|---|---|---|
| 1. | Members F.S.M.<br>Creative Arts Freshmen | 61 |
| 3. | Humanities Freshmen | 55 |
| 4. | Berkeley Seniors | 52 |
| 5. | Social Science Freshmen | 47 |
| 6. | Physical Science Freshmen<br>Biological Science Freshmen | 45 |
| 8. | Engineering Faculty | 44 |
| 9. | Engineering Freshmen<br>Agriculture Freshmen | 42 |

*Complexity*

| | | |
|---|---|---|
| 1. | Members F.S.M. | 66 |
| 2. | Creative Arts Freshmen | 58 |
| 3. | Humanities Freshmen | 56 |
| 4. | Berkeley Seniors | 54 |
| 5. | Physical Science Freshmen | 51 |
| 6. | Biology Freshmen<br>Engineering Faculty<br>Social Science Freshmen<br>Engineering Students | 49 |

*Autonomy*

| | | |
|---|---|---|
| 1. | Members F.S.M. | 67 |
| 2. | Berkeley Seniors | 61 |
| 3. | Humanities Freshmen | 58 |
| 4. | Creative Arts Freshmen<br>Engineering Faculty | 56 |
| 6. | Physical Sciences Freshmen | 55 |
| 7. | Social Science Freshmen | 54 |
| 8. | Biology Freshmen<br>Engineering Freshmen | 53 |

| | | |
|---|---|---|
| 10. | Agriculture Freshmen | 47 |

*Impluse Expression**

| | | |
|---|---|---|
| 1. | Members of F.S.M. | 64 |
| 2. | Berkeley Seniors | 54 |
| 3. | Engineering Freshmen | 52 |
| 4. | Engineering Faculty | 47 |

*Degree of Experienced Anxiety**

| | | |
|---|---|---|
| 1. | Members of F.S.M. | 48 |
| 2. | Berkeley Seniors | 51 |
| 3. | Engineering Students | 54 |
| 4. | Engineering Faculty | 55 |

(low Scores = higher anxiety)

*Masculinity-Femininity**

| | | |
|---|---|---|
| 1. | Engineering Freshmen | 60 |
| 2. | Physical Science Freshmen | 59 |
| 3. | { Engineering Faculty / Agricultural Freshmen / Biological Freshmen } | 58 |
| 6. | { Social Science Freshmen / Humanities Freshmen } | 51 |
| 8. | Creative Arts Freshmen | 50 |

(Masculine high – feminine low)

| | | |
|---|---|---|
| 10. | Agriculture Freshmen | 50 |

*Religious Liberalism*

| | | |
|---|---|---|
| 1. | Members F.S.M. | 64 |
| 2. | Berkeley Seniors | 58 |
| 3. | Engineering Faculty | 56 |
| 4. | Engineering Students | 55 |

*Altruism**

| | | |
|---|---|---|
| 1. | { Social Science Freshmen / Humanities Freshmen / Engineering Faculty } | 51 |
| 4. | Biology Freshmen | 48 |
| 5. | Argriculture Freshmen | 47 |
| 6. | { Engineering Freshmen / Physical Science Freshmen } | 46 |

*Practical Outlook**

| | | |
|---|---|---|
| 1. | Agriculture Freshmen | |
| 2. | { Enginggering Freshmen / Biology Freshmen } | 53 / 50 |
| 4. | Physical Science Freshmen | 48 |
| 5. | Creative Arts | 46 |
| 6. | Engineering Faculty | 44 |
| 7. | { Humanities Freshmen / Social Science Freshmen } | 41 |

Notes:

1. Scales marked with * were not administered to all groups.
2. All groups except F.S.M. and Berkeley Seniors were located at Davis Campus.
3. On scales measuring Thinking Introversion, Estheticism, Complexity and Autonomy, gains of 1 to 6 points are usually made between Freshmen and Senior years.

Sources: "Personality Characteristics of Students and Faculty in the College of Engineering." by Mary C. Regan. University of California, Davis. Mimeo, 1966.

"Intellect and Commitment: The faces of discontent" by Paul Heist, in *Order and Freedom on the Campus: The Rights and Responsibilities of Faculty and Students.* O. W. Knorr and W. J. Minter (Eds.) Boulder, Col., Western Interstate Commission for Higher Education, 1965.

ambiguity and uncertainty, breadth of comprehension and the capacity for complex syntheses of ideas. Here again F.S.M. members are supreme, seventeen points above engineering students, *and faculty.* On Autonomy, a measure of open-mindedness, self and environmental exploration and non-authoritariansim the F.S.M. are easily first, with engineers, agriculture students, and the "hard" sciences bringing up the rear, well below students in arts and humanities subjects.

The rebels are highest in willingness to reveal their true needs and feelings, Impulse Expression, and highest in their tolerance of various beliefs and non-beliefs, Religious Liberalism. On both these, engineering students and faculty are far behind. Rebels also allow themselves to feel and confront the sharpest anxieties. Engineers are precisely the opposite. No womanish horror of suffering will faze them. They are, above all other groups, proud of their masculinity and practicality. We may also note how "successful" the social sciences have been in imitating the hard sciences rather than the humanities. Social science students are way down among engineers, physicists and agriculturists. What an achievement, to have all the cultural deprivation and human irrelevance and not even a science to show for it! But note that 50% of the F.S.M. were social science *rebels.*

It is interesting that Brzezinski contrasted the dominant Technotronic Man with the doomed Pastoral Man and the displaced intellectual dissenter. But Table 33 shows that engineers *and* the pastoral agriculturalists are the *most similar,* brothers in parochialism and cultural deprivation. In contrast the group of rebel dissenters and those studying "impractical" subjects like English and creative arts, enjoy relatively high levels of creativity, independence and intellectuality.

But perhaps the hard sciences, while getting the less cultured students initially, make more of them in the end? Surely the huge sums of money that bypass the humanities to fatten technology and anything with military potential must be helping to sweep students from backgrounds of poverty to the pinnacle of achievement and mastery of the world?

Donald MacKinnon tested a large number of groups with Terman's Concept Mastery Test. This measures verbal intelligence, breadth of knowledge and interest, the capacity to deal with ideas at an abstract level, to associate meanings, think divergently via analogies, and to converge logically.[36] The scores are summarized below in Table 34.

Creative writers lead the field by a considerable margin. Yet such persons are widely ignored by national policy making. To whom do we principally turn? Why to two groups virtually at the bottom of the index, electronics engineers and scientists ( this group was working with guided missiles) and military officers. If, in a few years, these two groups are joined by independent inventors and student engineers, we will have a Rump Consortium of the Conceptually Underprivileged. When we permit military

Table 34

**MEAN SCORES AND STANDARD DEVIATIONS FOR VARIOUS GROUPS ON THE CONCEPT MASTERY TEST, FORM T**

| Group | N | Mean | S.D. |
|---|---|---|---|
| Creative Writers | 20 | 156.4 | 21.9 |
| Subjects of Standford Gifted Study | 1004 | 136.7 | 28.5 |
| Women Mathematicians | 41 | 131.7 | 33.8 |
| Graduate Students | 125 | 119.2 | 33.0 |
| Research Scientists | 45 | 118.2 | 29.4 |
| Creative Architects | 40 | 113.2 | 37.7 |
| Undergraduate Students | 201 | 101.7 | 33.0 |
| Spouces of Gifted Subjects | 690 | 95.3 | 42.7 |
| Electronics Engineers and Scientists | 95 | 94.5 | 37.0 |
| Engineering College Seniors | 40 | 80.4 | 27.9 |
| Military Officers | 344 | 60.3 | 31.6 |
| Independent Inventors | 14 | 50.8 | 34.7 |

Source: "Fostering Creativity in Students of Engineering" by D.W. MacKinnon. *Journal of Engineering Education,* Vol. 52. No. 3.

officers to make our policy, as in Vietnam, we rely on persons with conceptual mastery *nearly three times smaller* than those of creative writers, who seem mostly to dissent from our foreign policies. Is it any wonder that those of greatest sensitivity and humane intelligence are in widespread revolt against a disastrous policy? Only in internally stimulated Cold War psychoses keeps anti-developmental forces in control of the national destiny, and these are the men whose instruments are to shape our future in the year 2,000. To this "imperative" the futurologists and strategic thinkers have asked us to submit.

It will be claimed, inevitably, that I am "against technology" and that I advocate a retreat to a pastoral age. Or worse, I shall be accused of elitism in regard to those "Middle Americans" who rely on technological training to improve their economic conditions. Readers may even infer that technological perspectives are *inevitably* corrosive to psycho-social development.

| *Segments of the Cycle* | *Attitudes and Motivations* | REFORMERS | PRACTICALS | NO COLLEGE |
|---|---|---|---|---|
| b) IDENTITY | IN THE SENSE OF REJECTING A CONTRIVED PERSONA | | | |
| | Cannot accept outward respectability for career advancement | 83 | 61 | 46 |
| | Cannot accept conformity of dress and appearance | 72 | 55 | 35 |
| c) COMPETENCE | My success = bringing needed changes to society | 71 | 53 | 49 |
| d) INVESTMENT *authentic* and *intense* | Success = doing your own thing | 73 | 57 | 58 |
| | More emphasis on self-expression | 90 | 68 | 69 |
| e) SELF-SUSPENSION and RISK | De-emphasis upon status concerns | 80 | 75 | 57 |
| | De-emphasis upon money and materialism | 80 | 53 | 57 |
| | De-emphasis upon racial origins | 76 | 54 | 39 |
| | De-emphasis upon middle-class origins | 65 | 32 | 35 |
| | De-emphasis upon national or ethnic origins | 74 | 55 | 46 |
| f) BRIDGING THE (wide) DISTANCE | IN THE SENSE OF EXPERIENCING THE DISTANCE | | | |
| | There is a large generation gap | 69 | 56 | 48 |
| | Feel *very* great distance between self and parents | 24 | 11 | 15 |
| | IN THE SENSE OF SEEKING TO BRIDGE THE DISTANCE | | | |
| | Have love and respect for parents | 69 | 82 | 82 |
| | We should have more acceptance of others' peculiarities | 93 | 75 | 60 |
| | Have sympathy for the Vietcong | 21 | 8 | 11 |

Table 35

**THE ATTITUDES AND MOTIVATIONS OF THREE CONTRASTING GROUPS OF COLLEGE-AGE SUBJECTS**

1. College students seeking chiefly to reform society (42%): "REFORMERS"
2. College students seeking chiefly personal and practical advantages from society (58%): "PRACTICALS"
3. A control group of young persons not at college: "NO COLLEGE"

| *Segments of the Cycle* | *Attitudes and Motivations* | REFORMERS | PRACTICALS | NO COLLEGE |
|---|---|---|---|---|
| *Existence* | IN THE SENSE OF "TURNING OF" RECEIVED ORDERS AND INDUCEMENTS | | | |
| | Draft Resistance is justified | 67 | 36 | 17 |
| | No necessary obligation to serve country | 80 | 61 | 45 |
| | Rejects all 3 Presidential candidates (Nixon, Humphrey, Wallace) | 50 | 25 | 15 |
| | IN THE SENSE OF PLACING ONE'S OWN PERSONAL SYNTHESIS FOREMOST | | | |
| | Puts personal conscience above the law | 24 | 14 | 7 |
| | Suppprts more vigorous (non-violent) protest | 64 | 41 | 35 |
| | Greater freedom for individual | 84 | 69 | 65 |
| | Greater sexual freedom | 48 | 35 | 19 |
| a) PERCEPTION | IN THE SENSE OF BEING ABLE TO FOCUS ON PAINFUL PROBLEMS AND ABSURDITIES | | | |
| | Too little is being done for Blacks | 71 | 38 | 35 |
| | Our society lacks humanity | 34 | 31 | 27 |
| | We are a sick society | 50 | 32 | 44 |
| | Disgust with America on Viet Nam | 54 | 40 | 30 |
| | IN THE SENSE OF A CONCERN WITH BEAUTY | | | |
| | More emphasis on the arts | 84 | 55 | 42 |

**Table 35 (Continued)**

| *Segments of the Cycle* | *Attitudes and Motivations* | REFORMERS | PRACTICALS | NO COLLEGE |
|---|---|---|---|---|
| g) SELF-CONFIRMING SELF-TRANSCENDING IMPACT on others | Important that my job makes a meaningful contribution | 80 | 71 | 55 |
| | Seeks stimulation through the work itself | 77 | 70 | 52 |
| | Oriented to work which teaches and/or helps other people | 52 | 28 | 2 |
| h) *dialectic* leading to HIGHER SYNERGY | More freedom needed to debate and to disagree openly | 92 | 73 | 68 |
| | IN THE SENSE OF REJECTING AUTHORITARIAN RELATIONSHIPS | | | |
| | Condemns beating of Chicago demonstrators by police | 72 | 53 | 32 |
| | "Dove" on Viet Nam Issue | 69 | 45 | 37 |
| | *Intense* dislike of Mayor Daley | 50 | 27 | 5 |
| i) INTEGRATION of FEEDBACK and COMPLEXITY | IN THE SENSE OF SOCIAL RESPONSIBILITY | | | |
| | More must be done to combat poverty | 87 | 78 | 73 |
| | (no data on complexity) | | | |

Source: "What They Believe," A *Fortune* survey conducted by Daniel Yankelovich, in *Youth in Turmoil*, Time-Life Books, New York, 1969.

I believe none of these things, for they all contradict major tenets of this book, namely, that scientific and business concerns *can* be harnessed to human development, that improving one's own position need not be inconsistent with enhancing others', and that man can rebel and resynthesize "fixed sub-assemblies" to render them humane. Of course technology can be humanized and the technologist can be humane, but not until he realizes that technological development *by itself* can be quite antithetical to human development.

What matters most, therefore, is not so much the proportion in which persons have been liberally or technically educated, nor even their formal role, but their capacity *to free their life styles from formal or technical dictation.* Daniel Yankelovich made a 1969 survey which discriminated two kinds of college students. The REFORMERS sought to remake society in the image of their own values, while the PRACTICALS saw their educations as tools by which to extract from society the greatest personal benefit and prestige. Now most of the REFORMERS were in liberal arts, social sciences, and teaching, and most of the PRACTICALS were in technological and business pursuits, but not all. There were substantial minorities of reforming engineers and practical artists. It was their different life styles and outlooks upon the world that made the considerable differences we see in Table 35.

The PRACTICALS seem to suffer a diminished humanity that stems directly from their view of themselves as self-satisfying, extractive-and-consuming mechanisms. Over 60% of them believe that "enough" or "too much" is being done for Black Americans. 69% deny that American society lacks humanity. 64% cannot comprehend any justification for draft resistance. 46% identify themselves by their racial origins, and 68% by their middle class position. 47% refuse to criticize the Chicago police for beating fellow college students. Overall the PRACTICALS are closer to those who have not gone to college at all than they are to college REFORMERS.

The answer as to how we should treat technology is implicit in the two aspects of segment (h) in the model. There should be a dialectic, followed by synergy. That is, we should first consider all the ways in which technology seems quite apart from, or even opposed to, psycho-social development. We should assert our humanity over and against this technology. Only then can a just reconciliation be achieved. In this chapter I have been mostly concerned with the first step, for unless the values of human development are researched, understood with conviction, and thrust boldly into the environment, then any integration with technology will overwhelm our human values.

## NOTES FOR CHAPTER XI

1. "America in the Technetronic Age" by Zbigniew Brzezinski, *Encounter,* Jan., 1968, p. 16.

2. "How Technology will shape the Future" by Emmanuel G. Mesthene, *Science,* Vol. 161, July 12, 1968, pp. 135-143.

3. *The Technological Society* by Jacques Ellul, New York: Vintage, 1967, pp. 79-80.

4. See "AMA's Sorry Record" in *Boston Globe,* July 12, 1969. See also *World Handbook of Political and Social Indicators* by Bruce M. Russett, Yale University Press, 1964.

5. *Challenge to Reason* by C. West Churchman, New York: McGraw-Hill, 1968, pp. 156-117, quoted by Erich Fromm in *The Revolution of Hope,* New York: Bantam, 1968, p. 38.

6. "America in the Technetronic Age" by Zbigniew Brzezinski in *Encounter,* Jan. 1968, p. 22.

7. *Ibid.,* p. 20.

8. "The Next Thirty-three Years" by Herman Kahn and Anthony J. Wiener in *Daedalus,* Vol. 96, No. 3, 1967, p. 707.

9. *Ibid.*

10. *On Thermonuclear War* by Herman Kahn, Princeton University Press, 1960, p. 86.

11. *Strategy and Conscience* by Anatol Rapoport, New York: Harper and Row, 1964, p. xx of preface.

12. *Ibid.,* p. xxi.

13. *Eichmann in Jerusalem* by Hannah Arendt, New York: Viking Books, 1964, last page.

14. From the introduction to "Society and Ecology," *American Behavioral Scientist,* Vol. II, No. 6, 1968, p. 2.

15. "America in the Technetronic Age," *op. cit.,* p. 19.

16. *Ibid.,* pp. 22-23.

17. "Some Psychological Perspectives on the Year 2,000" by George A. Miller *Daedalus,* Vol. 96, No. 3, 1967, p. 893.

18. *Ibid.,* p. 886.

19. *Ibid.,* p. 890.

20. *Ibid.,* p. 886.

21. "Vitae Lampda" by Sir Henry Newbolt.

22. "Some Psychological Perspectives on the Year 2,000," *op. cit.*, p. 893.

23. Quoted by Senator Clark in *The Congressional Record,* July 27, 1967, also quoted by Noam Chomsky in "The Menace of Liberal Scholarship," *The New York Review of Books,* Jan. 2, 1969, p. 29.

24. "Some Psychological Perspectives. . ." *op. cit.,* p. 892.

25. "America in the Technetronic Age," *op. cit.,* p. 24.

26. "An End to History," speech delivered by Mario Savio in Sproul Hall, reprinted in *The Berkeley Student Revolt,* Lipset and Wolin, (eds.), *op. cit.,* p. 216.

27. *The Uncommitted, op. cit.,* p. 257.

28. "Some Psychological Perspectives," *op. cit.,* p. 893.

29. *Archives Europeennes de Sociologie*, No. 7, 1966.

30. "America in the Technetronic Age," *op. cit.,* p. 25.

31. *Ibid.,* p. 21.

32. See *Daedalus,* Vol. 96, No. 3, p. 852.

33. *The Revolution of Hope* by Erich Fromm, *op. cit.,* p. 44.

34. "Personality Changes in College Students, by Webster, *et. al., op. cit.*

35. *Occupations and Values* by Morris Rosenberg, Glencoe: The Free Press, 1957.

36. "Fostering Creativity in Students of Engineering" by Donald W. MacKinnon, *J. Engineering Education* Vol. 52, No. 3, 1961.

## *Chapter XII*

## The Student Radicals

Although this chapter on student radicals appears to climax my book, it should not be thought that I regard these students as paragons of everything that is meant by Radical Man. On the contrary, contemporary student radicalism is but one manifestation of a developmental theme as old as history which is constantly changing its content and style. Many descriptions in this chapter will be out of date before you read them, but the underlying theme is always there.

The radical succeeds only by being elusive and confounding predictions about his behavior. What "worked" yesterday is abandoned tomorrow lest opponents learn to counter it. Moreover, quite different styles of development are appropriate to different cultural, political, and organizational settings. It does not follow because physical confrontation is appropriate to persons in school whose words and petitions go unheeded, that it is a universally applicable model for all those with difficulty in communicating. Hence in this chapter I can only try to catch a passing glimpse of *one* contemporary form of student radicalism, namely the middle-class elements of the New Left. I have chosen these mainly because data are available, while very little is known about Black Power adherents and there are only impressionistic accounts of Hippies and the psychadaelic Left.

I intend to proceed as follows:

1) A research profile of student radicals
2) The years of unrest – why now?
3) The developmental themes in radical tactics
4) The rationales for repression
5) The dominant culture's thesis and the radicals' antithesis
6) The choice of fires

### *1. A research profile of the student activist*

Data on student radicals have already been presented. In Table 10, Chapter V, a large proportion of the sample of members from the British Campaign for Nuclear Disarmament were students. In Chapter IX, I presented findings on the New Left at Boston University. In Chapter X we examined some seriously regressed radicals. In Table 33, Chapter XI, the superior psychological ratings of the Free Speech Movement were evident. In most of these studies the outline of the developed helix has been pronounced, and other comparison groups, political and apolitical, have made relatively poor showings.

At least one objection has been made to this whole style of personality research. Are Left activists merely form fillers? Along with their greater cultural sophistication, their penchant for the social sciences and humanities, and their stated intention of radicalizing the faculty, do they seize upon the opportunity of being researched to put over their ideology?

The notion that only a shallow capacity for psychological self-advertisement and skillful form filling is being tapped by psychometric tests hardly survives the data presented in Table 36. Here we find a remarkable degree of consistency between psychometric tests, reported and observed habits of life, observation of student meetings, and the inner feelings and anxieties expressed in group interviews. That all these different methods arrive at internally consistent findings, that these patterns extend far beyond self-consciously political behavior to characterize the whole cultural style of the students' lives, greatly reduces the probability that researchers are measuring a carefully fabricated ideology. In any event it would take something close to genius to fool all the psychologists all of the time on over two dozen different tests and instruments.

As an example of this internal consistency, Table 36 reveals high scores on Belief in Man's Aloneness, and this is accompanied by a fierce independence from the family and even from fellow radicals, unsafe and uncertain career choices, a continual willingness to redefine one's identity in relation to society, the relative lack of structure and "free disorder" during meetings, and a tendency to identify with free thinking intellectuals, to shun formal and organized activities, to read copiously beyond course requirements, and to regard one's college career as a personal quest for meaning.

Note especially the radical rejection of those repetitive and predictable games, which do not permit the player to transcend the rules. Radicals have minimal interest in card games, war games, athletic contests, fraternity rituals, public ceremonies and receptions, the Dating Game, tinkering with automobiles, subjects like Law and Engineering which impose complex rules and systems upon the individual, watching Westerns and Light Comedy (perhaps the most routinized forms of entertainment) and of course T.V. from which these radicals turned with disgust, watching less than half an hour a day, while the conservative students averaged over two hours a day.

Another interesting aspect is the relative *balance* within the cycles of radicals, despite much speculation that they are unbalanced if not actually insane. Student leftists are more independent *and* more intimate, more liable to rebel *and* to participate with others in egalitarian relationships, more sensitive to beauty *and* more aroused by cruelty and ugliness, more impulsive *and* more intellectually efficient, more flexible in the suspension of their basic premises *and* more fiercely committed to those ethical principles that have survived a thousand suspensions to be constantly rediscovered and reaffirmed.

**Table 36**

**BEHAVIOR, STYLES, AND CHARACTERISTICS OF NEW LEFT ACTIVISTS AT BOSTON UNIVERSITY**

| *Segments of the Cycle* | *As Compared with Right Activists, non-Activists and Center Activists, New Left Activists were:* |
|---|---|
| *Man exists freely* | *Highest on Existentiality and Moral Freedom Scales* (see Chapter IX).<br>Least committed to an existing professional slot in professional society<br>Most free and spontaneous in their public meetings<br>Most likely to live off-campus and away from home<br>Least committed to formal religious practices and organizations<br>Least likely to suppress rebellious feelings<br>Least likely to support "school spirit" organization<br>Least conventional in career choices<br>Least interested in legal career |
| a) PERCEPTION | *Lowest on Scale of Perceptual Narrowing*<br>Most interested in Music (especially Folk Music)<br>Most interested in Modern Art and History of Art<br>Most interested in "Art" Movies<br>Least interested in Westerns, Light Entertainment and Satire<br>Lowest on index of T.V. watching<br>Highest in belief in Humanism<br>Most likely to be studying Liberal Arts |
| b) IDENTITY | *Highest on Scale of "Sensitivity to Own Feelings"*<br>Deepest appreciation of poetry<br>Greatest concern with personal identity<br>Highest in concern with self-discovery and personal search for meaning<br>Most psychologically minded |
| c) COMPETENCE | *High on Scale of Social Dominance* (Center was highest)<br>Most secure in social status<br>Most upwardly, least downwardly mobile families<br>Highest evaluation of persons with power *through* others<br>Lowest evaluation of persons with power *over* others |

**Table 36 (Continued)**

| | |
|---|---|
| d) INVESTMENT | *Highest on Scales of Inner Direction and Achievement via Independence*<br>Most likely to live away from home after graduation<br>Most independent from parents<br>Most likely read outside course requirements<br>Most likely to have demonstrated publicly |
| *authentic and intense* | Least likely to show discrepancy between feeling and action<br>More spontaneous, open and confiding<br>Least difficulty in self-expression<br>Less "hung-up" and inhibited sexually |
| e) SELF-SUSPENSION and RISK | 1) *IN THE SENSE OF EXISTENTIAL DESPAIR Highest on Scale Measuring Belief in Man's Aloneness*<br>Most anxious about acheiving personal development and identity<br>Most anxious for others and for society<br>Least likely to seek "quiet" or "graceful" life |
| | 2) *IN THE SENSE OF BEING FLEXIBLE Highest on Flexibility Scale, Lowest on Dogmatism Scale*<br>Longer reflection before answering questions<br>Most likely to regard college as moratorium |
| | 3) *IN THE SENSE OF SUSPENDING SELF CONCERN*<br>Lowest in expressing exclusive personal concerns<br>Highest membership in altruistic organizations for social betterment |
| f) BRIDGING THE (wide) DISTANCE TO OTHERS | *Lowest on "Intolerance toward Disbelievers" Scale*<br>Most likely to come from large city and least likely to come from small town<br>Highest contact with opposite sex<br>Most likely to identify with "far flung" personalities of many creeds and colors<br>Least likely to identify exclusively with white Americans or Europeans<br>Most likely to have global concerns<br>Lowest fraternity membership |

Table 36 (Continued)

| | |
|---|---|
| g) SELF-CONFIRMING | *Highest on Self-Actualization Scale*<br>Highest in reporting self-discovery<br>Highest in reporting close and long friendships<br>Highest in sexual experience<br>Lowest in uncomsummated sexual fantasy |
| SELF-TRANSCENDING IMPACT | IN THE SENSE OF REFUSING TO PLAY REPETITIVE GAMES<br>Least playing of card games<br>Least interest in cars<br>Least participation in sports<br>Least concern with sports<br>Rejection of the "Dating Mill" and "mutual con-game of going through the motions of dating" |
| h) *Dialectic* leading to higher SYNERGY | Highest in persistance under criticism<br>Highest rejection of parental demands as overriding one's own<br>*Lowest on "Fear of Compromise" Scale* and *Highest in Capacity for Intimate Contact*<br>More "mother-centered" homes<br>Highest frequency of informal "bull sessions" with friends<br>Most participatory democracy at meetings<br>Highest in *living with,* not just visiting sexual partners<br>*Lowest on Authoritarianism Scale*<br>Least identification with national figures wielding power |
| i) INTEGRATION OF FEEDBACK AND COMPLEXITY | *Highest in Intellectual Efficiency Scale*<br>*Lowest on Isolation, and Non-Integration within Belief System*<br>Highest in "personal search for truth"<br>High in ownership of books<br>High in pursuit of knowledge as an end in life<br>Low in objections to being tape-recorded<br>Highest in linking public with private concerns and self with the environment |

N.B. "Highest", "lowest", etc., mean that neither Center, Right nor Non-Activists rated as high or as low.
"High", "low", etc., mean that *one* other group usually the Center, and occasionally non-activists, rated as high or as low.

Source: "A Study of a Sampling of Boston University Student Activists" by Irvin Doress, Unpublished Doctoral Dissertation, Boston University. 1968. (Additional analyses of the raw data were undertaken by Charles Hampden-Turner,

Nor is there any evidence that these young men reject the old, out of hand. Their liking of modern art goes hand in hand with their greater knowledge of the history of art. They know and enjoy classical music and folk music more than do Right activists or non-activists. The radicals' nominations for "Greatest Living American" are nearly all over thirty-five years old and vary from the nominations of other groups, not with regard to age but in being more intellectual and more persuasive, while being less physically powerful and less likely to occupy prestigious roles. The conservative students were precisely opposite in their nominations.

Before the current surge of protest there were harbingers of the new style. In the early Sixties Frank Barron conducted a study of the correlations between aspects of personal creativity and attitudes to nuclear disarmament among students of the Rhode Island School of Design. He found that students judged as high creative were significantly more likely to favor a "SANE" nuclear policy of negotiation and disarmament, a fact which strengthens the impression that the art of reconciling ourselves with opponents is related to creativity, imagination, and developmental radicalism in general. The findings are set out in Table 37.

Among the more interesting details in this study was the "feminine" component in the personalities of dissenters, a tenderness towards others that in no way detracts from strong convictions and ego strength. Notice also the touch of psychasthenia, periodic instability and disorganization, but one that facilitates "bouncing back" with even stronger convictions than before. These and other characteristics closely resemble those of creative writers (Table E, Chapter III). The correlations appear rather modest, perhaps because of the poor overall knowledge of the "brinkmanship" being pursued at that time by John Foster Dulles, and the non-political nature of most design students at smaller colleges. Most of those who did not favor a "Sane" nuclear policy had no knowledge of America's nuclear policy at all.

In fact there is much evidence that civil rights activity and protest against the Viet Nam War are correlated with the academic quality of college institutions. A study of professors' opposition to the war found much higher degrees of dissent in those colleges with the best academic reputations.[1] In a second study, questionnaires on student protest were circulated to all accredited four-year colleges in the country. Based on an 85% return by Deans of Students it was found that incidence of Viet Nam protests correlated .43 with an index of academic excellence, and a number of similar correlations were found between left-wing activity and academic quality.[2]

Findings very similar to those at Boston University and the University of California were made by Richard Flacks and Charles Derber at the University of Chicago. These are set out in Table 38. The method used was to record open-ended discussions of personal values with the protesting students, their parents, and a control sample of non-activist students and parents. The

**Table 37**

**PERSONALITY CORRELATES AND FACULTY RATINGS OF STUDENTS FAVORING "SANE NUCLEAR POLICY" AT THE RHODE ISLAND SCHOOL OF DESIGN**

| *Segments of the Cycle* | *Scale or Faculty Rating* | *Correlation with "Sane Attitude"* |
|---|---|---|
| *Existence* | Barron-Welsh Creativity Test | .24 |
| | Independence of Judgment | .19 |
| | Originality | .19 |
| a) PERCEPTION | Knowledge concerning nuclear weapons | .90 |
| | Esthetic sensitivity | .20 |
| | Curiosity (faculty rating) | .23 |
| b) IDENTITY | Inward Looking (Extraversion | −.21) |
| c) COMPETENCE | Ego Strength | .16 |
| | Achievement oriented (faculty rating) | .17 |
| d) INVESTMENT *authentic & intense* | Vitality | .21 |
| e) SUSPENSION & RISK | Flexibility of independence - minus self-control | .20 |
| | Psychasthenia | .19 |
| f) BRIDGING THE DISTANCE | (No data) | |
| g) SELF-CONFIRMING SELF TRANSCENDING IMPACT | *Rated by faculty as:* | |
| | Achieves self-development | .23 |
| | Achieves independence | .22 |
| | Does creative and original work | .18 |
| h) *Dialectic* leading to | (no data) | |
| SYNERGY | Nurturant, tender and "feminine" in human relationships | .33 |
| i) INTEGRATED FEEDBACK & COMPLEXITY | Complexity and ideational fluency | .16 |

Source: *Creativity and Personal Freedom* by Frank Barron. New York Van Nostrand. 1968.

**Table 38 (Continued)**

| Segments of the Cycle | Values | Saliency of Values among: ACTIVISTS Hi-Activism % | ACTIVISTS % | ACTIVISTS Medium-Hi % | NON-ACTIVISTS % |
|---|---|---|---|---|---|
| e) SELF-SUSPENSION | Suspends concern with own status and materialism. | 100 | | 100 | 62 |
| | Absence of moralism and concern with self-control | 96 | | 100 | 46 |
| f) BRIDGING (wide) DISTANCES to others | Strongly Humanitarian concerned with wide spectrum of persons | 35 | | 29 | 0 |
| g) SELF CONFIRMING, SELF-TRANSCENDING IMPACT | Concern with Self-Realization | 44 | | 35 | 9 |
| | Seeks extreme depth in intimate relations | 18 | | 23 | 5 |
| h) *Dialectic* leading to SYNERGY | *Hostility to unilateral coercion:* | | | | |
| | Against Bombing N. Vietnam | | 91 | | 27 |
| | Against sending troops to Dominican Republic | | 94 | | 35 |
| | Against House UnAmerican Activities Committee | | 97 | | 27 |
| | *Degree of Agreement between father and son* against Bombing N. Vietnam | | 80 | | 37 |
| | against H.U.A.C. | 93 | | | 57 |
| | Belief in highly Nurturant and Cooperative Relationships[3] | 35 | | 29 | 0 |
| i) INTEGRATION of FEED-BACK and COMPLEXITY | Complex Intellectuality[2] and abstract thinking | 32 | | 29 | 3 |

Sources: "The Liberated Generation: An Exploration of the Roots of Student Protest". by Richard Flacks. *Journal of Social Issues,* Vol. 23 No. 3 1967
"An Exploration of the Value System of Radical Student Activists and Their Parents" by Charles Derber and Richard Flacks. Univ. of Chicago, mimeo

*Notes*

1. Romanticism – Esthetic and Emotional Sensitivity were scored together on a single scale.
2. Intellectual effectiveness – Complex Intellectuality also on one scale.
3. Humanitarianism – Belief in Nurturant Relationship also on one scale.

Table 38

COMPARATIVE VALUES OF STUDENT ACTIVISTS AND NON-ACTIVISTS AT THE UNIVERSITY OF CHICAGO

| Segments of the Cycle | Values | Saliency of Values among ACTIVISTS: Hi-Activism % | ACTIVISTS % | ACTIVISTS Medium-Hi % | NON-ACTIVISTS % |
|---|---|---|---|---|---|
| *Existence* | Approves civil disobedience in Civil Rights protests | | 97 | | 28 |
| | Approves Student protest demonstrations | | 100 | | 61 |
| | Concerned with existential philosophy and outlooks | | 53 | | 28 |
| a) PERCEPTION | Concerned with Humanistic philosophy. | | 64 | | 43 |
| | Esthetic and Emotional sensitivity[1] | 35 | | 47 | 10 |
| b) IDENTITY | Degree of fluidity in occupational choice | | high | | low |
| c) COMPETENCE | Intellectual effectiveness[2] | 32 | | 29 | 3 |
| d) INVESTMENT *authentic & intense* | Degree of Activism | | high | | low |
| | Authenticity towards self and others, acute sensitivity to hypocricy | 44 | | 35 | 11 |
| | Romanticism – orientation to feeling and spontaneous affective experience | 35 | | 47 | 10 |

interview records were coded and then shuffled and finally content-analyzed by politically neutral judges who did not know the type of student or parent who was speaking.

It is of interest that results obtained by researchers known to be partial to radicalism, like Paul Heist at Berkeley and Richard Flacks at Chicago, are so similar to those of Irvin Doress, who had hypothesized that activists of the Center would show superior mental health, followed by the Left and Right "extremes." Hence the predilection of the particular researcher did *not* explain the findings in at least one major study.

The Chicago study has features of additional interest. Activist students are much more likely to be influenced by existential philosophy, as well as humanism. They differ greatly from non-activists in rejecting material rewards and in their substantially lower evaluation of the virtues of self-control. The view of radicals as father-haters and as rejectors of authority in general receives a set-back with the discovery that they are *more* likely to agree with their fathers and mothers in a variety of political and cultural issues than were non-activists. In this study there was evidence for rather warmer filial relationships than those enjoyed by non-rebels. (However at Boston University no significant differences were found between groups on this issue.)

When the Chicago University radicals disagreed with their parents, it was usually on tactical questions rather than on the ends themselves and on the discrepancy between highly principled parental behavior within the family, and the parents seeming tolerance of injustice in the wider world. Typically radicals would question the attitudinal liberalism of their parents when it was unaccompanied by action. They seemed determined to perpetuate the ethical principles taught to them in their homes, and extend these to the much wider "distances" in university, urban and international relationships. Radicals were much more likely than non-activists to come from mother-centered, compassionate, and permissive homes and to have humanitarian, liberal, professional, highly educated, and socially concerned parents. Flacks suggests that radicals are less in revolt against their upbringing and nurture than they are the logical, developmental result of this process.

Almost identical conclusions were reached by Kenneth Keniston (see Table 39) in his depth study of a small group of radicals who were organizing the anti-war "Viet Nam Summer" campaign of 1967 from its headquarters in Cambridge, Mass.

This study is perhaps the most perceptive and multi-dimensional of all. He found that the sense of continuity within the lives of these young men was much stronger than any revolutionary discontinuity. They had simply left their former friends and associates far behind. So far from making self-conscious decisions to "become radicals," these young men had consummated the principles of their upbringing and later "woke up" to find themselves labeled radicals, finally accepting this label after a puzzled interval. Often it was a shock, as for this youth.

## TABLE 39

## A DEPTH STUDY OF THE RADICAL ORGANIZERS OF THE 1967 "VIET NAM SUMMER" CAMPAIGN

| *Segments of the Cycle* | *Childhood and Adolescent Experience* | *Current Attitudes and Behavior* |
|---|---|---|
| *Existence* | Held unpopular views at grade school.<br>Moral and political precocity from earliest age.<br>Rebellion against parents during adolescence on issues of unfairness and injustice. | An extraordinary distinctiveness and separateness of personhood.<br>Very independent.<br>Deliberately attempting to change themselves as people. |
| a) PERCEPTION | Family has marked concern with moral dimensions of life.<br>Is socially conscious and politically liberal (occasionally radical). | Unusual capacity to get ambivalence about their parents and to present differentiated portraits.<br>Strongly oriented to people, who are viewed with empathy and compassion.<br>Keen perception of the organized hypocrisy in society. |
| b) IDENTITY | Strong and warm identification with principled parents. | Very "psychologically minded" and self-analytical.<br>Possessed the quality of self-insight usually found only in those with extensive psycho-therapy. |
| c) COMPETENCE | Socio-economically priviledged.<br>Little difficulty in doing outstanding work at school. | A basic feeling of self-respect and adequacy.<br>"Successful" by all conventional criteria. |
| d) INVESTMENT<br>*authentic and intense* | | Commitment which is personal and moral, not formal and ideological.<br>Intimate connection between inner life and social action.<br>Unusually open, candid and trusting.<br>Vivid and expressive manner. |
| e) SELF-SUSPENSION and RISK | *In the sense of existential despair*<br>"My father would sit down and cry."<br>A "European type" adolescence, tumultous and complex with anguish and turmoil.<br>Occasionally haunted by the possibility of moral wrong, deformity and deviation. | "I feel proud that I can still cry, that things really dig me up inside."<br>Endurance of great tensions in Movement work.<br>Falls sick with shame and horror when America first escalates Viet Namese war. |

## Table 39 (Continued)

| | | |
|---|---|---|
| | *In the sense of flexibility* | |
| | | Absence of concrete visions or intellectual ideology.<br>Future open, fluid, undefined and indeterminate.<br>Highest tolerance for uncertainty and ambiguity. |
| | *In the sense of trust and vulnerability* | |
| | Unusually close and trusting relationships with parents. | Very open and unthreatened by interviews.<br>Ready to discuss the painful, the personal and private aspects of their lives. |
| | *In the sense of suspending self-concern* | |
| | Championed the underdog in grade and high schools. | Appalled at the condition of the poor and oppressed. |
| f) BRIDGING THE (wide) DISTANCE to others | A very early sense of "specialness" of being apart from others.<br>Avoidance of adolescent "in-groups" and peer culture. | The greatest tolerance for isolation and a loneness.<br>Work with the poor and deprived while knowing they will never be truly "at home" in this environment. |
| g) SELF-CONFIRMING SELF-TRANSCENDING IMPACT | Early family life is warm, close, idealistic.<br>Consistently elected to leadership in grade school.<br>*But* "success" proves gradually less meaningful.<br>Shift towards more relevant and idealistic goals. | Great personal satisfaction found in Movement work.<br>Great affection for co-workers and discovery of meaning.<br>Intimacy with opposite sex seen as landmark of personal growth.<br>Highly ambivalent about technology and "academic games". |
| h) *dialectic* leading to | Tremendous "shouting matches" with parents and use of parents' own principles against them. | Disagreements very openly stated and above board. |
| higher SYNERGY | Disciplined through reasoning and explaining.<br>Often played the "peace maker" and reconciler of family conflicts.<br>Strong sharing and openness between parents and children. | Love and respect for parents survives periodic conflict and reconciliation.<br>Dedication to the norms of participatory democracy. |
| i) INTEGRATION of FEEDBACK and COMPLEXITY | Gut reactions *preceded* articulate intellectual positions.<br>Described as "too cosmopolitan" in early job interviews.<br>The sensation "leaving others behind in development."<br>At each stage of growth a strong sense of continuity. | Powerful fusion of conscious and unconscious motives, personality and politics, will and conscience, ego and super-ego, self and principle.<br>More emotional *and* more reflective, intellectual, etc.<br>High self-confidence *and* deep self-doubts. |

Source: *The Young Radicals: Notes on Committed Youth,* by Kenneth Keniston, New York: Harcourt, Brace and World, 1968.

> One night when I was in college, I had dinner with (a conservative professor) and he proceeded to get quite drunk, and he said, "You know, you're a fucking traitor. You're going to be one of *those* guys. You're going to be a quisling for your own country." I was really stunned. But already, even then, there were differences developing.[3]

Joining the Movement was for these radicals a natural outcome of their past experience. They had come into their own, in a cycle of eternal return wherein novelty and familiarity were fused.

> Then for the first time, I really began to feel a part of the Movement. I began to be able to trace my own roots. . . The types of people that were being involved, and the goals that were being put forward – I began to feel I was *of* these, that in terms of my background, that this was the thing *from which I had sprung.* That was a really good feeling. I began to feel for the first time, that there was a kind of continuity to my whole political development. . . The continuity was always there, but my being able to appreciate it, being able to use it. . . that came later.[4]

*No* fundamental changes in core values were found in the transition of these radicals from adolescence to their present state of mind. As adolescents they had rebelled whenever they saw their parents as acting inconsistently towards them. In dialectic, described as "shouting matches," the adolescents had used their parents' own proclaimed values against them, much as they now used America's own proclaimed values to protest the war. Out of the intense disagreements in the home had come synergistic reconciliations, so that now they mostly held their parents in deep respect, mixed with a keen discernment of their parents' weaknesses. Again the attitude of these young radicals towards their country suggested the same sequence, a deep sense of outrage, a sincere wish for reconciliation, but no let-up in their anger until they were heeded.

As before we find an intense vulnerability and a tendency to "disintegrate" in the face of pain, disconfirmation, and loss of innocence, combined with an extraordinary phoenix-like capacity to rise from the ashes of their own existential despair with a new vigour. Having survived a stormy, "European type" adolescence, full of passionate discovery and awakenings, they mostly believed President Johnson's pledge to limit and resolve the Viet Nam dispute. Then come the bombs, shattering not only Asian bodies, but the consciences of all those Americans with the developed capacity to feel for distant others. The Great Mutilation of self and other had begun.

> Well my hypothesis was really destroyed. . . I was convinced Johnson would (stop the war). The bombings of February, 1964, were a real shake-up for me. I went to bed for two days. It seemed to me to utterly close the door. . .[5]

The very brief collapse of this young man, followed by energetic self-renewal, is the most singular characteristic of radical man. One could describe his youthful faith in Johnson's campaign promises as hopelessly naive, but developing man has no alternative *but* to trust and suffer. The anguish of betrayal is at least a sign of life, while the armour of cynicism leads to a self-fulfilling process of regression, incapable of generating or discovering the humanity of others.

Notice also how these young men seemed to feel first, then articulate and generalize later, in a process which exemplifies the axiom of existence preceding essence. Yet in no sense were they anti-intellectual, for both their scholarship and intelligences were profound. Rather there was a belief and trust in the capacity of their feelings to point towards intelligible truths. Within them the potential opposites of emotion and reason, conscious and unconscious commitment and flexibility were well integrated and reconciled into a remarkable complexity of personality.

It might be argued that this was an elite group of Harvard based graduate students, and that since the summer of 1967 the New Left has thrown more embittered legions into the fray, who have no illusions about America's goodness to lose. Perhaps we shall see yet another revolution betrayed, as the conservative opposition slowly eats away the emotional resources of the young, and the most bitter and pessimistic among them prove the better prophets. Radicalism is seldom a stable phenomenon.

My impression during 1969 is that anxiety is overwhelming at least some young radicals whose minds and speech are visibly calcifying around pre-fabricated ideologies. Although the research from 1964 to mid-1968 is overwhelmingly favorable to college radicals, the fate of Icarus remains their occupational hazard. By the time you read these words, a magnificant flight may have ended in a flurry of singed feathers.

But there is no evidence that the "worst elements" are most active and are duping well-meaning moderates. The Chicago University study found that those who protested most actively were the most socially concerned, humanitarian, and complex. While certain S.D.S. students were somewhat materialistic, self-seeking and lacking in compassion, these identified themselves quite distinctly by being *less* prominent in any protest activity. In the crunch they were conspicuously absent, while non-members who joined the protest had characteristics markedly similar to those of protesting members. The pain of protest seems to weed out of the ranks the faint-hearted and fair-weather friends and is a further illustration of the phoenix-like process of self-purgation and renewal. Radical students seem to have rediscovered the wisdom of William James.

> No matter how full a reservoir of *maxims* one may possess, and no matter how good one's *sentiments* may be, if one has not taken advantage of every concrete opportunity to *act,* one's character may remain entirely unaffected for the better. . .[1]

The profiles of white student radicals seem to vary little from campus to campus. A 1967 study of leaders of student bodies at the University of Indiana replicated much of the data already presented. The Left activists were more volatile, more aesthetic, better informed, more imaginative and more inclined to experiment in many areas of their lives, than were fraternity and religious leaders. In comparing groups of conservative and radical leaders, the researchers concluded

> The results indicated that liberal leaders tend to have lower superego strength, less concern for conventionalities and more interest in radical conditions and circumstances. . . Other differences suggest that liberal leaders tend to be more sober and serious in temperament, more emotionally sensitive, more forthright and unpretentious in social relationships. They also seem more confident and secure in meeting the daily demands of life than do conservative leaders.[7]

It was these Left activists whom the Dean of Students described as "headline hunters, egotists, and compensating personalities." Let us turn to some of the reasons for this extraordinary conflict in judgments.

2. *The Years of unrest – why now?*

> We are people of this generation, bred in at least modest comfort, housed now in universities, looking uncomfortably to the world we inherit.
>
> *The Port Huron Statement*

In attempting to answer this question one must be careful to avoid assuming that tranquility is a more natural state than dynamism or disturbance. It is not necessary to assume that something unusually harsh or repressive must have happened *to* students in order to "agitate" them. It is only necessary for growing organisms to press against the limits of the structures that contain them for protest activity to occur.

Yet one principal cause of student rebellion lies not in *their* discontinuity but in a strange unevenness within American cultural traditions. Coming to this country from England, early in the Sixties, I was almost immediately struck by the strength of developmental and humanist themes in American educational and child rearing philosophies, and the relative weakness of these same themes in commerce and in politics. In comparison to America the English public and grammar schools in which the elite are trained are relatively authoritarian, while the political and business worlds are relatively humane. It has long seemed to me only a matter of time before the developmental themes in American life confronted the repressive themes, and before those students nurtured in the better homes and schools came to regard the opportunities offered by business and government as an insult to their achieved levels of psycho-social development.

For an elder generation of Americans it was perfectly natural to grapple for money and prestige in a commercial or political arena during the day, and in the evenings and week-ends sanctify these tactics by bestowing the spoils upon the family and neighborhood charities. The battles were fought in the decaying cities. The largesse was distributed in the garden suburb. But this system is being undermined by the very affluence it creates. Despite what economists tell us, there is a limit to an educated man's appetite for the passive consumption of goods. The nobility of robbing Peter to feed young Paul is significantly reduced when Paul joins the millions of overweight children.

When satiation threatens, who remains in desperate need? Why, the very persons stomped upon in the initial battle. This being so, *why compete in a battle of self-interests in the first place?* The original rationale was that of scarcity. With scarcity disappearing, competition becomes a residual game, played for tokens of status and prestige, a game demanding consensus among players that such tokens are meaningful.

Young radicals are the children of affluence, the first of many to be satiated by the "consumer paradise" of upper middle class America. They have mostly received non-instrumental educations, often in the humanities and social sciences, which despite the best efforts of "value free" academics, tend to evoke social criticism. Now students are looking beyond the university to a wasteland culture of capitalist commerce and politics, not to mention a foreign policy whose savagery would shame a jungle, and they are appalled. Nothing in their past experience persuades them that it is necessary to live like this, that the rewards for competing are remotely meaningful, that national "honor" necessitates the killing of thousands of persons each week in Viet Nam. For students trained to compare symbols with reality the credibility gap grows to the dimension of a canyon.

Imagine, then, the disgust of these young people faced with the prospect of leaving the developmental milieu of home and school to take up privileged positions in a cultural meat-grinder. What is more natural than the insistence of these students that the universities, their last major staging post before entering the "other culture," should use all its resources to criticize and reform that culture?

Actually we know something of what happens to high school students when they leave the humanistic culture and enter the corporate one. Two large groups of students, the first destined for college and the second for employment, were closely matched on indices of Thinking Introversion, Complexity, Non-Authoritarianism and Social Maturity. Between them, these scales cover most of the segments of cycle. While the college sample had gained between 5 and 10 points on each of these scales four years later, the employed group had made only one small gain on Thinking Introversion and *had decreased significantly upon the other measures,* so that they were as much as a dozen points behind the college group.[8]

These findings provide clues as to what is angering students. First it suggests that after school or college those locked into roles, statuses, and jobs in the corporate culture do *not* necessarily develop and may often regress. A young trainee executive who has decided to distribute detergents for the rest of his days has surely placed a ceiling upon the amount of meaning and social value that can reside in his work. His value to the company may increase and the company may call this "development" but it is unlikely to be psycho-social development save in very modest degrees.

Second these findings suggest that most Americans may reach the pinnacle of psycho-social development in the early part of their adulthood, so that the current generation of students are probably more mature, as defined by the cycle model, than the vast majority of their critics. While sheer content and accumulation of knowledge is positively related to age, skills of communication, empathy and creativity among adults may be inversely related. We have seen, for instance, in Table 33, Chapter XI, that students in the Free Speech Speech Movement score significantly above the faculty of the Engineering School. Longitudinal studies with Kohlberg's Moral Judgment Scale show a decline in judgment with fatherhood.[9] Other clues come from the work of Herbert McClosky on *anomie* described in Chapter IV. Starting at the age of 21 and going upwards, he found in a large national sample of respondents that seniority correlated +.29 with Acquiescence, +.24 with Anomie, +.29 with Chauvinism, +.34 with Conventionality, +.24 with Elitism and anti-egalitarianism, +.25 with Ethnocentrism, +.34 with Authoritarianism, +.35 with Conservatism, +.29 with Need Inviolacy, and +.27 with Rigidity. Younger people, it seems have shaken off many of the crippling fears and inadequacies of their elders. Yet in view of the fact that McClosky found slightly higher correlations between these same characteristics and low education, we may infer that superior development of younger adults is due mostly to their longer schooling and superior education, and that when this education ends, development ends too for the vast majority of people.

So what students are protesting so vehemently *is the threatened end of their development as people.* Persons in high places within the University are seen as hand in glove with corporate and political interests, who arrange for suitable students to be channeled via the university into ready-made slots in the meat-grinder.

This would explain why the Left activists at Boston University had the vaguest career plans of any group. The Chicago protesters had highly diffused occupational identities. *None* of the group studied by Keniston had a clear idea of what they would be doing when the summer was over. Only in the Movement or in some marginal academic position did these young persons see any prospect of doing socially relevant work and thereby furthering their own and others' development.

But one could legitimately ask why the developmental culture of home and school did not earlier clash with the regressive culture of politics and commerce. One reason was the relative weakness of the educational sector and its designation was a mere training ground for the "real world," which financed it from its own surplus. But the importance of education in society has been growing apace. From the point of view of businessmen it is *the* commercial opportunity and bandwagon of the future, "the fastest growing sector of the economy." For politicians education has assumed prime importance as a patriotic symbol of the "Free World," an indicator of whether we are winning or losing the international horse-race with Russia, and a prime resource to feed the multi-billion defense industries. Hence the enormous expansion of education and its emergence as a distinct culture have coincided with the urgent desire of commercial and governmental agencies to *use* the universities and their human products for the furtherance of national and commercial policies.

The intent of certain students to radicalize the universities is shrewdly aimed at preparing these institutions to realize their own countervailing strength through the reformation of the wider culture and to infuse that culture with the ideals of humanism, social conscience, and self-expression. We are witnessing the opening rounds of a battle for the commanding heights of national influence. It is from the universities that the latest knowledge, technologies, and ideals increasingly flow. The coming battle will decide whether universities are to have the *initiative* in persuading government and commerce to struggle for a more humane society, or whether the universities are to remain as technical job-shops, supplying the "know-how" for the implimentation of regressive policies. In their present situation academics are mostly the servants of power. They could become the civilizers of power.

The increasing emphasis on education has also lengthened the post-adolescent moratorium. It is now possible for young people to consider and reconsider, to experiment with and to alter the relationship of their personal identity with the larger society. We saw in Chapters VII and VIII that this opportunity was most important to the induction of development. The longer young persons can wait before their career identity freezes into a final decision, the more ambitious and meaningful is that envisioned identity likely to be, and the more do society's existing institutional slots fall short of this ideal. The humanistic themes in American culture are probably *growing away* from the stagnant pool of power politics, represented by the National Democratic Convention of 1968.

Increasingly young people are encouraged to take short-term, potentially developmental jobs with Vista, The Peace Corps, Civil Rights groups and foundation-sponsored community action projects. Aged 23 you dream and plan and work for a better world at twenty-five dollars a week. Five years later you are worth two hundred dollars or more if you will only "grow up," "be practical" and turn your talents to the starry future of a certain brand of throat lozenges. The moratorium has only postponed and sharpened your confrontation with absurdity. The individual's profit motive is used to lure him into meaningless jobs. As for the few meaningful jobs, anyone who insists on meaning in his work will usually do it for commensurately less. Supply and demand tells the profit maximizer that the socially concerned can be bought on the cheap.

During the earlier periods the interval between school and work often with wars, depressions, or major crises. If you wanted your family to eat during the Thirties you took a job as soon as you could find it, and for radicals the best hope for the future lay in government institutions. From the early Forties to early Sixties, hot or cold wars dominated the national conscience and were widely regarded as regrettable necessities.

Now while there is nothing better for conservatism and for social control than a justified war, hot or cold, there is nothing worse for these mechanisms of discipline than a war widely regarded as unjust. The Viet Nam War, and the consistent failure of national leaders to predict its course, all this finally laid bare the connections between domestic repression, corporate enrichment, and foreign adventurism. Under criticism these same leaders showed unmistakable signs of rigidity, intolerance and super-patriotism. The two cultures in American life were polarizing. The enemies of Civil Rights were among those cheering for the war. Many of the younger generation who had grown to political awareness after the death of Stalin saw the "communist menace" explanation of the war as an outright hoax, a mere excuse to perpetuate the tactics of international and domestic manipulation. It also became increasingly clear that the Viet Cong had some psychological and developmental dynamism on their side, something that the "Hawks" and their academic clerks were conceptually ill-equipped to comprehend, a force which, as I. F. Stone expressed it, "was more than steel and chrome could bear." All the facts had been fed into the Saigon computers except the human spirit and its capacity to refuse.

Within the university the conflict between the developmental and regressive themes in American culture is being fought out in a microcosm. During the years at the University the students' appetites for liberty grow apace. At Berkeley it was found that 21% of the freshmen scored in the top third of an index of Libertarianism; by senior year this has grown to 40% and among graduate students it was 54%.[10] But even as the appetite grows, signs multiply that it will not be fulfilled. The job recruiters, the industry and government funds, the distraction of the faculty from student concerns, all can be traced to a disproportionate interest by the external culture in certain kinds of students and certain kinds of services produced by the University.

Table 40 shows the contribution to the Berkeley Free Speech Movement of students from different areas of concentration. The lines are fairly clearly drawn. Business School students make no contribution at all to the rebels' ranks, while earth sciences, engineering, physical sciences and mathematics are all under-represented. Many of these students already have their eyes fixed on lucrative employment. The system wants them. They want the system. In contrast the creative arts, humanities and social sciences are over-represented in the F.S.M. This breakdown is quite close to that in Tables 33 and 41, where we find rebels and students from the humanities consistently higher on a number of developmental indices than engineers, agriculturalists, and "hard" scientists. The interest of industrial and military recruiters is in the *least* psycho-socially developed students who are needed to service and perfect the machinery of the *status quo*. Those with saleable, technical skills which corporations can buy in a self-contained package and use in their own way are very much in demand. Those with critical, intellectual and humanistic skills which are not easily separable from the conscience of the individual are in significantly *less* demand.

If the university is a microcosm of cultural conflict, the social sciences are a microcosm within a microcosm. Here the humanities and sciences meet. Here you can choose to employ the "toolbox" borrowed from the physical sciences and sell your expertise in the prediction and control of human beings behavior or you can join in an unpredictable, rule-transcending dialogue with other human beings. Money, prestige, employment and patronage by the external culture all tend to reward the former option and punish the latter. Respectability and conscience meet head on. In the words of one F.S.M. song

I write theses
About feces
And it greases
My way up the line.

The great post-Sputnik emphasis on science and technology has undermined the humanism of universities in other ways. The continual branching out of scientific and technical specialities within a university is an overwhelmingly *differentiating* force. The myriad of departments and sub-departments have small occasion for dialogue and little to say to one another which would be comprehensible. "The process cannot be stopped. The results cannot be foreseen. It remains to adapt," as Clark Kerr put it referring to science and engineering.[11] Hence he characterized the university as "a mechanism held together by administrative rules and powered by money."[12] The humanities, general education, and certain of the softer social sciences are potentially *integrating* forces, which help the university to form a conscious identity and to make some semblance of a social and ethical stance in relation to the wider culture.

If agents in this wider culture were intent upon weakening the universities politically and socially, while exploiting to the full their technical resources, then no better policy could be devised than strengthening the hard sciences as against the humanities, and offering every material inducement to the most culturally deprived segments of the university, while ignoring those natural leaders with the greatest verbal, social and communicative skills. The university comes to resemble a huge, over-extended, uncoordinated milch-cow, helplessly twitching while industry and government alternately stuff it with food and milk it dry.

Consider, for instance, the findings of a 1969 study comparing the characteristics of a group of student draft resisters at the University of California at Berkeley, and a group of R.O.T.C. students enrolled in the college of military science. The contrasts in Table 42 are dramatic.

The R.O.T.C. cadet sees himself as a pawn of the system but is not uncomfortable in this role. For him, independence involves a loss of self-control, a suspension of conventional morality, and so he avoids any change-inducing experience. He tends to treat women as objects of conquest, and as subjects for conversation with his male friends. Strongly "masculine," egotistical and aggressive, he sees risk-taking as a gamble with death to achieve masculinity. College has influenced him little. He remains anti-intellectual, underdeveloped and routinized in his habits. On the other hand the draft resisting group shows most of the characteristics of radical man: intellectuality, autonomy, nurturance and intimacy with the opposite sex, and a strong sense of personal responsibility.

Surely it goes without saying that in the latter group are the persons who could turn the universities into a genuine Community of Scholars demanded by the F.S.M. or even the City of Intellect suggested by Clark Kerr. The presence on campus of military recruiters, Dow Chemical and R.O.T.C. with their consistent encouragement of the more regressive traits in the more regressed students cannot help subverting the basic principles of education which are also those of psycho-social development.

I am not trying to urge the subordination of business, engineering and the hard sciences. On the contrary, the health of these subjects is greatly *advanced* by the psycho-social development of their practitioners. Consider the research engineering companies in Table 14, Chapter VI, or the chemical companies in Table 12 of the same chapter. The most creative companies were also those which were more egalitarian, democratic, socially skilled, and

**Table 40**

**AREAS OF CONCENTRATION CHOSEN BY F.S.M. REBELS COMPARED WITH THOSE OF TOTAL STUDENT BODY AT UNIVERSITY OF CALIFORNIA AT BERKELEY**

| *Concentration* | *% choice by F.S.M.* | *% choice by student body* | *F.S.M. over or under represented in concentration* |
|---|---|---|---|
| Social Sciences | 50.6 | 36.8 | over |
| Business School | 0 | 5.0 | under |
| Creative Arts | 5.6 | 2.8 | over |
| Earth Sciences | 1.3 | 2.8 | under |
| Education | 1.3 | .7 | over |
| Engineering | 1.3 | 12.8 | under |
| Humanities | 18.8 | 16.4 | over |
| Mathematics | 3.8 | 5.7 | under |

Source: W.A. Watts and D. Whittaker. "Some socio-psychological differences between highly committed members of the Free Speech Movement and the student population at Berkeley." *Journal of Applied Behavioral Science,* 1966, 2.

**Table 41**

**AREAS OF CONCENTRATION OF BERKELEY STUDENTS SCORING "HIGH" UPON AN INDEX OF LIBERTARIANISM**

| *Concentration* | *% "High" (= Top 1/3rd) in Libertarianism (Men Only)* |
|---|---|
| Social Sciences | 63 |
| Humanities | 62 |
| Life Sciences | 41 |
| Physical Sciences (+Math.) | 39 |
| Engineering | 30 |
| Education | 29 |
| Business Admin. | 24 |

Source: Selvin, H.C. and Warren Hagstrom. "Determinants of Support for Civil Liberties." *The British Journal of Sociology,* March 1960.

**Table 42**

**DRAFT RESISTERS AT THE UNIVERSITY OF CALIFORNIA AT BERKELEY**

| *Segments of the Cycle* | *R.O.T.C. Students* | *Student Draft Resisters* |
|---|---|---|
| *Existence* | "Nice, conventional, good kid". "Respects mother, father cherry pie."<br>Sees himself as agent of traditional institutions.<br>Strict upbringing. | Strongly independent.<br>Values autonomy for self and others.<br>Marches, demonstrates, rebels resists.<br>More permissive family. |

**Table 42 (Continued)**

| | | |
|---|---|---|
| a) PERCEPTION | Shelters self from environment and from change-inducing experiences. | Unusually high concern and caring for others.<br>Very concerned with political, social and moral issues. |
| b) IDENTITY | Anti-intraceptive and defensive.<br>Strong concern with masculinity.<br>Uses alcohol to embalm and avoid contact with self. | Open and self-aware.<br>Unconcerned with proving masculinity. |
| c) COMPETENCE | Feels that he is a pawn and powerless to change the actions of his country.<br>Sexually inadequate and troubled. | Believes he can change society, that he can and should help others.<br>Sexually potent. |
| d) INVESTMENT<br>*authentic* and *intense* | Defines independence as loss of self-control. | Sees self as an actor with conscience who can cause effects in the world.<br>Poetic, literate and emotionally sensitive. |
| e) SELF SUSPENSION and RISK | Fears loss of control and self-exposure.<br>Well-ordered, routinized existence within structured settings.<br>Self-centered and admittedly egotistical.<br>Plans to take *physical* risks with death, not *emotional* risks. | Generally "hangs loose".<br>Lets things happen and prefers unstructured relationships.<br>More altruistic and unselfish. |
| f) BRIDGING THE (wide) DISTANCE | Shy with girls but boasts of his conquests with "the fellas." | Open relationships with members of the opposite sex. |
| g) SELF-CONFIRMING SELF-TRANSCENDING IMPACT | Poor relationships, treats females as objects, little real intimacy. | Achieves deep and genuine intimacy with others. |
| h) *dialectic* leading to SYNERGY | Seeks domination/submission relationships.<br>Aggressive and in bare control of impulses.<br>Father dominant in family with strict control. | Egalitarian relationships emphasizes companionship.<br>Rejects authority relationships with others.<br>Mother centered, nurturant family life. |

**Table 42 (Continued)**

| | | |
|---|---|---|
| i) INTEGRATION of FEEDBACK and COMPLEXITY | Accepts little personal responsibility for his own or his country's actions. Non-intellectual. | Accepts fullest responsibility for own and country's actions. Relatively intellectual, literate and sophisticated. Highly developed conscience. |

Source: Edward E. Sampson, Paper read before American Orthopsychiatric Association, April 1, 1969.

**Table 43**

**PROFILES OF MICHIGAN STATE UNIVERSITY STUDENT GROUPS ON COLLEGE STUDENT QUESTIONNAIRE**

1. *Cultural Sophistication*
   Left Activists 33.5
   Non-Activist (Controls) 29.2
   Student Govt. Leaders 23.8

2. *Social Conscience*
   Left Activists 33.3
   Non-Activists 28.8
   Student Govt. Leaders 27.3

3. *Liberalism*
   Left Activists 36.5
   Non-Activists 28.5
   Student Govt. Leaders 26.8

4. *Independence from Peers*
   Left Activists 29.8
   Non-Activists 26.0
   Student Govt. Leaders 23.6

5. *Independence from Family*
   Left Activists 33.0
   Non-Activists 27.1
   Student Govt. Leaders 25.0

6. *Involvement in "Collegiate Life"*
   Student Govt. Leaders 27.5
   Non-Activists 19.0
   Left Activists 14.8

7. *Study Habits*
   Non-Activists 26.0
   Left Activists 25.7
   Student Govt. Leaders 22.2

8. *Satisfaction with Faculty*
   Left Activist
   Non-Activists
   Student Govt. Leaders 21.6

9. *Satisfaction with Administration*
   Non-Activists 24.1
   Student Govt. Leaders 22.9
   Left Activists 15.5

N.B. On Scales 1 to 5 Left Activists consistently average above the 84th percentile.

Source: Unpublished Doctoral Dissertaion by George Paulus, University of Michigan. His data are summarized by Richard E. Peterson, "The Student Left in American Higher Education" in *Daedalus* vol. 97, No., 1968.

better integrated. We saw at the end of Chapter XI that "creative concept mastery" was not only a characteristic more developed in the humanities than in the hard sciences, but more developed *in the most creative scientists and architects themselves.* No area of concentration is without need of psycho-social development, and those concentrations with non-human subject matters need a developmental perspective as a kind of supplementary diet.

But any discussion of the regressive forces pressing in upon the university is incomplete without considering the role played by college administrators. When universities become over-differentiated through a concentration on technical expertise, and when dialogue and informal understandings between departments cease, the administrator becomes the link in the total organism, and administrative procedures tie the milch-cow's joints together in semblance of life.

The college administrator finds himself in an anomolous position. People who wield the greatest power in organizations are often regarded as the most able persons, a fact which legitimizes their power. Yet given the values of a university, the faculty are generally considered the most brilliant, so that administrators find themselves ruling over persons more highly valued and more visible within the community than they are themselves.

Much of the power wielded by administrators comes to them by default. The more creative a professor the more bored he is likely to be with any kind of routine or maintenance activity. Ex-faculty administrators or administratively oriented faculty tend to select themselves over a period of time, and Professor S. M. Lipset has observed that this process tends to encourage mediocrity.[13]

Upon administrators falls the task of managing the boundaries of the university system including its contacts with the outside world. Not unnaturally there is a tendency for administrators to assume some of the political coloration and general attitudes of those with whom they deal, especially if these persons are rich alumni or influential sources of aid.

But there is nothing like the same quality of contact between administrators and students. The administration has no exposure to the ferment of student ideas in the classroom and they encounter students mostly on bureaucratic and procedural issues about which students know little and usually care less.

But when agents of the outside culture intrude upon the campus to solicit certain kinds of students, it is the college administration that is regarded as having let them in and approved their mission. These agents are as dedicated to organized action, as the faculty, a potential countervailing force, are dedicated to scholarly detachment and collective inaction. Thus does the university become used for military and commercial ends, while administrators coordinate the uneasy whole.

In fact college administrators have a vested interest in the smoothest possible operation of the administrative machinery. They remain powerful, unchallenged and uncriticized by the faculty only so long as tranquility keeps them away from the more critical intellects of those who prefer dynamism and emotional risk taking. For just as routine activity attracts the relatively unimaginative and repels the more brilliant minds, so any crisis or change provoked by students throws the administration into a hornet's nest of academic scrutiny and judgment. In retrospect, there is hardly an academic who will not proclaim that the crisis should have been handled differently. At least a dozen doctoral theses, as many books, and a hundred articles probe every administrative decision during the crisis and examine every sign of inadequacy.

In these circumstances radical students have an equally high stake in producing disorder. The answer to uncreative leadership is to produce a stormy dialectic wherein the creative will rise in influence and the ritualists will sink. The answer to a faculty obsessed with consulting fees and private research, is to produce a much more interesting problem in the midst of the university itself which will attract their attention, their voices, their pens and their publishers. The answer to an alienated university with no humane dialogue is to shake the foundations until a hurried dialogue begins. The answer to academics who proclaim lofty principles of freedom from the lectern, but do nothing to translate these into action is to precipitate a crisis where action upon these principles becomes mandatory.

Ironically the long periods of administrative tranquility which characterized the universities in the fifties and early sixties appear to have visited a kind of psychological violence upon the student body. In Table 43 we see a comparison between three groups at Michigan University, Left Activists, Student Government leaders and a sample of ordinary non-activist students. By now it should come as no surprise that the Left rates higher in Cultural Sophistication, Liberalism, Independence from Family and Peers, Social Conscience, etc. The more extraordinary finding is the abysmal showing of Student Government leaders who presumably work with the Administration. They are the least sophisticated, the most lacking in compassion, and the most conforming. While the stressful activity of Left activists does not interfere with their study habits, the collegiate routines of student government leaders interfere substantially, and they are generally dissatisfied with the faculty (and the faculty with them, I imagine).

The doctrine of *in loco parentis* has proved self-fulfilling by attracting to the administration those students least independent of their parents, or one another, or the administration.

In a recent confrontation with Morris Abram, President of Brandeis University, Michael Rossman (earlier an F.S.M. leader) accused the universities of perpetuating "an oppressive social context," less physical in its violence than verbal and psychological.

> The difference between you and me is that we are both equally violent persons, and that I am deeply conscious of it. . . and you are, with pitiful blindness, unconscious of yours.[14]

I think this is more than metaphor and hyperbole. When a student body is "governed" by its saddest specimens, when you are told to "go through the proper channels" and these channels are clogged by semi-literate seekers for substitute daddies, who supposedly "represent" you, then the whole student social system has been twisted out of shape. It may not have been done deliberately or by physical force but the perversion is just as real. It happens because only the immature will work with the existing system, and like Uncle Toms in the ghetto, a whole culture is linked to the Establishment by those who collaborate with their culture's impotence. We may note in passing that the student government leaders at Michigan do not even *like* their administrators, being less satisfied with them than the average student. Now when the most sophisticated students on campus reject the administration in the greatest degree, and when the least sophisticated embrace it only to discover they had made a mistake, then something is very seriously wrong.

The best available evidence suggests that this situation is not confined to the University of Michigan. The same questionnaire has been used in a number of colleges where "Non Conformists" and "Academics" score consistently higher in sophistication, conscience, autonomy, etc., than "Collegiates" and "Vocationalists."[15] Yet the two latter categories are those which cooperate most readily with university officials and the external culture. Psycho-social development appears to accompany *minimal* cooperation with large parts of the university system, a shocking state of affairs.

Many years ago the universities struck an implicit bargain with the political and commercial culture. The universities would be free to think and discuss "dangerous ideas" with minimal interference, so long as these ideas did not impede politicians and businessmen from pursuing their practical affairs. This bargain has begun to break down, chiefly because commerce and politics have persuaded selected parts of the university to become staff departments to industry and government, and so the unselected parts of the university have decided to be influential as well in their own critical and dialectical manner. It seems the only way in which they can rebalance the very uneven use to which the university has been put, and which has precipitated a crisis of character for the university itself. The present system has subordinated the natural and creative leaders among the student body. Students have been subjected to the mass scheduling, social engineering and the technological conservatism discussed in the last chapter, and so the most creative spirits are in widespread revolt. As one prophet before the storm wrote to his fellow students

> You *perform.* But when do you think? Dutifully and obediently you follow, as a herd of grade-worshiping sheep. If you are strong at all you do this with a sense of shame, or if you are weak you do it with a studied cynicism . . . as jaded youth with parched imaginations that go no further than the oak-paneled rooms at the end of the line. . . BUT WHETHER YOU ARE STRONG OR WEAK YOU PERFORM LIKE TRAINED SEALS, AND LIKE SHEEP YOU FOLLOW . . . WITH THE THOROUGHBRED PHI BETA KAPPA SHEEP LEADING YOU! up the golden stairway to the omnipotent A, to the Happy Consciousness, to success and a very parochial mind. This . . . is your homage to respectability. Reluctantly or otherwise, you permit it to be applied by administrators who use computers on you as much because they are afraid of personal contact with you as for the reason they wish to keep the assembly line moving efficiently.[16]

*3. The developmental themes in radical tactics*

From the very first, the New Left has had remarkable and intuitive grasp of the principles of psycho-social development. Anyone caring to read the Port Huron Statement will find that it includes most, if not all, the principles of the developmental cycle.[17] This statement, generally attributed to Tom Hayden, is a founding charter of the Students for a Democratic Society.

The contemporary student Left is in some ways without precedent. Whereas earlier radical groups wanted to break into society and were chiefly angered by their deprivation and handicaps, these young men have triumphed in the early laps of the Great American Race. Now they are throwing off their gold medals and are vomiting conspicuously during award ceremonies. They have tasted in abundance what millions compete for, and are denouncing the race as fraudulent and the prizes as worthless. We have a new intellectual class whose "property" is their education and their conscience, rather than money or land. Politics is slipping out of the realm of economics into a psychology of self-expression and self-fulfillment.

Since virtually all the psycho-social data indicate that these young radicals are remarkably gifted, developed and creative, it behoves us to examine the style and tactics of their revolt. What may appear to us initially as shocking deviation from the norms of polite society may in reality be a new consciousness, which in time we shall come to share. Gardner Murphy recently observed

> Creative leaders of all sorts – and in particular religious, moral, and ideal leaders, fulfill that which is implicit but not explicit in the ideal demands of society. Because the formulations were not

> explicit, these leaders are often persecuted or destroyed, but because they express that which belongs to the active, but not yet consciously grasped, component in the society, their self-realization becomes in time a self-realization for others. . .[18]

If the disruptive tactics of radical students are as nihilistic and barbaric as so many experts claim, then we must believe that the best educated fringe of the best educated generation has suddenly and unaccountably gone mad. Let us examine some of the functions of their disruption.

In Chapters VII and VIII some general conclusions were reached about the necessary conditions for educing psycho-social development in six different organizational settings. In *every* case we found a *severe shock to the social system,* a feeling prior to developmental change, that whatever happened things could not continue as they had before. For instance, the managers in the Texas plant (Chapter VII, Table 16) failed to improve unless they had been at least moderately "shaken up" and disconfirmed in face-to-face small-group confrontations. Those managers who succeeded in finessing the encounter and keeping things polite and smooth, like gentlemen scholars at the university, failed entirely to develop or show any increased understanding of their employees. Would the Hawthorne experiment have been such a success if the researchers had *not* messed up and been obliged to ask the girls what was happening?

So the tactic of seizing the temporary initiative, and telling hard truths in physical confrontations is very far from being crazy or merely destructive. With no one to teach them, radicals have worked this out for themselves.

But surely it is unforgiveable to stop a whole university? What possible good can come of this? In T-groups we saw that considerable good came of this. In the first place a social vacuum "sucks out" into the environment the inner resources of most participants. It produces in time a "natural hierarchy," in which persons are held in esteem according to their capacities to help, nurture, inspire, and educe development in others, *not* because the armaments industry has a paternal eye on them, or because they have an inside track to the Dean.

The belief that one's given environment is in some respects absurd is an essential prerequisite to thinking and acting in creative ways so as to fill the vacuum surrounding one. This is partly the function of social criticism. Nor can people develop when they are busily engaged in bureaucratic routines, wherein A must act predictably in order to ensure a smooth fit with the routinized activities of B, C, D, and E. It is difficult for any single part of the machine to stop. It is only when the whole department or larger system is halted, so that nothing is routinely expected, that anything and everything become possible.

I can think of few better ways of reforming a bureaucracy than stopping it dead, and many corporations using sensitivity training do just that. The scope of their reform may be very modest compared with the opportunity for reform, but that has to do with characters of the participants and the limits of corporate imagination.

If radicals seem to hate everything America represents, at least part of the reason is that freedom, democracy, love of neighbor and the appreciation of heritage *must be rediscovered in action, not learnt by rote.* Genuinely free men create their own heritage, they doubt received wisdoms until these are proved *in situ.* There is an absurd contradiction in being lectured *about* freedom while sitting in straight rows and taking feverish notes. There are similar contradictions in the social sciences which know *about* people without knowing them, because research is split from teaching, perception is split from action, truth is split from communicability, and intellect is split from emotional experience. No wonder the Berkeley campus exploded shortly after students were told that "Free Speech" was permitted but not if it had any consequences in political action beyond the campus. Academic traditions and administrative rules fragment the developmental cycle into isolated segments. This is psychological and verbal violence at its worst.

The students counter this by use of all the T-Group and developmental principles we studied in earlier chapters, the prolonged face-to-face confrontations, the insistence on personal authenticity through action, the small group climate, the rebellion against authority, the suspension of structure, the creation of a social vacuum, the expression and acceptance of strong personal feelings, the intense dialectic, and the insistence upon the fullest participation in democratic decision-making.

Moreover what the radicals seek is what the university and the culture desperately need. If modern chemical companies cannot afford decisions unilaterally dictated from the top (see Chapter VI, Table 12) how much less can a modern university? If the most creative companies have the most confrontation and sharing of feelings in their decision-making, if they are characterized by much higher influence at lower levels, then what students are demanding seems essential to any healthy, complex system. We have seen that ordinary workers with grade school educations increase their morale and productivity by over 20%, as a result of joining in the creation of their own social and technical environment. This at the very least should be the right of every college student. It is precisely the best rules and the highest principles which *can* be suspended, because they will be personally rediscovered by sudents, who will *then* believe in them.

To understand the radicals' tactic of declaring publicly their existential rebellion, occupying buildings and making demands, we have only to follow the sequence of the cycle. First they *exist* on the basis of a radical PERCEPTION of some issue (e.g., the cooperation of Columbia University with the Institute of Defense Analysis and construction of a "racist" gym). But it is not enough to speak or write. To show *intensity* and *authenticity* of

INVESTMENT, one must RISK and SUSPEND one's academic status, and gamble for the DISTANT support of other students, faculty, and Harlem residents. If one is successful, alienation is overcome, SELF-TRANSCENDENCE is achieved and HIGHER SYNERGY is the consequence of rebellion. "I rebel, therefore we exist."

This higher synergy is often discovered following rebellions. For example Nathan Glazer, a severe critic of the F.S.M., had this to say of the climate on the Berkeley Campus following the disturbances:

> A great wave of energy has been released here, particularly among the students, by the crisis of the past few months, and it has been wonderful to see what prodigies of work – in organization, in research, in writing – have been evoked from them by the struggle. Certainly many professors have been given quite a start to discover what stores of energy are locked in our students and untouched by the normal educational routine. This is a moment that should be seized, for there are only a few moments in the history of an institution when large changes are possible. It is also clear that the chancellor welcomes proposals for change.[19]

The only mystery is where Glazer imagines that this energy came from, if not from the courage of a few students to rebel and thereby unlock the energies in others which were untouched by normal routines.

A similar rebellion at Columbia University brought out a similarly energetic and vociferous response. The Cox Commission failed to find the trace of a conspiracy.

> By the final days the revolt enjoyed both wide and deep support among the students and junior faculty and in lesser degree among senior professors. The grievances of the rebels were felt equally by a still larger number, probably a majority of the students. . .
>
> The existence of broad underlying unrest is also shown by the progress of the seizures. The action of the black students in Hamilton Hall was entirely independent of S.D.S. The seizure of Avery Hall by architectural students was their own movement. The occupation of Fayerweather Hall, in which a large part of graduate study in the social sciences is centered, was apparently spontaneous; no evidence of an S.D.S. connection has come to our attention.[20]

The commission reported that a poll of the student body was taken, although this failed to include the 1,000 students in the occupied buildings.

74% favored the end of the gym construction. 66% favored the severance of ties with the Institute of Defense Analysis. 37% favored amnesty for all protesting students. If we add to these proportions the 1,000 in the buildings, the percentages and numbers are respectively 78% (5,093), 72% (4,572) and 48% (3,054).[1]

But sheer numbers do not reflect the quality of the synergy and ecstatic levels of new experience following a successful rebellion. Those in the Columbia "communes" will probably never forget the deep bonds of affection and the heady excitement which follow an act of conscience. Do what you believe is right, despite the consequences, and behold! You have a thousand friends with all the colorful qualities of personality that characterize radicals. Those who look for a conspiracy miss the whole point. The point is to act spontaneously from the deepest ethical and human impulse and then to discover yourself in a fervent embrace with the complementary human impulse touched off in others. The basic dichotomy of individuality and intimacy is transcended when the lonely act calls forth a warm response.

Into the "liberated" buildings at Columbia came parcels of food donated by local stores, groups of physicians and medical students set up a free clinic nearby, the names of various professionals willing to give free service were chalked up on boards. In nearby Avery Hall architecture students worked with instructors to build special barricades. Girls came over from Sarah Lawrence and Barnard to join the rebels. In Fayerweather Hall performances of "guerilla theatre" were held by the light of a hundred candles. As a grande finale a couple were married by the college chaplain who pronounced them "children of a new age."[22]

The "bust" at Harvard in April of 1969 was similar in many ways, except that the occupation lasted only a few hours. One participant, Nicholas Gagarin, relates:

> There were two kinds of emotions in University Hall. The first were dreamlike and euphoric. They came from the weird realization that now at the University, Mr. Big, Harvard U, we finally had a building. They came from the carnival, open, free-wheeling, life-style inside. They came from the fact that one student found a memo on Dean Glimp's desk saying "Draft statement on limits of student dissent". . .
>
> What was most euphoric, however, was us and what we were to each other. For those few hours we were brothers and sisters. We did reach out and hold onto each other. You couldn't be flip about it. "I haven't seen so many friends together in two years," one girl said. But you had to realize – whatever your politics and tactics – that we were very beautiful in University Hall, we were very human, and we were very together. . .

> We had been together at the peak of human experience. Suddenly we were together at its pit – as the gut, uncontrollable horror of what the cops were doing jammed its way down into our bowels. I was in the line behind Dick Hyland. "They've got Mace," he shouted. With that, I quit, and jumped from one of the windows. Dick was braver. He stayed, and for that the cops would club him unconscious. . .

This particular student exemplified the cultural revolution, less consciously political, but the strands of which interweave with the New Left.

> What is really at stake . . . is not a political revolution, but a human one. And if we could bring that about, if we could bring ourselves into that beautiful human togetherness that existed inside the Hall, if we could end the inhumanity, competitiveness and alienation that the University teaches us so that we may fit neatly into an inhuman, competitive, alienated society – then such things as the war, ROTC, and slumlording would be inconceivable. They would be criminal acts, instead of merely crimes against conscience.[24]

At Columbia the prolonged occupation acted like an incubator to this humanizing process. More students joined and more buildings were occupied.

In the days that followed many of the students' heroes came to visit them and congratulate them (just as during the Hawthorne experiment a stream of visitors came to admire and inquire of the girls and the researchers). There was Dwight Macdonald, Conor Cruise O'Brien, Stephen Spender, Allen Ginsberg, Rap Brown and Stokely Carmichael. Later Harold Taylor and Erich Fromm would join with others to speak at a "counter commencement."

Now this is a rather amazing thing, that a small handful of twenty-year olds can communicate to a large campus in a way that brings thousands to their cause and the ad hoc faculty group within an inch of recommending amnesty. It is just nonsense to claim that anyone can do this who is mad or ruthless enough to seize a building. Police have hustled away such persons a score of times without major resentment. The capacity to rally half a campus or more against a President and Vice President who have dedicated the best part of their lives to political science tells us much about what is lacking in the academic culture, and what the young are intent upon supplying.

Some months later the Cox Commission informed their readers that the crisis at Columbia had provided "a creative source of renewal." So part of the students' message had come across. It remained only to execute the messengers.

4. *The rationales for repression*

So many reasons have been given for the immediate crushing of student protest that only a small selection of the more common arguments can be discussed here.

*It is seldom, if ever, permissible in a democratic society to circumvent existing channels of petition and redress of grievances.*

This axiom would severely cripple psycho-social development for the simple reason that "proper channels" are designed to admit only as much opposing power as rulers and managers feel they can tolerate. Such channels often permit rulers to say fifty words for every one heard in dissent. Moreover these channels often cannot accommodate protests directed at the channels themselves. The reform of the House Rules Committee cannot get through the House Rules Committee. A social system will censor messages critical of the system itself.

We saw in Chapter VI that the current level of development attained by a group tends to be frozen into structures and rules. With the passage of time these structures come to represent an *earlier* consensus about the "right" levels of behavior. The degree of participation in decision-making permitted by the structure is often much lower than the members could achieve by using their recently developed resources. Only a right of protest *which transcends the logic of the structures themselves* can enable a society to develop. It is a fallacy to think of societies as either democratic or undemocratic. They are more or less democratic and only effective protests can make them more democratic still.

*While many of the ends sought by protesting students are noble and visionary, nothing can justify the use of means that negate and contradict these ends.*

These critics seem to assume that means must at all times be similar in style and form to ends sought. Thus if the desired end is a rational, humane, affectionate and understanding culture, the means of achieving this should have the same qualities.

This argument totally ignores the dynamic opposites within the cycle. To achieve a higher order, men must risk and to some extent suspend their present order, to raise their competences they must flirt with humiliation. Individual daring is the prelude to more intense relationships. Each potentially contradictory element is *both* an end in itself *and* a means to an end. Each is a sharply contrasting opposite capable of reconciliation.

Just like a human being, a group or corporation can benefit from temporary disintegration as a means of achieving better reintegration. But so long as we insist that disintegration is bad *per se* and that anyone producing it can only wish to "destroy the university," we shall fail to understand the growth process itself.

The smooth, unbroken climb, sought by many administrators and social engineers, is a mechanistic analogue. It is not in the nature of living things.

*But rebel students are elitist, manipulating and anti-democratic. By what right do they attempt to change us?*

The accusation of elitism could, of course, be made against every truly creative person or group. A man rebels, presents a novel synthesis and inevitably irritates or enrages a large proportion of his audience. If he gave up with the first pangs of alienation and rejection society would have only accidental changes. In any dispute the creative person is bound to assume that much of the opposition to him is mistaken.

In this restricted sense rebel students are elitist, and elite as well. However, they are not elitist at all in seeking hierarchical relationships or official status and prestige. Kenneth Keniston witnessed a "revolt of the secretaries" against radical leaders coordinating the Viet Nam Summer campaign. The leaders were challenged by their rank and file who wanted a greater share in the decision-making. The leaders conceded at once, as they did to Black Power demands at the Conference of New Politics a few months later.

My own definition of manipulation is where a leader, at relatively no risk and danger to himself and without permitting himself to be influenced, moves many people like pawns on a chess board. But the great influence occasionally exercised by radicals is quite different from this. They run the highest risks in gambling not only with their continued leadership but their very existence as students. They leave themselves very wide open to a total, devastating and ignominious rejection by those to whom they appeal. Their subsequent influence is only purchased by first delivering themselves into the power of their intended constituency. If no one rallies to the issues they proclaim, they are lost.

Moreover manipulation is a tactic which the most gullible and least sophisticated fall for. They lack the capacity to think or choose for themselves. But a survey of Berkeley students which divided them into three degrees of support for the F.S.M., "militant," "moderate" and "conservative," found that nearly half the militants (45%) but only 10% of conservatives had a grade point average of B+ or better. In contrast more than a third of the conservatives but only 15% of the militants had an average of B– or worse. The militants were also higher on indicators of libertarianism.[25] What kind of "manipulation" is this, when the most free and the most intelligent respond to it? Here, as at the University of Michigan, it was the administration, not radical students, which was relatively popular with the less liberal and intelligent students.

*Rebel students are shrill, insulting, over-emotional and highly dogmatic. Problems can only be solved in a calm, reasonable atmosphere of mutual, scholarly respect.*

The older generation bewails the decline of good manners and moderation. Senior citizens seem haunted by image of "the beast in man," and every example of anger and immoderate language arouses their concern that the beast is breaking loose. They tend to assume that open mindedness and flexibility can only be achieved in an atmosphere of reasoned calm, and that "emotional outbursts" herald the break-up of civilization.

This thesis is flatly contradicted by our research findings which show positive correlations between openness, flexibility, impulse expression, and volatile dialectics. Even if we assume that these tests are all wrong and that the tough bargaining positions of student radicals are so obviously dogmatic as to require no further investigation, we are still confronted with their procedures of participatory democracy. How can rebel students in occupied buildings in Columbia, and in similar tight situations, make their decisions in open debate? The capacity to hold final decisions in abeyance *under strong external threat,* until all opinions have been heard must require an unusual tolerance for anxiety and uncertainty. This process so infuriated the black students in Hamilton Hall that it was one of their chief reasons for asking the white radicals to leave. All that we know about even moderately dogmatic persons suggests that they could never tolerate democratic decision-making under emergency conditions.

If, then, radicals appear inflexible in dealings with their opponents the explanation must lie elsewhere. Perhaps it is not their *personalities* which necessitate hard bargaining, but the *situation* of relative powerlessness in which they find themselves. Watts and Whittaker used a number of research instruments to measure flexibility and rigidity and found that Berkeley rebels were extremely flexible but also very highly committed.[26] By now it occurs to readers that the segments of the cycle model can never tell you how *much* of each quality, for example how much suspension versus how much firm integration, should be exhibited in any given situation. All we can say is that highly developed persons have a record of bringing the right combination of strengths to the demands of particular situations. In most arguments each party feels that the other is "dogmatic" for not yielding to him, but it does not follow that this is so.

The impression of student dogmatism can in part be traced to a misunderstanding between the generations concerning the necessary conditions of open mindedness. Older people tend to assume, I believe wrongly, that a state of emotional excitement necessarily imposes severe limits upon judgment. This view originates in the idea of scientific detachment. But the detached observer is genuinely open, *only when the object being studied is in fact a thing apart from the observer.* In all cases where we are participating and our feelings and attitudes influence the environment, *openness will be accompanied by personal suspension and emotional spasms of anxiety.* Calm and detached reason is a rigid form of interpersonal relationship, for it assumes that moral premises are already agreed upon and only the most rational means of achieving these ends are open for discussion. Noam Chomsky has been particularly perceptive on this aspect of liberal rigidity and the frightful toll it has caused in Viet Nam.

> A striking feature of the recent debate on Southeast Asian policy has been the distinction that is commonly made between "responsible criticism" on the one hand, and "sentimental" or "emotional" or "hysterical" criticism, on the other. There is much to be learned from a careful study of the terms in which this distinction is drawn. The "hysterical critics" are to be identified apparently, by their irrational refusal to accept one fundamental political axiom, namely that the United States has the right to extend its power and control without limit, insofar as is feasible. Responsible criticism does not challenge this assumption, but argues, rather, that we probably can't "get away with it" in this particular time and place.[27]

Chomsky cites the example of Henry Kissinger in a television debate: "he observed, rather sadly, that what disturbs him most is that others question not our judgment but our motives. . ."[28] It is the extraordinary dogmatism of scholar-liberals that they will re-examine everything which is at *a distance from themselves,* but not the moral premises and assumptions which comprise their own identities. These remain as unsuspended as America's self-interest. And of course the maximization of self-interest, unqualified by the suffering and opinions of others, is the perfect recipe for a rigidity of mind with brutal consequences. As we have seen in chapter after chapter, even self-interest itself suffers when unquestioned and unsuspended.

The pseudo-objective "liberal" begins by denying his own impulses in the name of rationality, and ends up punishing "aggression" in others, assuming this to be a characteristic of the environment and not himself. In fact the direct expression of anger, even tears at the appalling waste and destruction of our policy in Viet Nam is the *beginning* of true dialogue between people. Problems cannot be solved by abstract rationality based upon inhuman, inadequate premises. Appeals to calm reason only block attempts to re-examine our premises, and this re-examination will be an *agonizing* process, especially humiliating for those who loosed so great a holocaust upon a small nation. The present rudeness of radical students is only a foretaste of how much it is going to hurt once we see ourselves from the perspectives of our victims. The end of the war will see a flood of articles, films and books about America's conduct that will shame a whole generation. In the meantime radical students are trying to pry open our tightly closed minds.

*Student Rebels are mainly nihilists and anarchists intent upon destroying the university. They have no desire to substitute persuasion for violence.*

This was the substance of Grayson Kirk's complaint at Columbia University. There is certainly a self-proclaimed nihilist fringe among student rebels, but it does not seem extensive enough to register in research surveys.

The difficulty in attributing a sinister longing for physical violence to radical students is the tremendous advantage they have in verbal dialectic. They are much more skilled in the combative use of words and ideas than most of their opponents, while policemen and the many athletes or "jocks" among conservative students excel in strong-arm tactics.

So when radicals say that force is only used to achieve a proper and extensive hearing for their views, in situations where authorities decline to hear them out, one must either believe them, or believe that they are *so* stupid as to wish to play the game in their opponent's strongest suit. The following description of Columbia University before the uprising shows what students were up against.

> Many students had attacked Kirk's policies on a wide variety of problems, but the president remained coldly aloof, almost disdainful. When contact was with some other official of the administration results were equally frustrating. Students and faculty were told by high University officials that issues such as the gym or I.D.A. were none of their business, that their thoughts on these problems simply did not matter. Discussing the role of students in the University decision-making process, Herbert Deane (vice president for academic affairs) had phrased the problem this way almost one year to the day before the start of the spring uprising: "Whether students vote 'yes' or 'no' on a given issue means as much to me as if they were to tell me they like strawberries."..."You're only transitory birds," Kirk had once told a group of students who confronted him in his Low Library sanctuary, "and therefore should have no voice."[29]

The question left unanswered by critics of rebel students is how does one influence an administration of this kind? The tactic of the Cox Commission in criticising the administration as "authoritarian" and then condemning the revolt against authoritarianism, is unhelpful to say the least. Nor does it help to say that S.D.S. should have picketed and petitioned peacefully, for this is precisely what it did. Their leader gambled upon influencing the administration peacefully, and when rebuffed for the third time his followers deposed him. What greater sacrifice can any political group make in the cause of peaceful persuasion, than shattering its own structure upon a rock of indifference?

In fact it is rarely useful to attribute violence to specific persons until it is *first* attributed to relationships. Only the most naive would suppose that the first to strike physically is necessarily the origin of violence. Insofar as a violent relationship can be laid to either combatant, he with the most power and hence possibility of altering the relationship to yield greater mutual satisfaction should carry most blame. The subordinate is far more often "locked in" by structures and imposed expectations.

I think the common conviction that radicals wish to destroy the University is based on a simple misunderstanding, traceable to different styles of problem solving among students and administrators. We have seen that radicals have a very high tolerance for anxiety, uncertainty and dialectic. By contrast a study in the late fifties which measured the anxiety levels of many different professional groups found that creative writers suffered the highest anxiety and college administrators the lowest![30]

The group of radicals studied by Keniston revealed not only periodic "shouting matches" but the *reconciliation of conflict by this means.* I think administrators experience this style of student dialectic as destructive to their dignity and their quieter style of life. They feel control slipping from their grasp, so they predict the imminent destruction of the university by students.

At bottom is the question of tranquility as against ferment and whether we can really re-examine our fundamental premises without getting excited and severely pricking each others' consciences. But I think this is more than a matter of taste and life-style. I might grant conservatives their tranquility if America was not disfiguring the face of Viet Nam, so that one flyer exclaimed that "it looked like someone had caught smallpox and died." Is it not the function of conscience to disturb us when we commit unspeakable acts? The mainstay of humanitarian conduct is that when we hurt others we "break up inside," and this painful process often saves the other and in the longer run ourselves. Perhaps the greater obscenity would be an America that killed thousands of helpless peasants *without* breaking up.

The disorder and violence which "over emotional," "nihilistic" and "moralistic" students inflict upon this country is the merest shadow of the blood bath that rational, "reasonable," conventional, obedient All-American exponents of law and order are inflicting on Viet Nam, in dialogue with "responsible critics." I look forward to the day when America cannot commit such acts without even worse upheaval and nausea within its body politic. This seems to be a far more effective and humane deterrent to cruelty than threats of nuclear retaliation. If the discomfort students cause us today deters our leaders from embarking upon new foreign adventures in the future, it will have been worth it a thousand times over.

*Radical students exhibit too much youthful impatience with the necessary gradualism of democratic politics.*

This is perhaps the most crucial criticism of all. The dynamics of the cycle model can operate gently as in liberalism with mostly verbal protests, medium distances and moderate degrees of self-suspension, or they can operate with stormy upheavals, high risks, great tragedies and great triumphs. At some point the risk must be regarded as unacceptable and the anxiety generated as so great that the general population may be driven into a frenzy. Merely because the radical finds in disorder some exciting opportunities for new order, does not necessarily justify a level of disorder in which others simply cannot function. Besides disorder is usually more terrifying for those who did not initiate it, and upon whom it breaks unexpectedly. The artist and writer can go into a corner with their own creative disorder and the many who find both the process and results repellent do not have to experience them. But social and political creativity jumbles up people instead of words and there is no choice of remaining unaffected.

To put the argument another way, "regression in the service of the ego," or temporary suspension in order to achieve a higher synergy is a theory of growth which however true, remains exceedingly perilous. On the face of it, regression is regression and the service to the ego or the later synergy is at best problematical. It is no coincidence that there are many superficial resemblances between the radical Left and radical Right. Both rebel. Both are romantic, intense, idealistic. Both appeal to the heart and demand sweeping changes and hold out a vision of alienation overcome. The similarity comes about in part because regression is the temporary means to radical growth and the means *and permanent end* of right wing reaction.

There are at least two major perils to the tactics of developmental radicals who "shake the foundations" in order to reform the system. The first danger is that they do at least half the job that the radical right is seeking to do, and that if, following an initial regression, the forces of reaction take over, the regression becomes permanent rather than temporary and the system is worse off than before.

The second peril comes from dogmatic pseudo-radicals, those who wish to lose themselves not in order to find themselves, but to lose themselves. The genuine radical says "who will help me shake the foundations?" Those who volunteer may or may not have the same motivations as he. If they do not, he is likely to discover this only *after* the foundations are badly shaken, when he may discover to his horror that his allies are oblivion seekers.

The elder generation of liberals who lived through fascism and Stalinism cannot forget that there *are* oblivion seekers, hysterical destroyers, and not just a few but many who seem to infect one another during periods of disorder. If creativity is close to madness, if each of us can grow only by leaping over a widening abyss, then it makes sense to pause occasionally and consider that we are not single mountaineers but roped together. My admiration for those who make long, lonely leaps is occasionally tempered by two considerations. Do they *want* to reach the other side? If and when they fall, will they pull others into the abyss with them?

But the perils of impatience and excessive dynamism must be measured against the less immediate but possibly graver risks of gradualism. Auden once said, "We must love one another or die." I think we must radicalize (which includes love) or die. I regard the process of psycho-social development as competing with blind technological acceleration which yearly boosts our capacity to threaten, manipulate, depersonalize, obfuscate, kill and avoid confrontation with our still living victims. It was once fashionable to regard man as cast adrift in a slowly leaking row-boat upon a chartless sea. But today man seems to have fastened a number of powerful outboard motors to the front, back and sides of his row-boat so that it careens crazily sideways, backwards, forwards. One relatively small motor is attached beneath the rudder and enables us to steer. It is this that radical students are trying to develop and unless they succeed I cannot see very much future for the human race.

Perhaps, too, radical students, with their psychological mindedness, have sensed an infinitely greater calamity of which most of us are unaware. When a country acts with unimaginable cruelty as America has done in Southeast Asia, some of the most insidious damage is right here at home within our minds. I suspect that those cruelties we see without protest, and most appeals from which we turn in helpless resignation, leave their sicklied mark deep within us. So do not ask a screaming student what he hopes to gain. His is a holding action on behalf of humanity, and when this nightmare is over, the quickness of his compassion will have survived. It is the rest of us who will have slipped imperceptibly backwards into deadness. How can many of us ever feel deeply or sincerely for poor people again, if the sympathy conjures up, as it must, the true dimensions of our prior indifference and our crimes? Thank God there are people with the sensitivity to cry for the corruption of our national conscience.

5. *The societal thesis and the student antithesis*

If we are to heed what students are trying to tell us, it is essential to comprehend the one-sided, exaggerated nature of thesis and antithesis. The apparent "extremism" of radical students can only be understood if we see them as intent upon supplying certain elements lacking in the dominant culture (see Figure 4). Nothing is more infuriating than being told about what is missing in one's own character. Americans have invented a vast pseudo-scientific discourse largely aimed at keeping social facts separate from the personality of actors. The social sciences became bureaucratized long before they became useful and the result has been a division into non-viable departments, individual psychology, group psychology, sociology, etc., each discipline hugging and boosting its own amputated piece of man. Students are trying to tell us what is missing from these "scientific" images of man.

In the resulting dialectic each contestant tends to use his "best" weapons, those sanctioned by his philosophy. Students shout at their elders that they are power-mad and repressive, "up-tight" and compulsive in their legalism and morality, aloofly and pretentiously detached, selfishly nationalistic, narrowly

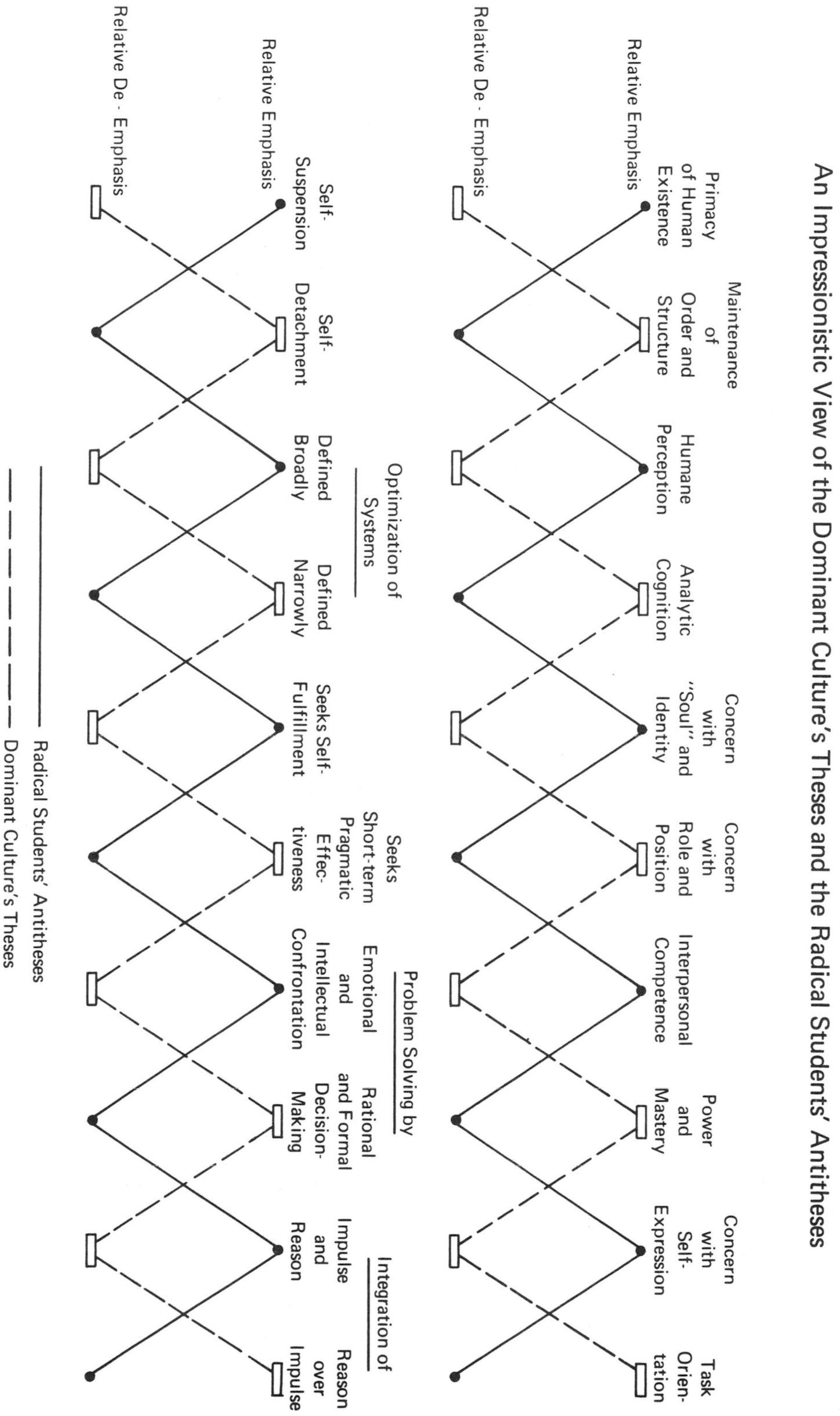
An Impressionistic View of the Dominant Culture's Theses and the Radical Students' Antitheses
Relative Emphasis
Relative De - Emphasis
Primacy of Human Existence
Maintenance of Order and Structure
Humane Perception
Analytic Cognition
Concern with "Soul" and Identity
Concern with Role and Position
Interpersonal Competence
Power and Mastery
Concern with Self-Expression
Task Orientation
Relative Emphasis
Relative De - Emphasis
Self-Suspension
Self-Detachment
Optimization of Systems
Defined Broadly
Defined Narrowly
Seeks Self-Fulfillment
Seeks Short-term Pragmatic Effectiveness
Problem Solving by
Emotional and Intellectual Confrontation
Rational and Formal Decision-Making
Integration of
Impulse and Reason
Reason over Impulse
Radical Students' Antitheses
Dominant Culture's Theses

concerned with short-term pay-offs and vulgar pragmatism, and aridly intellectual. Their elders reply in a pained, long-suffering voice that the short-comings of students are quite evident in their present demeanor, a shocking disregard for law and even common courtesies, a delusional belief in their own moral insight, an hysterical perversion of self-expression, a lamentable lack of detachment, and ignorance of empirical realities.

The more strenuous the argument becomes the more each contestant is convinced that his opinion of the other is being confirmed before his very eyes. The rebels at Columbia could show their fellow students that the administration was every bit as repressive and brutal as was originally claimed. The administration called upon trustees and the New York Times to witness that radical students were utterly without responsibility or restraint. This was where Decency and Moderation took their stand. If Columbia fell – so would Higher Education. The nihilistic nature of student rebellion, long suspected, proclaimed (and created?) by Grayson Kirk necessitated his rallying the rich and influential to his cause, thereby exemplifying the conspiracy of the power elite, long suspected, proclaimed (and created?) by the student Left.

In the tension aroused by the conflict the administration, always somewhat reminiscent of an icicle, froze hard into a perfect specimen, while the students always close to burning with an existential frenzy pronounced that the revolution had come.

Although these antics sound a trifle foolish, the rhetorical entrapment is very real. There is good logic in emphasizing these constituents which are missing from a relationship. No synergy following dialectic can come without a "just balance." The more your opponent ignores your thesis and inflates his antithesis, the more you need to stress your thesis to achieve a semblance of balance. Moreover an increasing number of waverers come to your banner as the other escalates his half-truth into a nightmarish lopsidedness. How can each side break out of this vicious circle? In practice the administration often backs away from the "fire" and calls for the police. I think the contestants have to go through the "fire."

6. *The choice of fire or fire*

In his poem *Little Gidding* T. S. Eliot suggested that mankind faced a choice of fires. One was represented by the Nazi scourge then devastating Europe, the second was an agony of the soul, a deep, terrifying realization of one's own capacities for good and evil.

In our modern hedonistic and technological culture we have become proud of reducing human pain and effort. We have suspected, often rightly, that advocates of suffering were moved by a secret desire to punish. Only gradually is it dawning upon us that the minimization of social conflict and the evasion of emotional turmoil is like asking a plasterer to seal a volcano.

There is, of course, no easy answer to the hundreds of problems raised in this and previous chapters. But insofar as any single problem holds other problems in its thrall, I would say that the central issue is our individual capacity to tolerate the fires of existential anxiety. I believe that one principal reason that radical students lack access to administrators, why black Americans lack access to white Americans, and why we would rather spend $70 billion on arms than negotiate with communists, is that the avoiding parties guess what they might hear, and they cannot bear to hear it. I think if we locked up some administrators in a room with some radical students for sixteen hours, the former would be changed men and perhaps the latter too. I doubt there would be any physical violence. I doubt if this is the real threat that radicals pose. I think radicals would prevail verbally, creatively, emotionally, and politically, and *that* is the substance of the terror they inspire.

The real reason we have been so backward in helping black people, in reversing our policy in Viet Nam, in aiding the Third World and in confronting communists, is our total underestimation of the virtues of vulnerability, anxiety and pain. When we do meet our enemies we typically turn it into a "rational discourse" or a televised verbal joust, not directed at the other at all, but at heartening our own supporters. We generally start to negotiate only *after* we have failed to kill, and then we wonder why the process is frustrating!

The confrontation students seek is much different from this. It is a baring of souls, a deeply emotional dialogue upon fundamental issues, an angry puncturing of pretension and paternalism. The kind of courage these students admire is seen in the man who can break down and cry for the opportunities he missed and for all those he could have helped. In Jonathan Kozol's book, *Death at an Early Age,* there is one passage I found especially moving. The older instructors at the school were saying to each other about Kozol and the defiance surrounding his dismissal:

> If this young man is right – if all these younger people are right – if the educational scholars are right. . .if Martin Luther King is right – then we are not merely in some error which may perhaps have to be somehow corrected but rather – and far more inexorable and terrible – our entire view of the world has been shattered and our entire lives may have been a waste.[31]

It is when the little doses of anxiety and suspension are evaded year after year, and when pat assurances are made that everyone's motives are the best, that we reach the point of total non-suspension and no return. The only answer is to plunge periodically into existential fire and like the phoenix renew ourselves. For years men have dichotomized peace and war, associating mental peace with physical peace and mental turmoil with physical warfare. This dichotomy is patently false. We must confront each other's psycho-social fire or be consumed by the fire of war.

The dove descending breaks the air
With flame of incandescent terror
Of which the tongues declare
The one discharge from sin and error
The only hope, or else despair,
Lies in the choice of pyre or pyre
To be redeemed from fire by fire.[32]

## NOTES FOR CHAPTER XII

1. "Professors' Attitudes toward the Vietnam War" by D. J. Armor, *et al, Public Opinion Quarterly,* No. 31, 1967, pp. 159-175. Opposition varied around 50% in large public and private universities, but dropped to 33% in small private schools, and to 17% in Catholic Universities.

2. "The Student Left in American Higher Education" by Richard E. Peterson, *Daedalus,* Vol. 97, No. 1, p. 311f.

3. *The Young Radicals* by Kenneth Keniston, New York: Harcourt, Brace and World, 1968, p. 95.

4. *Ibid.,* p. 123.

5. *Ibid.,* p. 124.

6. *Masters of Political Thought, op. cit.,* p. 70.

7. "Personality Characteristics of Campus Leaders" by B. B. Windborn and D. G. Jansen, *Journal of Counselling Psychology,* Vol. 14, No. 6, 1967, pp. 509-513.

8. "Commitment and Conformity in the American College" by James W. Trent and Judith L. Craise, *Journal of Social Issues,* Vol. 23, No. 3, pp. 43-44.

9. "Continuities and Discontinuities in Childhood and Adult Moral Development," Harvard University School of Education, Mimeo.

10. "Determinants of Support for Civil Liberties" by H. C. Selvin and W. O. Hagstrom, *op. cit.,* p. 503.

11. Quoted by Sheldon S. Wolin and John W. Shaar in "The Abuses of the Multi-University," (see also Clark Kerr's "Reply to Wolin and Shaar") in *The Berkeley Student Revolt, op. cit.,* pp. 350-366.

12. *Ibid.,*

13. "Violence and Power on the Campus" in *Change in Higher Education*, March-April 1969, p. 41.

14. *Ibid.* p. 31.

15. "The Student Left in Higher Education" by Richard E. Peterson, op. cit., pp. 299-302.

16. "Letter to Undergraduates" by Bradford Cleveland, reprinted in *The Berkeley Student Revolt, op. cit.*, p. 68.

17. Available from *Our Generation,* Literature Department, 3837 St. Laurent Blvd., Montreal 18. Excerpts appear in *The New Student Left* by Mitchell Cohen and Dennis Hale, Boston: Beacon Press, 1966.

18. *Human Potentialities* by Gardner Murphy, New York: Basic Books, 1958, p. 171, also in *Interpersonal Dynamics,* Bennis *et al.,* (eds.), *op. cit.,* p. 659.

19. "Reply to Selznick" by Nathan Glazer, *Commentary,* March 1965, reprinted in *The Berkeley Student Revolt, op. cit.,* p. 315.

20. *Crisis at Columbia* (The Cox Commission Report), New York: Vintage, 1968, pp. 190-191.

21. *Ibid.,* p. 191.

22. For this and similar descriptions see *Up Against the Ivy Wall* by Jerry L. Avorn, *et. al.,* New York: Atheneum, 1968, pp. 117-131.

23. "Non-Politics on the Battlefront" by Nicholas Gagarin, *The Harvard Crimson,* April 12, 1969, pp. 3-4.

24. *Ibid.,* p. 4.

25. "Mainsprings of the Rebellion" by Robert H. Somers in *The Berkeley Student Revolt, op. cit.,* p. 544.

26. See "Some Socio-psychological differences between highly committed members of the F.S.M. and the student population at Berkeley," *op. cit.*

27. "The Responsibility of Intellectuals" (originally in *New York Review of Books,* Feb. 23, 1967), reprinted in *American Power and the New Mandarins,* New York: Pantheon Books, 1969, p. 333.

28. *Ibid.,* p. 330.

29. *Up Against the Ivy Wall* by Avorn *et. al., op. cit.,* p. 119.

30. This was reported "The Anatomy of Angst," *Time Magazine,* March 31, 1961. The article refers to the work of Raymond B. Cattell and Irvin H. Sheier. I have been unable to find their original research.

31. *Death at an Early Age,* New York: Bantam Books, 1968, p. 211.

32. *Four Quartets,* by T. S. Eliot, New York: Harcourt, Brace and World, 1943, p. 37.

# SELECTED BIBLIOGRAPHY


Adler, A. *Understanding Human Nature.* Philadelphia: Chilton, 1926.

Adorno, T.W. *et al. The Authoritarian Personality.* New York: Harper & Bros., 1950.

Aiken, M., N. J. Demerath, and G. Maxwell. "Conscience and Confrontation." University of Wisconsin, Mimeo, 1966.

Aiken, M., and J. Hage. "Organizational Alienation." *American Sociological Review,* Vol. 31, No. 4, 1966.

Allport, G.W. *The Psychology of Prejudice.* New York: Anchor Books, 1954.

Allport, G.W. *Becoming.* New Haven: Yale University Press, 1955.

Allport, G.W. *Pattern and Growth in Personality.* New York: Holt, Rinehart and Winston, 1961.

Almond, G., and S. Verba. *The Civic Culture: Political Attitudes and Democracy in Five Nations.* Princeton: Princeton University Press, 1963.

Angyal, A. *Foundations for a Science of Personality.* New York: The Commonwealth Fund, 1941.

Arendt, Hannah. *The Origins of Totalitarianism.* Cleveland: World Publishing, 1958.

Arendt, Hannah. *Eichmann in Jerusalem.* New York: Viking, 1963.

Argyris, C. *Interpersonal Competence and Organizational Effectiveness.* Homewood, Ill.: Irwin-Dorsey, 1962.

Argyris, C. "T-Groups for Organizational Effectiveness." *Harvard Business Review.* March-April, 1964.

Argyris, C. *Integrating the Individual and the Organization.* New York: John Wiley.

Armor, D. J., *et al.* "Professors' Attitudes Toward the Vietnam War." *The Public Opinion Quarterly,* Vol. 31, Summer 1967.

Aron, R. *Marxism and Existentialism.* New York: "World Perspectives," Harper and Row, 1969.

Avorn, J.L. (plus staff members of the *Columbia Spectator). Up Against the Ivy Wall.* New York: Atheneum, 1969.

Bandura, A., and R. Walters. *Social Learning and Personality Development.* New York: Holt, Rinehart & Winston.

Banfield, E.C. *The Moral Basis of a Backward Society.* New York: Free Press, 1958.

Barnes, L.B. *Organizational Systems and Engineering Groups.* Boston: Harvard Business School Division of Research, 1960.

Barron, F. *Creativity and Psychological Health.* Princeton: Van Nostrand, 1963.

Bateson, G., *et al.* "Toward a Theory of Schizophrenia" in *Behavioral Science.* Vol. 1, No. 4, 1956.

Bay, C. "Political and Apolitical Students: Facts in Search of a Theory." *Journal of Social Issues* Vol. 23, No. 3, 1967.

Beckett, S. *Waiting for Godot.* New York: Grove Press, 1954.

Bell, D. *The End of Ideology.* Glencoe: Free Press, 1960.

Bell, D. (ed.) *The Radical Right.* New York: Anchor Books, 1964.

Bennis, W. E., H. Schein, D. E. Berlew, and F. I. Steele. *Interpersonal Dynamics.* Homewood, Ill.: The Dorsey Press, 1964.

Berdyaev, N. *Slavery and Freedom.* New York: Charles Scribner's Sons, 1944.

Berelson, B., and G. Steiner. *Human Behavior: An Inventory of Scientific Findings.* New York: Harcourt, Brace & World, 1964.

Berkowitz, L. "The Effects of Observing Violence." *Scientific American*, Vol. 210, No. 2, 1964.

Bernanos, G. *Diary of a Country Priest.* New York: Macmillan, 1937.

Berne, E. *Games People Play.* New York: Grove Press, 1964.

Bertalanffy, L. von. *Problems of Life.* New York: Harper Torchbooks, 1960.

Bertalanffy, L. von. *Robots, Men and Minds.* New York: George Braziller, 1967.

Bertocci, P.A., and R. M. Millard. *Personality and the Good.* New York: McKay, 1963.

Blake, R. R., Jane Mouton, L. B. Barnes, and L. E. Greiner. "Breakthrough in Organization Development." *Harvard Business Review* November-December, 1964.

Blake, R. R., H. A. Shepard, and Jane S. Mouton. *Managing Intergroup Conflict in Industry.* Houston: Gulf Publishing, 1965.

Blau, P. *Exchange and Power.* New York: John Wiley, 1964.

Blauner, R. *Alienation and Freedom: The Manual Workers in Industry.* University of Chicago, Mimeo, 1962.

Blumberg, P. *Industrial Democracy: The Sociology of Participation.* London: Constable.

Bogdonoff, M. *et al.* The modifying effect of conforming behavior upon lipid responses accompanying C.N.S. arousal. *Clinical Research* No. 9, 1961.

Bolt, R. *A Man for All Seasons.* New York: Random House, 1966.

Bradford, L. P., J. R. Gibb, and K. Benne. *T-Group Theory and Laboratory Method.* New York: John Wiley, 1964.

Bramson, L., and G. W. Goethals (eds.). *War.* New York: Basic Books.

Bruner, J. S. *On Knowing: Essays for the Left Hand.* Cambridge: Harvard University Press, 1964.

Brzezinski, Z. "America in the Technetronic Age." *Encounter,* January 1968.

Buber, M. "Distance and Relation." Trans. by R. A. Smith in *Psychiatry,* Vol. 20, No. 2, 1957.

Buber, M. *I and Thou.* Trans. by R. G. Smith. New York: Charles Scribner's Sons, 1958.

Buber, M. *The Knowledge of Man.* Trans. by M. Friedman and R. G. Smith. New York: Horizon.

Buchanan, P. C. "Evaluating the effectiveness of laboratory training in industry." Paper read at American Management Association seminar in New York, February 1964.

Bugental, J. F. T. *The Search for Authenticity.* New York: Holt, Rinehart & Winston, 1965.

Bugental, J. F. T. (ed.). *Challenges of Humanistic Psychology.* New York: McGraw-Hill, 1967.

Buhler, Charlotte. "The Reality Principle," *American Journal of Psychotherapy* No. 4, 1954.

Bunker, D. R. "Individual Applications of Laboratory Training," *Journal of Applied Behavioral Science* Vol. 1, No. 2, 1965.

Bunker, D. R., and E. S. Kowles. "Comparison of Behavioral Changes Resulting from Human Relations Training Laboratories of Different Lengths." Harvard Business School. Mimeo, 1967.

Butterfield, H. *History and Human Relations.* London: Collins.

Camus, A. *The Plague.* Trans. by Stuart Gilbert, New York: Alfred Knopf, 1948.

Camus, A. *The Rebel. An Essay on Man in Revolt.* Trans. by Anthony Bower. New York: Vintage, 1956.

Camus, A. *The Fall.* Trans. by Justin O'Brien. New York: Alfred Knopf, 1957.
Camus, A. *Exile and the Kingdom.* New York: Vintage, 1958.
Camus, A. *Caligula and Three Other Plans.* New York: Vintage, 1958.
Camus, A. *The Stranger.* Trans. by Stuart Gilbert. New York: Vintage, 1958.
Camus, A. *Resistance, Rebellion and Death.* Trans. by Justin O'Brien. New York: The Modern Library.
Camus, A. "Neither Victims nor Executioners." Trans. by Dwight MacDonald in *Seeds of Liberation,* Paul Goodman (ed.). New York: George Braziller, 1964.
Caplan, G. *An Approach to Community Mental Health.* New York: Grune and Stratton, 1961.
Carmichael, S., and C. Hamilton. *Black Power: The Politics of Liberation in America.* New York: Vintage, 1968.
Cheek, F. E., and Maureen Rosenhaupt. "Are Sociologists Incomprehensible?" *American Journal of Sociology,* Vol. 73, No. 5, 1968.
Chein, I. "The Awareness of Self and the Structure of the Ego." *Psychological Review,* No. 51, 1944.
Chinoy, E. *Automobile Workers and the American Dream.* New York: Doubleday, 1955.
Chomsky, N. "The Menace of Liberal Scholarship." *The New York Review of Books,* January 2, 1969.
Chomsky, N. *American Power and the New Mandarins.* New York: Pantheon, 1969.
Coles, R. "Social Struggle and Weariness." *Psychiatry, 27* 1964.
Combs, A., and D. Snygg. *Individual Behavior.* New York: Harper Bros., 1961.
Cooper, D. *Psychiatry and Anti-Psychiatry.* London: Tavistock Publications, 1967.
Coser, L. (ed.). *Sociology Through Literature.* Englewood Cliffs: Prentice-Hall, 1963.
Cox Commission Report. *Crisis at Columbia.* New York: Vintage, 1968.
Cox, H. *The Secular City.* New York: Macmillan, 1965.
Coxe, L., and R. Chapman. *Billy Budd* (drama). New York: Hill & Wang, 1949.
Crowne, D. P., and D. Marlowe. *The Approval Motive.* New York: John Wiley, 1964.
Crutchfield, R. S. "Conformity and Character." *American Psychologist, 10,* 1955.
Delgado, J. "Manipulation of Behavior by Direct Stimulation of the Brain." Paper presented at Columbia University Seminars on Technology and Social Change, November, 1966. Mimeo.
Deutch, K. W. *The Nerves of Government: Models of Political Communication and Control.* New York: Free Press, 1967.
Dewey, J. *Human Nature and Conduct.* New York: Henry Holt, 1922.
Dewey, J. *The Public and its Problems.* New York: Henry Holt, 1927.
Dewey, J. *Reconstruction in Philosophy.* New York: Henry Holt, 1935.
Doress, I. "A Study of a Sampling of Boston Student Activists." Unpublished doctoral dissertation, Boston University, 1968.
Dostoevsky, F. *The Brothers Karamazov.* Trans. by Constance Garnett. New York: The Modern Library.
Draper, H. *Berkeley, the New Student Revolt.* New York: Grove Press, 1965.
Einstein, A., and L. Infield. *The Evolution of Physics.* New York: Simon and Schuster, 1967.

Eliot, T.S. *Four Quartets.* New York: Harcourt, Brace & World, 1943.
Ellul, J. *The Technological Society.* New York: Vintage, 1967.
Elms, A. C., and S. Milgram. "Personality Characteristics Associated with Obedience and Defiance Toward Authorative Commands." *Journal of Experimental Research in Personality,* Vol. 1, No. 4, 1966.
Erikson, E. H. *Childhood and Society.* New York: Norton, 1950.
Erikson, E. H. "Identity and the Life Cycle." *Psychological Issues,* Vol. 1, No. 1. New York: International Universities Press, 1959.
Erikson, E. H. *Insight and Responsibility.* New York: Norton, 1964.
Eysenck, H. J. *The Psychology of Politics.* London: Routledge and Kegan Paul, 1954.
Festinger, L. *A Theory of Cognitive Dissonance.* Evanston, Ill.: Row Peterson, 1957.
Fingarette, H. "The Ego and Mystic Selflessness." *Psychoanalytic Review,* Vol. 45, No. 1, 1958.
Fitzgerald, S. *The Crack-Up.* New York: New Directions, 1945.
Flacks, R. W. "The Liberated Generation." *Journal of Social Issues,* Vol. 23, No. 3, 1967.
Flacks, R. W., and C. Derber. "An Exploration of the Value System of Radical Student Activists and Their Parents." Youth and Social Change Project. University of Chicago, Mimeo, 1967.
Foote, N. N., and L. S. Cottrell. *Identity and Interpersonal Competence.* University of Chicago Press, 1955.
Frank, J. D. *Persuasion and Healing.* New York: Schocken, 1961.
Frank, J. D. *Sanity and Survival: Psychological Aspects of War and Peace.* New York: Vintage, 1968.
Frankl, V. *Man's Search for Meaning.* New York: Washington Square Press, 1963.
Freud, Anna. *The Ego and the Mechanisms of Defense.* London: Hogarth Press, 1961.
Freud, S. *The Problem of Anxiety.* New York: Norton, 1936.
Friedman, M. (ed.) *The Worlds of Existentialism.* New York: Harper and Row, 1963.
Friedman, M. *To Deny Our Nothingness.* New York: Delacorte Press, 1967.
Fromm, E. *Escape from Freedom.* New York: Rinehart, 1941.
Fromm, E. *Man for Himself.* New York: Holt, Rinehart & Winston, 1947.
Fromm, E. *The Sane Society.* New York: Holt, Rinehart & Winston, 1955.
Fromm, E. *The Art of Loving.* New York: Harper and Row, 1956.
Fromm, E. *The Revolution of Hope.* New York: Harper and Row, 1968.
Gagarin, N. "Non-Politics on the Battlefront," *Harvard Crimson,* April 12, 1969.
Getzels, J. W., and P. W. Jackson. *Creativity and Intelligence.* New York: John Wiley, 1962.
Gibb, J. R., and Lorraine, M. "Humanistic Elements in Group Growth" in *Challenge of Humanistic Psychology.* J. F. T. Bugental (ed.).
Gilbert, W. S. *The Mikado.* New York: Random House.
Glazer, N. See his various contributions in *The Berkeley Student Revolt.* Lipset and Wolin (eds.).
Glover, E. "Medico-psychological aspects of normality." *British Journal of Psychology,* Vol. 23, 1932.

Goffmann, E. *The Presentation of Self in Everyday Life.* New York: Doubleday, 1959.
Goldstein, K. *The Organism.* New York: American Books, 1939.
Goldstein, K. *Human Nature in the Light of Psychopathology.* Cambridge: Harvard University Press, 1940.
Goldwater, B. *The Conscience of a Conservative.* New York: McFadden, 1961.
Goodman, P. *Compulsory Mis-education.* New York: Horizon Press, 1964.
Goodman, P. (ed.). *Seeds of Liberation.* New York: George Braziller, 1964.
Goodman, W. *All Honorable Men.* Boston: Little Brown.
Gouldner, A. W. "Metaphysical Pathos and the Theory of Bureaucracy." *American Political Science Review,* Vol. 49, 1955.
Gouldner, A. W. "Anti-Minotaur: The Myth of Value-Free Sociology," in *Sociology on Trial.* Stein and Vidich (eds.).
Gracia, S. de. *The Political Community: A Study of Anomie.* University of Chicago Press, 1948.
Green, P. *Deadly Logic: The Theory of Nuclear Deterrence.* New York: Schocken Books, 1968.
Greening, T. C., and H. S. Coffey. "Working with an 'Impersonal' T-Group." *Journal of Applied Behavioral Science,* Vol. 2, No. 4, 1966.
Greiner, L. "Organization Change and Development." Unpublished doctoral dissertation, Harvard Business School, 1965. (See also Blake *et al.*, 1964.)
Grusky, O. "Authoritarianism and Effective Indoctrination," *Administrative Science Quarterly,* Vol. 31, No. 4, 1962.
Gusfield, J. R. *Symbolic Crusade.* Urbana: University of Illinois Press, 1963.
Haan, Norma, M. Brewster Smith, and Jeanne Block. "Moral Reasoning of Young Adults," *Journal of Personality and Social Psychology,* Vol. 10, No. 3, 1968.
Hacker, F. J. "The Concept of Normality and its Practical Significance." *American Journal of Orthopsychiatry,* Vol. 15, 1945.
Hampden-Turner, C. M. "An Existential Learning Theory and the Integration of T-Group Research." *Journal of Applied Behavioral Science,* Vol. 2, No. 4, 1966.
Hampden-Turner, C. M. "Black Power: A Blueprint for Psycho-Social Development?" In *Social Innovation in the Ghetto,* R. Rosenbloom and R. Maris (eds.). Cambridge: Harvard University Press, 1969.
Harlow, H. F. "The Heterosexual Affectional System in Monkeys." In *Interpersonal Dynamics,* Bennis, W., *et al.* (eds.), 1964.
Hartmann, H. "On Rational and Irrational Action," in Geza Roheim (ed.), *Psychoanalysis and the Social Sciences.* New York: International Universities Press, 1947.
Heider, F. *The Psychology of Interpersonal Relations.* New York: John Wiley, 1958.
Heist, P. "Intellect and Commitment: The faces of discontent." In *Order and Freedom on the Campus: The Rights and Responsibilities of Faculty and Students,* Knorr and Minter (eds.), 1965.
Hendrick, I. "A Discussion of the Instinct to Master." *Psychoanalytical Quarterly,* Vol. 12, 1943.
Herzberg, F., B. Mausner, and B. Snyderman. *The Motivation to Work.* New York: John Wiley, 1959.
Hess, E. H., and J. Polk. "Pupil Size as Related to Interest Value of Visual Stimuli." *Science,* Vol. 132, 1958.

Hilgard, E. R. *Theories of Learning.* London: Methuen, 1958.

Hofstadter, R. *The Paranoid Style in American Politics.* New York: Alfred Knopf, 1965.

Homans, G. C. *Social Behavior: Its Elementary Forms.* New York: Harcourt, Brace & World, 1961.

Hora, T. "The Process of Existential Psychotherapy." *Existential Inquiry,* Vol. 1, No. 1, 1959.

Harney, Karen. *Neurosis and Human Growth.* New York: Norton, 1950.

Horowitz, I. L., (ed.). *The New Sociology.* New York: Oxford University Press, 1964.

Horwitz, M. "Training in Conflict Resolution." In *T-Group Theory and Laboratory Method.* Bradford, Gibb and Benne (eds.), 1963.

Huxley, A. *The Devils of Loudon.* New York: Harper, 1959.

Jacobs, P., and S. Landau. *The New Radicals.* New York: Vintage, 1966.

Jahoda, Marie. *Current Concepts of Positive Mental Health.* New York: Basic Books, 1958.

James, W. *The Principles of Psychology.* New York: Henry Holt, 1890.

James, W. *Essays in Pragmatism.* New York: Haffner Publishing Co., 1949.

Jaspers, K. *Reason and Existence.* New York: The Noonday Press, 1955.

Jonas, H. "The Practical Uses of Theory." *Social Research,* Vol. 26, No. 2, 1959.

Jones, M. R. (ed.). *Current Theory and Research in Motivation.* University of Nebraska Press, 1954.

Josephson, E., and Mary Josephson (eds.). *Man Alone: Alienation in Modern Society.* New York: Dell Publishing, 1962.

Jourard, S. M. *The Transparent Self.* Princeton: Van Nostrand, 1964.

Jung, C. *The Integration of Personality.* New York: Farrar and Rinehart, 1939.

Jung, C. *Memories, Dreams and Reflection.* New York: Pantheon, 1963.

Kafka, F. *The Penal Colony.* New York: Schocken Books, 1945.

Kafka, F. *The Trial.* Harmondsworth, Middlesex: Penguin Books, 1954.

Kafka, F. *Metamorphosis and Other Stories.* Harmondsworth, Middlesex: Penguin Books, 1961.

Kahn, H. *On Thermonuclear War.* Princeton: Princeton University Press, 1960.

Kahn, H., and A. J. Wiener. "The Next Thirty-Three Years," in *Daedalus,* Vol. 96, No. 3, 1967.

Kahn, R., *et al. Organization Stress: Studies in Role Conflict and Ambiguity.* New York: John Wiley, 1964.

Kaplan, A. *The Conduct of Inquiry.* San Francisco: Chandler, 1964.

Kaufman, A. S. *The Radical Liberal: New Man in American Politics.* New York: Atherton.

Kaufman, W. (ed.). *Existentialism from Dostoyevski to Sartre.* New York: Meridian Books.

Kelly, G. A. *The Psychology of Personal Constructs.* New York: Norton, 1955.

Keniston, K. *The Uncommitted: Alienated Youth in American Society.* New York: Harcourt, Brace & World, 1965.

Keniston, K. *The Young Radicals: Notes on Committed Youth.* New York: Harcourt, Brace & World, 1968.

Key, V. O. "Interrelations of Opinion," in *Readings in American Political Behavior.* R. E. Wolfinger (ed.).

Kierkegaard, S. *The Concept of Dread.* Trans. by W. Lowrie. Princeton: Princeton University Press, 1944.

Kierkegaard, S. *Fear and Trembling* and *Sickness Unto Death.* Trans. by W. Lowrie. New York: Anchor Books, 1954.

Knorr, O. W., and W. J. Minter (eds.). *Order and Freedom on the Campus.* Boulder, Col.: Western Interstate Commission for Higher Education, 1965.

Koch, S. "Psychology and the Emerging Conceptions of Knowledge as Unitary." In *Behaviorism and Phenomenology.* T. W. Wann (ed.).

Koestler, A. *The Yogi and the Commissar.* New York: Macmillan, 1945.

Koestler, A. *The Act of Creation.* New York: Macmillan, 1966.

Koestler, A. *The Ghost in the Machine.* New York: Macmillan, 1968.

Kohlberg, L. "The Development of Children's Orientations toward a Moral Order: 1. Sequence in the development of moral thought." *Vita Humana,* Vol. 6, pp. 11-33; 1963.

Kohlberg, L. "Moral and Religious Education and the Public Schools: A Developmental View." In *Religion and Public Education.* T. Sizer (ed.). Boston: Houghton Mifflin, 1967.

Kohlberg, L. "Education for Justice: A Modern Statement of the Platonic View." Ernest Burton Lecture at Harvard University, 1968. (School of Education, Mimeo.)

Kohlberg, L. "Stage and Sequence: The Cognitive-Developmental Approach to Socialization." In *Handbook of Socialization Theory and Research,* David A. Croslin (ed.). New York: Rand McNally, 1969.

Kohlberg, L. *Stages in the Development of Moral Thought and Action.* New York: Holt, Rinehart & Winston (in press).

Kohler, W. *The Mentality of Apes.* Harmondsworth, Middlesex: Pelican Books, 1957.

Kolakowski, L. *Towards a Marxist Humanism.* New York: Grove Press, 1968.

Kopkind, A. "The New Left: Chicago and After." *The New York Review of Books,* September 28, 1968.

Kornhauser, A. *Mental Health of the Industrial Worker.* New York: John Wiley, 1965.

Kozol, J. *Death at an Early Age.* New York: Bantam Books, 1968.

Krech, D., R. S. Crutchfield, and E. L. Ballachey. *Individual in Society.* New York: McGraw-Hill, 1962.

Kunen, S. *The Strawberry Statement: Notes of a College Revolutionary.* New York: Random House, 1969.

Laing, R. D. *The Self and Others.* London: Tavistock Press, 1961.

Laing, R. D. *The Divided Self.* Baltimore: Penguin, 1965.

Laing, R. D. *The Politics of Experience.* New York: Pantheon, 1967.

Laing, R. D., and D. G. Cooper. *Reason and Violence: A Decade of Sartre's Philosophy.* London: Tavistock Press, 1964.

Laslett, P. "The Sovereignty of the Family." *The Listener.* April, 1960.

Lasswell, H. *Politics: Who Gets What, When, How.* New York: Meridian Books, 1958.

Lawrence, P. R. *et al. Organization Behavior and Administration: Cases, Concepts and Research Findings.* Homewood: Irwin and Dorsey, 1965.

Lawrence, P. R., and J. W. Lorsch. *Organization and Environment.* Boston: Harvard Business School, Division of Research, 1967.

Leach, E. *Runaway World?* (The Reith Lectures). London: British Broadcasting Company, 1968.

Lecky, P. *Self-Consistency–A Theory of Personality.* New York: Island Press, 1945.

Lesieur, F. G. (ed.). *The Scanlon Plan.* Cambridge: M.I.T. Press, 1958.
Lessing, Doris. "Each His Own Wilderness." *New English Dramatists.* Harmondsworth, Middlesex: Penguin Books, 1959.
Levinson, D. "The Authoritarian Personality and Foreign Policy." *Journal of Conflict Resolution,* Vol. 1, 1957.
Lewin, K. *Field Theory in Social Science.* New York: Harper, 1951.
Lewin, L. C. *Report from Iron Mountain on the Possibility and Desirability of Peace.* New York: Dial Press, 1967.
Lewis, S. *Babbitt.* New York: Signet Classic, 1961.
Lipset, S. M. *Political Man.* New York: Anchor Books, 1963.
Lipset, S. M. "Three Decades of the Radical Right." In *The Radical Right,* Daniel Bell (ed.), 1964.
Lipset, S.M., and S.S. Wolin (eds.). *The Berkeley Student Revolt.* New York: Anchor Books, 1965
Lipsitz, L. "Mass Production and Political Attitudes." Unpublished Ph.D. thesis, Yale University, 1963.
Lohmann, K., *et al.* "Some Perceptual Changes During Sensitivity Training." *Journal of Educational Research,* Vol. 53, 1959.
Louch, A.R. *Explanation and Human Action.* Berkeley: University of California Press.
Lynd, Alice. *We Won't Go.* Boston: Beacon Press, 1968.
Lynd, Helen M. *On Shame and the Search for Identity.* New York: Harcourt, Brace & World, 1958.
Lyons, G. "The Police Car Demonstration: A Survey of Participants." In *The Berkeley Student Revolt,* Lipset and Wolin (eds.), 1965.
Machlup, F. "Are the Social Sciences Really Inferior?" In *Philospohy of the Social Sciences,* M. Natanson (ed.), 1965.
MacKinnon, D.W. "Fostering Creativity in Students of Engineering." *Journal of Engineering Education,* Vol. 52, No. 3.
MacKinnon, D.W. "The Highly Effective Individual." In *Explorations in Creativity.* Mooney and Razik (eds.), 1967.
Maddi, S.R. *Personality Theories.* Homewood, Ill.: The Dorsey Press, 1968.
Magee, B. *The New Radicalism.* New York: St. Martin's Press, 1962.
Mailer, N. *The Armies of the Night.* New York: New American Library, 1968.
Mann, J., and H. Otto (eds.). *Ways of Growth.* New York: Richard S. Grossman, 1968.
Marcuse, H. *One Dimensional Man.* Boston: Beacon Press, 1964.
Maritain, J. *Existence and the Existent.* New York: Doubleday, 1956.
Martin, J.C. *The Tolerant Personality.* Detroit: Wayne State University Press, 1964.
Maslow, A.H. "The Authoritarian Character Structure." *Journal of Social Psychology,* Vol. 18, 1943.
Maslow, A.H. *Motivation and Personality.* New York: Harper, 1954.
Maslow, A.H. *Toward a Psychology of Being.* Princeton: Van Nostrand, 1962.
Maslow, A.H. "Synergy in Society and the Individual." *Journal of Individual Psychology,* Vol. 20, 1964.
Maslow, A.H. *Eupsychian Management.* Homewood, Ill.: Irwin-Dorsey, 1965.
Maslow, A.H. *The Psychology of Science.* New York: Harper, 1966.
Matson, F.W. *The Broken Image.* New York: George Braziller, 1964.
Matson, F.W., and A. Montague (eds.). *The Human Dialogue.* New York: Free Press, 1967.

May, R. *Existential Psychology.* New York: Random House, 1961.
May, R. (ed.). *Existence: A New Dimension in Psychiatry and Pscyhology.* New York: Clarion Books, 1967.
McClelland, D.C. *The Achieving Society.* Princeton: Van Nostrand, 1961.
McClosky, H. "Conservatism and Personality." *American Political Science Review,* Vol. 42, 1958.
McClosky, H., and J. Schaar. "Psychological Dimensions of Anomy." *American Sociological Review.*
McDermott, J. "Intellectuals and Technology." *The New York Review of Books,* July 31, 1969.
McGregor, D. "The Scanlon Plan Through a Psychologist's Eyes." In *The Scanlon Plan.* F. Lesieur (ed.), 1958.
McGregor, D. *The Human Side of Enterprise.* New York: McGraw-Hill, 1960.
Mead, A. H. *Mind, Self and Society.* University of Chicago, 1934.
Melman, S., and R. Falk (eds.). *In the Name of America.* Published by Clergy and Laymen Concerned about Vietnam. Distributed by E. P. Dutton, New York, 1968.
Merton, R.K. *Social Theory and Social Structure.* Glencoe: Free Press, 1949.
Mesthene, E.G. "Man and His Tools." Address to Grinnell College. Harvard University Program on Technology and Society, Mimeo.
Mesthene, E.A. "How Technology Will Shape the Future." *Science,* Vol. 161, July 12, 1968.
Miles, M. "Human Relations Training: Processes and Outcomes." *Journal of Counseling Psychology,* Vol. 7, 1960.
Milgram, S. "Behavioral Study of Obedience." *Journal of Abnormal and Social Psychology,* Vol. 67, No. 4, 1963.
Milgram, S. "Some Conditions of Obedience and Disobedience to Authority." *Human Relations,* Vol. 18, 1965.
Mill, J.S. *Autobiography.* New York: Oxford University Press, 1924.
Mill, J.S. *On Liberty.* London: G.A. Watts, 1946.
Miller, G.A. "Some Psychological Perspectives on the Year 2,000." *Daedalus,* Vol. 96, No. 3, 1967.
Mills, C. W. *The Sociological Imagination.* New York: Grove Press, 1961.
Mooney, R., and T. Razik (eds.). *Explorations in Creativity.* New York: Harper and Row, 1967.
Moreno, J.L. "The Dilemma of Existentialism, Daseinanalysis and Psychodrama, with Special Emphasis on Existential Validation." *International Journal of Sociometry and Sociatry,* Vol. 1, No. 1, 1956.
Morton, R.B. "The Uses of the Laboratory Method in a Psychiatric Hospital." In *Personal and Organizational Change Through Group Methods,* Shein and Bennis (eds.), 1965.
Murphy, G. *Human Potentialities.* New York: Basic Books, 1958.
Natanson, M. (ed.). *Philosophy of the Social Sciences.* New York: Random House, 1963.
Neumann, F. *The Democratic and the Authoritarian State.* Glencoe: The Free Press, 1957.
Nietzsche, F. *Thus Spake Zarathustra.* New York: The Modern Library.
Newfield, J. *A Prophetic Minority.* New York: Signet Books.
Olson, R. *An Introduction to Existentialism.* New York: Dover Press, 1962.
Osborn, R. *The Vulgarians.* Greenwich Conn.: The New York Graphic Society.

Osborne, J. *Inadmissable Evidence.* London: Faber & Faber, 1965.
Osgood, A., and H. Tannenbaum. "The Principle of Congruity in the Prediction of Attitude Change." *Psychological Review,* Vol. 62, 1955.
Parkin, F. *Middle Class Radicalism.* New York: Frederick A. Praeger, 1968.
Parnes, S. J., and H. F. Harding. *A Source Book for Creative Thinking.* New York: Charles Scribner's Sons, 1962.
Paulus, A. "A Multivariate Analysis Study of Student Activist Leaders. Student Government Leaders, and Non-Activists." Cited in "The Student Left in Higher Education," by R.E. Peterson. *Daedalus,* Vol. 97, No. 1.
Pepitone, Albert. *Attraction and Hostility.* New York: Atherton Press, 1966.
Perry, R.B. *General Theory of Value.* New York: Longman's Green, 1926.
Perry, R.B. *Realms of Value.* Cambridge: Harvard University Press, 1954.
Peterson, R.E. "The Student Left in American Higher Education." *Daedalus,* Vol. 97, No. 1, 1968.
Piaget, J. *The Moral Judgment of the Child.* London: Kegan Paul, 1932.
Polyani, M. *Personal Knowledge.* New York: Harper Torchbook, 1964.
Rainwater, L., and W.L. Yancey. *The Moynihan Report and the Politics of Controversy.* Cambridge: M.I.T. Press, 1967.
Rank, O. *The Trauma of Birth.* New York: Harcourt, Brace & World, 1929.
Rapoport, A. *Strategy and Conscience.* New York: Harper & Row, 1964.
Regan, Mary C. "Personality Characteristics of Students and Faculty in the College of Engineering." Davis: University of California. Mimeo, 1967.
Rest, J.R. "Developmental Hierarchies of Comprehension and Preference in Moral Thinking." Paper read at the meeting of the Society for Research in Child Development at Santa Monica, California, March, 1969.
Rest, J.R., E. Turiel, and L. Kohlberg. "Level of Moral Development as a Determinant of Preference and Comprehension of Moral Judgments made by Others." Harvard School of Education. Mimeo, no date.
Riesman, D. *The Lonely Crowd.* New Haven: Yale University Press, 1950.
Robinson, J. *Honest to God.* London: S.C.M. Press, 1963.
Roethlisberger, F., and J. Dickson. *Management and the Worker.* Cambridge: Harvard University Press, 1939.
Rokeach, M. *The Open and Closed Mind.* New York: Basic Books, 1960.
Rogers, C.R. *On Becoming a Person.* Boston: Houghton-Mifflin, 1961.
Rogers, C.R. "Toward a Modern Approach to Values." *Journal of Abnormal and Social Psychology,* Vol. 68, No. 2, 1961.
Rogers, C.R. "The Process of the Basic Encounter Group." LaJolla: Western Behavioral Sciences Institute, 1966.
Rogers, C.R., W.L. Knell, and Helen McNeil. "The Role of Self Understanding in the Prediction of Behavior." In *The Self in Growth, Teaching and Learning,* Don E. Hamachek (ed.). Englewood Cliffs: Prentice-Hall, 1965.
Rosenberg, M. *Occupations and Values.* Glencoe: Free Press, 1957.
Rosenberg, M. *Society and the Adolescent Self-Image.* Princeton: Princeton University Press, 1965.
Rosenthal, R., and Lenore F. Jacobson. "Teacher Expectations of the Disadvantaged." *Scientific American,* Vol. 218, No. 4, 1968.
Rosenthal, R., and Lenore F. Jacobson. *Pygmalion in the Classroom.* New York: Holt, Rinehart & Winston, 1969.
Roszak, T. (ed.). *The Dissenting Academy.* New York: Pantheon, 1968.
Royce, J. *The Encapsulated Man.* Princeton: Van Nostrand, 1964.

Rubin, I. "The Reduction of Prejudice Through Laboratory Training." *Journal of Applied Behaviorial Science.*
Ruskin, J. *Unto This Last.* J.D.C. Monfries and G.E. Hollingsworth (eds.). London: University Tutorial Press.
Sampson, E.E. (ed.). *Stirrings Out of Apathy.* Special issue of the *Journal of Social Issues,* Vol. 23, No. 3, 1967.
Sanford, M. (ed.). *The American College.* New York: John Wiley, 1962.
Sargent, S.S. "Humanistic Methodology in Personality and Social Psychology." In *Challenges of Humanistic Psychology,* J.F.T. Bugental (ed.), 1967.
Sartre, J.P. *No Exit and Three Other Plays.* New York: Vintage Books, 1955.
Sartre, J.P. "Portrait of an Anti-Semite." In *Existentialism from Dostoyevsky to Sartre.* Walter Kaufmann, (ed.), 1956.
Sartre, J.P. *Existential Psychoanalysis.* Chicago: Regnery, 1962.
Schachtel, E.G. "On Alienated Concepts of Identity." *American Journal of Psychoanalysis,* November, 1961.
Schein, E.H., and W. Bennis. *Personal and Organizational Change Through Group Methods.* New York: John Wiley, 1965.
Schiff, L.E. "The Obedient Rebels: A Study of College Conversions to Conservatism." Journal of Social Issues, Vol. 20, No. 4, 1964.
Schneir, W. (ed.). *Telling it Like it Was. The Chicago Riots.* New York: New American Library, 1969.
Schutz, A. "Concepts, Constructs and Theory Formation." *Journal of Philosophy,* April, 1959.
Schutz, W.C. *Joy.* New York: Grove Press, 1968.
Schutz, W.C., and V. Allen. "The Effects of a T-Group Laboratory on Interpersonal Behavior." *Journal of Applied Behaviorial Science,* Vol. 2, No. 2, 1966.
Seeley, J.R. "Social Science? Some Probative Problems." In *Sociology on Trial,* M. Stein and A. Vidich (eds.), 1963.
Seeley, J.R. *The Americanization of the Unconscious.* New York: Science Books.
Seeman, M. "On the Meaning of Alienation." *American Sociological Review,* Vol. 26, No. 6, 1959.
Selvin, H.C., and W.O. Hagstrom. "Determinants of Support for Civil Liberties." In *The Berkeley Student Revolt,* S.M. Lipset and S.S. Wolin (eds.), 1965.
Shaw, G.B. *Saint Joan.* Maryland: Penguin, 1963.
Shaw, G.B. *Back to Methusulah.* Harmondsworth, Middlesex: Penguin Books, 1961.
Silberman, C.E. *Crisis in Black and White.* New York: Vintage Books, 1964.
Silone, I. *The Seed Beneath the Snow.* Trans. by Frances Frenaye. New York: Harper Bros.
Simmons, J.L. "Tolerance for Divergent Attitudes." *Social Forces,* Vol. 43, No. 3.
Skinner, B.F. *Science and Human Behavior.* New York: Macmillan, 1953.
Skinner, B.F. "Behaviorism at Fifty." In *Behaviorism and Phenomenology,* T.W. Wann (ed.). University of Chicago Press, 1964.
Slater, P.E. *Microcosm.* New York: John Wiley, 1966.
Smith, D. *Conservatism: A Guide to its Past, Present and Future.* New York: The Hearst Corporation, 1963.

Smith, H.P., and Ellen W. Rosen. "Some Psychological Correlates of World-Mindedness and Authoritarianism." *Journal of Personality,* Vol. 26, 1958.
Smith, M.B., J.S. Bruner, and R.W. White. *Opinions and Personality.* New York: John Wiley, 1960.
Solomon, F., and J.R. Fishman. "Youth and Peace: A Psychosocial Study of Student Peace Demonstration in Washington, D.C. *Journal of Social Issues,* Vol. 20, No. 4, 1964.
Somers, R.H. "The Mainsprings of the Rebellion." In *The Berkeley Student Revolt,* S.M. Lipset and S.S. Wolin (eds.), 1965.
Spender, S. *The Year of the Young Rebels.* New York: Vintage Books, 1969.
Stark, R., and C.Y. Glock. "Will Ethics be the Death of Christianity?" *Transaction,* June, 1968.
Steele, F.I. "Personality and 'Laboratory Style' " *Journal of Applied Behavioral Science,* Vol. 4, No. 1.
Stein, M., A.J. Vidich, and D.M. White. *Identity and Anxiety.* Glencoe: Free Press, 1960.
Stein, M., and A.J. Vidich. *Sociology on Trial.* Englewood Cliffs: Prentice-Hall, 1963.
Stouffer, S. *Communism, Conformity and Civil Liberties.* New York: Doubleday, 1955.
Sullivan, H.S. *The Interpersonal Theory of Psychiatry.* New York: Norton, 1953.
Taguiri, R., and L. Petrullo (eds.). *Person, Perception and Interpersonal Behavior.* Palo Alto: Stanford University Press, 1958.
Taylor, C.W. "A Tentative Description of the Creative Individual." In *A Source Book of Creative Thinking,* S.J. Parnes and H.F. Harding (eds.).
Teilard de Chardin. *The Phenomenon of Man.* New York: Harper, 1959.
Terman, L.M. *Concept Mastery: Test Manual.* New York: Psychological Corporation, 1956.
Thomas, D. *The Collected Poems of Dylan Thomas.* New York: New Directions.
Tillich, P. *The Courage to Be.* New Haven: Yale University Press, 1959.
Tillich, P. *The Shaking of the Foundations.* Harmondsworth, Middlesex: Penguin Books, 1962.
Tiryakian, E.A. *Sociologism and Existentialism.* Englewood Cliffs: Prentice Hall, 1962.
Tomkins, S. "Left and Right: A Basic Dimensions of Ideology and Personality." In *The Study of Lives,* R.W. White (ed.), 1963.
Trent, J.W., and Judith L. Craise. "Commitment and Conformity in the American College." *Journal of Social Issues,* Vol. 23, No. 3, 1967.
Trow, M. "Some Implications of the Social Origins of Engineers." Paper read at annual meeting of American Association for the Advancement of Science, December, 1958.
Valiquet, M.I. "Contribution to the Evaluation of a Management Training Program." Unpublished doctoral dissertation, Massachusetts Institute of Technology, 1964.
Verba, S. *Small Groups and Political Behavior.* Princeton: Princeton University Press, 1961.
Vidler, A.R. (ed.). *Soundings: Essays Concerning Christian Understanding.* Cambridge University Press, 1963.

Vispo, R.H. "On Human Maturity." *Perspectives in Biology and Medicine,* Vol. 9, No. 4.

Wann, T.W. (ed.). *Behaviorism and Phenomenology.* University of Chicago Press, 1964.

Watson, J. *Behaviorism.* New York: Norton, 1924.

Watts, A.W. *The Two Hands of God: The Myths of Polarity.* New York: Collier, 1969.

Watts, W.A., and D. Whittaker. "Some Socio-psychological differences between highly committed members of the Free Speech Movement and the student population at Berkeley." *Journal of Applied Behavioral Science,* Vol. 2, 1966.

Webster, H., M. Freeman, and P. Heist. "Personality Changes in College Students." In *The American College,* N. Sanford (ed.), 1962.

Wesker, A. *The Kitchen* (a play). London: Jonathan Cape, 1961.

Westby, D., and R. Braungart. "Class and Politics in the Family Backgrounds of Student Political Acitivists." *American Sociological Review,* Vol. 31, 1966.

White, R.W. "Motivation Reconsidered: The Concept of Competence." *Psychological Review,* Vol. 66, 1959.

White, R.W. *Lives in Progress.* New York: Holt, Rinehart & Winston, 1961.

White, R.W. (ed.). *The Study of Lives. Essays in Honor of Henry J. Murray.* New York: Atherton Press, 1964.

Whyte, W.H. *The Organization Man.* New York: Simon and Schuster, 1956.

Wild, J. *Existence and the World of Freedom.* Englewood Cliffs: Prentice Hall, 1963.

Williams, H. "Theology and Self-Awareness." In *Soundings: Essays Concerning Christian Understanding,* A.R. Vidler (ed.), 1963.

Wilson, C. *Introduction to the New Existentialism.* Boston: Houghton Mifflin, 1967.

Windborn, B.B., and D.G. Jansen. "Personality Characteristics of Campus Leaders." *Journal of Counseling Psychology,* Vol. 14, No. 6, 1967.

Winthrop, H. "Cultural Determinants of Psychological Research Values." In *Journal of Social Psychology,* Vol. 53, 1961.

Wishner, J. "A Concept of Efficiency in Psychological Health and Psychopathology." *Psychological Review,* Vol. 62, No. 1, 1955.

Wolff, K.H. "Surrender and Religion." *Journal for the Scientific Study of Religion,* Fall, 1962.

Wolfinger, R.E. (ed.). *Readings in American Political Behavior.* Englewood Cliffs: Prentice Hall, 1966.

Wolin, S.S., and J.W. Schaar. "The Abuses of a Multi-University." In *The Berkeley Student Revolt,* S.M. Lipset and S.S. Wolin (eds.), 1965.

Wright, R. *Black Boy.* New York: Harper & Row, 1945.

Yankelovich, D. "What They Believe." *Youth in Turmoil,* by the editors of Fortune Magazine. New York: Time-Life Books, 1969.

Zaleznik, A., and D. Moment. *The Dynamics of Interpersonal Behavior.* New York: John Wiley, 1964.

Zinn, H. *S.N.C.C. The New Abolitionists.* Boston: Beacon Press, 1965.

Zinn, H. *Democracy and Disobedience.* New York: Vintage Books, 1968.

# SUBJECT INDEX


A.B.M. (Anti-Ballistic Missile System), 282, 286, 289
Abstracted idols, 79, 141, 150, 159
Abstraction, 7, 79, 88, 141, 163, 178, 274
Absurd, The, 86, 97, 157
    encounter with, 86, 157-160, 186, 378
Absurdity, 22, 37, 39, 47, 53
    rebellion against, 103, 107, 158
Abyss, 50, 74, 86, 392
Academic quality and protest, 354
Achievement, need for (Scale), 133
    and personality modification, 322
Achievement via Independence (Scale), 242-43, 352
Activisim, high/medium/low/non, 238-63, 356-57
    and British C.N.D., 119-120
    and scholastic performance, 265, 354, 374-75, 384
Administration, college and mediocrity, 374
    satisfaction with (Scale), 373, 375
    popular with less liberal students, 384
Administrators, college, 374-75
    in a moral dilemma, 140
    and anxiety, 388
Aesthetic (see Estheticism)
Affect (See Emotion)
A.F.M. (All Four Models)
    includes:
    M.P.D. (Model of Psycho-social Development), 31f, 102, 155
    M.A.C. (Model of Anomic Cycle), 68f, 209-11
    M.F.S. (Model of Formal System Structures), 128-29
    M.R.C. (Model of Radical-Conservative Dimension), 230-31, 304f
Aggression (see Hostility and Violence)
Alienation, 74, 142, 253
    (Scale), 71, 72, 78, 84, 226, 236
Aloneness, Belief in Man's (Scale), 244-45, 350, 352
Altruism (Scale), 15, 339
Ambition and Aspiration (Scale), 133
Ambiguity, Intolerance of, 13
    (Scale), 70, 74, 103, 226
"Americanism," 79, 248, 280 (See also Patriotism)
Americans for Democratic Action, 285-88
Analogies, economic, 246-47
    (See M.R.C.) Mechanistic, 383
Anomic Cycle, 68
Anomic persons, defined, 67-69, 79, 81
    in industry, 140-41, 145
    in T-Groups, 159, 172-73
Anomie, 67-93
    (Scale), 67, 70-72, 73, 81, 84, 142, 145-47, 156, 365
    manager as healer of, 207-14
    of right and left, 226-27, 233, 235-36
    and seniority, 365
Anti-Ballistic (See A.B.M.)

Anti-Communism, 248, 252, 255
(See also Communist "menace" etc.)
Anti-Intraception, 75, 109, 239, 372
Anti-Semitism, 85
(Scale), 70, 73, 78, 84
Antithesis (see Thesis)
Anxiety, existential (see also SUSPENSION), 106-07, 136, 207, 393
in academia, 316
among college administrators, 388
experienced anxiety (Scale), 338
and openness to experience, 385
in conflict situations, 275-76
reduced by violence, 280
tolerance for, 208, 212
(Scale), 385
Aquiescence, 77, 81, 242, 365
(Scale), 70, 72, 73, 78, 84, 140, 226, 365
Asch technique, 97, 101-13
Astronauts, 317
Autonomy, 44, 131
(Scale), 338-40
(see also existence and Freedom)
Authenticity, defined, 45
(See A.F.M.)
Authoritarian Belief in Great Cause (Scale), 258-59
Authoritarian Conformance, 115
(Scale), 242, 259
Authoritarianism, 74, 112, 116
(Scale), 70-78, 84, 86, 136, 145-47, 227, 353, 365
and anomie, 88-91, 207, 209-11
and conservatism, 226-27, 258-60
and counterfeit development, 260-61
and engineering students, 336-38
Non-authoritarianism (Scale), 365
and seniority, 365
Authority(ies), 86, 105, 107, 108, 118
(See also M.R.C. segment g)
Balance, among faculties, 58
as justice, 57, 392
as synergistic integration, 57-61, 256
(see also M.P.D.)
Basic Drives, 20-21
Basic Encounter Group, 157
Behaviorism, 9, 19-26, 105
Being-for-itself and in-itself, 53, 161-62
Belief in Man's Aloneness (see Aloneness)
Belief system, isolation and non-communication within, 264-65, 353
rejection on the basis of, 249-50
Bewilderment (Scale), 71, 93, 253
Billy Budd, 136-40, 151
Black Americans, 45, 50, 89, 90, 130, 172
Black Power, 45
Bomb, The, 120
"clean bomb," 186, 188, 265
(see also Nuclear)

Boston University Study, 233-64, 275, 349-52
BRIDGING THE DISTANCE, defined, 48-50
(See A.F.M.)
British Campaign for Nuclear Disarmament, 116, 118-19
Business Administration Students, 133, 174, 253, 368-70
Business Attitudes (Scale), 133
California F. Scale, 221
(See Authoritarianism)
Calvinism (Scale), 70, 72, 78, 84-85, 91, 226
Campaigns for Nuclear Disarmament (See British and SANE)
Cartesian dichotomy, 26-27
Chaos, 107
(See also Absurdity)
Chauvinism, 85, 91, 244, 365
(Scale), 70, 72, 78, 84, 140, 226, 365
Christ, 48, 68, 104, 107
Civil Libertarianism (See Libertarianism)
Classical Conservatism, 233
Cognitive consistency, Theories of, 65, 202
Columbia University, 15, 91-92, 380-81
Committment, 43, 49, 359
(See also Anti-Communism)
Communism, 74, 172, 232
Communist "conspiracy," 92, 248, 255
"menace," 252, 255, 367
Communist students, 221, 224, 233-38
Companies, automobile, 146-47
chemical and container, 142-44
engineering, 148-49
Scanlon, 205-06
simple v. complex and high performing v. low, 142-46
(See also Organizations)
COMPETENCE, defined, 43-45
(See A.F.M.)
Competition, as a game, 329-30, 364
as non-synergistic, 176-77, 331-32
and scarcity, 364
as a win-lose-compromise dilemma, 321
Complex v. simple environments, 141-49
COMPLEXITY, defined, 56, 59-60
(See A.F.M.)
Complexity (Scales), 336-40, 357, 365
behavioral v. technological, 142
Compulsive-obsessive characteristics, 8, 77
(Scale), 70, 72, 78, 84
Computer, as a closed mind, 322
and creative workers, 195
and freedom to learn, 321, 330
Concentrations (see Students by different concentration)
Concept Mastery Test (see Terman's C.M.T.)
Conceptual Development (Scale), 122
Concern with People, and Productivity (Scales), 168-70
Conflict, and the cross, 48
and the "cross-over effect," 275-76
between "inner" and "outer cycles," 137-38
and win-lose conflict, 175-78

within and between persons, 48, 55, 254, 262
(See also Competition, Dialectic and Domination/Submission)
Conformity, 4
in experiments, 97-118, 140-41
and T-Groups, 157-58
and strategic deterrence, 332
and war, 321
(See also Aquiescence, Conventionality, Obedience and Party-Lining)
Confrontation, 144, 161-63, 186, 194
in student rebellion, 378-79, 393
(See also Dialectic)
Congress, Houses of, 79, 80, 281-95
Conscience, 45, 106, 116, 137, 152
constituency of, 123
and principle orientation (See M.M.J. stage 6)
Social Conscience (Scale), 375-76
and student revolt, 381
Consensus, false, 97-8
politics
Conservative church members, 252
Conservative formal systems, 134-35
Conservative Man, 13-14, 94, 174, 195
as the better prophet, 273
and technological thinking, 303-35
Conservative-Radical dichotomy (See M.R.C.)
Conservative Rejection of Existence (Scale), 233-36, 240-53
Conservative Students, 179, 233-64
Conservatism, 13
(Scales), 70, 72, 78, 84, 226, 235
and authoritarianism, 226-27, 258-60
in different disciplines, 229-30, 336
and Left wing pathologies, 269-73
and seniority, 365
and socializing children, 272-73
and votes in Congress, 281-95
(See Classical Conservatism, Situational Conservatism)
Consistency (See Cognitive Consistency)
"Conspiracies," communist, 92, 248, 255
Jesuit, Zionist, etc., 69-70
of Power Elite, 393
Contempt for Human Frailty (Scale), 70, 72, 78, 83, 85, 226-27, 236, 249
Contempt for Human Weakness (Scale), 70, 73, 78, 86, 91
Contradiction, 37-38, 55, 58, 103-04
and conservative ideology, 265
and non-integration of beliefs (Scale), 263-64
and technological thinking, 334-35
in universities, 382
Contrast (see counterfeits of)
Conventionality (Scale), 69-70, 72, 78, 84, 140, 226-27, 255, 365
Cooperation (See Participation, SYNERGY)
Corporate Cycle, 128
Corporation, 132, 135, 142-51
(See also Company and Organizations)
Counselling Program, 188, 192
Counterfeits, of creativity, 261
of contrast, 260
of radicalism, 275

Creative persons, 37-39, 52-53, 112, 114, 119, 179, 331
who are: leaders, 377-78
students, 354-55, 374, 384
workers, 195-200
writers, 48-49, 112, 119, 340-41
Creativity, 19-28, 35, 48-50, 69
in corporations, 145, 148-49
counterfeits of, 260-61
and SANE, 354-55
and stormy dialectic, 375
Cultural Sophistication (Scale), 373, 375
Custodial Liberalism (seeLiberalism)
Death, 22, 47-48, 244, 260, 261
death fear, 160
(See also SUSPENDING)
Democracy, 295-300
participatory, 359, 383
Dependency (Scale), 71, 91
Description v. prescription, 12, 183
Detachment, from self, 5-6
from self-concern, 27-28
and flexibility-rigidity, 385-86
(See also SUSPENDING)
Determinism, 25-26
"soft," 315, 318
Development (See A.F.M. and M.M.J.)
Developmental environments, 142-44
Dialectic, defined, 53, 57-58
(See A.F.M.)
Dialogue, 23, 50, 57, 79, 85
versus napalm and rightsticks, 90
as a non-game, 320
radical-conservative, 273
and tears over Viet Nam, 386, 393
Dichotomies, false, 60, 199, 262, 393
between Radicalism and Conservatism (See M.R.C.)
unreconciled, 261
(See Opposites)
Differentiation and integration, 34, 129, 143-44, 368, 371
DisINTEGRATION, defined, 93-95
(See M.A.C.)
Disorganization (Sclae), 71, 93
Dissent, 97-101
Dissenters, 111-115, 118
(See also Students: by type)
DISTANCE (See BRIDGING THE . . . )
Dizziness of Freedom, 47, 159
Dogmatic Left, and Developmental Left, 274-277
and Dogmatic Right , 220-25, 304
Dogmatism, 112, 220-29
(Scale), 221, 224, 233
and subsections of Scale, 233-34, 258, 263
and emotional excitement, 384-87
and opinionation, 221
Domination/Submission (See M.A.C. segment h)

Double-bind, 80-81, 94, 97
Double-heli (cycle) model, 32-33, 109, 128, 130
(See also M.P.D.)
Draft resisters, 261
DyinGartist, 52
Economic analogies, 246-47
(See M.R.C. segment e)
Education (Scale), 71, 73, 78, 84, 93, 227
Ego-control v. Anxiety (Scale), 122
Ego-strength, 43, 112, 354
(Scale), 49, 355
Electric shock, 98-100, 279
Elitism, 74, 90, 135, 365
(Scale), 70, 72, 78, 84, 91, 226
and rebel students, 384-85
and risk reduction, 79-80, 159, 244
Emotion, 13
and dogmatism, 384-86
subordinated to reason, 333-35
and strategic deterrence, 323-26
(See also Feeling and Intensity)
Empathy, 35, 111, 271-72
Encounter with the Absurd (see Absurd)
End of history, 329, 334
End of ideology, 314
Ends (see Means)
Engineering students, 174, 253, 335-37, 369-70
(See also students by concentration)
Engineering Companies (see Companies)
Estheticism, 50, 133, 336
(Scale), 338, 356-58
Ethnocentrism, 50, 65
(Scale), 70, 72, 78, 84, 226, 365
and anomie, 85, 87, 91
and obedience, 116
and symbols of discrepant belief, 248-49
Existence, 19, 90, 103
failure of, 67-69
Rejection of (Scale), 233-36
Existential anxiety, 36, 47, 106-07, 136, 260, 393
Existential despair, 352, 360, 361, 363
Existential leap, 50, 111, 260
Existential nothingness, 50, 157-60
(see also Nothingness)
Existential philosophy, 22, 25-26, 356, 358
Existentiality (Scale), 233, 234, 351
Exists freely, man, 19, 23, 34, 37
(See also M.P.D., M.R.C., and Rebel)
Expansion of consciousness, 23, 36
of pupils, 12-13
Experimentation and manipulation, 3-10, 97-117, 183
in life style, 163-64, 188
Exploring capacities, 19-20
Faith-in-People, 44, 81
(Scale), 48, 70, 336
(See also Trust)

Fear of Compromise (Scale), 256-57, 353
Feeling Reactivity (Scale), 237-39, 351
FEEDBACK, defined, 56, 59-61
    (See A.F.M.)
Feedback loop, 131, 201, 213-15
Fires, image and choice of two, 160, 392-94
Flag, 79, 158, 252
Flexibility, 107, 156
    (Scales), 48, 49, 62, 245
    and anxiety in radicals, 244-45, 275-76, 352, 360
    and emotional outbursts, 385-86
    (See also Inflexibility and SUSPENSION)
Formal system (See M.F.S.)
Free Speech Movement, 15, 380, 384
    and Moral Judgment, 40, 271-72, 336-38
Freedom, 25-27, 43, 61
    and computers, 321-22, 330
    dizziness of, 47, 159
    in radical-conservative rhetoric, 242-43
    and technological games, 321-22, 334-35
    and universalism, 330
    within the law, 25-26
    world of, 26
    (See also Autonomy and Exists Freely)
Futility, Sense of (Scale), 71, 88
Futurology, 304-05, 311-14
Game, of dating, 350-53
    designers and players, 331
    how you played the, 320
    Prisoners Dilemma and Zero-sum, 12-13, 306
    technology as a, 319
    and war, 12, 306
Games, and rationality, 320
    Rebels refusal to play, 350, 353
    strategic and racist, 324
Goals, sanctioned by authority (See M.R.C. segment g)
God, alleged access to, 80
    deciding against, 69
    hath joined together, 11
    in man v. above man, 252
    waiting for, 39
    word of, 48
Group (small) climate of, 160, 188, 194, 379
Group confrontation, 161, 186, 378
    (See also Training Group synonyms)
Group cycles, 124-25
Guilt, 76, 240
    (Scale), 70, 72, 76, 78, 84, 226, 235
Hawthorne Experiment, 184-92, 378, 382
Hell, 86, 161
    descent into, 48
    fire, 50
    is other people, 162
Heroism of Vulnerability, 325-26
Hierarchy, 13, 87
    in corporations, 141-42, 144-45

(See also M.F.S. segment c)
disliked by radicals, 384
inside and outside the mind, 92, 261-65, 334
used to settle conflict, 178, 212
Holons, 56, 61
Hostility, 91, 227, 236
(Scale), 89
(See also Authoritarianism and Violence)
House Un-American Activities Committee, 79-80, 248, 293-94
Houses of Congress, 281-95
Humanism, 148, 273, 356, 358
Humanistic liberals, 292-95
Humanitarianism, 133
(Scale), 356-57
"Humpty-Dumpty Dilemma," 10
I and me, 57
I-Thou, 52, 55
IDENTITY, defined, 39-42
(See A.F.M.)
Ideology, 88
and academic disciplines, 229-30, 336
end of, 314
and radicalism/conservatism (see M.R.C.)
and societal contradictions, 333
Idols, 90, 141
as abstractions, 79, 150
a Moloch, 79
Impulse, Expression (Scale), 338-40
Repression (Scale), 240
(See also Emotion, Feeling, Intensity)
Inauthenticity, defined, 76-79
(See M.A.C.)
in COMPETENCE, defined, 75-76
(See M.A.C.)
Independence v. conformity, 97-110
from parents, 352
from present stimuli, 35
seen as loss of self control, 372
Independence of Judgment, 112
(Scale), 49, 62
Independence from Family/Peers (Scales),
(See also Achievement via Independence), 373, 375
Independent variables, 5, 11, 13, 184-87
Individual principles orientation (See M.M.J.)
Inflexibility (Scale), 72, 81
Inner Directed (Scale), 242-43, 352
Insecurity, holy, 48
ontological, 47
Instrumental Relativism (See M.M.J.)
Intellectual(s), the, 60, 89-90, 119
dissenter, 312, 315
Intellectual, Effectiveness (Scale), 357-58
Efficiency, 264
(Scale), 264-65, 353

Intellectuality, 93
(Scale), 71, 73, 78, 80, 84
(See also INTEGRATION)
INTEGRATE FEEDBACK, defined, 56, 59-61
(See A.F.M.)
Integration (See differentiation and . . . )
Internationalism (Scale), 50
Intersecting cycles, 32, 128, 155
Intensity, defined, 45
(See A.F.M.)
Intimate Contact (Scale), 256-57, 353
Intolerance of Ambiguity, 74
(Scale), 70, 72, 78, 84
Intolerance towards the Renegade, etc. (Scale), 249-50
Intuition, 174
(Scales), 49, 174-75
Inverted trees of language, 56, 59, 61
INVESTS, 19
defined, 43-46
(See A.F.M.)
"Is," and "ought," 12, 27-28, 53, 56, 159
Isolation, Contradiction and Non-Integration within the Belief System (Scale), 264-65, 353
Isolationism, 74, 85, 146, 249
(Scale), 70, 72, 78, 84, 226
Job Codification (Scale), 141
Just, to make, 37
(See M.R.C. segment h)
Justice, 57, 60-61, 88, 90, 109, 163, 392
(See also Balance and SYNERGY)
Law and Order, 91, 123
Orientation (Scale) (See M.M.J. stage 4)
Law(s), freedom within, 25-26
of the heart and soul, 52
waiting to receive, 39
Leap (see Existential Leap)
Learning Theory, 19-23
Left, Dogmatic v. Developmental, 220-25, 274-76
escalation by the, 274-75
masturbation fantasies of, 279
New v. Old, 157, 221-225, 233, 240, 249
pathologies of, 269-73
(See Radical, Rebel, M.R.C.)
Left v. Right, in academic disciplines, 229-30
in basic ideology, 230-31
their similarity of tact, 389
Left-wing Ideology (Scale), 226-27
Legitimacy, 225-29
Liberals, humanistic v. custodial, 292-95
like a moth, 247-48
and pseudo-objectivity, 386
Liberalism Quotient of the A.D.A., 285-88, 290-91, 293
Liberalism (Scales), 256, 373, 375
(See also Religious Liberalism)
Libertarianism (Scale), 153, 174, 253, 367-68, 370

Life, basic property of, 24
Fear, 159
a state of organization, 24
Love and anxiety, 160
excursus on, 11
one another or die, 389-90
and surrender, 47
M.A.C. (Model of Anomic Cycle), 67f, 209-11
Man, exists freely, 19, 23, 31, 34, 37, 103, 127
(See also A.F.M.)
the measure, 229
as morally competent/incompetent (See M.R.C. segment c)
is the product of known forces (See M.R.C.)
Managerial Grid Seminars, 157, 168-70
Manifest Anxiety (Taylor's Scale), 70
v. Ego Control (Scale), 246
(See also Anxiety)
Masculinity, 244, 336
(See M.R.C. segment e)
concern with (Scale), 371-72
Matrix of thought, 21-23, 25, 53, 88
Meaninglessness, 5, 59
(See also Absurd)
Means and ends, 57, 132, 135
in technology, 308, 321
in strategic thinking, 331-32
and student rebellion, 383
Mental Health (See Positive M.H.)
Metaphysical rebel, 60-62
M.F.S. (Model of Formal System Structures) 128-29
M.M.J. (Model of Development in Moral Judgment), 120-21, 139, 160, 269-70
Models (See A.F.M. and M.M.J.)
Moloch, every idol a, 79
of mechanism, 151
Moral Acceptability (Scale), 233-34
Moral choice, 28, 30, 35, 49
Moral Freedom (Scale), 233-34, 351
Moral Judgment (Scale) (See M.M.J.)
Moratorium, in a T-Group, 163-64
in corporations, 186, 194
college as a, 352
and post-adolescence, 366-67
M.P.D. (Model of Psycho-social development) 31f, 102f, 155
M.R.C. (Model of Radical-Conservative Dimensions), 230-31, 306f
Mysticism (Scale), 71-72, 91
National Training Laboratories, 157
Nazis, 22, 75, 76, 158
Need Inviolacy, 75, 81, 240
(Scale), 70, 74, 78, 84, 226, 235, 365
New Left (See Left)
Non-SUSPENDING, defined, 79-81
(See M.A.C.)
Norms, choosing, making, testing, 67
integrated v. polarized v. compromised, 169-71
of rightness, 10

Nothingness, 50, 81, 86, 107
in T-Groups, 157-60
Beast of, 255
(See also Absurd)
Nuclear war, and "acceptable" losses, 313
and annihilation, 37, 82
and disarmament campaign, 82, 118-120
and simulation games, 320
Obedience Experiment, 98-113, 157
Obedience and Punishment Orientation (See M.M.J. stage 1)
Objectivity, 16-17, 50, 58, 132
Pseudo-objectivity, 313-17, 324
Obsessive, 13, 77, 88-91, 242
(Scale), 70, 72, 78, 84, 226
Official policies (See M.F.S.)
Old Left (See Left)
Open Mindedness, 3, 47, 105, 384-86
Open partisanship (Scale), 296, 300
Opinionation (Scale), 221, 223
Organizations, 127f
high performing v. low, 143-44, 148-49
development of relationships in, 188-91, 202-06, 209-12
(See also Companies, Corporations)
Originality (Scale), 111
Ought (See "Is")
Outer-cycle, 130-31, 158
(See also M.F.S.)
Parables, Biblical, 11, 56
of Kafka, 39
Paranoid Tendencies (Scale), 71, 73, 78, 84, 227, 236
Participation (See Democracy and SYNERGY)
Participatory Democracy, 364, 383, 385
Party Lining (Scale), 233-34
Party Loyalty (Scale), 85
Patriotism, 79, 87, 92, 101, 141, 248
Peace, march, 77
and mental conflict, 393-94
as a non-game, 320
(See also Draft Resistors and SANE)
PERCEPTION, defined, 37-39
(See A.F.M. and M.M.J.)
Perceptual Narrowness (Scale), 237-38, 351
Permissiveness (See Moral Freedom and Sexual)
Personal Concordance (See M.M.J. stage 3)
Personality Orientation Inventory (See Bosces A to I Chapter IX)
Pessimism, 5, 76, 240
(Scale), 70, 72, 78, 84, 226
Phoenix, 48, 393
"effect," 49, 361, 362
Phonemes, 56, 59
P.O.I. (See Personality . . . )
Police, 91-92
Political, Cynicism/Impotence/Indifference/Moral Indulgence/Suspicion (Scales), 70, 72, 78, 84, 226
Political and Economic Conservatism (Scale), 239
Political and Social Awareness (Scale), 235

Populism (Scale), 70, 73, 78, 86, 91
  and Left/Right Ideology, 227, 249
Port Huron Statement, 363, 377
Positive Mental Health, 34-36, 48, 145
Power, Black, 45
  "Polish," 185
Power over man v. through man, 3, 105, 135, 351
Practical Outlook (Scale), 339
PRACTICALS v. Reformers, 342-45
Praxis, 53
Prescription (See Description)
Prisoner's Dilemma Game, 12-13
Prejudice, 4, 81, 141, 172
  and strategic thinking, 324-25
  (See also Dogmatism and Rigidity)
Protest (See Activism, Dissent, Rebellion)
Psychological Mindedness, 359
  (Scale), 49
Psycho-social development (See M.P.D.)
Punishment Orientation (See M.M.J. stage 1)
*Quantum satis,* 55
Racism and strategic thinking, 324-25
Radical orientation, defined, 229-31
  v. conservative orientation (See M.R.C.)
Radicalism, problems in defining, 217-29
  Dogmatic v. Developmental, 220-25
  counterfeit of, 225
  (See Activism, Dissent, Rebellion and Student: by type)
Rebel, I rebel therefore we exist, 52, 56, 109, 171, 256, 380
Rebels: by type, against absurdity, 22, 37
  against death and injustice, 61, 90
  metaphysical, 60-61
  obedient v. developmental, 218-19
  against technological trends, 305-06
  against trainers in T-Groups, 164-65
  against torture in laboratory, 115-17
Rebellion, free exchange following, 55, 90
  and fulfillment, 253
  and higher student synergy, 380-82
Rebellion Issues in Congress, 284-85, 288
Reconciliation, of conflict, 60, 111
  of opposites, 57-60, 109, 119, 122, 260, 332, 383
  (See also SYNERGY and Unity of Contraries)
REFORMERS v. Practicals, 342-45
Regression, deliberate periodic, 49
  in service of growth, 164, 180, 392
  in Plant Y, 208
  in win-lose contests, 176-78
Reinforcement, 19-23, 26-27
Religiosity, 69
  (Scale), 70, 72, 78, 84, 226
Religious Liberalism (Scale)
Renegade (See Intolerance towards . . . )
Resolution (See Reconciliation)
Responsibility (See Social Responsibility)

Right, the political, 13
  in academic disciplines, 229-31
  in ideology (See M.R.C.)
  students of the, 233-65
  (See also Conservative)
Right-wing Ideology (Scale), 226-27, 230-31
Rigidity, 81, 110
  (Scale), 70, 72, 78, 84, 226, 235
  and besiegement, 248
  and dogmatism, 244-46
  and emotional outbursts, 296, 385
  and seniority, 365
RISKING, defined, 45-48
  (See A.F.M.)
RISK-reducing strategies, defined, 79-81
  (See M.A.C.)
Role (See M.F.S.)
Romanticism (Scale), 356, 357
Rule(s), followers/rejectors/worshipers, 67
  orientation to (See M.M.J.)
SANE nuclear policy, 354-55
Satisfaction with, Administration/faculty (Scale), 373, 375
Scanlon Plan, 192-207
Segregation, 84, 131, 145-46
  (Scale), 70, 72, 78, 84, 226
  (See also Votes in Congress)
SELF-CONFIRMING/TRANSCENDING, defined, 51-53
  (See also A.F.M.
SELF-SUSPENDING, defined, 45-48
  (See A.F.M.)
Self-Acceptance, 35, 172
  (Scale), 49
  (See also IDENTITY)
Self-Actualization, 36, 53-54, 353
  (Scale), 250, 253
Self-Confidence, 51, 76
  (Scale), 70, 72, 235
Self-Consistency, 36, 53, 65, 202
Self-Control, 111, 194
  (See Ego Control and M.R.C. segment e)
Self-Detachment (See Detachment)
Self-Disclosure, 44-46, 171
Self-Esteem, 35
  (Scale), 43-44
Self-Expression, 35, 51, 53, 106
Self-fulfilling prophecy, 5, 13, 193, 325, 362, 375
Self-ideal congruence, 271
Self-Insight, 35, 39, 42, 51, 62, 359
Self-Surrender, 36, 45-48
Senate, the (See Houses of Congress)
Sensation-Intuition (Scale), 173-74
Sexual, experience, 353
  inadequacy, 372
  inhibition, 256
  permissiveness, 233
Siege conditions, 248, 260-61

Simple (See Complex)
Simulation game, 320-21
(See also Games)
Situational Conservatism, 273, 285
Situational Morality, 233-34
Skill level, 145-47
Small group climate (See Group)
Social Conscience, 14
(Scale), 373, 375
Social Contract Orientation (See M.M.J. stage 5)
Social Dominance (Scales), 235, 238, 240, 351
Social Maturity (Scale),
Social Presence (Scale), 49
Social Responsibility, 74, 93, 116
(Scale), 71, 73, 78, 84, 226, 237
Social science students, 14-15, 174, 179, 253, 338-40, 368-71
Social scientists, 5, 9, 13-15, 134-35
Social status, 128, 254, 390
(Scale), 49
(See M.F.S.)
Social structures, 128-29, 142-45, 148-52
Social vacuum, 158-59, 378
Solitary and solidary, 52, 57, 109
Specialization and technique, 150-51
Standards, external, 197-199
(See also M.R.C.)
Status Frustration (Scale), 71, 72, 78, 84, 88, 226, 253
Strategic Thinking, 303, 314
and prejudice, 323-25
Stimulus, 19, 26-27
Structure (See Social Structure)
Students: by different concentrations, 14-15, 253, 336-44, 368-71
by type: Academics, 376
activists, Hi/Lo, 356-57
collegiates, 376
draft resistors, 372-73
freshmen, 338-39
fraternity, 363
graduate, 368
non-conformists, 376
PRACTICALS v. REFORMERS, 343-45
Rebels, 336-40, 350-53, 356
R.O.T.C., 369, 371-73
SANE supporters, 354-55
student government, 373-75
vocationalists, 376
Surrender (See Self-Surrender and Vulnerability)
SUSPENDING (See A.F.M.)
Suspension of self-concern, 36, 47
structure, 47, 129
SYNERGY, defined, 53, 55-58
Techniques, automatism and monism of, 307
for controlling controllers, 327
decree our future, 305
which disguise feelings, 314-16
and specialization, 150-51

Technology and blind acceleration, 390
and burning people, 101-02
as creating opportunities, 321
as a force apart from man, 306-07
and the formal system, 132
hostile to myth, metaphor and ideal, 333
its means become its ends, 308, 321
no way to guide, 317
Television (See T.V.)
Terman's Concept Mastery (Scale), 49, 340-41
T-Group (See Training Group)
Theories of cognitive consistency, 36, 202
Theory Y, 193-94
Thesis and antithesis, 58, 390 -92
Thinking Introversion (Scale), 336, 338, 365
Tolerant Personality, the, 51
Toleration (Martin's Scale), 50-51
McClosky's (Scale), 70, 72, 78, 84, 220
Totalitarianism (Scale), 234
Trades Union, 170, 200, 207, 213
Trainer, in Obedience experiments, 98-100
in T-Groups, 157, 164-65
Training Groups, defined with synonyms, 157, 194, 378
TRANSCENDING (See A.F.M.)
Trust, 4 building of, 50, 112, 118
among radical groups, 274
(See also Faith)
Trust in People (Scale), 336
Truth, as communicability, 274
realized through paradox, 57
T.V. quiz scandals, 241
students' viewing, 350
violence, 280
Uncertainty, 142-44, 148, 151
Unifying philosophy, 36, 61-63
Unity of contraries, 55, 57
(See Reconciliation of opposites, and SYNERGY)
Universalism, 330-31
Universities, attempt to radicalize, 366
as microcosms of conflict, 367-68
as milch-cows, 371
stopping dead, the, 378-79
destroying, the, 386-88
Unselfishness, 107, 156
(See also SUSPENSION)
Vacuum (See Social vacuum)
Value-free science, 12-13, 132, 305, 331
v. value-full investigation, 27-28
Viet Nam Summer, 358-62
Viet Nam War, 89, 92
appropriation for, 284, 288, 292-93
and "breaking-up inside," 388
and domestic repression, 367
and "liberal" rigidity, 385-86
and obedience experiments, 99-102
protest against, 354, 361-62, 364

Violence, attributed to relationships, 387
justified v. unjustified, 279-81
psychological violence, 375-77
as a radical tactic, 277-81
Votes in Congress, 281-95
Vulnerability, 361
heroism of, 325-26
strength through, 280
(See also Surrender)
War, 37, 151
as a conservative game, 12, 320
and "counterfeit contrast," 259-61
destroying love, 281
hero of, 326
as an "iron lung," 87
and miscommunication, 138
and obedience, 99-102, 118
Oh, What a Lovely, 87
and social control, 367
win-lose psychology of, 87-88, 175-78
Wasteland, 66, 158
Western Electric, 184, 187, 192
Win-lose psychology, 87-88, 176-78
(See Games, Strategic Thinking and War)
Workers, 76, 119
creativity among, 195-200
high-low skilled, 145-47

# NAME INDEX


Abram, M., 375
Adorno, T., 44, 267, 268
Agnew, H., 327
Aiken, M., 153
Allen, V., 172-73
Allport, G., 15, 35, 36
Almond, G., 295, 300
Angyal, A., 36
Archimedes, 8
Arendt, H., 346
Argyle, M., 215
Argyris, C., 35, 153
Armor, D., 394
Asch, S., 97-98, 101-13, 125
Avorn, J., 395
*Babbitt, G.*, 69, 76, 83, 85, 115
Bacon, F., 2, 23
Ballachey, E., 113 125
Bandura, A., 29
Barnes, L., 149, 168-70
Barrett-Lennard, 35
Barron, F., 35, 48, 49, 64, 112, 113, 354-55
Bateson, G., 94
Beckett, S., 64, 94
Bell, D., 266, 305, 314
Belloc, H., 151
Benne, K., 180
Bennis, W., 16, 94, 181
Bergman, I., 281
Bergson, H., 50
Berkowitz, L., 15, 302
Berlyne, D., 13
Bernanos, G., 67
Berne, E., 17
Bertalanffy, L. von, 10, 17, 34
Binger, C., 35
Binswanger, L., 26, 36
Blake, R., 168-70, 176-78
Blau, P., 11, 17
Boch, Jeanne, 41
Boelen, B., 36
Bogdonoff, M., 125
Bohr, N., 14
Bolt, R., 93
Boss, M., 36
Bowie, R., 305
Bradford, L., 180
Branson, L., 268
Brown, R., 382
Bruner, J., 185
Bryan, W., 317
Brzezinski, Z., 305, 312, 314, 319, 328-29, 333, 335-36

Buber, M., 36, 52, 55, 57, 69, 76
*Budd, Billy,* 136-40, 151, 375
Bugental, J., 35, 36
Bunker, D., 166-67
Butterfield, H., 11
Camus, A., 22, 28, 52, 56, 57, 60, 64, 74, 77, 86, 88, 90-91, 108, 179, 180
Caplan, G., 180
Carmichael, S., 65, 382
Cattell, R., 395
Chapman, R., 153
Cheek, F., 16
Chein, I., 36
Chomsky, N., 347, 385-86
Christie, R., 266
Churchill, W., 185
Churchman, C., 346
Clark, J., 347
Cleveland, B., 395
Coffey, H., 181
Cohen, M., 394
Combs, A., 35
Cook, L., 125
Cooley, Mathew, 207-15
Cooper, D., 66, 94
Coser, L., 94
Cottrell, L., 35
Courant, R., 266
Cox, A., 395
Cox, H., 95
Coxe, L., 153
Craise, Judith, 394
Cromwell, O., 309
Crutchfield, R., 15, 98, 101-15
Deane, H., 387
Delgado, J., 20-21, 26
Derber, C., 354, 357
Descartes, R., 26-27
Dewey, J., 52, 57
Dickson, J., 191-92
Doress, I., 224-50, 257-59, 264, 353, 358
Dostoevsky, F., 180
Dulles, J.F., 354
Eichmann, 45, 316
Einstein, A., 20, 229, 168
Eliot, T.S., 57, 68, 160, 392, 394, 395
Ellul, J., 307, 346
Elms, A., 117
Erikson, E., 36, 64
Eulau, H., 302
Eysenck, H., 260
Fairbairn, W., 36
Fanon, F., 328
Festinger, L., 66
Fingarette, H., 36
Fishman, J., 267, 268

Fiske, D., 66
Fitzgerald, S., 37
Flacks, R., 152, 354, 358, 359
Flynn, J., 268
Foote, N., 35
Frankl, V., 22, 35, 158
Freud, S., 74
Friedman, M., 58, 65, 86, 93, 94
Fromm, E., 35, 36, 50, 58, 76, 94, 335, 347, 382
Gagarin, N., 381, 395
Garroway, D., 241
Gibb, J., 181
Gilbert, W., 152
Gilliat, Penelope, 15
Ginsberg, A., 382
Glazer, N., 380, 394
Glimp, F., 381
Glock, C., 268
Goddard, J., 265, 281
Godot, 39
Goethals, G., 268
Golden, C., 216
Goldwater, B., 115, 229, 237, 244, 249, 303, 311, 334
Goodman, P., 95, 331
Gorham, W., 305
Goslin, D., 125
Gouldner, A., 11, 17
Green, P., 17
Greening, T., 181
Greiner, L., 168-71
Grenville, C., 37
Grusky, O., 153
Guest, R., 211, 216
Guntrip, H., 36
Gusfield, J., 266
Gutenberg, J., 21-22
Haan, Norma, 37, 153, 302
Haigh, D., 87
Hage, J., 153
Hagstrom, W., 153, 370, 394
Hale, D., 394
Hamilton, C., 65
Hampden-Turner, C., 353
Harding, H., 38
Harlow, H., 15, 28, 29
Harris, O., 241
Hartmann, H., 35
Hawkes, Jaquetta, 125
Hayden, T., 377
Heffner, H., 87
Hegel, A., 58
Heidegger, 76
Heider, F., 66
Heisenberg, 12
Heist, P., 181, 358

Herzberg, F., 153
Hess, E., 17
Hess, K., 268
Hilgard, E., 28
Hitler, A., 303
Hofstadter, R., 266, 267
Homans, A., 16, 17
Hora, T., 36
Horney, Karen, 35
Horwitz, M., 180, 266
Howard, A., 153
Huntington, S., 305
Huxley, A., 79
*Hyde, Mr.*, 4
Hyland, D., 382
Infield, L., 267
Jacobson, Lenore, 215
Jahoda, Marie, 36
Janowitz, M., 302
Jansen, D., 394
James, W., 36, 50, 52, 56, 362
Jaspers, K., 268, 302
*Jekyll, Dr.*, 4
Johnson, D.L., 215
Johnson, L.B., 99
Jonas, H., 2, 15
Jones, M., 29
Josephson, E., and Mary, 33
Jourard, S., 45, 46
Juliet, 11
Jung, C., 35, 57
Kafka, F., 39, 64, 86, 95
Kahn, H., 305, 312, 313, 335-37, 346
Kahn, R., 276
Kaplan, A., 16
Kaufmann, W., 94
Kelly, A., 65
Keniston, K., 74, 93, 330, 358-61, 366, 384, 388, 394
Kennedy, J.F., and R.K., 37, 285
Kepler, 16
Kerr, C., 368, 371, 394
Key, V., 266
Kierkegaard, S., 43, 47, 50, 74
King, M.L., 88, 123, 392
Kissinger, H., 386
Kirk, A., 386-87, 391
Knell, W., 42
Knorr, O., 339
Knowles, E., 173
Koestler, A., 2, 7, 21, 26, 28, 37, 56, 57, 61, 89, 164
Kohlberg, L., 39, 120-25, 139-40, 269, 302, 365
Kohler, W., 20-21
Kolakowski, L., 232, 267
Kornhauser, A., 145-47
Kozol, J., 392
Krech, D., 113, 125

Kroeber, T., 36
Kubie, L., 35
Laing, R., 16, 66, 94
Laski, H., 105
Laslett, P., 85
Lasswell, H., 266
Lawrence, P., 144, 216
Leach, E., 6, 333
Lean, A., 267
Lecky, P., 36
Lesieur, F., 205, 215
Lessing, Doris, 82, 94
Lipset, S., 153, 266, 268, 374
Lorsch, J., 144
Lucier, J., 239, 267
Lunn, A., 267
Luther, M., 45
Lynd, Alice, 268
MacDonald, D., 382
Machlup, F., 16
MacKinnon, D., 216, 340-41, 347
Maddi, S., 66
Magee, B., 66
Maitland, 92
Mann, J., 180
Marcuse, H., 55, 183, 265, 302
Martin, J., 50-51
Marx, K., 9, 236, 333
Maslow, A., 36, 39, 53-54, 55, 260
Matson, F., 25, 29, 95
Mausner, B., 153
May, R., 26, 29, 58, 65
Mayman, M., 35, 38
Mayo, E., 184, 187
McCarthy, J., 89, 98, 251, 254
McClelland, D., 55, 152, 266
McClosky, H., 13, 67-93, 133, 227, 236, 242, 249, 259, 361, 365
McGregor, D., 193, 215
McNeil, Helen, 42
Mead, G., 57
Melville, H., 8, 136
Mersault, 158, 261
Merton, R., 16
Mesthene, E., 15, 305, 336, 346
Milgram, S., 15, 98-100, 122-25
Mill, J.S., 43, 58
Miller, Arthur, 24
Miller, G.A., 321-22, 327, 330-31, 346
Mills, C.W., 29
Minter, W., 339
Mischel, W., 260
Moment, D., 215
Montague, A., 95
Mooney, R., 216
More, Sir T., 81
Moreno, J., 35

Mouton, Jane, 168-70, 176-78
Moynihan, D., 14, 16, 17
Murphy, G., 377, 395
Mussolini, B., 303
Natanson, M., 16
Neumann, F., 93
Newbolt, Sir H., 347
Newton, 16
Nietzche, F., 47
Nissen, H., 29
Nixon, R., 89
O'Brien, C., 382
Orwell, G., 279
Osborn, R., 94
Osborne, J., 92
Osgood, G., 28
Otto, H., 180
Overstreet, B., 35
Parkin, F., 119, 266
Parnes, S., 38
Parsons, T., 29
Paulus, G., 375
Pavlov, I., 7
*Pease,* 80
Pepitone, A., 66, 302
Perry, R.B., 58
Peterson, R., 375, 395
Poincare, H., 229
Polyani, M., 10
Pool, I., deS., 135, 305
Powell, A., 293-94
Price, D., 305
Quarton, G., 334-35
Rainwater, L., 16, 17
Rank, O., 159
Rapoport, A., 315-16, 323, 346
Razik, T., 216
Regan, Mary, 339
Rest, J., 125, 153, 302
Reuther, W., 74
*Reynolds,* 80
*Rieux, Dr.,* 158
Rim, Y., 153
Robbins, H., 266
Robinson, J., 229
Roethlisberger, F., 191-92, 215
Rof-Carballo, 35
Rokeach, M., 65, 221-23, 232, 244, 266, 267, 268
Rogers, C., 35, 42
*Romeo,* 11
Rosen, Ellen, 65
Rosenberg, M., 43, 44
Rosenhaupt, Maureen, 16
Rosenthal, R., 217
Rossman, M., 374

Roszak, T., 153
Rubin, I., 181
Ruskin, J., 133
Russett, B., 346
Sampson, E., 373
Sanford, N., 181
Sartre, J.P., 22, 58, 61, 66, 76, 158, 161-62, 308
Savio, M., 329, 347
Scanlon, J., 193, 214
Schaar, J., 67-71, 227, 395
Schachtel, E., 93
Schein, E., 181
Schiff, L., 271, 272
Schutz, A., 16
Schutz, W., 172, 173, 180
Seeley, J., 16, 17
Selvin, H., 153, 370, 394
Shakespeare, W., 20
Shaw, G.B., 104, 110, 285, 302
Silberman, C., 69, 93
Sillitoe, A., 216
Silone, I., 75, 83
Simmons, J., 268
Slater, P., 180
Smith, D., 267, 268
Smith, H.P., 65
Smith, M. Brewster, 41, 153
Snyderman, B., 153
Snygg, D., 35
Socrates, 91, 152
Solomon, F., 267, 269
Somers, R., 395
Spender, S., 382
Stalin, J., 73, 303
Stager, M., 126
Stark, R., 268
Steele, F., 173
Stein, M., 13, 16, 93
Stone, I.F., 367
Strausz-Hupe, R., 305, 317-18
Sullivan, H., 35, 36
Sullivan, E., 125
Tannenbaum, H., 66
Taylor, C., 38
Taylor, H., 382
Teilard de Chardin, 58
Terman, L., 49
Thomas, D., 65
Tillich, P., 35, 47, 52
Tomkins, S., 233-34, 270
Trent, J., 394
Trow, M., 336-38
Valiquet, M., 181
VanDoren, C., 241
Verba, S., 215, 295, 300

*Vere, Captain,* 136-40, 278
Vidler, A., 93
Vidich, A., 16, 93
Vispo, R., 36
Waldeck, R., 268
Walters, R., 28
Wann, T., 29
Watts, A.W., 58, 369
Webster, H., 181, 347
Weiner, A., 346
Wesker, A., 76
White, D., 93
White, R., 35, 266
Whittaker, D., 369
Whittinton, R., 94
Whorf, B., 56
Wild, J., 23
Williams, H., 74
Windborn, B., 390
Wolff, K., 36, 47, 58
Wolfinger, R., 266
Wolin, S., 153, 268, 395
Wright, R., 80
Yancey, W., 16, 17
Yankelovich, D., 342-345
Zaleznik, A., 215